Essentials

of Psychological Ass

Everything you need to know to administer, score, and interpret the major psychological tests.

I'd like to order the following *Essentials of Psychological Assessment:*

- ❑ WAIS®-IV Assessment (w/CD-ROM) / 978-0-471-73846-6 • $46.95
- ❑ WJ III™ Cognitive Abilities Assessment / 978-0-471-34466-7 • $36.95
- ❑ Cross-Battery Assessment, Second Edition
  (w/CD-ROM) / 978-0-471-75771-9 • $46.95
- ❑ Nonverbal Assessment / 978-0-471-38318-5 • $36.95
- ❑ PAI® Assessment / 978-0-471-08463-1 • $36.95
- ❑ CAS Assessment / 978-0-471-29015-5 • $36.95
- ❑ MMPI-2™ Assessment / 978-0-471-34533-6 • $36.95
- ❑ Myers-Briggs Type Indicator® Assessment, Second Edition
  978-0-470-34390-6 • $36.95
- ❑ Rorschach® Assessment / 978-0-471-33146-9 • $36.95
- ❑ Millon™ Inventories Assessment, Third Edition / 978-0-470-16862-2 • $36.95
- ❑ TAT and Other Storytelling Assessments, Second Edition
  978-0-470-28192-5 • $36.95
- ❑ MMPI-A™ Assessment / 978-0-471-39815-8 • $36.95
- ❑ NEPSY®-II Assessment / 978-0-470-43691-2 • $36.95
- ❑ Neuropsychological Assessment, Second Edition / 978-0-470-43747-6 • $36.95
- ❑ WJ III™ Tests of Achievement Assessment / 978-0-471-33059-2 • $36.95
- ❑ Evidence-Based Academic Interventions / 978-0-470-20632-4 • $36.95
- ❑ WRAML2 and TOMAL-2 Assessment / 978-0-470-17911-6 • $36.95
- ❑ WMS®-III Assessment / 978-0-471-38080-1 • $36.95
- ❑ Behavioral Assessment / 978-0-471-35367-6 • $36.95
- ❑ Forensic Psychological Assessment, Second Edition / 978-0-470-55168-4 • $36.95
- ❑ Bayley Scales of Infant Development II Assessment / 978-0-471-32651-9 • $36.95
- ❑ Career Interest Assessment / 978-0-471-35365-2 • $36.95
- ❑ WPPSI™-III Assessment / 978-0-471-28895-4 • $36.95
- ❑ 16PF® Assessment / 978-0-471-23424-1 • $36.95
- ❑ Assessment Report Writing / 978-0-471-39487-7 • $36.95
- ❑ Stanford-Binet Intelligence Scales (SB5) Assessment / 978-0-471-22404-4 • $36.95
- ❑ WISC®-IV Assessment, Second Edition (w/CD-ROM)
  978-0-470-18915-3 • $46.95
- ❑ KABC-II Assessment / 978-0-471-66733-9 • $36.95
- ❑ WIAT®-III and KTEA-II Assessment (w/CD-ROM) / 978-0-470-55169-1 • $46.95
- ❑ Processing Assessment / 978-0-471-71925-0 • $36.95
- ❑ School Neuropsychological Assessment / 978-0-471-78372-5 • $36.95
- ❑ Cognitive Assessment with KAIT
  & Other Kaufman Measures / 978-0-471-38317-8 • $36.95
- ❑ Assessment with Brief Intelligence Tests / 978-0-471-26412-5 • $36.95
- ❑ Creativity Assessment / 978-0-470-13742-0 • $36.95
- ❑ WNV™ Assessment / 978-0-470-28467-4 • $36.95
- ❑ DAS-II® Assessment (w/CD-ROM) / 978-0-470-22520-2 • $46.95
- ❑ Executive Function Assessment / 978-0-470-42202-1 • $36.95
- ❑ Conners Behavior Assessments™ / 978-0-470-34633-4 • $36.95
- ❑ Temperament Assessment / 978-0-470-44447-4 • $36.95
- ❑ Response to Intervention / 978-0-470-56663-3 • $36.95

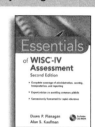

Please complete the order form on the back.
To order by phone, call toll free 1-877-762-2974
To order online: www.wiley.com/essentials
To order by mail: refer to order form on next page

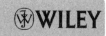

Essentials

of **Psychological Assessment** Series

ORDER FORM

Please send this order form with your payment (credit card or check) to:
John Wiley & Sons, Attn: J. Knott, 111 River Street, Hoboken, NJ 07030-5774

QUANTITY	TITLE	ISBN	PRICE
_____	_____	_____	_____
_____	_____	_____	_____
_____	_____	_____	_____
_____	_____	_____	_____
_____	_____	_____	_____

Shipping Charges:	Surface	2-Day	1-Day
First item	$5.00	$10.50	$17.50
Each additional item	$3.00	$3.00	$4.00

For orders greater than 15 items,
please contact Customer Care at 1-877-762-2974.

ORDER AMOUNT _____

SHIPPING CHARGES _____

SALES TAX _____

TOTAL ENCLOSED _____

NAME_____

AFFILIATION_____

ADDRESS_____

CITY/STATE/ZIP _____

TELEPHONE _____

EMAIL_____

❏ Please add me to your e-mailing list

PAYMENT METHOD:

❏ Check/Money Order   ❏ Visa   ❏ Mastercard   ❏ AmEx

Card Number _____ Exp. Date _____

Cardholder Name *(Please print)* _____

Signature _____

*Make checks payable to **John Wiley & Sons.** Credit card orders invalid if not signed.*
All orders subject to credit approval. • Prices subject to change.

To order by phone, call toll free 1-877-762-2974
To order online: www.wiley.com/essentials

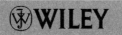

Essentials of Forensic Psychological Assessment
Second Edition

Essentials of Psychological Assessment Series
Series Editors, Alan S. Kaufman and Nadeen L. Kaufman

Essentials of 16 PF® Assessment
by Heather E.-P. Cattell and James M. Schuerger

Essentials of Assessment Report Writing
by Elizabeth O. Lichtenberger, Nancy Mather, Nadeen
L. Kaufman, and Alan S. Kaufman

Essentials of Assessment with Brief Intelligence Tests
by Susan R. Homack and Cecil R. Reynolds

Essentials of Bayley Scales of Infant Development-II Assessment
by Maureen M. Black and Kathleen Matula

Essentials of Behavioral Assessment
by Michael C. Ramsay, Cecil R. Reynolds, and
R. W. Kamphaus

Essentials of Career Interest Assessment
by Jeffrey P. Prince and Lisa J. Heiser

Essentials of CAS Assessment
by Jack A. Naglieri

*Essentials of Cognitive Assessment with KAIT and Other
Kaufman Measures*
by Elizabeth O. Lichtenberger, Debra Broadbooks,
and Alan S. Kaufman

Essentials of Conners Rating Scales Assessment
by Elizabeth P. Sparrow

Essentials of Creativity Assessment
by James C. Kaufman, Jonathan A. Plucker, and John Baer

Essentials of Cross-Battery Assessment, Second Edition
by Dawn P. Flanagan, Samuel O. Ortiz, and Vincent
C. Alfonso

Essentials of DAS-II® Assessment
by Ron Dumont, John O. Willis, and Colin D. Elliot

Essentials of Evidence-Based Academic Interventions
by Barbara J. Wendling and Nancy Mather

Essentials of Forensic Psychological Assessment, Second Edition
by Marc J. Ackerman

Essentials of Individual Achievement Assessment
by Douglas K. Smith

Essentials of KABC-II Assessment
by Alan S. Kaufman, Elizabeth O. Lichtenberger,
Elaine Fletcher-Janzen, and Nadeen L. Kaufman

Essentials of Millon™ Inventories Assessment, Third Edition
by Stephen Strack

Essentials of MMPI-A™ Assessment
by Robert P. Archer and Radhika Krishnamurthy

Essentials of MMPI-2™ Assessment
by David S. Nichols

*Essentials of Myers-Briggs Type Indicator® Assessment,
Second Edition*
by Naomi Quenk

Essentials of NEPSY® Assessment
by Sally L. Kemp, Ursula Kirk, and Marit Korkman

Essentials of Neuropsychological Assessment, Second Edition
by Nancy Hebben and William Milberg

Essentials of Nonverbal Assessment
by Steve McCallum, Bruce Bracken, and John Wasserman

Essentials of PAI® Assessment
by Leslie C. Morey

Essentials of Processing Assessment
by Milton J. Dehn

Essentials of Response to Intervention
by Amanda M. VanDerHeyden and Matthew K. Burns

Essentials of Rorschach® Assessment
by Tara Rose, Nancy Kaser-Boyd, and Michael P. Maloney

Essentials of School Neuropsychological Assessment
by Daniel C. Miller

Essentials of Stanford-Binet Intelligence Scales (SB5) Assessment
by Gale H. Roid and R. Andrew Barram

Essentials of TAT and Other Storytelling Techniques Assessment
by Hedwig Teglasi

Essentials of Temperament Assessment
by Diana Joyce

Essentials of WAIS®-IV Assessment
by Elizabeth O. Lichtenberger and Alan S. Kaufman

Essentials of WIAT®-II and KTEA-II Assessment
by Elizabeth O. Lichtenberger and Donna R. Smith

Essentials of WISC-III® and WPPSI-R® Assessment
by Alan S. Kaufman and Elizabeth O. Lichtenberger

Essentials of WISC®-IV Assessment, Second Edition
by Dawn P. Flanagan and Alan S. Kaufman

Essentials of WJ III™ Cognitive Abilities Assessment
by Fredrick A. Schrank, Dawn P. Flanagan, Richard W.
Woodcock, and Jennifer T. Mascolo

Essentials of WJ III™ Tests of Achievement Assessment
by Nancy Mather, Barbara J. Wendling, and Richard
W. Woodcock

Essentials of WMS®-III Assessment
by Elizabeth O. Lichtenberger, Alan S. Kaufman, and
Zona C. Lai

Essentials of WNV™ Assessment
by Kimberly A. Brunnert, Jack A. Naglieri, and Steven
T. Hardy-Braz

Essentials of WPPSI™-III Assessment
by Elizabeth O. Lichtenberger and Alan S. Kaufman

Essentials of WRAML2 and TOMAL-2 Assessment
by Wayne Adams and Cecil R. Reynolds

Essentials

of Forensic Psychological Assessment
Second Edition

Marc J. Ackerman

 John Wiley & Sons, Inc.

Copyright © 2010 by John Wiley & Sons, Inc. All rights reserved.

Published by John Wiley & Sons, Inc., Hoboken, New Jersey.
Published simultaneously in Canada.

Library of Congress Cataloging-in-Publication Data:
Ackerman, Marc J.
  Essentials of forensic psychological assessment / Marc J. Ackerman. — 2nd ed.
    p. cm. — (Essentials of psychological assessment series)
  Includes bibliographical references and index.
  ISBN 978-0-470-55168-4 (pbk.)
  1. Forensic psychology.   I. Title.
  RA1148.A28 2010
  614'.15–dc22

                                      2009046303

Printed in the United States of America

10 9 8 7 6 5 4 3 2 1

Contents

Series Preface

In the *Essentials of Psychological Assessment* series, we have attempted to provide the reader with books that will deliver key practical information in the most efficient and accessible style. The series features instruments in a variety of domains, such as cognition, personality, education, and neuropsychology. For the experienced clinician, books in the series will offer a concise yet thorough way to master utilization of the continuously evolving supply of new and revised instruments, as well as a convenient method for keeping up to date on the tried-and-true measures. The novice will find here a prioritized assembly of all the information and techniques that must be at one's fingertips to begin the complicated process of individual psychological diagnosis.

Wherever feasible, visual shortcuts to highlight key points are utilized alongside systematic, step-by-step guidelines. Chapters are focused and succinct. Topics are targeted for an easy understanding of the essentials of administration, scoring, interpretation, and clinical application. Theory and research are continually woven into the fabric of each book, but always to enhance clinical inference, never to sidetrack or overwhelm. We have long been advocates of "intelligent" testing—the notion that a profile of test scores is meaningless unless it is brought to life by the clinical observations and astute detective work of knowledgeable examiners. Test profiles must be used to make a difference in the child's or adult's life, or why bother to test? We want this series to help our readers become the best intelligent testers they can be.

There has been a tremendous amount of growth in the field of forensic assessment since the publication of Marc Ackerman's popular and influential first edition of *Essentials of Forensic Psychological Assessment* more than a decade ago, necessitating an updated edition on the topic. Due to the major changes in the field since the publication of the first edition, every chapter in this volume has been substantially revised, and an entirely new chapter on "dangerousness" and risk assessment has also been added. Like the first edition, this volume provides a summary of the parameters of assessing individuals in divorce, child custody, personal injury, sexual abuse, and substance abuse evaluations. In addition, areas of civil commitment, competency to stand trial, and juvenile circumstances are addressed. Each chapter provides the reader with the ability to pursue additional sources of information to enhance knowledge of these specific areas.

Alan S. Kaufman, Ph.D., and Nadeen L. Kaufman, Ed.D., Series Editors
Yale University School of Medicine

Acknowledgments

Counting all of the editions of all of the books that I have written, this is the fifteenth time in the last 19 years that I have undertaken such a task. Not to be political, but I fully understand the concept of "it takes a village" to make the process of this task as easy as possible. Unfortunately, the past year has been fraught with difficulties that have interfered significantly with completing the second edition. It is only because of the people around me that I was able to accomplish this task.

I would first like to acknowledge the authors who contributed chapters to this book. Andrew W. Kane, Ph.D. not only authored two chapters for this volume, but has co-authored many other texts with me over the past 20 years. He has always added a dimension to my work that has been appreciated. Ned Rubin, Psy.D. has been a friend and colleague for my entire professional career. His diligence in authoring the substance abuse chapter was much appreciated. Melissa Westendorf, J.D., Ph.D. has once again demonstrated her skills in her chapter on competency to stand trial assessment. Sheryl Dolezal, Psy.D. was my practice partner for 10 years and stepped in at a late date to competently help me co-author the chapter on juvenile assessment. Elizabeth Waisanen co-authored the new chapter to the second edition about dangerousness and risk assessment. Her clear and concise writing style is definitely a significant contribution to this text.

Throughout the production of this second edition, I have consulted with many colleagues who have provided valuable information. They include Yosef Ben-Porath, Ph.D.; Donald Bersoff, J.D, Ph.D.; James Bow, Ph.D.; Jay Flens, Psy.D.; Jonathan Gould, Ph.D; Roger Greene, Ph.D., Randy Kamphaus, Ph.D.; Kathryn Kuehnle, Ph.D.; Leslie Morey, Ph.D.; and Randy Otto, Ph.D. I would also like to thank Susan Madden of Western Psychological Services, Julie Alexander of Psychological Assessment Resources, and Krista Isakson of Pearson Assessment.

Needless to say, a book of this nature could not be successful without the support and encouragement of publishers and editors. Including the various editions of books, this is the seventh time that I have worked with John Wiley & Sons. Over much of that period of time, I have watched Isabel Pratt grow to her current role of editor. She is a genuine pleasure to work with and one who has mastered the art of being supportive, encouraging, and appropriately assertive when necessary. It is clear that without her help, this book would not have been completed. In addition, I would like to thank Kara Borbely and Susan Moran for help in the final stages of the text.

Not only did Elizabeth Waisanen co-author one of the chapters of this book, but she served as my director of this project. She spent countless hours researching, chasing after sources, and assembling the manuscript. I believe she now has a full understanding of what writing a book is all about. However, just as was true with Isabel Pratt, it is very clear to me that without Liz's support, this task would not have been completed. Finally, I continually thank my wife Stephanie for her understanding of my drive to continue performing research and writing books, even though at times it is disruptive to her life and the piles of materials exceed her comfort level.

To all of the above people who make up my "village," my sincere deep gratitude for their support during this project and hopefully in the future.

One

INTRODUCTION TO ESSENTIALS OF FORENSIC ASSESSMENT

Marc J. Ackerman

The psychologist's role in forensic assessment has been present for decades. However, it is only in recent years that the psychologist's involvement in court cases has become as prominent as it is. Psychologists have become involved in all aspects of the courts, including divorce, personal injury, criminal, children's court, and even in some cases, probate court.

For years expert psychological testimony was considered to be admissible based on the *Frye* test from the Supreme Court case *Frye v. United States* (1923). The point at which a scientific principle or discovery crosses the line between the experimental and demonstrable stages is difficult to define. Somewhere in this twilight zone the evidential force of the principle must be recognized, and while courts will go a long way toward admitting expert testimony deduced from a well-recognized scientific principle or discovery, the principle from which the deduction is made must be sufficiently established to have gained *general acceptance* in the particular field in which it belongs (Ackerman & Kane, 2005).

In June 1993 the United States Supreme Court decided *Daubert v. Merrell Dow Pharmaceuticals*. The Court declared that the *Frye* "standard, absent from and incompatible with the Federal Rules of Evidence should not be applied in federal trials." Although the *Daubert* ruling has not been accepted by all states (Arizona, California, Florida, Nebraska, and New York have explicitly rejected that model), and other states have not adopted the model, psychologists must be aware of whether the state in which they practice is a "*Daubert state.*" If the *Daubert* criteria must be met, certain requirements should be adhered to with regard to use of specific instruments. (See Rapid Reference 1.1.)

Two Supreme Court cases followed Daubert and clarified some of the Daubert ruling. In *General Electric Company v. Joiner* (1997), the U.S. Supreme Court reaffirmed the conclusions in *Daubert* and stated, "Nothing in either *Daubert* or the Federal rules of Evidence requires a district court to admit opinion evidence which is connected to existing data only by the *ipse dixit* (he said it himself) of the expert (139L.Ed.2d@520). The trilogy of cases concluded with *Kuhmo Tire Company v. Carmichael* (1999), in which the U.S. Supreme Court stated that individuals may be considered experts if they have any specialized knowledge or experience that may contribute to the fact finders' understanding of the case.

The trilogy of *Daubert, Joiner,* and *Kuhmo* cases has formed the basis for how forensic psychologists should operate in the forensic arena. The Supreme Court allowed each state to determine whether it would use the *Daubert* standard or continue to use the *Frye* standard. It is commonly accepted among forensic psychologists (Ackerman, 2005; Gould, 2006) that the *Daubert* standard should be used by the forensic psychologist, whether practicing in a *Daubert* state or not.

The influence of *Daubert* has not only been felt in the 2002 iteration of the American Psychological Association Code of Ethics, but has significantly impacted academics as well. In the past decade, there has been a proliferation of "evidence-based" textbooks, professional books, and professional literature that addresses evidence-based issues.

When giving evidence in a case, a psychologist will be asked to state whether the opinions given are to a "reasonable degree of psychological/professional certainty/probability." Although no legal or psychological standard has been established to instruct the psychologist or lawyer as to what "reasonable degree" represents, the accepted standard from the legal perspective is the 51st percentile, or anything that occurs more than 50% of the time. Psychologists are likely to be more conservative, having been taught in the course of their education to look at research at the .05 or .01 confidence level. However, in the legal arena it is acceptable to opine that something occurring more than 50% of the time will be to a "reasonable degree of certainty."

≡ *Rapid Reference 1.1*

Daubert Criteria

- Use theoretically and psychometrically adequate data-gathering instruments.
- Draw conclusions using scientifically validated theoretical positions.
- Weigh and qualify testimony on the basis of the adequacy of theory and empirical research on the question being addressed.
- Be prepared to defend the scientific status of your data-gathering methods during the process of qualification as an expert witness.

Table 1.1 Criteria of Psychological Tests for Use in Forensic and Custody Evaluations

Otto, Edens, and Barcus (2000, p. 100)	Melton, Petrila, Poythress, & Slobogin (2007, p. 48)
1. Is the test commercially published?	1. Is the test commercially published?
2. Is a comprehensive test manual available?	2. Is a comprehensive user's manual available?
3. Are adequate levels of reliability demonstrated?	3. Have adequate levels of reliability been demonstrated?
4. Have adequate levels of validity been demonstrated?	4. Have adequate levels of validity been demonstrated?
5. Is the test valid for the purpose for which it will be used?	5. Is the instrument valid for the purpose for which it will be used?
6. What are the qualifications necessary to use this instrument?	6. What are the qualifications necessary to use this instrument?
7. Has the instrument been peer reviewed?	7. Has the instrument been subjected to peer review?
	8. What construct is to be assessed?
	9. How directly does the instrument assess the construct of interest?
	10. Are there alternative methods of assessment that assess the construct of interest in more direct ways?
	11. Does the use of this instrument require an unacceptable degree of inference between the construct it assesses and the psycho-legal issue(s) of relevance?
	12. Does the instrument include measures of response style?

CRITERIA FOR THE USE OF TESTING

In an ideal world, all these criteria could be fully met. In practice, psychologists may use a test that does not quite meet the ideal—for example, a test that, although the best test, is too new to appear in the *Mental Measurements Yearbook* or published research. The psychologist is responsible for acknowledging this fact, however, and for indicating how a given test addresses the psychological and legal issues (Ackerman & Kane, 2005, pp. 148–149).

The psychologist should read the test manual of any unfamiliar tests in an effort to determine how many of the Otto et al. (1998) and Melton et al. (2007) criteria are met. A test that meets few of the criteria will have difficulty in gaining acceptance according to *Daubert* requirements.

CAUTION

When giving evidence in a case, do not rely on "junk science," which cannot meet the *Frye* or *Daubert* test.

Codes

Many organizations have developed codes or guidelines to be utilized in performing different types of forensic work. The forensic psychologist must be aware of the existence of these codes and guidelines and be familiar with many of them. (See Rapid Reference 1.2.)

Although these codes and guidelines are not necessarily considered mandatory by the American Psychological Association (APA), they tend to be viewed by the courts and legal profession as the standard of practice or standard of care. As a result, any psychologist engaging in professional activity different from what the codes or guidelines would suggest is likely to be subjected to a rigorous cross-examination about the standard of practice or standard of care. Therefore, it is recommended psychologists take a conservative approach and view the guidelines as if they represent the standard of practice, even though the sponsoring organization may not state that this is the case.

The 2002 American Psychological Association Ethical Principles of Psychologists and Code of Conduct, which can be found in full at www.apa.org, has been strongly influenced by *Daubert, Joiner,* and *Kuhmo.*

When reading the new Code of Ethics it is apparent that the revision committee was aware that psychologists are involved in forensic psychology in ever-increasing numbers and that the Code is being used by non-psychologists in many appropriate and inappropriate ways, especially in litigation. The previous iteration of the Code (APA, 1992) had a separate section for forensic psychology. The latest revision has eliminated the section on forensic psychology and has incorporated the forensic issues within each of the 10 ethical standard areas.

A second major change in the code can be found in the second to last paragraph in the Introduction. It states,

> The modifiers used in some of the standards of the Ethics Code (e.g., reasonably, appropriate, potentially) are included in the standards when they would (1) allow professional judgment on the part of psychologist,

≡ *Rapid Reference 1.2*

Codes and Guidelines

- American Psychological Association's (2002) "Ethical Principles of Psychologists and Code of Conduct"
- American Psychological Association's (1987) "General Guidelines for Providers of Psychological Services"
- The American Psychology-Law Society's (in press) "Specialty Guidelines for Forensic Psychologists"
- American Psychological Association's (2007) "Record Keeping Guidelines"
- Association of State and Provincial Psychology Boards' (2005) *Code of Conduct*
- American Professional Society on the Abuse of Children's (1997) "Guidelines for Psychosocial Evaluation of Suspected Sexual Abuse in Children"
- Academy of Family Mediators' (2001) "Standards of Practice for Family and Divorce Mediation"
- American Psychological Association's (2009) "Guidelines for Child Custody Evaluations in Family Law Proceedings"
- American Psychological Association's (1997) Patients' Bill of Rights (adopted by 14 health care providing organizations)
- American Psychological Association's (1998) "Guidelines for Psychological Evaluations in Child Protection Matters"
- Association of Family and Conciliation Courts' (2007) "Model Standards of Practice for Child Custody Evaluations"
- American Academy of Matrimonial Lawyers' Guidelines (in preparation)

(2) eliminate injustice or inequality that would occur without the modifier, (3) ensure applicability across the broad range of activities conducted by psychologists, or (4) guard against a set of rigid rules that might be quickly outdated. As used in the Ethics Code, the term reasonable means the prevailing professional judgment of psychologists engaged in similar activities, in similar circumstances, given the knowledge the psychologist had or should have had at the time. (2002, p. 2)

Whereas in the past, psychologists had little or no discretion in following the APA Code, the new Code allows psychologists to make choices based on the circumstances that are presented. Examples of these choices will be demonstrated in the discussion of the standards, infra.

The Codes and Guidelines that are published by governing organizations are considered to be *aspirational* and not *mandatory*. As a result, from an ethical perspective, the psychologist can engage in behavior that is outside the Standards, Codes, or Guidelines. However, since these documents are promulgated by professional governing bodies, they are often viewed by the legal profession and the courts as the "Standard of Practice" for psychologists. Therefore, the psychologist must be aware that the legal profession may look at these Standards and Codes differently than the psychologists.

This section will address each of the standards and subsections of the Code that are applicable to forensic psychology settings and discuss them. Other standards can be found by reading the Code in its entirety.

Code Section 1.02

1.02 Conflicts between Ethics and Law, Regulations, or Other Governing Legal Authority

If Psychologists' ethical responsibilities conflict with law, regulations, or other governing legal authority, psychologists make known their commitment to the Ethics Code and take steps to resolve the conflict. If the conflict is unresolvable via such means, psychologists may adhere to the requirements of the law, regulations, or other governing legal authority. (p. 1063)

There will be times that court orders ask psychologists to engage in an activity that is contrary to the APA Code of Ethics. The court order supersedes the Code. However, it is the psychologist's obligation to explain to the court that they are being asked to violate the Code and to make a record in the event that a complaint would be filed against the psychologist. Attorneys should be willing to help psychologists make this record.

Code Section 2.01

2.01 Boundaries of Competence

(a) Psychologists provide services, teach, and conduct research with populations and in areas only within the boundaries of their competence, based on their education, training, supervised experience, consultation, study, or professional experience. (p. 1063)

Psychologists are often willing to testify in areas where they may not have training or competence. It is not unusual for an attorney who is interested in obtaining as much information through his or her expert witness as possible, to ask a psychologist to testify in areas about which they have little or no expertise. However, it is the psychologist's responsibility to educate the attorney, and not the attorney's obligation to know the Code. Lyn Greenberg and her colleagues discuss forensic psychologist's obligations in 2004, stating, "Psychologists practicing in forensic cases have an ethical obligation to be thoroughly familiar with research relevant to the populations they are serving." (p. 19)

Code Section 3.04

3.04 Avoiding Harm

The first obligation of any healthcare provider is "do no harm." However, there are legitimate activities that may lead to harm, one of them being conducting a child custody evaluation in a case where the judge determines that one of the parents must relinquish custodial rights. (p. 1065)

Code Section 3.05

3.05 Multiple Relationships

(a) A multiple relationship occurs when a psychologist is in a professional role with a person and (1) at the same time is in another role with the same person, (2) at the same time is in a relationship with a person closely associated with or related to the person with whom the psychologist has the professional relationship, or (3) promises to enter into another relationship in the future with the person or a person closely associated with or related to the person. A psychologist refrains from entering into a multiple relationship if the multiple relationship could reasonably be expected to impair the psychologist's objectivity, competence, or effectiveness in performing his or her functions as a psychologist, or otherwise risks exploitation or harm to the person with whom the professional relationship exists. Multiple relationships that would not reasonably be expected to cause impairment or risk exploitation or harm are not unethical. (p. 1065)

This section states that "a multiple relationship occurs when a psychologist is in a professional role with a person and at the same time is in another role with the same person." This would include situations where a psychologist serves as a therapist and evaluator, therapist and mediator, or evaluator and mediator. A psychologist can assume one of those roles, but not more than one. This standard also addresses the issue of the "psychologist's objectivity or effectiveness in performing his/her functions as a psychologist." Since the psychologist's objectivity may already be impaired, it is helpful if the psychologist has engaged in peer review with a trusted colleague to obtain additional input as to whether the situation rises to the level of an ethical concern or not. There are times that multiple relationships are unavoidable, such as in rural areas, small towns, or on military bases.

Code Section 3.06

3.06 Conflict of Interest

Psychologists refrain from taking on a professional role when personal, scientific, professional, legal, financial, or other interests or relationships could reasonably be expected to (1) impair their objectivity, competence, or effectiveness in performing their functions as psychologists or (2) expose the person or organization with whom the professional relationship exists to harm or exploit. (p. 1065)

Multiple relationships and conflict of interest are often confused since they both involve impairment of objectivity, competence, and effectiveness in performing functions. Conflicts of interest can involve seeing both members of a couple in therapy, performing a custody evaluation on someone who may have other interests with the psychologist, such as a banker, insurance salesman, stockbroker, or real estate agent.

Code Section 3.07

3.07 Third-Party Requests for Services

When psychologists agree to provide services to a person or entity at the request of a third party, psychologists attempt to clarify at the outset of the service the nature of the relationship with all individuals or organizations involved. This clarification includes the role of the psychologist (e.g., therapist, consultant, diagnostician, or expert witness), an identification of who is the client, the probable uses of the services provided or the information obtained, and the fact that there may be limits to confidentiality.

(*See also* Standards 3.05, Multiple Relationships, and 4.02, Discussing the Limits of Confidentiality.) (p. 1065)

Code Section 3.10

3.10 (a) Informed Consent

When psychologists conduct research or provide assessment, therapy, counseling, or consulting services in person or via electronic transmission or other forms of communication, they obtain the informed consent of the individual or individuals using language that is reasonably understandable to that person or persons except when conducting such activities without consent is mandated by law or governmental regulations or as otherwise provided in this Ethics Code. (p. 1065)

As part of obtaining informed consent, it is necessary for the psychologist to indicate to the subject, who requested the services, which are paying for services, what will happen with the results of the evaluation? Failure to obtain informed consent of the party may invalidate the evaluation, and as a result, disqualify its use in the court. (See Rapid Reference 1.3.)

 *Rapid Reference 1.3*

Obtaining Informed Consent

Psychologists are ethically bound to inform evaluation participants of the following:
- Nature and purpose of the evaluation at the beginning of an evaluation.
- Extent of the evaluation.
- Cost of the evaluation.
- Amount of time the evaluation will take.
- Any fee arrangements in writing (if the participant is not paying for the evaluation, inform the participant who is paying for the evaluation and what the relationship is between the evaluator and the payor).
- Who will receive the report and how the information will be used.
- Concept of confidentiality and whether the results of the evaluation will be confidential.
- Duty to warn or protect where applicable.

Code Section 4.01

4.01 Maintaining Confidentiality

Psychologists have a primary obligation and take reasonable precautions to protect confidential information obtained through or stored in any medium, recognizing that the extent and limits of confidentiality may be regulated by law or established by institutional rules or professional or scientific relationship. (*See also* Standard 2.05, Delegation of Work to Others.) (p. 1066)

Confidentiality is the cornerstone of the therapeutic relationship. However, it has little applicability in the forensic setting. In most requests for forensic evaluations, the court orders the evaluation, thus requiring that the report be supplied to the court, the attorneys, or some other agency or individual. The forensic psychologist needs to inform the participant in the evaluation that the results are not confidential. The psychologist is best protected by having the individual sign a statement recognizing that the report is not confidential.

Code Section 6.01

6.01 Documentation of Professional and Scientific Work and Maintenance of Records

Psychologists create, and to the extent that records are under their control, maintain, disseminate, store, retain, and dispose of records and data relating to their professional and scientific work in order to (1) facilitate provision of services later by them or by other professionals, (2) allow for replication of research design and analyses, (3) meet institutional requirements, (4) ensure accuracy of billing and payments, and (5) ensure compliance with law. (*See also* Standard 4.01, Maintaining Confidentiality.) (p. 1067)

The American Psychological Association has developed Record Keeping Guidelines (APA, 2007). The record keeping guidelines can be found by going to the American Psychological Association web site at www.apa.org.

Code Section 6.03

6.03 Withholding Records for Nonpayment

Psychologists may not withhold records under their control that are requested and needed for a client's/patient's emergency treatment solely because payment has not been received. (p. 1068)

One of the more difficult components of performing child custody work can be receiving payment. Psychologists usually attempt to receive payment on a retainer basis. However, there are times when work is performed pursuant to court orders prior to receiving a payment, and at a later date there is a request for a release of information obtained during that period. Psychologists are not obligated to disseminate the information if payment has not been received unless that information is needed for the "patient's emergency treatment."

Code Section 6.04

6.04 Fees and Financial Arrangements

(a) As early as is feasible in a professional or scientific relationship, psychologists and recipients of psychological services reach an agreement specifying compensation and billing arrangements.

(b) Psychologists' fees practices are consistent with law.

(c) Psychologists do not misrepresent their fees.

(d) If limitations to service can be anticipated because of limitations in financing, this is discussed with the recipient of services as early as feasible. (See also Standards 10.09, Interruption of Therapy, and 10.10, Terminating Therapy.) (p. 1068)

Code Section 9.0

9.0 Assessment

The standards on assessment as represented by Section 9 of the APA Code may be the most important collective set of standards as it applies to forensic psychology and custody evaluation.

Section 9.01

9.01 Bases for Assessments

(a) Psychologists base the opinion contained in their recommendations, reports, and diagnostic or evaluative statements, including forensic testimony, on information and techniques sufficient to substantiate their findings. (*See also* Standard 2.04, Bases for Scientific and Professional Judgments.) (p. 1071)

This standard is a reflection of the *Daubert* standard. In today's world of forensic psychology, a psychologist should not render an opinion that cannot be supported by scientific data to substantiate the findings. Assessment techniques that in the past were referred to as "junk science" are no longer acceptable for the bases of opinions.

(b) Except as noted in 9.01(c), psychologists provide opinions of the psychological characteristics of individuals only after they have conducted an examination of the individuals adequate to support their statements or conclusions. When, despite reasonable efforts, such an examination is not practical, psychologists document the efforts they made and the result of those efforts and clarify the probable impact of their limited information on the reliability and validity of their opinions (Boundaries of Competence, and 9.06, Interpreting Assessment Results). (p. 1071)

As noted in the American Psychological Association Guidelines for Conducting Child Custody evaluations, a psychologist should not render an opinion about the psychological characteristics of an individual who they have not personally evaluated. The most flagrant example of a violation of this standard is when a psychologist tests one parent and then proclaims, based on those test results, that that parent should be the custodial or placement parent, without testing or evaluating the other parent.

(c) When psychologists conduct a record review or provide consultation or supervision and an individual examination is not warranted or necessary for the opinion, psychologists explain this and the sources of information on which they based their conclusions and recommendations. (p. 1071)

This does allow for record review to provide consultation to an attorney in cases. Consultation or responding to hypothetical questions in testimony is not the same as rendering an opinion without evaluating individuals.

Code Section 9.02

9.02 Use of Assessments

(a) Psychologists administer, adapt, score, interpret, or use assessment techniques, interviews, tests, or instruments in a manner and for the purposes that are appropriate in light of the research on or evidence of the usefulness and proper application of the techniques. (p. 1071)

This standard addresses the issue that the instruments that are used should be applicable to the setting within which they are used. As a result, using tests in custody evaluations that have no research about their applicability to that setting is not appropriate.

(b) Psychologists use assessment instruments whose validity and reliability have been established for use with members of the population tested. When such validity or reliability has not been established, psychologists describe the strengths and limitations of test results and interpretation. (p. 1071)

Section 9.02b indicates that if reliability and/or validity cannot be established, it becomes the reporting psychologist's obligation to indicate what limitations are for the use of that particular instrument.

Code Section 9.03

9.03 Informed Consent in Assessments

(a) Psychologists obtain informed consent for assessments, evaluations, or diagnostic service, as described in Standards 3.10, Informed Consent, except when (1) testing is mandated by law or governmental regulations; (2) informed consent is implied because testing is conducted as a routine educational, institutional, or organizational activity (*e.g.,* when participants voluntarily agree to assessment when applying for a job); or (3) one purpose of the testing is to evaluate decisional capacity. Informed consent includes an explanation of the nature and purpose of the assessment fees, involvement of third parties, and limits of confidentiality and sufficient opportunity for the client/patient to ask questions and receive answers. (p. 1071)

The same issues that apply to general informed consent apply to informed consent for assessments in custody cases since most of the work that is done in a custody case is assessment oriented.

Code Section 9.04

9.04 Release of Test Data

(a) The term test data refers to raw and scaled scores, client/patient responses to test questions or stimuli, and psychologists' notes and recordings concerning client/patient statements and behavior during an examination. Those portions of test materials that include client/patient responses are included in the definition of test data. Pursuant to a client/patient release, psychologists provide test data to the client/patient or other persons identified in the release. Psychologists may refrain from releasing test data to protect a client/patient or other persons identified in the release. Psychologists may refrain from releasing test data to protect a client/patient or others from substantial harm or misuse or misrepresentation of the data of the test, recognizing that in many instances release of confidential information under these circumstances is regulated by law. (*See also* Standard 9.11, Maintaining Test Security.) (p. 1071–1072)

There probably is not a standard that has a greater impact on the relationship between psychologists and lawyers than 9.04(a). For decades psychologists and lawyers have been in a professional "tug-of-war" about the release of "raw data." The Revision Committee was obviously aware of these concerns when 9.04a was written. The most important statement in 9.04(a) is the qualification given about what is required to release information, which states, "Psychologists may refrain from releasing test data to protect a client/patient or others from substantial harm or misuse or misrepresentation of the data or test," indicating that it is the psychologist's belief that the attorney is not qualified to interpret the data, and as a result, is likely to misuse or misrepresent it. The common practice of sending the raw data to another psychologist of the attorney's choice is still the best resolution of this concern.

Code Section 9.06

9.06 Interpreting Assessment Results

When interpreting assessments results, including automated interpretations, psychologists take into account the purpose of the assessment as well as the various test factors, test-taking abilities, and other characteristics of the person being assessed, such as situational, personal, linguistic, and cultural differences that might affect psychologists' judgment or reduce the accuracy of their interpretations. They indicate any significant limitations of their interpretations. (*See also* Standard 2.01b and c, Boundaries of Competence, and 3.01, Unfair Discrimination.) (p. 1072)

There is a dilemma that arises out of Ethical Standard 9.06. As a result, technically, anyone using the MMPI-2 interpretation programs would be violating this standard. However, from a practical issue that is not likely to carry any weight.

Code Section 9.08

9.08 Obsolete Tests and Outdated Test Results

(a) Psychologists do not base their assessment or intervention decisions or recommendations on data or test results that are outdated for the current purpose.

(b) Psychologists do not base such decisions or recommendations on tests and measure that are obsolete and not useful for the current purpose. (p. 1072)

Too often, psychologists do not keep up to date by ordering new tests because they are very costly ($1,000–$1,200 per intelligence test), there is a comfort level with using tests the psychologist is familiar with, and the psychologist may not use the test frequently enough to warrant spending the time to develop familiarity with a new test. However, the standard of practice indicates that after a new test has been out for a year, it should replace the old test.

Code Section 9.09

9.09 Test Scoring and Interpretation Services

(a) Psychologists who offer assessment or scoring services to other professionals accurately describe the purpose, norms, validity, reliability, and applications of the procedures and any special qualifications applicable to their use.

(b) Psychologists select scoring and interpretation services (including automated services) on the basis of evidence of the validity of the program and procedures as well as on other appropriate considerations. (*See also* Standard 2.01b and c, Boundaries of Competence.) (p. 1072)

It indicates that when using automated interpretations, the problem with this standard is that there are some tests, such as the MMPI-2, that do not divulge their rationale, scoring, and interpretation methods, or other important information to determine whether the test fits these circumstances based on trade secrets, copyright laws, and other concerns.

Code Section 9.10

9.10 Explaining Assessment Results

Regardless of whether the scoring and interpretation are done by psychologists, by employees or assistants, or by automated or other outside services, psychologists take reasonable steps to ensure that explanations of results are given to the individual or designated representative unless the nature of the relationship precludes provisions of an explanation of results (such as in some organizational consulting, preemployment or security screenings, and forensic evaluations), and this fact has been clearly explained to the person being assessed in advance. (p. 1071)

This standard helps people recognize that ordinarily the results would be shared with the individual, but there are some settings such as forensic evaluations where sharing with the individual would be precluded by the evaluation.

Code Section 9.11

9.11 Maintaining Test Security

The term *test materials* refers to manuals, instruments, protocols, and test questions or stimuli and does not include *test data* as defined in Standard 9.04, Release of Test Data. Psychologists make reasonable efforts to maintain the integrity and security of test materials and other assessment techniques to this Ethic Code. (p. 1072)

We have now come full circle in that 9.04 allow psychologists to release test data with a valid release. However, in the spirit of the 2002 Code, the psychologist is allowed to make the ultimate decision of whether releasing the test data will cause "substantial harm or misuse or misrepresentation of the test data." Recent informal surveys of experienced forensic psychologists yielded virtual unanimity that they would use the qualifier about harm, misuse, or misrepresentation to prevent the release of test data in custody cases. Note that even though the Ethical Code allows for release of test data, it still protects test materials (manuals, instruments, protocols, and test questions) and affirms the necessity for psychologists to maintain the integrity and security of these materials. (p. 1072)

Rule of Conduct H.4 of Association of State and Provincial Psychology Boards (1991) "Code of Conduct" states, "Psychologists shall not reproduce or describe in popular publications, lecture, or public presentations, psychological tests or other assessment devices that might invalidate them." (p. 26)

Responding to Attorney's Demands

- When an attorney requests or subpoenas raw test data from a psychologist, the psychologist's ethical obligation is to inform the attorney that the integrity and security of the tests must be maintained and to offer to send the raw test data to any licensed psychologists of the attorney's choice.
- The attorney should have his or her client sign an informed consent form requesting release of information from the evaluation or therapy or both, including the name of the psychologist to whom the raw data should be sent, if possible.

- If the attorney seeks a court order to personally review the raw test data, rather than sending it to a psychologist retained as a consultant for that purpose, the judge could be asked to review the test data in camera (instead of permitting discussion in open court) and narrow the subpoena as much as possible.
- The court should also be asked to issue a protective order
  - Prohibiting parties from making copies of the materials.
  - Requiring that the materials be returned to the psychologist at the conclusion of the proceedings.
  - Requiring that the materials not be publicly available as part of the record of the case, either by sealing part of the record or by not including the material in the record at all.

DON'T FORGET

- Do not transcend the boundaries of your expertise. (Code: Principle A, Standard 12.1; Testing: 2.01(a); Custody Guidelines: 5A)
- Do not misrepresent your qualifications. (Code: Principle B, Standards 2.01(a), 5.01)
- Avoid dual/multiple relationships. (Code: Principle B, Standards 3.05, 3.06; Specialty Guidelines: IV.D (1,2); Custody Guidelines)
- Discuss fees from the outset. (Code: Standard 6.04; Custody Guidelines: 15; Specialty Guidelines: IV.B)
- Do not release raw data to unqualified individuals. (Code: Standards 9.04; 9.11)
- Do not use obsolete tests. (Code: Standard 9.08; Custody Guidelines: 5B)
- Do not violate test security. (Code: Standard 9.11; Testing: Standards 11.7 and 5.7)
- Inform patient/client of limits of confidentiality. (Code: Standards 3.10, 9.03; Specialty Guidelines: V.B.; Custody Guidelines: 10)
- Report previously unreported child abuse. (Code: Standard 4.05)
- Understand state laws regarding duty to warn and protect. (Code: Standard 4.05)
- Do not withhold records for lack of payment. (Code: Standard 6.03)
- Do not make recommendations without seeing both parents. (Code: Standards 7.02(a,b,c), 7.04(b); Specialty Guidelines: VI.H; Custody Guidelines: 8, 13)
- Do not work on a contingency fee basis. (Specialty Guidelines: IV.B)
- Maintain records. (Code: Standard 6.01; Custody Guidelines: 16; Record Keeping Guidelines)

- Requiring that testimony regarding the content of the items be sealed or not included in the record.
- Sealing any references to test items in pleadings or other documents filed by the parties.
- Requesting that the judge's opinion, including both findings of fact and conclusions of law, not include descriptions or quotations of the actual items or responses.

Note: From Ackerman, 2006, p. 49

The Health Insurance Portability and Accountability Act (HIPAA)

The provisions of HIPAA do not control any aspect of forensic psychological evaluations. Forensic services are provided to respond to a legal and not a therapeutic question: They are provided at the request of a third party (not the client himself/herself) and fall outside the health care system and, as a result, are not covered by health insurance. The only exception would be if protected health information is received by the forensic evaluator from another party as part of record review. The forensic psychologist must maintain the security of those protected health information records.

PRESENCE OF THIRD PARTIES DURING EVALUATIONS

It is not unusual for attorneys or courts to request that a third party be present during a forensic psychological evaluation. This is often done under the guise of wanting to make sure that a child is not "harmed" or an adult is not "badgered." Parents have also requested to be present when their children are evaluated, especially when abuse allegations have been made. However, research indicates that such "third party observers" (TPOs) should not be present because of the effect such observers are likely to have on the results of the evaluation. In order for a standardized psychological instrument to be valid and reliable, it must be administered according to specific criteria that were utilized during the standardization process. There are no tests that are standardized with third party observers present. Kramer and Brodsky (2007) state "the examiner must ensure that the attorney does not actively or passively interfere with the examination itself."

"Impression management" is an additional area of concern. Examinees alter their performance depending on their perception of how they should or want to come across, ways they want to avoid coming across, whom they want to please (or avoid pleasing) with their performance, and so forth. Parties may increase the statements they make that are designed to get the TPO to like them, or approve of them, may avoid disclosure of sensitive or negative (especially embarrassing) information, or may otherwise fail to be forthright with the evaluator (Ackerman & Kane, 2008, p. 21).

KNOW YOUR STATE LAW

Every state has different laws and regulations that govern how forensic psychologists are allowed to practice within that state. A copy of temporary practice laws in the United States and Canada can be found on pages 3–8 of Ackerman and Kane (2008). Before beginning practice in your jurisdiction, it is essential to determine what state laws govern your professional forensic psychology activity. The following list is a guide to specific laws that you should inquire about within your jurisdiction.

- Determine if your jurisdiction has incorporated the APA Child Custody Guidelines into state law or any other guidelines or codes.
- Before you attempt to practice in another state for a specific case, check the state laws in that state to determine what you are and are not allowed to do.
- Determine if your state has a law that specifically identifies what should be included in a child custody evaluation.
- Determine if your state has laws that specifically identify the type of training you need in order to perform a child custody evaluation.
- Determine if your state law allows courts to order significant others (new spouses, live-in partners, grandparents) to participate in the evaluation or if it must be voluntary.
- Determine the role of the guardian ad litem by statute and if the guardian ad litem must be an attorney or can be a mental health professional or other nonattorney.
- If a guardian ad litem is involved in the case, are you allowed to meet with the children without the guardian ad litem's permission?
- Determine the current state law regarding *Tarasoff*-type warnings.
- Determine if your state has a law regarding maintaining test security or releasing test data.
- With regard to placement issues, find out if any "rebuttable presumptions" are mandated by law when making placement decisions and determine if your state has a law that requires starting from a position of "substantially equal placement."
- Determine what domestic violence laws exist in your state and whether you are required to include domestic violence issues as part of your evaluation.

- Determine whether your state's law(s) regarding mandated child abuse reporting has any areas in which "permissive" reporting is allowed instead of "mandated" reporting.
- Determine if your state has some form of information system allowing you to check for current or previous court cases in which parties or significant others have been involved.
- Is your state a *Daubert* state, a *Frye* state, or neither?
- Does your state prohibit dissemination of medical and/or educational records to parents who have been denied placement of their children pursuant to court order?

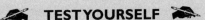

TEST YOURSELF

1. **Dual or multiple relationships are becoming an increasing concern in the practice of forensic psychology.**
   True or False?

2. **Raw data should readily be turned over to attorneys when a subpoena is issued.**
   True or False?

3. **When raw data are subpoenaed, the psychologist should**
   (a) attempt to quash the subpoena.
   (b) encourage the judge to review the records in camera.
   (c) request the judge order that the data be returned after the case is completed.
   (d) ask the judge not to include any raw data in the findings of fact and court orders.
   (e) all of the above.

4. **Which of the following is not one of *Daubert* requirements?**
   (a) Use of tests found in the Mental Measurements Yearbook
   (b) Use theoretically and psychometrically adequate data-gathering instruments
   (c) Draw conclusions using scientifically validated theoretical physicians
   (d) Weigh and qualify testimony on the basis of adequacy of theory and empirical research
   (e) Be prepared to defend the scientific status of your data gathering

5. **There is no difference between the psychologist's role as a therapist and forensic evaluator.**
   True or False?

6. Tests such as the MMPI-2 can be sent home with subjects in an effort to save time.

True or False?

7. Informed consent includes all of the following, except informing the participants

(a) of the nature and purpose of the evaluation.

(b) the extent of the evaluation.

(c) the cost of the evaluation.

(d) the location of the evaluation.

(e) the amount of time the evaluation will take.

8. The original Duty to Warn or Protect case was

(a) *Egly v. University of South Carolina.*

(b) *Tarasoff v. Regents of the University of California.*

(c) *Schuster v. Altenberg.*

(d) *Jaffe v. Redmond.*

Answers: 1. True; 2. False; 3. e; 4. a; 5. False; 6. False; 7. d; 8. b

Two

ESSENTIALS OF CHILD CUSTODY EVALUATIONS

Marc J. Ackerman

HISTORY OF CUSTODY DECISION MAKING

Prior to the 1900s children were viewed as property. As a result, fathers automatically received placement of children since women were not allowed to own property. In the unlikely event a mother gained custody, the father was no longer held financially responsible for the support of the children. Following the Industrial Revolution, an increasing awareness of the mother's role in caring for children resulted in the "tender years" doctrine. This assumed that fathers lacked the ability to be sensitive to children's needs in the "tender years" and resulted in a change that automatically favored mothers in custody disputes. In the late 1960s and early 1970s the "best interest standard" was adopted (Goldstein, Freud, & Solnit, 1973), and with the enactment of the Uniform Marriage and Divorce Act (UMDA) in the early 1970s, custody issues focused on the best interest of children. Rapid Reference 2.1 cites several factors that were considered in determining a child's best interest.

Psychology became aware of its ever-increasing role in child custody evaluation cases. In 1994 the APA developed guidelines to be utilized in child custody evaluation proceedings.

The APA Guidelines for child custody evaluations were revised in 2009. As was true of the 1994 Guidelines, the 2009 Guidelines are considered to be aspirational and not mandatory. It should be pointed out that many of the Guidelines were taken directly from the APA Code of Ethics, and specifically referenced in the body of the Guidelines. There appears to be a contradiction between the intent of the ethics quoted in the APA Code of Ethics and in the custody evaluation Guidelines. The number of Guidelines has been reduced from 16 to 14 between 1994 and 2009.

Many practicing psychologists already follow the Guidelines, and for psychologists who do, the Guidelines are both validating and affirming. Psychologists who have not met the standards of these Guidelines in the past must consider improving the quality of their work product.

≡ *Rapid Reference 2.1*

UMDA Factors

- Wishes of the parents regarding custody
- Wishes of the child
- Interaction and interrelationships of the child with the parents, siblings, and anyone else who significantly affects the child's adjustment to home, school, and community
- Mental and physical health of the parties
- Other factors that may be deemed relevant to each individual case

Particular attention should be paid to Guidelines 10 and 12. Guideline 10 states, "Psychologists may seek corroboration of information gathered from third parties, and are encouraged to document the bases of their eventual conclusions." This supports the notion that psychologists should not rely on "he said/she said" information without corroboration. Guideline 12 states, "Psychologists provide an opinion of an individual's psychological characteristics only after they have conducted an examination of the individual adequate to support their statements and conclusions.... If a desired examination cannot be arranged, psychologists document their reasonable efforts and the result of those efforts, and then clarify the probably impact of this limited information on the reliability and validity of their overall opinions, limiting their forensic conclusions and any of their recommendations appropriately. When psychologists are not conducting child custody evaluations, per se, it may be acceptable to evaluate one parent, or only the child, or only another professional's assessment methodology as long as the psychologists refrain from comparing the parents or offering opinions or recommendations about the apportionment of decision-making, caretaking, or access."

Too many psychologists are willing to make custody and placement recommendations after having evaluated only one parent and not seeing the children. In many states, licensure boards perceive this to be "an actionable offense." An example is found at the end of a recent report, which states, "The following recommendation is made with the awareness that the mother was evaluated without evaluating the father. Nevertheless, I am confident and comfortable in stating that the mother has the intellectual and emotional resources to be a competent parent to her two sons. ... Therefore it is my recommendation that the mother be granted primary placement, although in joint custody with the father of her two young sons"(Ackerman, 2006, p. 302).

It appears as if the new Guidelines are less stringent than the previous Guidelines, which will leave some psychologists wanting more guidance. To that end, the Association for Family and Conciliation Courts (AFCC) Standards or the American Psychological-Law Society (AP-LS) Specialty Guidelines should be consulted.

In 1986, Keilen and Bloom published the seminal study about child custody evaluation practices. Ackerman and Ackerman (1997) replicated the Keilen and Bloom study, which set the standard of practice for child custody evaluations for a decade. The Ackerman and Ackerman study was replicated by Ackerman and Brey (in press). The results of that study state:

- The sample is mostly males, mostly PhDs, with virtually no formal academic training in the area of custody evaluations.
- Half of the respondents had at least one licensure board complaint, with 20% of the respondents having three or more complaints, while 91% and 81% stated they did not have any state ethics board complaints or malpractice suits, respectively.
- The length of time devoted to performing custody evaluations has increased approximately 50% over the last ten years. This is represented by an increase of approximately five hours in report writing, five hours in interviewing, and three hours in reviewing materials.
- In spite of the fact that there has been an increase of criticism of custody evaluation specialty tests, there has been an increase in their usage by two-and-a-half times over ten years ago.
- The hourly fee for testing and testifying has increased approximately 50% over the past ten years, while the overall fee for an evaluation of four has doubled over the same period.
- Evidence of abuse, alcohol-and-drug related problems, emotional instability, and alienation remain the most frequent reasons for sole custody.
- Parents' ability to communicate and cooperate, having good parenting skills, and attachment remain the most frequent reasons for joint custody.
- The wishes of a fifteen-year-old have dropped from the twelfth most important variable in 1997 to the sixteenth most important variable in 2010. The study also suggests that the wishes of five- and ten-year-olds should not be listened to.
- The sexual preference of the parent has become a complete non-issue, being the thirty-seventh most important variable out of forty variables to be addressed.
- "Substantially equal placement" was defined as anywhere from 60/40 in one direction to 40/60 in the other direction.

THE EVALUATION

The evaluation process itself includes interviews, gathering of collateral information, testing, report writing, and dissemination of information (see Table 2.1).

Gindes (1995) suggests that psychologists performing child custody evaluations should have competence in the following areas: (1) research, theory, policy, and practice regarding divorce and child custody issues; (2) the psychological assessment of adults and children; (3) developmental psychology; (4) family psychology; (5) psychopathology of adults and children; (6) the effects of divorce and custody arrangements on adults and children; (7) relevant aspects of the legal system; (8) relevant aspects of forensic psychology; and (9) the *Ethical Principles and Code of Conduct for Psychologists*.

The Parent Interview

Interview of parents should include basic demographic information. This author commences every interview with the same open-ended statement: "I guess the best place to start would be for you to tell me a little about what you know about why we are meeting today." This allows interviewees to start at any point that feels comfortable. Clinically, the first thing the parent brings up is often significant.

When basic demographic information has not been obtained through a questionnaire, it should be obtained during the interview process. In addition, Ackerman (2006, pp. 119–121) has determined that information in several other areas should be pursued as well.

Place of Residence
The interview should also address the number of times that the individual has moved and what the current living environment is like.

Place of Employment
This section should also discuss job satisfaction, ability for promotion, and duration of employment.

Employment History
The employment history does not need to include part-time jobs held during school. However, if the interviewee has only had part-time jobs, then clarification should be sought as to why. Similarly, if an individual has changed jobs more than once every few years, that should be discussed, with consideration given to calling former employers to verify information.

Table 2.1   Minimum Standards of Practice in Conducting Child Custody and Visitation Evaluations

Standard	Foundation
1. Child custody evaluations are by definition "forensic evaluations"	AACAP (1997): Galatzer-Levy, Kraus, & Galatzer-Levy (2009); Gould (2006); Heilbrun (2001); Melton, Petrila, Poythress, & Slobogin (2007); Otto et al. (2003)
2. The purpose of the evaluation is to assess the psychological best interest of the child	APA (2009); California Rules of Court (2003); Martindale (2001)
3. The court is the evaluator's primary client	AACAP (1997); AFCC (2006); Melton, Petrila, Poythress, & Slobogin (2007); NCPA (1994)
4. The evaluator is either court-appointed or assigned by consent	Ackerman (2006); AACAP (1997); Committee on Ethical Guidelines for Forensic Psychologists (1991); Gould (2006); Heilbrun (2001); Melton, Petrila, Poythress, & Slobogin (2007)
5. The scope of the evaluation is anchored to specific referral questions	Ackerman (2006); APA (2009); Gould (2006); Heilbrun (2001)
6. The evaluator obtains informed consent from all parties	AACAP (1997); APA (2009); AFCC (2006); California Rules of Court (2003); Committee on Ethical Guidelines for Forensic Psychologists (1991); Heilbrun (2001); Martindale (2001)
7. The skills, knowledge, and expertise needed to conduct a competent evaluation requires that the evaluator gain specialized forensic competence	Ackerman (2006); American Academy of Psychiatry & Law (AAPL, 1995); APA (2009); AFCC (2006); Committee on Ethical Guidelines for Forensic Psychologists (1991); Gould (2006); Heilbrun (2001)
8. Record keeping is of the highest standard and one's records should be retained	Committee on Ethical Guidelines for Forensic Psychologists (1991); Gould (2006); Martindale (2001)
9. The evaluator uses multiple avenues of data gathering	Ackerman (2006); California Rules of Court (2003); Galatzer-Levy, Kraus, & Galatzer-Levy (2009); Heilbrun (2001); Melton, Petrila, Poythress, & Slobogin (2007)

Table 2.1 (Continued)

Standard	Foundation
10. Opinions are not given about the psychological functioning of any individual who has not been personally evaluated	AAPL (1995); APA (2009); AFCC (2006); Committee on Ethical Guidelines for Forensic Psychologists (1991)
11. The evaluator clarifies with the parties in advance his or her contractual arrangements for conducting the evaluation	Ackerman (2006); APA (1994); California Rules of Court (2003); Committee on Ethical Guidelines for Forensic Psychologists (1991); Martindale (2001); Melton, Petrila, Poythress, & Slobogin (2007); Stahl (1999); Strassburger, Gutheil & Brodsky (1997)
12. The evaluator acknowledges any implicit or explicit limitations of psychological knowledge and techniques used in the evaluation	APA (2009); Heilbrun (2002); Melton, Petrila, Poythress, & Slobogin (2007)
13. The evaluator avoids ex parte communication with counsel or the judge	California Rules of the Court (2003); NCPA (1994); Stahl (1999)
14. The evaluator avoids accepting allegations as facts	Gould (2006); Melton, Petrila, Poythress, & Slobogin (2007); NCPA (1994)
15. It is important to assess the family factors that assess the child(ren)	APA (2009); AFCC (2006); Otto et al. (2003)
16. Evaluators shall have a minimum of a master's degree in a mental health field	AFCC (2006); California Rules of Court (2003)
17. The evaluator shall be knowledgeable about the relevant statutes and case law governing child custody	Ackerman (2006); Heilbrun (2001); Melton, Petrila, Poythress, & Slobogin (2007)
18. Comparable evaluation techniques should be used to evaluate each litigant	Ackerman (2006); AFCC (2006); Gould (2006)
19. Appropriate and relevant collateral information is obtained	Ackerman (2006); APA (1994); AFCC (2006); Gould (2006); Heilbrun (2001); Melton, Petrila, Poythress, & Slobogin (1997); NCPA (1994); Otto et al. (2003); Skafte (1995)

(continued)

Table 2.1 (Continued)

Standard	Foundation
20. The quality of the relationship between parent/caretaker and child should be assessed	Ackerman (2006); AFCC (2006); Galatzer-Levy & Kraus (1999); Gould (2006); Stahl (1999)
21. Evaluators should adhere to the ethical principles in their own professions	Ackerman (2006); AACAP (1997); AFCC (2006); Galatzer-Levy, Kraus, & Galatzer-Levy (2009); Martindale (2001); Melton, Petrila, Poythress, & Slobogin (1997)
22. There are essential differences between traditional clinical practice and the performance of child custody evaluations	AACP (1997); Galatzer-Levy, Kraus, & Galatzer-Levy (2009); Gould (2006); Melton, Petrila, Poythress, & Slobogin (2007)
23. Evaluators need to be aware of and knowledgeable about special considerations in child custody evaluations	Ackerman (2006); AACP (1997); Gould (2006); Stahl (1999)
24. Evaluators must be aware of relevant law, local rules, and rules of discovery	Committee on Ethical Guidelines for Forensic Psychologists (1991); Heilbrun (2001); Melton Petrila, Poythress, & Slobogin (2007)

Education History

This portion of the interview can be very straightforward but may require extensive discussion if the interviewee has dropped out of school, failed out of school, or not completed any high school or college program that was begun.

Names and Ages of Children, and Whether the Children Are Living at Home

In the case where children are residing in another residence, either exclusively or on a primary placement basis, discussion should include why, for how long, and the quality of contact.

Previous Psychological or Psychiatric Treatment

Releases should be sought from all previous or present therapists, counselors, or physicians who have prescribed psychiatric medications. This portion of the interview should discuss whether the treatment was inpatient or outpatient, what the diagnosis and treatment were, what the outcome was, and what the individual learned from the therapeutic process. It can also be beneficial to determine if the therapy was terminated by mutual agreement, by the therapist, or by the client/patient leaving prematurely. Furthermore, this section should also discuss whether any psychiatric medications have been taken previously or are currently being taken.

Alcohol or Other Drug Use/Abuse History

Although some individuals consider alcohol and other drug abuse as falling under the category of psychological or psychiatric treatment, it is frequently viewed as a separate category. It is important to obtain the parents' perceptions of the quantity of drinking and whether the drinking has ever interfered with employment, school, social relationships, or familial relationships. Discussions should also include whether the individual has ever been involved in any alcohol or other drug abuse treatment. When the answer is affirmative, it is essential to determine if the parent is still involved in aftercare. One of the most frequent indications of relapse in alcohol and other drug abuse patients is termination of aftercare less than two years posttreatment.

Problems with the Law

Ordinarily, this portion of the interview would not include problems that the parent had during teenage years or minor problems during college years. However, when there is considerable history of difficulty with the law during childhood and adolescence, this area needs to be explored in further detail. One of the more important components to be identified during this portion of the interview is whether these problems were isolated or are related to a chronic behavior pattern. When an individual has had three or four arrests for the same or similar crimes, it is significant, even when these arrests may have spread over a period of 20 or 25 years. The evaluator must also determine if the problems with the law were in any way related to psychological problems and, if they were, whether treatment was sought. Crimes against property may be viewed as less serious than crimes against persons in this context. Most states have a web site that can be utilized to determine what court actions an individual has been involved in. It is important to find out what this web site is and to access it for each party in the divorce.

Information About the Family of Origin

Questions in this area would include whether parents are living or deceased and if deceased, when they died and how the loss was grieved. Familial histories of alcoholism, suicide, mental illness, divorce, and other serious concerns should be discussed in detail. The types of occupations or professions the individual parents had and the relative success of their employment careers should also be discussed.

As part of discussions about the family of origin, ages of siblings, marital status of siblings, and closeness with siblings should also be discussed.

Any Problems with Developmental Milestones

Not only should the parents be interviewed about whether they had problems with any developmental milestones but also whether the children who are subjects of the custody evaluation had any problems with developmental milestones. Of interest is if the parents have different perceptions of the developmental milestones and any related problems that their children had. History of walking, talking, toilet training, eating patterns, sleeping patterns, unusual childhood illnesses, and seizure disorders are of particular interest.

History of Sexual Abuse or Assault

Since sexual abuse or sexual assault can have a profound, long-term negative impact on individuals (see Chapter 9), it is essential that this area be explored in detail when parents answer in the affirmative. Questions in the area should include particulars about when the abuse or assault occurred, who the perpetrator was, what the resolution was, if a protective services agency was involved, whether any legal action was taken, and whether the individual sought any therapeutic relief following the abuse or assault.

Current Medical Problems

When the medical problem is serious in nature, discussion must include how it is being treated and if the illness affects the parent's activities of daily living.

Major Stressors in Parents' Lives

Does the parent perceive that there are currently any major stressors in his or her life, other than the divorce or post-judgment dispute? Again, when the answer is affirmative, detailed questions must be asked about how these stressors affect the parent, the child(ren), employment, and/or social relationships.

Previous Marriage History

When parents have been previously married, the evaluator must determine whether there were children from that marriage. Questions should be asked about where those children are residing. If they reside with the parent being interviewed, questions should also address how much time the other parent is spending with the children, what the parent being interviewed feels about the relationship of these children with the other parent, and questions that would identify any other problems. In the case where the children are living with the other parent, questions should address how much time the parent being interviewed spends with those children and, specifically, whether or not any problems are associated with those contact times. If so, additional questioning should ensue. In cases where the parent being interviewed did not receive custody or placement of the children from a previous marriage, that parent should be questioned about whether placement was determined by a court order or stipulation, or through mediation. When the court ordered that the child be placed with the other parent, details should be sought as to why the court made that decision. It is not necessary to obtain detailed information as to why the previous marriage ended in divorce, but summary information would be beneficial. However, when there are major problems with the previous marriage, further questioning would be helpful.

Current Marital Situation

In addition to background questions, questions about the current divorce situation should also be asked. They include problems with visitation or periods of physical placement, reasons the parent feels he or she would make the better custodial or placement parent, concerns that the parent feels that the other parent has about him or her, what the parent considers the ideal placement schedule to be, reason for the current divorce, living environment, description of child, and discipline (Ackerman, 1995, pp. 86–87).

The interview process could be as short as an hour with individuals who have uneventful life histories. There are examiners who engage in 10 to 12 hours of interview covering the individual's life from birth until the time of the evaluation. Other interviewers are only interested in obtaining information that is directly or indirectly relevant to the divorce process. In most cases anything that is important enough to discuss can be obtained in two to three hours of interview. Generally, to interview beyond that leads to extraneous or less important information.

Psychologists are often put in the position of being asked to evaluate the importance that should be placed on the behavior(s) of an individual. This author advocates a two-pronged approach in assessing the importance placed on a particular behavior. The recency and frequency of the behavior should be assessed. The more recently the behavior(s) have occurred and the more frequently they have occurred over time, the more importance that should be placed on these behaviors.

The Child Interview

Kuehnle, Greenberg, and Gottlieb (2004) addressed the issue of interviewing children in divorce cases. They point out that relevant issues include "(1) reaction to the divorce; (2) perception of his or her role in the divorce; (3) view of his or her parents as they go through the divorce process; (4) perception of how the divorce has affected his or her relationships with parents, siblings, relatives, and friends; and (5) view of how he or she has been impacted by each parent's new social life" (p. 99). For younger children the evaluator should explore "(1) ability to separate from parent; (2) understanding of 'divorce'; (3) perception of relationship with each parent; (4) emotional status; and (5) self-concept" (p. 101). With children between 9 and 12 years of age, during the middle school years the child interview should include "(1) how the child learned of the divorce; (2) information about the divorce provided to the child (e.g., blame for the divorce, emotional injuries cased to one parent by the other, information from the court documents; (3) the child's perception of self-blame or blame of a specific parent, and the bases of the blame; (4) relationship and one-on-one time spent with each parent; (5) involvement with the parent in the child's school and extracurricular activity; and (6) how the child is coping with the parental separation and other stressors associated with a broken family" (p. 101).

Kuehnle, Greenberg, and Gottlieb suggest a six-step procedure in performing the interview. They include "(a) development of rapport; (b) assessment of the child's ability to answer questions and provide details; (c) identification of ground rules for the interview; (d) interview practice of non-essential questions; (e) introduction of the substantive topic beginning with open-ended and moving to more directive questions; and (f) interview closure" (p. 108).

All children three years of age and older should be interviewed individually. Certainly the younger the child, the less involved the interview process is likely to be. With very young children, interviews may actually be relatively short due to language limitations, lack of awareness of problems within the family, or unwillingness to respond. Even so, the attempt should be made.

Although children three to five years old may wish to have a parent present during the interview process, it is generally not a good idea to use this format. Any time a parent is in the interview room with the child, the child is likely to respond to questions in the direction that the child perceives the parent wishes. There is no harm in having the parent bring the child to the interview room and leave prior to the content-related questions. In situations where the child is unwilling to allow the parent to leave the evaluation room, it may be helpful to have the other parent bring the child on a different occasion and have that parent attempt to leave the child. It is of clinical significance, and should be noted, when the child is willing to be left with the psychologist by one parent but not the other. In situations where the child refuses to be left after this process has been attempted a number of times on several different occasions, it is appropriate to abandon attempts to interview that child. It is also of note when a child older than four or five years of age demonstrates the problem just described. When this is the case, it becomes essential for the interviewer to attempt to determine what has occurred in the child-rearing practices that has resulted in this immature behavior.

The child interview should include such questions as the following: "How would you feel if the judge said you should live with your father?" And next, "How would you feel if the judge said you should live with your mother?" When the child responds in either the affirmative or the negative, follow-up questions should be asked to clarify the reason for the response, unless the child has already given a detailed response in the original answer. When the child gives an ambivalent response, care must be taken to avoid pressuring the child to answer the question when he or she really does not want to.

> **CAUTION**
>
> Do not ever ask a child directly where he or she would like to live.

As a follow-up to the previously discussed area, the child can be asked, "Would you like to see your mother/father more time, less time, or about the same amount of time?" The answer should be explored in detail, especially if the child wants more or less contact when they have an ample amount of time or the answer is "about the same" if they do not have much time at present.

Another question to ask is, "When you do something bad, how does your mother/father punish you?" When a child responds with an answer that suggests physical punishment, it is essential to query about the extent of the punishment, the implements used for punishment, and whether any injury has resulted from the punishment. Certainly, if previously undisclosed physical abuse is identified at this time, it becomes necessary for the evaluator to report the findings to the child protective services agency in the community. As a follow-up to the discipline/punishment questions, the child would be asked, "Did your mother/father ever hurt you?" Again, if the answer is in the affirmative, details should be sought.

When talking about the subject of hurt or injury, questions like "Did your mother ever hurt your father?" or "Did your father ever hurt your mother?" should also be asked. In asking these questions, the examiner would have the opportunity to pursue any details that may be clinically significant. It is also important to know if the child witnessed this directly and, if not, from whom the information was obtained.

One of the areas of concern is whether either or both of the parents coached the child to say something that would be advantageous to that parent's case. Generally, this can be dealt with by asking the child directly, "What did your mother or father tell you to be sure to tell me today?" Coaching is generally easy to discern. In those cases where coaching has not taken place, the child is likely to look at the evaluator in a confused manner and say things like "I don't know" or "Nothing" or "Just be honest." However, in those instances where the parent has actually encouraged the child to share certain information, the child generally will respond with a long, rather well-rehearsed litany of statements. When asked to discuss this again at some point later in the interview, this child is likely to repeat the same information either verbatim or almost verbatim. In addition, ask questions like, "When your mother/father talks about your father/mother, what does she/he say?"

Concerns are often raised about substance abuse on the part of the parents. Questions like, "Have you ever seen your mother/father drunk?" are an important part of the interview process. An affirmative answer would be followed by questions about frequency and behavior of the parent when under the influence of alcohol.

Each child should be asked if he or she has talked about the divorce with anyone. This provides the examiner with the opportunity to determine if either or both of the parents are sharing appropriate information with the child. Since it is disadvantageous for the children to know more information than is necessary, parents' sharing such information would be a negative indicator.

A series of questions should be asked about parental involvement with the child. Not only should these questions deal with discipline (addressed earlier) but Ackerman (2006, pp. 128–129) suggests the following:

- What kinds of activities does your mother/father do with you?
- Who takes you to school?
- Who goes to school conferences?
- Who drives car pools?
- What activities do you go to with your grandparents/aunts/uncles/cousins?
- Who helps you with homework?
- Who takes you to the doctor?
- When you have a problem, who do you talk to about your problem?
- What are the household rules and who enforces them?
- Do you go to religious school? If so, who takes you?
- Who buys your clothes for you?
- When you stay at your father's house, what does he cook for dinner?
- When you stay at your mother's house, what does she cook for dinner?

Collateral Information

Collateral information from friends or relatives of the individual are likely to be relatively unreliable self-serving documents. However, if a friend or relative should write a letter that is unfavorable, particular attention should be paid to this letter. When looking at issues involving problems with the law, psychologically

≡ Rapid Reference 2.2

Obtaining Collateral Information

Collateral information can be obtained through interviewing or receiving information from:

- Stepparents
- Relatives
- Home visits
- Therapists
- School records/teachers
- Police records
- Employment records

maladaptive behavior, mental health histories, and substance abuse problems, the rules of recency and frequency should be applied. The more recent or frequent the event(s) are, the more attention should be paid to the problems. The less frequent or recent the events are, the less attention should be paid to the problem. Rapid Reference 2.2 lists forms of collateral information.

Tests of Cognitive Functioning

Tests of cognitive functioning should include intelligence tests, achievement tests, and psychoeducational tests. Some examiners feel that tests of cognitive functioning are not necessary, especially with well-educated individuals with advanced degrees. However, intelligence tests are not administered solely for the purpose of obtaining an IQ score. The subtests on an IQ test provide information about judgment, reasoning, memory, concentration, and many other factors that are relevant in evaluating an individual's ability to parent adequately. There is no event of greater importance for a child than education. If there is a significant discrepancy between the parent's ability and the child's ability, that parent may not be able to adequately support the child academically.

Personality Testing

The MMPI-2 remains the gold standard in personality testing. Every survey that has been performed identifies it as the most frequently used instrument. Most

≡ *Rapid Reference 2.3*

Frequent Elevation Interpretations

3–4 Elevations. These people tend to be very immature and may satisfy their own aggressions and hostilities through indirect acting out. They are often described as excitable, may have physical complaints, and may be passive-aggressive.

4–3 Elevations. The elevation of Scale 4 indicates the amount of aggressive hostile feelings present. When Scale 4 is higher than Scale 3, the controls are not always adequate. As a result, these individuals tend periodically to have violent episodes.

3–6 Elevations. These individuals tend to deny their hostilities, aggressions, and suspicions. They are hard to get along with because of their underlying egocentricity. Although their anger is seen by others, the individual is typically unaware of the level of anger.

6–3 Elevations. When Scale 6 is higher than Scale 3, suspiciousness and acting out behavior increases.

4–6/6–4 Elevations. These individuals may be hostile, resentful, and suspicious. They tend to transfer blame for their problems onto others. They are litigious and may threaten lawsuits. They have poor impulse control, are explosive, and have a propensity toward violence. Seriously disruptive relationships occur with the opposite sex. They also tend to have poor work records and demonstrate poor judgment.

recently, Ackerman and Brey (2010) find that psychologists use it 97.2% of the time in custody evaluations.

Individual Validity Scales in Child Custody Evaluations

The L, F, and K scales on the MMPI-2 remain the primary sources of information regarding the validity of the tests. Parents with high L scales are likely to be either excessively religious and moralistic or attempting to portray themselves in a very positive, "I'm perfect" light. This is particularly true when the L scale is elevated in conjunction with the K scale. With both the L and K scales elevated and a suppressed F scale, the resulting "V" pattern is commonly referred to as a *fake good* profile. If L is above 60 and K above 65 on the MMPI-2, the clinical scales may not be an accurate representation of the individual's psychological functioning, as there has probably been an overt attempt on the part of the subject to portray himself or herself in a highly favorable light. When the K scale is elevated alone, it represent defensiveness on the part of the parent. However, this defensiveness should not be considered significant unless the K scale is above 65 on the MMPI-2.

Research has demonstrated that the mean K scale of individuals involved in custody evaluations is 59 on the MMPI-2. This suggests that people involved in custody evaluations are more defensive than the general population, which is not surprising, given the legal battle being fought. When the F scale is elevated and the L and K scales are not, this suggests either confusion or "faking bad" on the part of the parent. Also, a difference between the F and F-back scores suggests that the individual was either more or less careful toward the end of the test or that there was an inconsistency in the individual's test-taking approach that may affect the overall validity of the results. When Scales F and 8 are both highly elevated, there is a strong suggestion of psychopathology. A very high F (90 or above) could be an indication of extreme psychopathology, extreme effort by the parents to make themselves look bad, poor reading ability, or random responding. It is necessary for the clinician to make this discrimination.

Medoff (1999) discussed this issue by stating that "it is critical to note that, while elevations have reached levels of statistical significance, they fall short of clinical significance" (p. 410). He goes on to state, "Nevertheless, it has become commonplace for psychologists engaged in this line of work to tender false casual attributions of clinically significant defensiveness to the divorce or custody dispute context" (p. 410). Their position essentially is, "We must take the divorce context into consideration, but cannot use it to excuse all defensiveness or lying" (p. 410).

Individual Clinical Scales in Custody Cases

Scale 1 (Hypochondriasis)
When Scale 1 is elevated, it is not likely to interfere with parenting skills unless the parent is significantly preoccupied with the physical symptomatology. In recent years, Chronic Fatigue Syndrome and Fibromyalgia are diagnostic labels that have been used with greater frequency. It is not unusual to see elevation on Scale 1 in chronic fatigue patients. These patients may engage in behavior that will interfere with their parenting skills.

Scale 2 (Depression)
Scale 2 is the most frequently elevated scale. When this scale is elevated in conjunction with Scale 7 (Psychasthenia), the parent is relatively unlikely to be able to

support the child's self-esteem development. Furthermore, if the depression has reached a vegetative state, it is likely that the parent will not be able to function adequately in parenting tasks.

Scale 3 (Hysteria)

An elevation on Scale 3 is likely to be found when an individual overreacts to and overinterprets events. As a result, reports of incidents that have occurred are likely to be overstated and must be weighted against tendencies to overreact and overinterpret. These individuals also tend to have an unforgiving aspect to their personality.

Scale 4 (Psychopathic Deviate)

Generally speaking, there is little "good news" associated with an elevation on Scale 4. An elevation on Scale 4 represents deviance in thinking and often in behavior. This elevation can be acceptable in highly educated individuals. However, the lower the education level, the greater the concern about an elevated Scale 4. In addition, when a 4–9 profile is found, it represents individuals who are likely to demonstrate antisocial tendencies and transfer these tendencies to their children through teaching and modeling. The 4–9 profile individual typically does not do well with children who need structure. Their lack of ability to connect interpersonally with other individuals will also interfere with child rearing. It is important to interpret the 4–9 profile in conjunction with the first Factor-Anxiety Scale, a supplementary scale. The lower the score on the first Factor-Anxiety Scale, the greater the likelihood that the individual is demonstrating antisocial tendencies. However, if the Anxiety Scale is elevated in conjunction with the 4–9 profile, it is less likely that there will be concerns associated with it. Individuals with elevated 4–9 profiles have a considerable amount of difficulty accepting responsibility for their own behavior. They tend to blame others. In custody cases, a person with an elevated 4–9 who loses the custody litigation is not going to be able to accept responsibility for the fact that his or her behavior is what led to losing custody. Instead, such claims will be made as, "My ex lied about me in court, and that's why I lost" or, "The judge didn't know what he/she was doing" or, "If my attorney had done a better job, we would have won this case."

When Scales 4 and 6 are elevated together, there should be concern about the amount of anger and hostility that may be present and how that anger will interfere with the individual's ability to function with children and interact with the ex-partner. It may be necessary, as a result, to evaluate the safety level of the child(ren) in the presence of individuals with high 4–6–8, 4–6–9, or 4–6–8–9 profiles. These generally represent the most dangerous of elevations and were found in the three MMPIs administered to Jeffrey Dahmer.

Scale 6 (Paranoia)

Elevations on Scale 6 are not unusual in child custody cases. Many activities occurring during divorce litigation can engender feelings of paranoia. The other side may be hiring someone to follow the individual and, in fact, plot against the individual, appropriately raising the individual's level of suspiciousness. However, it is unlikely that Scale 6 will elevate much above 65 unless there was already an underlying component of paranoia present in the individual's personality.

Scale 7 (Psychasthenia)

Since elevations on Scale 7 result from lack of confidence, feelings of insecurity and inferiority, anxiety, and worrying, these characteristics will interfere with the parent's ability to interact with the child(ren) effectively.

Scale 8 (Schizophrenia)

An elevation on Scale 8 can represent confusion in thinking on the part of the parent. The greater the confusion on the part of the parent, the greater the unpredictability, which will lead to difficulty in having the child understand the parent's wishes or desires. This could result in overburdening or parentifying the child.

Scale 9 (Hypomania)

The individual with an elevated Scale 9 is likely to be impulsive, need excitement, and not recognize the consequences of his or her own behavior. Obviously, all of these represent a potential danger to the child. This is particularly dangerous when the scale is elevated along with 4, 6, and/or 8. Scale 9 is often referred to as the "energizer bunny" of the MMPI-2. Any elevated scale on the MMPI-2 will be more pronounced or energized if 9 is elevated with it.

Scale 0 (Social Introversion)

An individual with an elevated Scale 0 could be so introverted that he or she will be unable to appropriately model prosocial behavior.

Effect of Child Custody Litigation

Many MMPI/MMPI-2 studies have been performed looking at the results of child custody litigation. The results of the Ackerman and Ackerman (1992) study have been reported previously. Segal (1996) found that custody litigants are likely to have elevated L and K Scales that like a "fake good" profile (p. 14).

Ben-Porath (1995) also report correlations between scores on various scales of the MMPI and custody determination. Relatively high correlations were found between the Paranoia and Depression scales and parents who lost legal custody of their children. In other words, parents with high scores on Scales

2 and 6 were likely to fail to get custody. Moderate correlations were found between the Depression Scale (2), the Social Introversion Scale (0), the Anxiety Content Scale (ANX), the Low Self-Esteem Content Scale (LSE), and the Family Problems Content Scale (FAM), and whether parents lost custody of their children. When looking at the validity scales, people motivated to "fake good" or "fake bad" were unable to avoid elevating the F Scales, the F-K score, and the Ds (Dissimulation Index) index scores. However, the faking did not elevate the VRIN (Variable Response Inconsistency) score (Ackerman & Kane, 2005, p. 459).

CAUTION

- Do not become concerned about elevations of the K Scale below 60 in custody cases.
- Determine how much of the 3, 4, and 6 Scale elevations are a function of the divorce case by reviewing critical items.
- Make sure a complete evaluation of the MMPI-2 results is undertaken.

A complete evaluation of the MMPI-2 results includes reviewing Validity scales, Clinical scales, Content scales, Supplementary scales, Subscales, Subtle and Obvious scores, and an interview about critical items.

Minnesota Multiphasic Personality Inventory—Second Edition—Restructured Form (MMPI-2-RF)

Many of the criticisms have been leveled against the MMPI-2. One of the greatest criticisms about the MMPI-2 Clinical Scales is that they are not separate and distinct in that there is considerable item overlap, with many items appearing on two or more of the scales.

In 2003, Auke Tellegen and his colleagues published a monograph about the MMPI-2 Restructured Clinical (RC) Scales. The RC Scales are designed specifically to be discreet scales without item overlap. As a result, the intent is to allow for a purer interpretation of the results.

The Restructured Clinical Scales have been incorporated into the new Minnesota Multiphasic Personality Inventory—Second Edition—Restructured Form (MMPI-2-RF). The overall objective in developing the MMPI-2-RF was to use a 338 item subset of the original MMPI-2 pool of items. As a result, the MMPI-2-RF should take less time to administer than the MMPI-2 itself. However, the authors have been informed that, even after the MMPI-2-RF is published, the University of Minnesota and Pearson Assessment has no intention of ceasing the publication and use of the regular MMPI-2.

There are three higher order scales that have been developed specifically to address the issue of psychopathology. They are:

1. The EID-Emotional/Eternalizing/Dysfunction
2. The THD-Thought Dysfunction
3. The BXD-Behavioral/Externalizing/Dysfunction Scales

The Validity Scales remain essentially the same with the L, K, VRIN, and TRIN (True Response Inconsistency) Scales; the main F-Scale; and the Fp (Infrequency-Psychopathology-Revised), which measures infrequent responses of psychiatric populations. There are a number of different F-Scales, including the FS (Infrequency-Somatic), which measures frequent somatic complaints in medical patient populations, and the FBS (the Fake Bad Scale-Revised), which addresses non-credible somatic and cognitive complaints.

Instead of the 10 main Clinical Scales, there are now eight restructured Clinical Scales on the MMPI-2-RF. In addition, there is the RCd: Demoralization Scale, which measures general unhappiness and dissatisfaction. The eight main RC Scales are:

1. RC1: Somatic Complaints—these diffuse physical health complaints
2. RC2: Low Positive Emotions—a distinctive, core vulnerability factor in depression
3. RC3: Cynicism—non-self-referential beliefs that others are bad and not to be trusted
4. RC4: Antisocial Behavior—rule breaking and irresponsible behavior
5. RC5: Ideas of Persecution—Self-referential beliefs that others pose a threat
6. RC6: Dysfunctional Negative Emotion—maladaptive anxiety, anger, irritability
7. RC7: Aberrant Experiences—unusual perceptions of thoughts associated with psychosis
8. RC8: Hypomanic Activation—overactivation, aggression, impulsivity, and grandiosity

It is relatively easy to see that the new RC Scales closely parallel the original MMPI-2 Clinical Scales in concept.

The MMPI-2-RF also has a number of Specific Problem (SP) Scales. These Specific Problem Scales are either divided into categories or parallel the underlying main RC Scale.

Specific Problem Scale
- Somatic
- HPC: head, pain complaints—head and neck pain

- NUC: neurological complaints—dizziness, weakness, paralysis, loss of balance, and so forth
- GIC: gastrointestinal complaints—nausea, recurring upset stomach, and poor appetite

Internalizing (RCd Facets)

- SUI: suicidal/death ideation—direct reports of suicidal ideation and recent attempts
- HLP: helplessness, hopelessness—belief that goals cannot be reached or problems solved
- SFD: self-doubt—lack of self-confidence, feelings of uselessness
- NFC: inefficacy—belief that one is indecisive and inefficacious
- COG: cognitive complaints—memory problems, difficulty concentrating

Externalizing (RC4 Facets)

- JCP: juvenile conduct problems—difficulties at school and at home, stealing
- SUB: substance abuse—current and past misuse of alcohol and drugs

RC9 Facets

- AGG: aggression—physical aggressiveness, violent behavior
- ACT: activation—heightened excitation and energy level

Internalizing (RC7 Facets)

- SNV: sensitivity/vulnerability—taking things too hard, being easily hurt by others
- STW: stress/worry—preoccupation with disappointments, difficulty with time pressure
- AXY: anxiety—pervasive anxiety, frights, frequent nightmares
- ANP: anger proneness—becoming easily angered, impatient with others
- BRF: behavior-restricting fears—fears that specifically inhibit normal behavior
- MSF: multiple specific fears—various specific fears involving blood, fire, thunder, and so forth

Interpersonal

- FML: family problems—conflictual family relationships
- IPP: interpersonal passivity—being unassertive and submissive
- SAV: social avoidance—not enjoying and avoiding social events

- SHY: shyness—feeling uncomfortable and anxious around others
- DSF: disaffiliativeness—disliking people and being around people

Interest Scales

- AES: Aesthetic-literary interest—literature, music, theater
- MEC: mechanical-physical interest—fixing and building things, the outdoors, sports

In 2006, David S. Nichols criticized the RC Scales, saying that:

> [T]he RC Scales selectively emphasize a single content theme embodied within each Clinical Scale. As such, they stand a considerable remove from the Clinical Scales because of the loss of the syndromal complexity that characterizes their parent scales.... In virtually all cases, the selected RC core dimensions are adequately, if not abundantly, represented in one or more of the numerous Content Based Scales of the MMPI-2.... As a result of the various problems, the RC Scales should be used with caution. Their application in medical, chronic pain, personnel, and forensic evaluations may be of particular concern because of the increased likelihood of forensic challenge.... Given the long history of the MMPI/MMPI-2 and the breadth of its use worldwide, it is unlikely that the RC project will be the final effort to find a sound and efficient means of establishing better control over the co-variation afflicting the Clinical Scales.... Future research will have a better outcome than the research that has been applied to the co-variation problem thus far.

Considerable research has been performed over the last two decades to determine the most frequently elevated scales on the MMPI-2 in divorce cases. Because of the newness of the MMPI-2-RF, there are no data that will help us understand what type of responses can be expected in custody evaluations utilizing the MMPI-2-RF. To that end, two research projects (Ackerman & Waisanen) and Ackerman & Kravit are currently under way to compare the results of individuals on the MMPI-2 and the MMPI-2-RF in child custody cases. It is hoped that we will have a better understanding of the efficacy of using the MMPI-2-RF in child custody cases. Although there is criticism of many of the RC Scales being similar to Content Scales, there is particular usefulness in the RC-4 and RC-8 Scales. The RC-4 Scale is a pool of items identifying antisocial conduct and addiction-related concerns. The RC-8 Scale is particularly sensitive to concerns about the possible presence of psychosis. (Until there is a substantial body of research on the RF Scales, the present author strongly recommends that they not be used in child custody evaluations.)

Millon Clinical Multiaxial Inventory-III

The MCMI has been in use for decades. The MCMI-III is the current offering and includes 175 true/false items. It can be differentiated from the MMPI-2 and Personality Assessment Inventory (PAI) in that most of its scales are devoted to diagnoses of personality disorders. Although there has been an attempt to coordinate the MCMI-III with DSM-IV diagnoses, this effort has not been altogether successful. Some of the scales (Avoidant, Dependent, Borderline, and Passive-Aggressive) have good to excellent convergence. However, inconsistent to poor convergence was found on the Obsessive-Compulsive, Antisocial, Histrionic, and Narcissistic scales.

Halon (2001) found the Desirability (Y), Histrionic (4), Narcissistic (5), and Compulsive (7) to be the most frequently elevated scales among custody litigants. Because these are the scales that have inconsistent or poor convergence, one has to question the utility of using the MCMI-III in child custody evaluations. McCann et al. (2001) found that scales 4, 5, and 7 did not overpathologize child custody examinees and recommended adjusting the scores accordingly. McCann et al. suggest that the MCMI-III should not be used alone and should be integrated with other test data.

Research (Hynan, 2004, p. 108) has also demonstrated that there are significantly different base rates between men and women on the Histrionic, Narcissistic, and Compulsive scales. As a result, women will score as significantly more pathological on those three scales than will men. Hynan concludes, "Practitioners need to be particularly cautious about using the MCMI-III in custody evaluations.... Also, the likelihood that an individual will be found normal on the MCMI-III is relatively small." Nevertheless, use of the MCMI in forensic work remains controversial (Lally, 2003; Rogers, 2003).

Pearson Assessments has attempted to address the issue regarding base rate score differences between men and women. Jay Flens reviewed the recent work by Pearson Assessment and states that he believes that Pearson's assessment does not adequately address the concerns about the base rate differences on the Histrionic, Narcissistic, and Compulsive scales. Flens also states that the new non-gendered norms have not been validated at this point. Using the new software update from Pearson will override the old software and the male/female norms will no longer be available to the consumer. He, too, seriously questions the use of the MCMI-III in custody cases and possibly other venues (personal communication, July 16, 2009).

Based on the recent concerns that have been generated about the use of the MCMI-III in child custody evaluations and in forensic evaluations in general, this author no longer recommends its use in child custody evaluations or other forensic settings. Instead, when the practitioner wants to use an additional personality assessment instrument with the MMPI-2, it is now recommended that the PAI be used instead of the MCMI-III.

The PAI

The Personality Assessment Inventory (PAI) was found to be the second most frequently used multiscale inventory in forensic evaluations of adults (Archer, Buffington-Vollum, Stredny, & Handel, 2006, p. 88). The PAI has been in use for almost two decades at this time. It has a strong advantage over the MMPI-2 and MCMI-III in that it contains nonoverlapping scales that enhance its discriminant validity. As discussed before, it is recommended that the PAI be used in conjunction with the MMPI-2 in performing forensic evaluations in general and child custody evaluations specifically. Rapid References 2.4 through 2.8 outline PAI indices.

"The PAI is a self-administered, objective test of personality and psycho-pathology designed to provide information on critical client variables" (Morey, 2003, p. 1). Like similar instruments, it has Validity Scales and Clinical Scales. In addition, it adds Treatment Scales and Interpersonal Scales.

Validity Scales

Inconsistency (ICN): Determines whether the client is answering consistently throughout the inventory. Each pair consists of highly (positively or negatively) correlated items.

Infrequency (INF): Determines whether the client is responding care-lessly, randomly, or idiosyncratically. Items are neutral with respect to psychopathology and have extremely high or low endorsement rates.

Negative Impression (NIM): Suggests an exaggerated unfavorable impression or malingering.

Positive Impression (PIM): Suggests the presentation of a very favorable impression or reluctance to admit minor flaws.

Clinical Scales

Somatic Complaints (SOM): Focuses on preoccupation with health matters and somatic complaints associated with Somatization or conversion disorders.

Anxiety (ANX): Focuses on phenomenology and observable signs of anxiety, with an emphasis on assessment across different response modalities.

Anxiety-Related Disorders (ARD): Focuses on symptoms and behaviors related to specific anxiety disorders—particularly phobias, traumatic stress, and obsessive-compulsive symptoms.

Depression (DEP): Focuses on symptoms and phenomenology of depressive disorders.

Mania (MAN): Focuses on affective, cognitive, and behavioral symptoms of mania and hypomania.

Paranoia (PAR): Focuses on symptoms of paranoid disorders and on more enduring characteristics of the paranoid personality.

Schizophrenia (SCZ): Focuses on symptoms relevant to the broad spectrum of schizophrenic disorders.

Borderline Features (BOR): Focuses on attributes indicative of a borderline level of personality functioning, including unstable and fluctuating interpersonal relations, impulsivity, affective lability and instability, and uncontrolled anger.

Antisocial Features (ANT): Focuses on history of illegal acts and authority problems, egocentrism, lack of empathy and loyalty, instability, and excitement-seeking.

Alcohol Problems (ALC): Focuses on problematic consequences of alcohol use and features of alcohol dependence.

Drug Problems (DRG): Focuses on problematic consequences of drug use (both prescription and illicit) and features of drug dependence.

Treatment Scales

Aggression (AGG): Focuses on characteristics and attitudes related to anger, assertiveness, hostility, and aggression.

Suicidal Ideation (SUI): Focuses on suicidal ideation, ranging from hopelessness to thoughts and plans for the suicidal act.

Stress (STR): Measures a lack of perceived social support, considering both the level and quality of available support.

Treatment Rejection (RXR): Focuses on attributes and attitudes indicating a lack of interest and motivation in making personal changes of a psychological or emotional nature.

Interpersonal Scales

Dominance (DOM): Assesses the extent to which a person is controlling and independent in personal relationships. This scale reflects a bipolar dimension with a dominant style at the high end and a submissive style at the low end.

Warmth (WRM): Assesses the extent to which a person is interested in supportive and empathic personal relationships. This scale reflects a bipolar dimension, with a warm, outgoing style at the high end, and a cold, rejecting style at the low end.

A several-step procedure is used in interpreting the PAI. The first step is determining the likelihood of profile distortion. All subsequent interpretive decisions are based on this determination (Morey, 2003, p. 27).

The ICN and INF scales can elevate as a result of a carelessly completed questionnaire, reading or language problem, confusion, or clerical scoring errors. Research suggests that the NIM Scale is better at detecting efforts to simulate severe psychopathology than it is at identifying malingering when milder forms of disorder are being simulated (Morey, 2003, p. 49).

DON'T FORGET

Do not attempt to interpret the PAI if 18 or more items on the test were left unanswered. Also, do not interpret individual scales if 20% of items on that scale were left unanswered (Morey, 2003, p. 23).

A malingering index has been developed by Morey (2003) and is discussed in Rapid Reference 2.4.

≡ Rapid Reference 2.4

Malingering Index

Source: Morey, 2003

Content: Sum of eight configural features of profile, involving comparisons among 12 PAI scales and subscales.

Descriptive statistics: Community sample mean of 0.46 features (SD = 0.74); clinical sample mean of 0.80 (SD = 0.98).

Correlates: Correlates moderately with NIM and MMPI F and inversely with PIM; correlates modestly with Rogers discriminant function.

Interpretation: Scores of 3 or above raise questions of overt efforts to malinger more severe mental disorders; scores of 5 or above are highly specific to malingering. Score appears to show moderate relationship to respondent's true mental health status; false positive elevations are more common among hostile, suspicious, and unempathic patients.

Source: From L. C. Morey, *Essentials of PAI Assessment.* Copyright © 2003 John Wiley & Sons, Inc. This material is used by permission of John Wiley & Sons, Inc.

≡ Rapid Reference 2.5

Rogers Discriminant Function

Source: Rogers, Hinds, and Sewell (1996).

Content: Weighted sum of features from 20 PAI scales and subscales.

Descriptive Statistics: Community sample mean of −1.00 (SD = 1.08); clinical sample mean of −1.15 (SD = 1.17).

Correlates: Correlates modestly with the Malingering index and INF; minimal correlations with NIM or MMPI's F scale.

Interpretation: Scores above zero suggest overt efforts to malinger mental disorder. Score appears to show little relationship to respondent's true mental health status; thus, elevations are unlikely to be produced by true psychopathology.

Source: From L. C. Morey, *Essentials of PAI Assessment.* Copyright © 2003 John Wiley & Sons, Inc. This material is used by permission of John Wiley & Sons, Inc.

A Defensiveness Index has also been developed (Morey, 2003) and is discussed in Rapid Reference 2.6.

Each of the scales has relevant subscales that are included in interpretation and are discussed in greater detail in Morey (2003).

A Personality Assessment Screener (Morey, 2003) has been developed and is discussed in Rapid Reference 2.7.

≡ Rapid Reference 2.6

Defensiveness Index

Source: Morey, 2003.

Content: Sum of eight configural features of profile, involving comparison among 13 PAI scales and subscales.

Descriptive statistics: Community sample mean of 2.81 features (SD = 1.52); clinical sample mean of 1.66 (SD = 1.54).

Correlates: Correlates moderately with PIM and MMPI's L; correlates modestly with the Cashel discriminant function, MMPI's K, and the Marlowe-Crowne Social Desirability Scale.

Interpretation: Scores of six or above raise questions of overt efforts to face good; sensitivity appears lower in individuals coached to produce believable positive impression profiles. Score appears to show moderate relationship to respondent's true mental health status.

Source: From L. C. Morey, *Essentials of PAI Assessment.* Copyright © 2003 John Wiley & Sons, Inc. This material is used by permission of John Wiley & Sons, Inc.

≣ *Rapid Reference 2.7*

Suicide Potential Index

Source: Morey, 2003

Content: Twenty configural features of the PAI profile involving information from 21 different scales and subscales related to suicide risk factors.

Descriptive statistics: Community sample mean of 3.14 features (SC = 3.22); clinical sample mean of 7.74 (SD = 5.30).

Correlates: Index correlates highly with BOR, DEP, ANX, and other markers of depression and demoralization, and it correlates strongly with overall profile elevation. Also correlates highly with NIM and can thus be influenced by negative profile distortion.

Interpretation: Scores of 13 or above suggest the presence of numerous risk factors for suicidality; scores of 18 or above represent an extreme configuration of risk factors.

Source: From L. C. Morey, *Essentials of PAI Assessment.* Copyright © 2003 John Wiley & Sons, Inc. This material is used by permission of John Wiley & Sons, Inc.

There is also a Suicide Potential Index and a Violence Potential Index, seen in Rapid References 2.8 and 2.9.

≣ *Rapid Reference 2.8*

Violence Potential Index

Source: Morey, 2003

Content: Twenty configural features of the PAI profile involving information from 24 different scales and subscales related to risk factors for violence.

Descriptive statistics: Community sample mean of 1.68 features (SD = 2.18); clinical sample mean of 4.40 (SD = 3.98).

Correlates: Highest correlates are BOR, ANT, AGG-P, and other markers of antisocial behavior and attitudes. Correlates strongly with overall profile elevation and also correlates with NIM; the index can thus be influenced by negative profile distortion.

Interpretation: Scores of 9 or above suggest the presence of numerous risk factors for dangerousness; scores of 17 or above represent an extreme configuration of risk factors.

Source: From L. C. Morey, *Essentials of PAI Assessment.* Copyright © 2003 John Wiley & Sons, Inc. This material is used by permission of John Wiley & Sons, Inc.

≡ *Rapid Reference 2.9*

Brief Description of PAS Scores

Total score: Assesses potential for emotional and behavioral problems of clinical significance and need for follow-up evaluation.

Negative Affect (NA) element: Suggests personal distress and the experience of unhappiness and apprehension.

Acting-Out (AO) element: Suggests behavior problems associated with impulsivity, sensation seeking, and drug use.

Health Problems (HP) element: Suggests somatic complaints and health concerns.

Psychotic Features (PF) element: Suggests risk for persecutory thinking and other psychotic phenomena.

Social Withdrawal (SW) element: Suggests social detachment and discomfort in close relationships.

Hostile Control (HC) element: Suggests an interpersonal style characterized by needs for control and inflated self-image.

Suicidal Thinking (ST) element: Suggests thoughts of death or suicide.

Alienation (AN) element: Suggests failures of supportive relationships and a distrust or disinterest in such relationships.

Alcohol Problems (AP) element: Suggests negative consequences related to alcohol use and abuse.

Anger Control (AC) element: Suggests difficulties in the management of anger.

Source: From L. C. Morey, *Essentials of PAI Assessment.* Copyright © 2003 John Wiley & Sons, Inc. This material is used by permission of John Wiley & Sons, Inc.

The strengths and weakness of the PAI will vary to a certain extent as a function of the application for which the test is being used. These strengths and weaknesses can be found in Rapid Reference 2.10.

Many psychologists report that they do not score the Rorschach, as their clinical experience and expertise over the years does not require scoring to help determine whether a Rorschach test taker is depressed, psychotic, has difficulty with emotional control, or is guarded. These same psychologists also report that the Rorschach is used as a structured clinical interview technique, as opposed to one that needs to be subjected to rigorous scoring and analysis. While these methods are certainly acceptable, they will not provide the in-depth analysis available through the Exner scoring system, and as a result they may not be as valuable in court proceedings.

≡ *Rapid Reference 2.10*

Other Personality Tests

Projective drawings, the Rorschach, TAT (Thematic Apperception Test), CAT (Children's Apperception Test), Roberts Apperception Test, and projective questions or sentence completion tests are used with frequency as part of the custody evaluation testing process (Ackerman & Ackerman, 1997). With the advent of the Exner scoring system, the Rorschach has become more than just a psychoanalytically based projective technique. If the Rorschach is to be scored, it must be scored according to the Exner system. The "structural summary" that Exner provides allows the examiner to generate many research-based hypotheses, an opportunity that was not available through previous scoring systems. Meloy, Hansen, and Weiner (1997) concluded that "the Rorschach has authority, or weight, in high courts of appeal throughout the United States" (pp. 60–61).

None of the projective techniques identified previously should be used as an instrument in isolation in generating hypotheses and drawing conclusions. Instead, they should serve as part of a battery of tests that collectively will provide information resulting in legitimate hypotheses and conclusions.

Specialized Instruments

Ackerman-Schoendorf Scales for Parent Evaluation of Custody (ASPECT)
Ackerman and Brey (2010) report almost a 250% increase in the use of the ASPECT over the Ackerman and Ackerman 1997 study, in spite of recent criticism. The ASPECT is designed to directly indicate appropriateness of a parent for custody of the child by identifying those characteristics reported in the psychological research as being determinative of fitness for custody or placement of a child. Fifty-six unweighted items are utilized to obtain a Parental Custody Index (PCI).

Interpretation of the ASPECT
The ASPECT is a compilation of many different components that have been reported in the professional literature to help identify who makes the best custodial parent. The PCI serves as a summary of all those components in the ASPECT. However, the results of the ASPECT should not be the single criterion used to determine who should be the custodial parent. In certain situations, the ASPECT results are irrelevant. For example, in a situation in which the father has been found guilty of sexually abusing his children, it is likely that the mother would be

awarded custody regardless of the ASPECT scores. For a parent who has acute ongoing substance abuse, active psychoses, or other blatantly disqualifying conditions, the results of the ASPECT would be more of interest value than a necessity to determine who the custodial parent should be. Interpretation of the ASPECT begins by comparing the PCIs of the two individuals.

With a standard deviation on the PCI of approximately 10, a difference in scores of 10 points or more between the mother and the father is considered to be significant. When a significant difference occurs, the examiner can report, for example, that based on the results of the ASPECT, the mother/father would make a better placement parent. However, before reaching this conclusion, the examiner must evaluate the significant difference based on cutoff score interpretation (scores above or below predetermined numbers).

It is assumed that the custody evaluation is performed in an effort to determine who would make the best placement parent, and that this determination is based on what is in the best interests of the child. When no significant differences are reported on the PCI, the results of the ASPECT suggest that neither parent would be a better placement parent than the other.

In such a case, if the best interests test is being utilized, there will likely be no substantial difference between the parents with regard to with whom the child resides. In these situations, it may be best not to make a recommendation for placement but instead to encourage the parents to try to mediate their differences. When mediation is successful, it saves the entire family the added psychological and financial burden of a custody dispute. The results of the psychological evaluation and the ASPECT can always be used to make a recommendation of a substantially equal placement schedule.

There are situations in which the scores can be significantly different yet be of no particular value. For example, if both scores fall above 85, which is the 80th percentile, both parents would make appropriate custodial parents, even if their scores are more than 10 points apart. When both scores fall below 65, which is the 12th percentile, it is likely that neither parent would make an appropriate custodial parent. As a result, interventions that include parenting classes, supervision, or even, in extreme cases, foster placement, must be considered. When a significant difference occurs, it can be helpful to look at the actual items to determine which items are scores in the critical direction for each individual.

Validity and Reliability of the ASPECT

With regard to validity, the ASPECT is considered to be content valid, because the questions were derived from the literature on custody issues. The gender study as well as the intercorrelation matrix gives evidence of construct validity. Predictive validity is measured in two separate ways. The first involves other psychologists' administering the ASPECT but not tallying the results until after they have already formulated custody recommendations. Their recommendations were compared with the ASPECT predictions to gain a measure of predictive validity.

A second predictive validity study involves comparing judges' custody decisions with the prediction made by the ASPECT. An outcome study of 56 cases compared the results of the ASPECT with the eventual outcome of the case, whether the outcome was the result of a stipulation or of a judge's order. In 59% of the cases the outcome was the result of a judge's order, whereas in 41% of the cases it was a result of a stipulation. The study compared results in cases where there was a 10-point or greater difference in ASPECT scores between the parents and cases where there was less than a 10-point difference. As mentioned earlier, a 10-point or greater difference is considered a significant difference and should be viewed as being predictive. Less than 10-point difference is not significant, and, as a result the ASPECT does not predict who would make the best custodial parent. In 30 of the cases, there was a 10-point or greater difference. In 28 of those 30 cases, or 93.3% of the time, the ASPECT results agreed with the judge's final order. In those 26 cases where there was less than a 10-point difference in the ASPECT scores, the ASPECT results agreed with the judge's decision 14 times and did not agree with the judge's decision 12 times. The 10-point difference cutoff was demonstrated as an accurate predictor of who would make the better custodial parent based on the judge's eventual recommendations after consideration of data from all relevant sources. Furthermore, the results substantiate the conclusion that a difference of less than 10 points is not interpretable in making a recommendation, as it represents close to an even split with the judge's ultimate decision.

Several research projects have been undertaken since the ASPECT was published. Ackerman and Ackerman (1992) utilized results from 262 parents who had been administered the ASPECT; these results are reported in Rapid Reference 2.4.

In 2000, the ASPECT-SF was developed for two reasons. In the 10 years since the ASPECT had been developed, there appeared to be less of an emphasis being placed on psychological testing in making custody and placement recommendations. Second, the ASPEC-SF can be used by all mental health professionals because no testing is required. The ASPECT-SF consists of 41 ASPECT items that are not tied to test results. ASPECT-SF PCI scores are highly correlated with ASPECT PCI scores ($r = .93$). The logical question that evolves from these data is why would one give the full ASPECT when the PCI-SF correlates .93 with the PCI (Ackerman & Schoendorf, 2000, p. 1).

≋ *Rapid Reference 2.11*

ASPECT RESEARCH

- The mean for all parents was 78.1, which was not significantly different from the mean for the standardization sample.
- However, all placement parents had significantly higher than mean (81.8) than did the nonplacement parents (74.3).
- The highest mean was found among all placement mothers (83.1), with the lowest mean found among all nonplacement fathers (73.6).
- Hubbard (1996) compared how the ASPECT results correlated with the newly developed Parent-Child Relationship Inventory (PCRI), which was purported by the publisher to be useful in custody evaluations. Adequate correlations were not found to support the use of the PCRI with the ASPECT.
- Beyer (1996) also performed a dissertation study that has extremely important implications for the validity of the ASPECT. Beyer compared the individual child's ratings on a life satisfaction scale of total satisfaction in each parent's home to the individual parent's PCI at the time that the ASPECT was administered. An average of three years after the divorce, 67% of individuals who found life with the father to be more satisfying had fathers with higher PCIs at the time of administration. Furthermore, 73% of children who saw life more satisfying with mothers an average of three years later had mothers with higher PCIs at the time of the administration. Caution must be taken when interpreting these results, as a relatively low total sample number was used in this study. Replication with a larger total sample would be desirable.

Wellman (1994) wrote a critique of the ASPECT indicating that "the items making up the ASPECT relate closely to the current literature on appropriate criteria for custody decisions. Further the measure uses criteria from many sources (intellectual, personality, and academic achievement tests, interviews and observations) creating a comprehensive data base" (p. 18).

When the ASPECT was originally developed it was reviewed in the *Mental Measurements Yearbook* and in other literature. Brodzinsky (1993) reviewed a number of instruments that have been used for custody evaluations. He states, "Two interesting and more quantitative approaches to the assessment of custody and visitation disputes have been developed by Bricklin (1984) and Ackerman and Schoendorf (1992)" (p. 213) and concludes:

Despite the limitations of these alternative assessment procedures, they represent a valuable addition to the field of child custody evaluations. Most important, they shift the focus from a more traditional clinical assessment to one in which the evaluator is focusing more on a functional analysis of the parties' competencies within specific childcare roles. As such, these instruments are likely to provide information that is particularly relevant to the issues before the court. (p. 218)

Otto and Edens (2003) and Otto et al. (2000) provide thoughtful critiques of the ASPECT. Otto et al. report three primary concerns. The basic concern that is identified throughout the literature is with regard to basic psychometric properties (Arditti, 1995; Melton, 1995; Wellman, 1994). In addition, concerns are generated that some of the items have "no clear relationship to custody outcomes," that some "key factors" relevant to final custody decision are not incorporated into the assessment process, and that the PCI "encourages clinicians to offer ultimate issue opinions" (p. 331).

Otto and Edens (2003) point out another common criticism with regard to using judges' decisions as a criterion for predictive validity. They state, "Moreover, although the PCI results apparently were not presented to the judges, it is unclear exactly what (if any) mental health information they were provided about the parents and whether or not this had any impact on their custody determinations" (p. 267).

Arditti (1995) reviewed the ASPECT, stating, "The ASPECT represents an important effort to quantify elements associated with parental effectiveness, as well as provide a sophisticated interpretation of test results. Its major shortcomings are its lack of internal validity and cumbersome administration, given the battery of tests deemed necessary" (p. 21).

Melton (1995) states:

In short, the ASPECT was ill-conceived: An instrument that results in a score showing the parent who should be preferred in a custody decision necessarily results in over-reaching by experts who use it. Even if the idea had merit, though, the psychometric properties of the ASPECT remain essentially unknown, and the item selection and scoring procedures appear to pull for often irrelevant conclusions. (p. 23)

Melton, Petrila, Poythress, and Slobogin (1997) raise several concerns about the ASPECT addressed later in the Otto and Edens and Otto et al. works. Melton and colleagues raise concerns about psychometric properties, item selection, averaging scores, and some factors being ignored (p. 503). While accurate, item-related concerns reflect fewer than 5 of the 56 items on the ASPECT. Psychometrically, these few items could be eliminated and the overall reliability of the PCI would not be affected. Although some of the psychometric concerns that Melton, Petrila, Poythress, and Slobogin raise may have merit, it does not seem prudent to throw out the baby with the bathwater because a few items may not be as reflective of parental capacity as once thought.

In previous publications, Melton has indicated that he does not believe that psychologists should be testifying to the ultimate issue in custody cases. Because the ASPECT is specifically designed to help the psychologist answer the ultimate issue for the court, it would be surprising if Melton supported use of the instrument. Furthermore, Arditti's comments are well taken.

However, the authors of the ASPECT do not apologize for a "cumbersome administration given the battery of tests deemed necessary" (Ackerman & Kane, 2005, p. 548). It is felt that one of the strengths of the ASPECT is its broad-based database that requires information from a wide battery of instruments. The best interest of the child criterion requires that the assessments be comprehensive.

Otto et al. (2000) and Otto and Edens (2003) raise some of the issues that Arditti (1995), Wellman (1994), and Melton (1995) had previously raised in their writings. They also address new issues. It must be remembered that there are 56 items on the ASPECT that were judged to be relevant to custody decision making in the early 1990s, when the instrument was developed. Some of these issues may not be as relevant in 2010 as they were in 1990. However, as the manual points out, 5 of the 56 items can be eliminated without affecting the overall PCI. Therefore, if several items are not as relevant today as they were 15 years ago or are deemed not to be related to parent competencies as suggested by Melton, Petrila, Poythress, and Slobogin and Otto et al., the overall PCI is not affected until the research or criticism reaches the level of demonstrating that more than seven items are not relevant.

Otto and Edens correctly point out that third-party interviews are not incorporated into the assessment process on the PCI. However, they state that "key factors" are not incorporated. They do not identify factors other than third-party interviews that are not included. Finally, they address the issue of psychologists offering ultimate issue opinions. Ackerman et al. (2004) indicate that approximately 70% to 75% of family law judges, family law attorneys, and psychologists support psychologists' testifying to the ultimate issue. Those not supporting psychologists' testifying to the ultimate issue are espousing a minority opinion not representing the standard of practice within the profession.

Bricklin Instruments

Criticisms have been leveled against the Bricklin Perceptual Scales (BPS) and the Perception of Relationships Test (PORT) based on lack of reliability and validity data, and that these measures are difficult to interpret. The results of the BPS are more defendable than the results of the PORT, but neither may meet Heilbrun's criteria, as outlined in Chapter 1. With regard to the Bricklin family of instruments, there has been so much negative literature for so long that the use of any of these instruments in child custody evaluations is questionable and risky, at best. For example, Otto and Edens (2003) evaluated the BPS, the PORT, and the Parent Perception of Child Profile (PPCP). They conclude that the BPS is "loosely standardized," the interrater reliability is not established and the normative sample is not evident. They indicate there is little evidence of reliability and no normative data available for the court, and that the PPCP and Parent Awareness Skills Survey (PASS) are not standardized and offer no indication that the results are reliable.

Parent-Child Relationship Inventory

The PCRI assesses parents' attitudes toward parenting and toward their children. The PCRI yields a quantitative description of the parent-child relationship that complements other assessment procedures used in clinical evaluations of children and families. Rather than replacing qualitative evaluation of parent-child interactions, the PCRI helps to put qualitative impressions in perspective by making normative comparisons possible.

Standardized on more than 1,100 parents across the United States, the PCRI identifies specific aspects of the parent-child relationship that may cause problems, as well as giving an overall picture of the quality of the relationship. In an era when fathers are increasingly expected to take an active role in parenting, the PCRI explicitly measures the attitudes and behaviors of both mothers and fathers. It is assumed that the PCRI will often be administered to couples, and there are separate norms for mothers and fathers.

Recent increases in child custody litigation and divorce mediation have created a demand for sophisticated assessment of the relationships between parents and children, and the PCRI may prove especially useful in child custody settings and in other institutions that specifically address the needs of children. Used in conjunction with interviews and other forms of clinical assessment, the PCRI can be an important element in the making of custody recommendations and in evaluating the possibility that a parent is abusive (Gerard, 1994, p. 1).

Research performed by Hubbard (1996) demonstrate acceptable correlations of the PCRI with the MMPI-2 and ASPECT results for fathers. However, the coefficients between the PCRI and these instruments from mothers were generally at or around zero. These results are yet unexplained and may call into question the efficacy of using the PCRI in custody evaluations.

Parenting Stress Index

Although the Parenting Stress Index (PSI) is not designed for forensic settings, it is being used increasingly in forensic contexts, especially divorce cases. Of custody evaluators, 65.7% use the PSI as part of a custody evaluation (Ackerman & Brey, 2010). It contains 101 items in two domains: Child Characteristics and Parent Characteristics.

The Child Characteristics Domain includes six subscales as follows:

Adaptability: difficulties adjusting to changes, inflexible.

Distractibility/Hyper: ADHD-type behaviors.

Demandingness: demands requiring accommodation or attention.

Mood: moodiness, crying, displays of unhappiness.

Acceptability: behaviors that do not match parent's expectations or hopes for child.

Reinforces Parent: parent does not experience positive reinforcement from interactions with the child.

The Parent Characteristics domain subscales are as follows:

Competence: sense of competence in the parenting role.

Isolation: lack of social support for his or her role as parent.

Attachment: assesses parent's sense of attachment to the child.

Health: the impact of physical health on parenting.

Role Restriction: impact of the restrictions parenting places on parent's choices and freedom.

Depression: impact of depression and feelings of guilt on parenting behavior.

Spouse: help and emotional support from the child's other parent.

The PSI model is based on several assumptions:

- All stresses in the parenting system, regardless of source, are multidimensional and summative.
- Stress results from important transactions between parent and child and the parent's social environment.
- All these transactions are cognitively appraised by the parent and given either a positive or negative stress value.
- Life events provide a context that may add to the stress load of a parent.
- Parents generally act as buffers for their children, and the most proximal sources of parenting stress will have the greatest impact on the parenting behavior exhibited.

- The total level of parenting stress is the best predictor of dysfunctional parenting and that portion of the child's development that is linked to parent-child transactions (Archer, 2006, p. 299–300).

USE OF THE PSI IN CHILD CUSTODY EVALUATIONS

The PSI has unique potential to contribute to the psychological testing data in a parenting evaluation because the variables being measured are similar to several statutory factors that most states require to be considered in these evaluations: the child's developmental status, the parents' psychological health, and the relationship between all the parties (Archer, 2006, p. 12). Variables that are measured by evaluators in a child custody case generally revolve around family relationship factors, which makes it logical to use the PSI as part of the assessment (Archer, 2006, p. 213). Table 2.2 provides preliminary descriptive data for the PSI in custody evaluations.

Interpretation of the PSI in a child custody case begins with a review of the response style by looking at the Defensive Responding indicator. A PSI profile is considered "defensive" when the Defensive Responding score is 24. After addressing the response style issues, the evaluator should address any domain and subscale elevations. At this point, the domain and subscales are considered elevated at or above the 85th percentile. The manual can be used to establish hypotheses about the various domains. As is true of all instruments, the domains and subscales should be used to generate hypotheses and not as stand-alone data (Abidin, 1995).

DO'S AND DON'TS IN THE CUSTODY PROCESS

There are a number of behaviors that parents should and should not engage in during a divorce. Without going through formalized testing, the evaluator or, for that matter, an attorney, can look through this list of do's and don'ts to determine how many of the do's a particular parent is engaging in and how many of the don'ts that particular parent is not engaging in. As a result, an individual can subjectively infer which parent is acting in the child's best interest.

Ackerman (2008, pp. 207–223) has compiled the following lists of custody do's and don'ts.

Custody Do's

1. Attempt mediation or collaboration before litigation.
2. Understand from the outset that two parents living apart will not see their children as often as two parents living together.

Table 2.2 Preliminary Descriptive Data for the PSI in the Child Custody Context

Scales and Subscales	Mean
Total Stress Score	185.5
Child Domain	87.4
Distractibility	20.9
Adaptability	23.2
Reinforces Parent	7.9
Demandingness	15.4
Mood	8.8
Acceptability	11.2
Parent Domain	98.1
Competence	21.2
Isolation	10.2
Attachment	10.1
Health	10
Role Restriction	14.1
Depression	15.1
Spouse	17.5
Life Stress	16.8
Defensive Indicator	27.3

Note: Total sample of custody litigants = 214 (male = 107, female = 107).

Source: Adapted from Table 11.1 (Archer, 2006, p. 316).

3. Anticipate that two adults living apart will have more expenses than two adults living together.
4. Consider a joint custody arrangement rather than sole custody.
5. Be willing to share holidays rather than alternating them.
6. Be together (with your spouse) when you tell your children about your separation and/or divorce.
7. Provide stability; don't move from one home to another more often than necessary.
8. Be sensitive to your children's needs as well as your own.

9. Plan and consult with each other in advance of placement/visitation time with your children.

10. Observe time schedules with your children as strictly as possible.

11. Be flexible regarding visitation times for each parent.

12. Do whatever is necessary to resolve angry feelings toward your ex-spouse.

13. Refrain from giving your children too much decision-making power.

14. Tell your children often that they are still loved and that they are not getting divorced from their parents.

15. Give children therapeutic opportunities if their psychological adjustment appears to be too problematic.

16. Create an emotional environment for your children that allows them to continue to love and spend time with the other parent.

17. Present a united front when handling problems with the children.

18. Encourage a good relationship between the children and the other parent's extended family.

19. Encourage children to remember the other parent on special occasions, allowing them to buy cards and gifts and to telephone.

20. Use discretion about the time and frequency of your calls to children.

21. Recognize that children will feel powerless and helpless, and don't demean them, because they are so vulnerable.

22. Recognize that children may feel insecure and exhibit regressive behavior; be prepared to get them therapy if these behaviors persist.

23. Provide an appropriate role model for your children.

24. Allow your children to see where the other parent is going to live after moving out of the house.

25. Put your differences aside long enough to be able to peaceably attend school conferences and activities.

26. Recognize the rights and responsibilities of the other parent to consult school authorities concerning school performance and the right to inspect and receive copies of student records and reports and school calendars and notices.

27. Notify the other parent of medical emergencies, and recognize his or her right to have input about surgery, dental care, hospitalization, or institutionalization.

28. Recognize the right of both parents to inspect and receive copies of children's medical and dental records and the right to consult with any treating physician, dentist, or mental health professional.

DON'T FORGET

Before and during custody proceedings, remember these key custody do's:

- Attempt mediation before litigation.
- Consider a joint-custody rather than sole-custody arrangement.
- Try to share holidays rather than alternating them.
- Avoid giving children too much decision-making power.
- Present a united front when handling your children's problems.
- Make plans directly with your children's other parent instead of using your children as a go-between.

29. Recognize that children need substantial contact with the same-gender parent during adolescence.
30. Allow all grandparents to continue having contact with the children whenever reasonable.
31. Communicate with the other parent openly, honestly, and regularly to avoid misunderstandings that could be harmful to your children.
32. Make plans directly with the other parent instead of using your children as go-betweens.
33. Live as close to one another as is practical, convenient, and reasonable.
34. Maintain household routines as much as possible to keep some stability in children's lives.
35. Maintain the same set of rules as much as possible at both homes.

Custody Don'ts

1. Don't agree to alternating, 50/50 placement arrangements.
2. Don't, if possible, allow overnight visitation for infants (birth to 12 months).
3. Don't foster feelings of guilt in children over divorce.
4. Don't allow children 9 to 12 years of age to refuse to visit the other parent.
5. Don't allow teenagers to become too parental.
6. Don't allow children to exhibit too much acting-out behavior in response to the divorce. If their behavior gets out of hand, don't deny them therapy.
7. Don't take sides about parenting issues in front of the children.

8. Don't put the children in the middle when arranging visitation.

9. Don't communicate with the other parent through the children.

10. Don't fight or argue with or degrade the other parent in front of the children.

11. Don't plan visitations with the children and then arrive late or not at all.

12. Don't withhold time with the other parent as punishment for the children and the other parent.

13. Don't discuss financial aspects of the divorce (support, maintenance, and late or back payments) with the children.

14. Don't assume, based on your children's communication, anything about what the other parent has said or done. Check it out.

15. Don't use children as pawns to express anger toward the other parent.

16. Don't overburden children by requiring them to have too much responsibility for their growing up and maintenance.

17. Don't overburden children by giving them responsibility for maintaining your psychological stability.

18. Don't overburden children by making them the focus of arguments between you and the other parent.

19. Don't allow your children to spend too much time with a parent who appears to be or has been diagnosed as being mentally ill.

20. Don't separate your children.

21. Don't introduce children to every person you date.

22. Don't allow children to see sexually intimate behavior between you and your partner.

23. Don't sleep in the same bed with school-age children except under unusual circumstances.

24. Don't ask children to keep secrets from your ex-spouse.

RECOMMENDED CHILD CUSTODY EVALUATION PRACTICES

As stated earlier in this chapter, there has been considerable research performed by Ackerman and his associates and Bow and his associates during the past decade since the first edition of this book was published that have helped define the standard of practice. As noted in the Ackerman and Brey study, significantly more time has been spent on evaluations than 10 years ago. Much of that time is spent with increased

> **DON'T FORGET**
>
> In contested custody cases, 76.4% of judges reported that they would not order a 50/50 placement schedule (Ackerman & Drosdeck, 2010).

testing. As a result, this author recommends the following tests be administered to each parent in a child custody evaluation:

- Intelligence test
- Achievement test
- MMPI-2
- PAI
- Rorschach
- PSI
- BASC 2
- ASPECT/ASPECT-SF

For children:
- Intelligence Test
- PAI-Adolescent (down to age 12)
- Rorschach
- BASC 2 (down to age six)

 TEST YOURSELF

1. **The American Psychological Association Ethics Codes and the American Psychological Association "Guidelines" for custody evaluations are completely separate documents.**
   True or False?

2. **What are the three most commonly elevated scales in custody evaluations on the MMPI-2?**

3. **Which of the following is not a specialized test developed for custody evaluations?**
   (a) Ackerman-Schoendorf Scales for Parent Evaluation of Custody
   (b) Clinician's Guide for Child Custody Evaluations
   (c) Bricklin Perceptual Scales
   (d) The Custody Quotient

4. **Which of the following is not a study that has identified the standards of practice in child custody evaluations?**
   (a) The wishes of the parents regarding custody
   (b) The wishes of the child
   (c) The mental and physical health of the parties
   (d) Geographic location
   (e) Interaction and interrelationships of the child with the parents, siblings

5. Sexual preference is an issue in determining custody and placement of the children.

True or False?

Answers: 1. False; 2. Scales 3, 4, and 6; 3. b; 4. c; 5. False

SELECTED INSTRUMENTS

Ackerman-Schoendorf Scales of Parent Evaluation of Custody (ASPECT)
Western Psychological Services: http://www.wpspublish.com
1–800–648–8857

Behavioral Assessment Scales for Children—2nd edition (BASC 2)
Pearson Assessments: http://www.pearsonassessments.com
1–800–627–7271

Minnesota Multiphasic Personality Inventory—2nd edition (MMPI-2)
Pearson Assessments: http://www.pearsonassessments.com
1–800–627–7271

Parent-Child Relationship Inventory (PCRI)
Western Psychological Services: http://www.wpspublish.com
1–800–648–8857

Parental Stress Index (PSI)
PAR: www.parinc.com
1–800–331–8378

Personality Assessment Inventory (PAI)
PAR: www.parinc.com
1–800–331–8378

Three

ESSENTIALS OF PERSONAL INJURY ASSESSMENT

Marc J. Ackerman

The general misconception that personal injury cases only involved individuals who suffer physical injury in some form of an accidental situation is one that is held by professionals and nonprofessionals alike. There are two parts to every personal injury lawsuit: Damages, which refers to how much damage has been caused by the injury, and liability, which refers to who is responsible for those damages. Personal injury cases can include any situation where an individual is injured physically or psychologically in which damages occur, including accidents resulting in physical or psychological injury; medical malpractice cases resulting in psychological injury; and sexual abuse, harassment, and/or misconduct cases resulting in psychological injury. Damages without liability or a liability without damages will render a personal injury legal action moot. Psychologists generally become involved in personal injury cases on the damages side. However, psychologists can be asked to address liability issues when the behavior of mental health professionals is called into question. When the injury occurs in the workplace, a personal injury case becomes a Worker's Compensation case.

A recent study has addressed the issue of test usage in personal injury cases (Archer, Buffington-Vollum, Stredny, and Handel, 2006). The instruments most commonly used, according to Archer and colleagues are in Rapid Reference 3.1.

The two primary areas that this chapter will address with regard to personal injury cases are Posttraumatic Stress Disorder (PTSD) and neuropsychological assessment. The PTSD area of concern addresses psychological damage resulting in trauma, while the neuropsychological testing addresses head injuries that can result in a decline in cognitive functioning.

≡ Rapid Reference 3.1

Instruments Frequently Used in Personal Injury Cases

Archer, Buffington-Vollum, Stredny, and Handel (2006) listed tests most frequently used in personal injury cases:

- MMPI-2
- WAIS-III, Wechsler Memory Scale, or Wechsler Intelligence Scales
- Rorschach Inkblot
- Bender Gestalt
- Sentence Completion

Archer and colleagues have also found the TAT to be commonly used.

POSTTRAUMATIC STRESS DISORDER

The diagnostic criteria for Posttraumatic Stress Disorder found in the DSM-IV (American Psychiatric Association, 1994, pp. 427–429) are:

A. The person has been exposed to a traumatic event in which both of the following were present:
   1. The person experienced, witnessed, or was confronted with an event or events that involved actual or threatened death or serious injury, or a threat to the physical integrity of self or others.
   2. The person's response involved intense fear, helplessness, or horror. Note: in children this may be expressed by disorganized or agitated behavior.

B. The traumatic event is persistently reexperienced in one (or more) of the following ways:
   1. Recurrent and intrusive distressing recollections of the event, including images, thoughts, or perceptions. Note: In young children, repetitive play may occur in which themes or aspects of the trauma are expressed.
   2. Recurrent distressing dreams of the event. Note: In children, there may be frightening dreams without recognizable content.
   3. Acting or feeling as if the traumatic event were recurring (includes a sense of reliving the experience, illusions, hallucinations, and dissociate flashback episodes, including those that occur in awakening

or when intoxicated). Note: In young children, trauma-specific reenactment may occur.

4. Intense psychological distress at exposure to internal or external cues that symbolize or resemble an aspect of the traumatic event.
5. Physiological reactivity on exposure to internal or external cues that symbolize or resemble an aspect of the traumatic event.

C. Persistent avoidance of stimuli associated with the trauma and numbing of general responsiveness (not present before the trauma), as indicated by three (or more) of the following:
   1. Efforts to avoid thoughts, feelings, or conversations associated with the trauma.
   2. Efforts to avoid activities, places, or people that arouse recollection of the trauma.
   3. Inability to recall an important aspect of the trauma.
   4. Markedly diminished interest or participation in significant activities.
   5. Feelings of detachment or estrangement from others.
   6. Restricted range of affect (e.g., unable to have loving feelings).
   7. Sense of a foreshortened future (e.g., does not expect to have a career, marriage, children, or a normal life span).

D. Persistent symptoms of increased arousal (not present before the trauma), as indicated by two (or more) of the following:
   1. Difficulty falling or staying asleep
   2. Irritability or outbursts of anger
   3. Difficulty concentrating
   4. Hypervigilance
   5. Exaggerated startle response

E. Duration of the disturbance (symptoms in B, C, and D) is more than one month.

F. The disturbance causes clinically significant distress or impairment in social, occupational, or other areas of functioning.

Posttraumatic Stress Disorder is most likely to occur during the young adult years, but it can occur at any age, including early childhood. At any point, each individual has a certain level of stress, coping ability, normal anxiety and autonomic arousal, and social support. Any preexisting mental disorder functions as both a stressor and a partial determinant of coping ability. These factors, in various combinations, will determine how the individual reacts to a serious traumatic incident (Ackerman & Kane, 1998, p. 588). Rapid Reference 3.2 provides information on the kinds of individuals who may be predisposed to PTSD.

≡ Rapid Reference 3.2

Individuals Who May be Predisposed to PTSD

Although no research unequivocally demonstrates that any particular personality type is predisposed to PTSD (Briere, 1997), the following people may be more susceptible than others:

- Individuals who are vulnerable because of environmental stressors (Scrignar, 1996)
- Individuals who develop persistent psychological symptoms following traumatic events (Scrignar, 1996)
- Individuals with prior psychological impairment who may be easy prey for someone who is predatory (Briere, 1997)
- Individuals who have suffered severe stress for sufficient duration (Meek, 1990)
- Individuals who have experienced prior trauma; prior adjustment, family history of psychopathology; perceived life threat; peritraumatic emotions, peritraumatic dissociation (Ozer, Best, Lipsey, and Weiss 2003)

PTSD Evaluations

Briere (1997, p. 147) has indicated that the following six areas must be assessed when evaluating PTSD claimants in personal injury cases:

1. Pretrauma functioning
2. Trauma exposure
3. Social supports
4. Comorbidity
5. Potential malingering or secondary gain
6. Posttraumatic response

Rapid Reference 3.3 cites the standard questions that must be asked of PTSD claimants in personal injury cases.

PTSD Testing

The MMPI-2 may be the most important test to administer in personal injury cases, not so much because of the clinical scales, but rather because of the validity scales to identify response style.

A number of important inferences can be drawn from individuals who are forthright on the validity scales of the MMPI-2. They did not attempt to

≡ *Rapid Reference 3.3*

What to Ask PTSD Claimants in Personal Injury Cases

Simon and Wettstein (1997, pp. 32–33) have noted five standard questions to ask PTSD claimants:

- Does the alleged PTSD claim actually meet specific clinical criteria for this disorder?
- Is the traumatic stressor that is alleged to have caused the PTSD of sufficient severity to produce this disorder?
- Is the diagnosis of PTSD based solely on the subjective reporting of symptoms by the client?
- What is the claimant's *actual* level of functional psychiatric impairment?

"fake good" or "fake bad"; they neither exaggerated nor downplayed their symptoms. These individuals answered honestly, and their answers on the balance of the test and other instruments are also likely to be honest. The examiner can believe, with a reasonable degree of certainty, what the test says about the individual's degree of depression, anxiety, and worry about physical problems.

Of course, the converse is also true. The individual whose validity scale scores suggest exaggeration, cover-up, and other attempts to obfuscate has provided a strong suggestion that other claims may also be false, or at least not completely true.

The Fake Bad Scale (FBS) and the Fp (Fake Pscyhopathology Scale) have been used to help determine the validity of the responses. The Fake Bad Scale is one that is used to determine malingering on the MMPI-2. It was developed by Lees-Haley in 1992. "It should be noted, based on available cutoff scores and a large data set, the majority of personal injury litigants do not appear to frankly exaggerate on the FBS" (Lees-Haley, 1997; Koch et al., 2006). A number of studies have been performed on the mean scores of personal injury litigants on the FBS. They are summarized in Table 3.1.

The F(p) Scale is referred to as the F psychiatric scale or the F psychopathology scale. It is designed to detect exaggeration and malingering by identifying items infrequently endorsed by the normative group, but also endorsed by fewer than 20% of psychiatric patients (Arbisi & Ben-Porath, 1995).

The F(p) Scale includes items infrequently endorsed by psychiatric patients. Individuals with scores of greater than 8 are overreporting the extent and severity of their psychopathology. This is particularly true if F-K is greater than 20.

Table 3.1 Mean FBS Scores in Personal Injury Cases

	N	Mean
Head Trauma, Chronic Pain, or Both	95	22.3
Unselected, Consecutive Litigants	492	20.8
Personal Injury Litigants	120	20.7
Atypical Mild Traumatic Brain Injury	159	24.8
Moderate to Severe Traumatic Brain Injury	68	17.6
Chronic Pain	100	22.7
Improbable Posttraumatic Stress	57	29.1
Major Trauma Posttraumatic Stress	32	24.3
Personal Injury Litigants	25	27.6
Litigants with Presumed Spurious PTSD Claims	55	27.1

Note: Adapted from Koch et al. (2006).

There is no single MMPI-2 clinical scale profile that defines PTSD. The Posttraumatic Stress Disorder Scale (Keane(Pk)) on the MMPI-2 measures negative responses to stressful situations. There is mixed review about whether the Pk Scale accurately measures PTSD. A meta-analysis by Wise (1996) found that 29% of the studies yielded 8/2–2/8 profile patterns on the MMPI-2. More recent studies have shown marked profile elevations on scales 1, 2, 3, and 7.

When the Anxiety Scales elevations are within $10T$ score points of the PTSD Scale, the results are most likely a function of anxiety and not PTSD. When the PTSD Scales are more than $10T$ Scale points above the Anxiety Scales, it is safe to interpret these results as being indications of genuine PTSD (Ackerman & Kane, 1998, 603–605).

Early studies on the Pk Scale had serious methodological problems. Some have not necessarily controlled for severity of distress and impairment, leaving open the possibility that Pk measures the severity of general psychological distress, rather than PTSD (Koch et al., 2006).

The PAI can also be used to diagnosis PTSD. The Anxiety subscale, ANX-P, is often significantly elevated in individuals with Posttraumatic Stress Disorder. The Anxiety/Related Disorders subscale ARD-T also has elevations with individuals diagnosed with Posttraumatic Stress Disorder.

Although many clinical groups demonstrate ARD-T scores above $70T$, PTSD, subjects will typically score at least $80T$ on this scale. However, the diagnosis of PTSD should not be based solely upon an ARD-T elevation

. . . all three DEP subscales may display elevations as a function of painful guilt feelings (DEP-C), recurrent distressing dreams leading to sleep disturbance (DEP-P), and diminished interest in significant activities (DEP-A). Other symptoms of PTSD include physiological anxiety reactivity, reflected on ANX-P; feelings of detachment or estrangement from others, manifested on SCZ-S and low WRM; hypervigilance, evidenced in PAR-H elevations; and irritability, which can be gauged using MAN-I; difficulty with concentration and focus often leads to prominent SCZ-T elevations. Finally, outbursts of anger are also common, reflected in AGG elevations (with AGG-A and AGG-P typically elevated to a greater extent than AGG-V). (Morey, 2003, p. 210–211)

It is not unusual to also see the Depression scale of the PAI elevated in PTSD cases. Individuals with PTSD often show signs of anger and resentment that can manifest itself in elevations of the Aggression scale.

Specialized Instruments

Instruments have been developed in recent years to test the level of trauma that an individual is experiencing. Three of these tests have been developed by Briere (1995, 1996) as the Trauma Symptom Inventory (TSI) and the Trauma Symptom Checklist for Children (TSCC), and also the Detailed Assessment of Posttraumatic Stress Scale (DAPS). Another instrument was developed by Foa (1995), entitled Posttraumatic Stress Diagnostic Scale (PDS). Blake et al. (1995) developed the Clinician-Administered PTSD Scale (CAPS), and Horowitz et al. (1979) developed the Impact of Experience Scale (IES).

Trauma Symptom Inventory

According to Briere (1995, p. 1), "The Trauma Symptom Inventory (TSI) is a 100 item test of posttraumatic stress and other psychological sequelae of traumatic events. It is intended for use in the evaluation of acute and chronic traumatic symptomotology, including, but not limited to, the effects of rape, spouse abuse, physical assault, combat, major accidents and natural disasters, as well as lasting sequelae of childhood abuse and other early traumatic events."

The TSI scales have demonstrated high internal consistency and good convergent validity, but somewhat lower discriminant validity. It is advised that the TSI be used in conjunction with at least one other general measure of psychopathology, such as the MMPI-2. Another possible weak point with the TSI involves gender-specificity that suggests the scale performs better with females.

The TSI strengths include: "(a) the clinically clear, internally consistent organization and quantification of diagnostic information useful in assessment of the known clinical PTSD cases; (b) the incorporation of critical items, indicating potential risks and clinical problems presented by the patient; and (c) satisfactory levels of convergent validity, which makes the TSI useful in situations not requiring differential diagnostic decisions" (Gebart-Eaglemont, 2001, p. 953).

McDevitt-Murphy, Weathers, and Adkins (2005) studied the effectiveness of the TSI measuring PTSD. They found a correct classification rate of 85.5% and concluded that the TSI demonstrated good convergent validity with other measures of PTSD, which supported the use of the TSI in the assessment of PTSD (p. 63).

The instrument has three validity scales and 10 clinical scales. Briere (1995, p. 2) has outlined the validity scales as follows:

1. *Response Level (RL)*. High scores on this scale reflect the tendency toward defensiveness, a general under-endorsement response set, or a need to appear unusually symptom-free.
2. *Atypical Response (ATR)*. High scores on this scale may reflect psychosis, extreme distress, general over-endorsement response set, or an attempt to appear especially disturbed or dysfunctional.
3. *Inconsistent Response (INC)*. High scores on this scale represent unusually inconsistent responses to TSI items that may reflect random item endorsement, attention or concentration problems, or reading/language difficulties.

Briere (1995, p. 2) has outlined the 10 clinical scales as follows:

1. *Anxious Arousal (AA)*. This scale measures symptoms of anxiety, especially those associated with posttraumatic hyperarousal.
2. *Depression (D)*. This scale measures depressive symptomotology in terms of both moods state (sadness) and depressive cognitive distortions (hopelessness).
3. *Anger/Irritability (AI)*. This scale measures self-reported anger, irritable affect, as well as associated anger cognitions and behavior.
4. *Intrusive Experiences (IE)*. This scale measures symptoms associated with posttraumatic stress, such as flashbacks, nightmares, and intrusive thoughts.
5. *Defensive Avoidance (DA)*. This scale measures the type of avoidance associated with posttraumatic symptomotology in both the cognitive and behavioral areas.
6. *Dissociation (DIS)*. Depersonalization, derealization, out-of-body experiences, and psychic numbing are measures of dissociative symptomatology seen on this scale.

7. *Sexual Concerns (SC)*. This scale measures self-reported sexual distress, such as sexual dissatisfaction, sexual dysfunction, and unwanted sexual thoughts or feelings.

8. *Dysfunctional Sexual Behavior (DSB)*. This scale measures behavior that is, in some way, dysfunctional, either because of its indiscriminate quality, its potential self-harm, or its inappropriateness to accomplish nonsexual goals.

9. *Impaired Self-Reference (ISR)*. This scale measures problems of the self-domain, such as identity confusion, self-other disturbance, and a relative lack of self-support.

10. *Tension Reduction Behavior (TRB)*. This scale measures the respondent's tendency to turn on external methods of reducing internal tension or distress, such as self-mutilation, anger outbursts, manipulative behavior, and suicidal threats.

The TSI not only measures concerns about Posttraumatic Stress Disorder but also Acute Stress Disorder. The Intrusive Experience Scale reflects the "B" group of symptoms associated with PTSD found in DSM-IV. The Defensive Avoidance Scale measure the "C" group of the PTSD symptoms in DSM-IV.

Two studies performed by Briere (1997) and Damare (1996) included 935 individuals and 1,249 individuals, respectively. The first study indicated that both physically and sexually abused individuals scored significantly higher on the 10 clinical scales than the nonabused individuals. Furthermore, persons of color had a higher incidence of PTSD. The authors hypothesized that this is based on the fact that they are exposed to more trauma. Age of first abuse was not predictive of adjustment, but age of last abuse was. The second study performed by Briere and Damare found that females reported higher symptoms of anxious arousal, depression, intrusive experiences, and defensive avoidance, while males had greater sexual distress and dysfunctional sexual behavior. They concluded that "it did not necessarily follow that greater endorsement of symptoms of dysphoria and posttraumatic stress by females means that women experience greater psychological distress at these domains for equivalent traumata. Alternatively, differences observed might result from sex-role specific differences in the expression of psychological distress" (Briere, 1995, p. 3).

The TSI is a standardized, reliable, well-validated instrument that can be useful in a wide variety of personal injury cases (Ackerman & Kane, 1998, pp. 416–418).

Trauma Symptom Checklist for Children

The TSCC is appropriate for children ages 8 through 16. Its two validity scales are:

1. Underresponse (UND)
2. Hyperresponse (HYP)

Its six clinical scales are:

1. Anxiety (ANX)
2. Depression (DEP)
3. Anger (ANG)
4. Posttraumatic Stress (PTS)
5. Dissociation (DIS)
6. Sexual Concerns (SC)

The TSCC has an alternate form referred to as the TSCC-A. The TSCC-A, which is used less frequently, excludes the sexual concerns items for children for whom it would be inappropriate to include these items. The sample kit does not come with the TSCC-A forms and must be requested separately. Critical items are also presented for both the TSCC and the TSCC-A. When interpreting the TSCC, a mean of 50 and a standard deviation of 10 is used, with scores above 65 being clinically significant on all scales except the sexual concerns scale, where scores above 70 are considered to be clinically significant.

Posttraumatic Stress Diagnostic Scale
Foa's (1995) PSD utilizes a different approach to measuring PTSD. It is a 49-item self-report structural questionnaire that asks specific questions about each of the diagnostic categories of PTSD. The score sheet allows the examiner to measure whether criteria A through F of DSM-IV are met by scoring the individual on each of these six areas. The standardization sample for the PSD is relatively small. However, since it is utilized specifically for the purpose of validating a PTSD diagnosis, it serves well as a "structured interview" type of assessment model for determining if the DSM-IV criteria for PTSD are met (Ackerman & Kane, 1998, p. 418).

The Detailed Assessment of Posttraumatic Stress Scale (DAPS)
The DAPS directly correlates with the PTSD criteria found in DSM-IV-TR. It includes two validity scales and assesses comorbid conditions often found with PTSD: dissociation, substance abuse, and suicidality (Briere, 2004).

The Clinician-Administered PTSD Scale (CAPS)
The CAPS was developed by Blake et al. (1995), which identifies 17 PTSD symptoms rated in severity from zero to four and in frequency from zero to four. Thus, each symptom can receive a rating from zero to eight. The traditional scoring rule requires a combined score of three to be counted toward a diagnosis (Koch et al., 2006, p. 650).

The CAPS has been referred to as the "gold standard" measure of PTSD in combat veteran populations. However, the psychometric properties of the CAPS in nonveteran populations are not well known (Blanchard et al., 1996; Foa & Tolin, 2000; in Young, Kane, & Nicholson, 2006).

Impact of Experience Scale

The Impact of Experience Scale (IES) was developed by Horowitz, Wilner, & Alvarez, 1979). Of 15 items split into subscales of intrusion (seven items) and avoidance (eight items), Joseph (2000) reviewed research on this scale and noted that "internal consistency and test/retest reliability are adequate for the IES. With respect to validity, there is some debate about whether all IES items can be considered measures of psychological distress." While it is still a PTSD measure, the IES does not contain any items from Criterion B and only sample symptoms from Criterion C. "In summary, the IES has some utility in the discrimination of stress versus non-distress, trauma survivors, but should not be used as a proxy for measures whether self-report or interview-based, that can reliably diagnosis PTSD and that provide a fuller coverage of the range." Young, Kane, and Nicholson (2006) state, "Given these concerns, the IES is not recommended for forensic evaluations" (p. 113).

Explaining PTSD to the Judge or Jury

Presenting the concept of PTSD to the trier of fact is often cumbersome and gets lost in the theoretical language of the DSM-IV criteria. Judges and juries appear to be better able to grasp the concept of PTSD when it is presented in a certain way.

NEUROPYSCHOLOGICAL ASSESSMENT

Myriad tests have been developed for use in neuropsychological testing. It is not possible to discuss all these tests in this format. Rapid Reference 3.4 summarizes tests currently used in neuropsychological assessment.

The Halstead-Reitan Neuropsychological Battery and the Luria-Nebraska Neuropsychological Battery were previously the most widely used neuropsychology batteries. They are currently only used 10% of the time. The Halstead-Reitan Battery was initially developed in the laboratory established in 1935 by Halstead to study neurosurgical patients, with a particular focus on frontal lobe functioning. Reitan was a student of Halstead's and was responsible for validating new tests that could be added to the standard battery. As a result of their work and that of

DON'T FORGET

To help judges and juries better understand PTSD:

- Explain that the individual is suffering from a severe anxiety disorder, perhaps the most severe form of anxiety possible.

- Identify the symptoms that the plaintiff is experiencing that represent PTSD diagnostic criteria without stating specifically that they are PTSD diagnostic criteria. For example, the expert witness could state, "As a function of this anxiety, Mr. Smith is experiencing difficulty concentrating, recurring thoughts about the accident, angry outbursts, nightmares. . ."

- After describing the symptoms that are present, explain that the collective label for these symptoms is Posttraumatic Stress Disorder. This is said somewhat in passing; the important element is the anxiety component of the disorder and not the technical label it is given (Ackerman & Kane, 1998, p. 610).

other researchers, a core battery was developed to address most areas of brain function/dysfunction. The precise content of that battery has changed periodically over the years, to add new tests and delete those found to be less valid than others were demonstrated to be, but at any point in time there is a relatively fixed set of tests bearing the title "Halstead-Reitan Battery."

The total time for administration of the battery is roughly 6–8 hours. Although the individual tests that constitute the battery are independent, it is necessary to administer a core battery and a certain number of tests in order to derive an impairment index (Goldstein, 1990, pp. 207–208).

Norms for the individual tests within the Halstead-Reitan Battery are available, but there is not a manual for the battery as a whole because it has never been published as a single procedure (Goldstein, 1990, p. 213). Both the individual tests and the Halstead-Reitan Battery as a whole validly and reliably distinguish between brain-damaged and non-brain-damaged individuals.

The Luria-Nebraska Neuropsychological Battery was first described in 1978 by Charles Golden and his associates. It was an attempt to take the work done by Luria in Russia and convert it into a standardized set of procedures for evaluation of individuals with possible neuropsychological impairment. This required development of a scoring system, data on reliability and validity, and a review of existing research on its procedures. The test battery was published in 1980 by Western Psychological Services, which continues to offer the battery in both adult and child forms (Goldstein, 1990, pp. 215–216).

The Luria-Nebraska has been shown to have discriminative validity regarding brain-damaged patients, normal controls, and chronic schizophrenics. Reliability

≡ Rapid Reference 3.4

Selected Psychological and Neuropsychological Test Instruments

Behavior

Behavior Assessment Scales for Children, Second Edition (BASC 2)

Achievement Measures

Basic Achievement Skills Individual Screener

Wide Range Achievement Test—4th edition (WRAT 4)

Woodcock Johnson—III

Affective States

Beck Depression Inventory

Attention, Concentration, and Conceptual Thinking

Paced Auditory Serial Addition Test (PASAT)

Seashore Rhythm Test

Trail Making Tests (Parts A and B)

Wechsler Adult Intelligence Scale—4th edition (subtests: Arithmetic, Digit Symbol)

Comprehensive Neuropsychological Test Batteries

Halstead-Reitan Neuropsychological Battery (adult and child versions)

Luria-Nebraska Neuropsychological Battery (adult and child versions)

Hand Dominance

Harris Test of Lateral Dominance

Language

Aphasia Screening Test

Boston Diagnostic Aphasia Exam

Multilingual Aphasia Examination

Peabody Picture Vocabulary Test—III

Memory and Learning

Boston Visual Retention Test

California Verbal Learning Test

Rey Auditory Verbal Learning Test (RAVLT)

Rey-Osterrieth Complex Design Test (Recall Mode)

Tactual Performance Test (Memory and Localization)

Wechsler Adult Intelligence Scale—4th edition (subtest: Digit Span)

Wechsler Memory Scale—4th edition

Motor Skills

Connors Continuous Performance Test (CPT)

Finger-Tapping Test

Grip Strength

Grooved Pegboard Test

Executive Functioning

Stroop

Test of Everyday Attention (TEA)

Tower of London

Strategy Application Test

Reasoning and Problem Solving

Categories Test

Wisconsin Card Sort Test

Visual-Spatial and Constructional Ability

Berry-Buktenica Test of Visual Motor Integration (VMI)

Bender Gestalt Visual-Motor Test

Benton Facial Recognition Test

Benton Visual Form Discrimination Test

Raven's Progressive Matrices

Rey-Osterrieth Complex Figure Test (Copy Mode)

Tactual Performance Test

Wechsler Adult Intelligence Scale—3rd edition (subtests: Block Design, Object Assembly, Picture Arrangement, Picture Completion)

of the 13 major scales, according to the test manual (p. 230), range from .78 to .96 (Golden, Hammeke, & Purisch, 1980).

The combination of the WAIS-IV and the WMS-IV provides the examiner with additional information that can be used in neuropsychological evaluations (see, e.g., Kaufman & Lichtenberger [1999] for WAIS-III assessment).

The Halstead-Reitan Battery and the Luria-Nebraska Neuropsychological Battery have been replaced with a number of individual tests. The examiner selects which tests are most applicable to the question at hand.

Executive Functioning

In addition, there has been a far greater emphasis placed on executive functioning in recent years. Executive functioning has become an umbrella term that includes a number of categories.

Sample executive functioning categories:

- Problem Solving
- Concept Formation
- Abstract Reasoning
- Planning
- Organization
- Goal Setting
- Hypothesis Generation
- Estimation
- Behavioral Regulation
- Common Sense
- Creativity
- Working Memory
- Inhibition
- Self-Monitoring
- Initiative
- Self-Control
- Attentional Control
- Anticipation

Adapted from Baron (2004, Table 6.1).

Selected Tests of Executive Functioning

Wisconsin Card Sort

The Wisconsin Card Sort test was developed as a measure of "flexibility in thinking." It measures effective hypothesis-testing, ability to maintain a set, and response flexibility.

Stroop Color Word

The Stroop is a brief measure of focused attention and the ability to shift from one perceptual set to another, in addition to the ability to inhibit responding.

Tests of Everyday Attention (TEA)

The Tests of Everyday Attention (TEA) has a child version referred to as the TEA-Ch. It includes nine subtests measuring everyday tasks, such as maps, searching, opposites, and the like. There is a much greater emphasis on practical applications of executive functioning.

Short Category Test

One of the problems with the Categories Test from the Halstead-Reitan Battery is that it can take up to two hours to administer. As a result, Western Psychological Services has developed the Short Category Test, published in 1987. "The Short Category Test, Booklet Format (SCT) thus represents the first successful effort to reduce the length and complexity of the Category Test while retaining its desirable psychometric properties" (Wetzel & Boll, 1987, p. 1). The test is intended for adults and adolescents 15 years and older. Prospective subjects for the test must be able to see clearly and should be alert enough to respond to the demands of the test situation. The SCT is best used as a measure of cognitive deterioration based on a previous normal level of ability, and is less appropriate for individuals with a well-documented history of mental retardation or subnormal intelligence. Validity data indicate that the correlation coefficients of .80 to .93 were found between the Short Category Test and the original Halstead Category Test, depending on order of presentation.

The Brief Neuropsychological Cognitive Examination

Most psychological batteries take hours to perform. The Brief Neuropsychological Cognitive Examination (BNCE) is an attempt to provide a neurological screen in less than 30 minutes.

The BNCE has proven to be useful in the brief assessment of the presence and degree of cognitive impairment in patients undergoing forensic evaluation. The BNCE is composed of 10 subtests that assess working memory, gnosis, praxis, language, orientation, attention, and executive functions. None of the tests require more than minimum reading skills. Five of the subtests measure the processing of conventional information and five focus on the processing of novel or incomplete information. The test helps to reliably uncover the mild impairment that is often missed by other brief cognitive screeners. In some cases, it may be more efficient than a lengthy neuropsychological battery. In others, it may indicate that testing with a lengthy battery is warranted.

In the last several years, the BNCE has been used in forensic assessment of more than 300 patients in the forensic unit of the State Hospital in Massachusetts. It has been used to identify patients with signs of cognitive impairment to be referred for a more comprehensive neuropsychiatric assessment. One such case was that of an 81-year-old patient without a psychiatric or criminal history who was admitted to the hospital after he set his house on fire, resulting in the death of his wife. He claimed not to recall the event, but no cognitive decline was revealed in the regular psychiatric evaluation of mental status. The BNCE showed mild cognitive abnormalities that consisted of relatively low aggregate scores for tasks that required processing new and unconventional information. It was suspected that he was in the early stages of Alzheimer's disease, but his head computed tomography, magnetic resonance imaging scan, and electroencephalogram turned out to be negative. A single photon emission computed tomography scan revealed temporoparietal hypoperfusion, a pattern typical in cases of Alzheimer's disease. Subsequent assessments with the BNCE in the following months showed progressive, fairly severe cognitive decline that was attributed to the further development of Alzheimer's disease.

The BNCE can be helpful in differentiating actual cognitive impairment caused by neurological diseases with psychiatric manifestations and primary psychiatric disorders from cases of malingering, especially in cases where substance abuse is a factor. Malingering should be suspected when an individual obtains low scores on tasks requiring conventional information processing in the presence of high scores for tasks requiring the processing of novel, unconventional information. In more obvious cases of malingering, a person may obtain uniformly low scores for all the BNCE tasks, and yet maintain a relatively high functional level of activity, fully oriented to his or her daily schedule and successfully accomplishing routine daily tasks. In the absence of malingering, such a situation is unlikely.

The Comprehensive Neuropsychological Screening Instrument for Children

The NCSIC was developed for children between 6 and 12 years of age who are suspected of having sustained a brain injury. "The authors intended its use for determining whether or not a child has sustained a neurologic insult, the severity of any impairment, whether further evaluation is needed, and how that evaluation should be focused" (Baron, 2004, p. 101). The test takes 20 to 30 minutes to administer and includes 20 subtests assessing memory, language, executive functioning, and motor control in both the visual and auditory modalities.

 **TEST YOURSELF**

1. **What are the diagnostic criteria for PTSD? (see pp. 67–68)**

2. **When assessing for PTSD, which of the following should not be considered?**
   (a) Pre-trauma functioning
   (b) Trauma exposure
   (c) Social supports
   (d) Previous conduct disorder
   (e) Comorbidity

3. **The Trauma Symptom Inventory (TSI) is used to help diagnose**
   (a) an eating disorder.
   (b) the presence of Posttraumatic Stress Disorder.
   (c) sexual deviation.
   (d) the presence of Acute Stress Disorder.

4. **Which instrument should not be used in assessing PTSD?**
   (a) The Minnesota Multiphasic Personality Inventory, 2nd edition
   (b) The Personality Assessment Inventory
   (c) The Millon Clinical Multiaxial Inventory, 3rd edition
   (d) The Impact of Experience Scale

5. **Executive functioning includes:**
   (a) concept formation.
   (b) goal setting.
   (c) inhibition.
   (d) behavioral regulation.
   (e) all of the above.

6. **Which of the following is not an instrument that would be used in neuropsychological testing?**
   (a) Wisconsin Card Sort
   (b) The Stroop Color Word Test
   (c) The Faces and Places Test
   (d) The Short Category Test

Answers: 1. see pp. 67–68; 2. d; 3. b; 4. c; 5. e; 6. c

SELECTED INSTRUMENTS

Brief Neuropsychological Cognitive Examination (BNCE)
Western Psychological Services: http://www.wpspublish.com
1–800–648–8857

Short Category Test
Western Psychological Services:http://www.wpspublish.com
1–800–648–8857

Trauma Symptom Checklist for Children (TSCC)
Western Psychological Services: http://www.wpspublish.com
1–800–648–8857

Trauma Symptom Inventory (TSI)
Western Psychological Services: http://www.wpspublish.com
1–800–648–8857

Wisconsin Card Sort
Western Psychological Services: http://www.wpspublish.com
1–800–648–8857

Stroop Color Word
Psychological Assessment Resources: www.parinc.com
1–800–331–8378

Personality Assessment Inventory
Psychological Assessment Resources: www.parinc.com
1–800–331–837

Trail Making
Psychological Assessment Resources: www.parinc.com
1–800–331–8378

Visual Motor Integration (VMI)
Western Psychological Services: http://www.wpspublish.com
1–800–648–8857

Four

ESSENTIALS OF MALINGERING ASSESSMENT

Andrew W. Kane

A significant concern in personal injury cases is that there is a financial incentive for malingering, either by exaggerating one's symptoms or by creating symptoms that are not actually present. In addition, some people will exaggerate symptoms (consciously or unconsciously), or malinger, to gain sympathy. These can be particularly problematic when there is alleged to be a significant psychological or emotional injury.

Evaluators must be very cautious in labeling individuals as malingering. Inaccurately labeling someone as a malingerer carries substantial stigma, can prevent the individual from receiving appropriate care, can present the individual so labeled with a severe psychological trauma, and can cause the person to lose employment benefits or disability income (Drob, Meehan, & Waxman, 2009). To avoid inaccurate labeling, the evaluator must conduct a comprehensive evaluation that takes into consideration the individual's characteristics, the environment, and evidence of a clear reason for the individual to malinger.

Shuman (2005) indicated that malingering is "the voluntary falsification or fabrication of physical or psychological symptoms.... The MMPI has been found to be the most helpful psychological test in identifying exaggeration and minimization of symptoms, although it will not identify all malingering.... Clinical observation and interviewing, while often relied on in judicial proceedings, have not been proven in the scientific literature to be effective in the detection of malingering" (pp. 9–14).

A distinction must also be made between exaggeration of symptoms and malingering. The former may be due to naiveté, to an unconscious quest for secondary gain (e.g., emotional support), or other factors discussed later. One of the tasks of an assessment is to distinguish, if possible, between conscious malingering and unconscious or naïve exaggeration (Sella, 1997). Rogers (2008a) recommends distinguishing among *malingering, factitious presentations,* and *feigning*. The first requires "fabrication or gross exaggeration of multiple symptoms" (p. 5), as well as the presence of external incentives. *Factitious presentations* are deliberate production of symptoms with the motivation to take on a sick role. *Feigning* should be used, Rogers indicates, to indicate "deliberated fabrication or gross exaggeration of psychological or physical symptoms without any assumptions about its goals" (p. 6). Psychological testing can be used to establish feigning, he indicates, but not malingering. Deception, per se, does not imply malingering, as the individual may have a variety of reasons for feigning. Malingering also does not preclude the presence of real disorders.

Young, Kane & Nicholson (2007) indicate that "[m]alingering levels in neuropsychological assessment have been estimated to range from 2% to as high as 64%. Unfortunately, with different definitions of malingering, different samples studied, and different objectives of the research, comparing rates of malingering across studies is difficult" (p. 28).

It should be kept in mind that an individual who exhibits feigning or malingering may also have one or more real, demonstrable psychological disorders. Any disorders present should be diagnosed by the evaluator (Ackerman & Kane, 1998; Drob, Meehan, & Waxman, 2009; Kane, 2007a; Rogers, 2008a).

COMPENSATION NEUROSIS

The term *compensation neurosis* was coined by C. T. J. Rigler in 1879 with regard to the increase in reports of disability following railroad accidents. The great weight of the research, however, indicates that patients do not become free of symptoms soon after the end of litigation, nor do they quickly return to work (Ackerman & Kane, 1998; Binder & Willis, 1991; Binder & Rohling, 1996; Binder, Trimble, & McNeil, 1991; Bryand & Harvey, 2003; Call, 2003; Hyler, Williams, & Spitzer, 1988; Nicholson & Martelli, 2007b; Resnick, 1997; Ryan & Warden, 2003; Samra & Koch, 2002; Shuman, 2000; Walfish, 2006; Wilson & Moran, 2004). Rapid Reference 4.1 outlines other research findings.

≡ Rapid Reference 4.1

Research on Compensation Neurosis

Specific research studies have found the following:

- Psychological responses to accidents, including speed of recovery, do not differ between countries that have laws permitting compensation for pain and suffering and those that do not.
- Few people report a significant reduction in symptoms upon resolution of litigation (except the amount due to the stress of the litigation itself).

- As many as 50% to 75% of people injured in compensable accidents are unable to return to work for two years or more after litigation ends; treatment time does not differ significantly for people who litigate and those who do not (Resnick, 1997).
- There is usually improvement in PTSD symptoms and work and other role performance over time, even when there is litigation (Blanchard et al., 1998).
- It should be noted that persons with real suffering and disability due to minor head trauma are especially likely to seek legal recourse when that is an option, and they are relatively unlikely to be discouraged or deterred by the time and effort needed to win in court (Heilbronner, 1993). A meta-analysis by Binder and Rohling (1996) found that "patients with *less* severe injuries, as measured by posttraumatic neurological data, are *more* likely to seek monetary compensation" (p. 9). Further, "a large number of patients report changes in cognition, emotion, and behavior after a blow to the head even if they are not pursuing litigation. There is also ample evidence in the head injury literature of patients whose PCS (Postconcussional Syndrome) symptoms persist even after their legal cases have been settled" (Heilbronner, 1993, p. 161).

Scrignar (1996) indicated that, while the incidence of malingering in personal injury suits is not known, "most experienced forensic clinicians believe that few fakers come to court. Personal injury litigants are carefully screened by plaintiff and defense attorneys, private investigators, physicians, and mental health professionals. This intense scrutiny identifies the pretender and forces malingerers out of the civil courts" (p. 208).

DSM-IV-TR

The DSM-IV-TR (American Psychiatric Association, 2000) has done little to shed light on the question of malingering. The DSM-IV-TR defines malingering as "the intentional production of false or grossly exaggerated physical or psychological symptoms, motivated by external incentives such as avoiding military duty, avoiding work, obtaining financial compensation, evading criminal prosecution, or obtaining drugs" (p. 739).

The DSM-IV-TR further indicates that one should suspect malingering if any of the following is present: (1) the person is being evaluated on referral from an attorney; (2) objective findings differ markedly from the level of stress or disability alleged by the patient; (3) failure of the patient to cooperate with diagnosis and treatment processes; and/or (4) evidence of an Antisocial Personality Disorder.

The first three criteria, unfortunately, are of little value. In personal injury law-suits, referrals to mental health professionals are common when the plaintiff is al-leging psychological or emotional injuries. Further, a discrepancy between claimed stress or disability and objective findings is common in a PTSD case, in part because it is the individual's unique experience of the trauma, not objective findings, that de-termines the degree of disability. It is also common for patients with chronic pain to lack objective medical findings to support the individual's claim of significant pain, yet the pain persists even in the absence of any evidence of personal gain. A lack of cooperation during diagnosis and treatment is also commonly found in PTSD cases and among people with relatively severe brain damage who, unaware of how severe the damage is, refuse to cooperate with treatment. That leaves the fourth criterion, diagnosis of an Antisocial Personality Disorder, as the only DSM-IV-TR criterion that would provide a clue regarding whether a person may be malingering. Nicholson and Martelli (2007a) and Vitacco (2008) indicate that the only empirical study of the validity of the DSM criteria found an 80% false positive rate.

NAIVETÉ

Some people naively make the *post hoc, ergo propter hoc* (after this, therefore because of this) error. That is, they assume that a psychological disability that follows an accident or other personal injury was caused by the accident or other trauma. People who believe this, out of ignorance, should be separated from people who are consciously attempting to malinger (Resnick, 1997).

THE PSYCHOLOGICAL MEANING OF COMPENSATION

While some people seek compensation through the courts in order to get money for its own sake, others have different motivation. A real victim may exaggerate real symptoms, looking for "justice" via redress for actual or perceived harm caused by an employer or the individual who caused the injury (Kane, 2007b; Resnick, 1997; Rogers, 2008d). Others have a goal of preventing injury to some-one else, particularly in cases involving sexual misconduct by professionals, sexual harassment, and driving while intoxicated. Others want to ensure that the evalua-tor and others recognize the importance and meaning of the trauma to the victim. Many also need assurance that others appreciate how terribly they have suffered, even if they have moved beyond the acute traumatization and are in fact suffering less at present (Resnick, 1997). Malingering is far more likely for the person seek-ing "money for its own sake" than in the other situations. In the other situations, simply winning the case is often sufficient reward.

OTHER NONMALINGERING CAUSES OF EXAGGERATION

It is also relevant that plaintiffs' lawyers ask questions that encourage injured people to think about possible injuries, and that may, intentionally or not, make the injured person perceive themselves as totally or permanently disabled. Unethical lawyers, of course, may directly try to foster this perception (Lees-Haley, 1997; Youngjohn, 1995). This pattern may be further reinforced by family members, physicians, and others who fail to insist that the individual function at the highest possible level under the circumstances. Further, "Physical injury and pain often produce a regression, characterized by a breakdown of the more mature coping mechanisms. Injured patients may become totally dependent on their families, physicians, and attorneys, even though they were formerly quite autonomous" (Resnick, 1988, p. 93).

DIFFERENTIAL DIAGNOSIS

It is necessary to be able to identify diagnostic errors and confirm accurate diagnoses. It should be noted that simulators sometimes have a good grasp of the psychological consequences of a postconcussional syndrome or PTSD, making simple knowledge of symptoms an inadequate basis for identifying malingerers (Resnick, West, & Payne, 2008).

A clinical model has been developed by Resnick et al. to identify malingered PTSD. (*See* Rapid Reference 4.2.)

≡ *Rapid Reference 4.2*

Identifying Malingering

A. Understandable motive to malinger PTSD

B. At least two of the following criteria:

1. Irregular employment or job dissatisfaction
2. Prior claims for injuries
3. Capacity for recreation, but not work
4. No nightmares or, if nightmares, exact repetition of the civilian trauma
5. Antisocial personality traits (not applicable to criminal-forensic cases)
6. Evasiveness or contradictions
7. Non cooperation in the evaluation

Source: Resnick et al., 2008 p. 123

Confirmation of malingering can be identified in a number of ways. If the individual confesses malingering, there is incontrovertible psychometric evidence that malingering occurred, *or* strong collateral evidence of malingering (such as audio or videotape contradicting reported symptoms) (Resnick, 2008).

Similarly, Wilson and Moran (2004, p. 628) developed a list of "critical cues to malingering" (as shown in Rapid Reference 4.3).

Rogers (2008b, 2008d) indicates that a detection strategy for a feigned (but not necessarily malingered) disorder could include: (1) reporting of rare symptoms, those that fewer than 5% of clinical populations report; (2) quasi-rare symptoms, those that may appear in clinical populations but are still relatively uncommon; (3) improbable symptoms, those that "have a fantastic or preposterous quality" (p. 19); (4) symptom combinations present that are very uncommon among clinical populations; (5) indiscriminant endorsement of symptoms; (6) endorsement of a large number of "severe" or "unbearable" symptoms; (7) obvious symptoms of mental disorders; (8) significant discrepancies between symptoms that are reported and those that are observed; and (9) endorsement of invalid symptoms of a claimed mental disorder; often based on a stereotype of the disorder.

Wilson and Moran (2004) identify critical cues that should be addressed when assessing if malingering takes place. Malingerers will often not be cooperative with psychological or medical assessment requests. They may also be evasive and vague in their ability to produce details about the traumatic event. It is not unusual for incorrect details or improbable or implausible information about the traumatic experience to be described. There is a general tendency to blame all symptoms on the traumatic event. It is not unusual for malingerers to be familiar with the diagnostic criteria for PTSD, which can result in overemphasizing certain aspects of the criteria in their descriptions, such as "flashback" experiences. Inconsistency in psychometric testing is also found with malingerers in that they do not have the knowledge about the instruments to know precisely what answers to give or not give to support a diagnosis of PTSD. The examiner must also look at previous history regarding previous claims, events that preceded the traumatic event, and history of antisocial behavior.

Preexisting Conditions

Any evaluation must involve consideration of preexisting conditions as part of a comprehensive evaluation. Medical records should be reviewed in detail. School records will be relevant for some evaluations. Information from personnel files, co-workers, spouses, and significant others may provide important data. Psychotherapy records, if any, may provide essential information. As much of this information as reasonably possible should be gathered prior to the evaluation of the plaintiff so that appropriate questions may be asked to follow up on hypotheses generated by the data.

Posttraumatic Stress Disorder, Panic Disorder, Generalized Anxiety Disorder, organic mental disorders, major depressive episodes, Adjustment Disorder, Obsessive Compulsive Disorder, Substance-Induced Disorders, Psychosis, and Somatoform Disorders must all be ruled in or out through differential diagnosis. Further confusing matters, Factitious, Conversion, and Somatization Disorders may overlap with one another and with Malingering (Nicholson & Martelli, 2007a).

Factitious Disorder

A Factitious Disorder involves the conscious production or fabrication of physical or psychological symptoms or signs in order to be able to take on the sick role, rather than some other type of gain or external incentive (DSM-IV-TR, 2000; Vitacco, 2008). Cunnien (1997, p. 44) has suggested that this diagnosis be considered when (1) the patient admits to voluntary control of symptoms; (2) the patient presents with "bizarre or absurd symptomatology"; (3) the patient presents with an "unusual symptomatic response to treatment that cannot otherwise be explained" (e.g., paradoxical response to medication); (4) there exists "suspicion of motivation to assume the sick role"; (5) there is a "past history of factitious symptoms"; and/or (6) there is evidence of pathological lying, or "use of an alias in medical settings." However, there are no unequivocal guidelines or psychological tests to assess motivation (Vitacco, 2008). It is necessary for the clinician to first determine that the patient is feigning, and then to explore the apparent motivation for the feigning (Vitacco, 2008). An individual who has a Factitious Disorder is not malingering; he or she has a significant psychological need to be seen as sick and suffering. The individual with a Factitious Disorder is not typically aware of his or her motivation for feigning (Nicholson & Martelli, 2007a).

Malingering

Per the definition at the beginning of this chapter, malingering involves the conscious production of "false or grossly exaggerated physical or psychological symptoms," motivated by some kind of personal gain. When malingering is found in a personal injury lawsuit, the gain usually sought is financial, though it may also be due to a desire to be taken care of or other forms of reinforcement.

EVALUATING FOR MALINGERING

Evaluation for malingering is primarily an evaluation of feigning, a conscious or unconscious attempt by the individual to present himself or herself in a way that is not an accurate portrayal of his or her status and symptoms. The evaluation should be comprehensive, addressing every relevant aspect of the individual's functioning. It should involve psychological testing, review of collateral data, and an interview of the individual. Multiple detection strategies should be utilized to address the many ways in which individuals may feign (Rogers, 2008d).

Martelli, Nicholson, Zasler, and Bender (2007) recommend that all evaluations include several elements in order to maximize the validity of the results:

1. Establish rapport and a basic working relationship with patients and examinees [...]. Valid data collection requires a collaborative effort. The possibility of dissimulation might be reduced given better rapport [...].
2. Ensure that emotional variables affecting motivation are adequately assessed during an interview that is conducted prior to the exam. Specifically, assess the impact of anger or blame and feelings of resentment or victimization, as well as the other variables shown in the literature to be associated with poor recovery and adaptation to impairment. Assess pain, fatigue or other factors that may actually interfere with optimal performance [...].
3. Make efforts to maximize validity of exam procedures. Where possible, utilize instruments with built-in symptom validity measures [...].
4. Employ shorter symptom validity tests in order to minimize possibility of negative reactions owing to the nature of protracted participation in easy, boring, or atypical tasks [...].
5. Remain aware that, in science and medicine, situations are rarely either-or, or clear-cut, or one-dimensional [...]. Cut-off scores, by their nature, always entail judgment, inherently result in misclassification and impose an artificial dichotomy on essentially continuous variables [...].

6. Utilize and devise models that measure the degree of apparent motivation and effort, using multiple data sources, and estimate confidence levels of inferences, given consideration of the multiple factors that contribute to exam findings [...]. (Martelli, Nicholson, Zasler, & Bender, 2007, p. 18)

PSYCHOLOGICAL TESTING

Choosing Tests

Tests should be chosen that have significant sensitivity and specificity with regard to assessment of feigning, and that add incremental validity to the accumulated data. There is no correct number of tests, but it should be small enough to permit the individual to complete the tests in a reasonable time without great fatigue, yet large enough to address the key issues (Kane, 2007c).

Sensitivity and Specificity

According to Melton, Petrila, Poythress, and Slobogin (2007, p. 738), "'[s]en-sitivity' reflects a test's capacity to select many or more of the individuals who possess the trait or exhibit the behavior that the test is designed to measure. 'Specificity' is an index of the degree to which the test selects only those individuals possessing the trait or expressing the behavior that the test is designed to detect." The most useful tests, in context, will accurately identify individuals who are feigning, while not identifying individuals who are not feigning. No test is nearly perfect in doing so, but many tests provide useful evidence of an individual's attempt to feign.

Response Style

A key factor in any evaluation is to address the response style of the individual. It is essential for evaluators to assess an examinee's response style, and how it affects test results and the evaluation as a whole, as part of a forensic evaluation (Otto, 2008). When tests and related instruments are involved, this may also be referred to as "test-taking attitude." According to Heilbrun (2001, pp. 165–166):

Response style has been defined to include four particular styles: (1) reliable/honest (a genuine attempt is made to be accurate; factual inaccuracies result from poor understanding or misperception), (2) malingering (conscious fabrication or gross exaggeration of psychological and/or physical symptoms, understandable in light of the individual's circumstances and not attributable merely to the desire to assume the patient role, as in Factitious Disorder), (3) defensive (conscious denial or gross minimization of psychological and/or physical symptoms, as distinguished from ego defenses, which involve intrapsychic processes that distort perception), and (4) irrelevant (failure to become engaged in the evaluation; responses are not necessarily relevant to questions and may be random). It is useful to broaden the fourth response style to include instances in which the individual refuses to respond, or responds minimally, and call this uncooperative rather than irrelevant.

Heilbrun, Warren, and Picarello (2003, p. 71) add two additional categories: "uncooperative, in which the individual responds minimally or not at all to assessment questions," and "impaired: it involves experiencing communication deficits resulting from young age, thought and speech disorganization, intellectual deficits, and/or memory problems."

Minnesota Multiphasic Personal Inventory, Second Edition (MMPI-2)

The MMPI-2 is the most widely utilized and researched objective psychopathology test in the world (Greene, 2008; Kane, 2007b). The MMPI-2 validity scales are particularly well-suited for addressing whether an individual is malingering or otherwise not answering questions in an open, forthright manner, although the results may be ambiguous, and interpretations must be carefully considered (Bender, 2008; Boccaccini & Brodsky, 1999; Fishbain, Cutler, Rosomoff, & Rosomoff, 2003; Greene, 2008; Greenberg, Otto, & Long, 2003; Kane, 2007b; Lees-Haley, 1992; Melton, Petrila, Poythress, & Slobogin, 2007; Otto, 2002; Pope, Butcher, & Seelen, 2006; Posthuma, Podrouzek, & Crisp, 2002; Rabin, Barr, & Burton, 2005; Resnick et al., 2008; Rogers, 2003; Rogers, Sewell, Martin, & Vitacco, 2003; Rogers & Shuman, 2005; Shuman, 1994, 2002 supplement). The validity scales of the MMPI-2 are the most frequently used scales for this purpose (Fishbain et al., 2003; Pope et al., 2006; Rogers, 2008a; Rogers, Jackson, Sewall, Tillbrook, & Martin, 2003). By assessing the individual's test-taking attitude (response style) with the MMPI-2 validity scales, the evaluator obtains data that identify whether (and to what degree) the individual was consistent, defensive, exaggerated symptoms, and so forth. This test-taking attitude can generally be extended, cautiously, to the whole evaluation. The person who produces a valid MMPI-2 is relatively likely to also produce valid results from other tests and various means of gathering information (Boccaccini & Brodsky, 1999; Graham, 2006; Pope, personal communication, May 14, 2006; Pope, Butcher, & Seelen, 2000; Rubenzer, 2009).

The MMPI-2 has a number of validity scales and one additional factor—the number of items to which no response was given or for which both "true" and "false" were marked, the "Cannot Say" or "?" Scale. Samuel, DeGirolamo, Michals, and O'Brien (1995) indicate that significantly more blanks are left by people involved in personal injury litigation than among people who are not so involved. They also indicate that the closer the evaluation is to the date of the injury, the more likely it is that the individual will leave more than 30 items blank, producing a profile that is likely to be invalid, or, at the least, questionable. It is often possible to address this problem by asking the person to answer the questions left blank, either by reading from the test booklet or by reading the items to the individual. This small variation in the standardized procedure should be noted in the report, but would not be expected to adversely affect the validity of the test.

Next, the consistency of responding is addressed with two scales. The Variable Response Inconsistency Scale (VRIN) consists of 67 paired items, with the two items in each pair being either similar or opposite in meaning. An individual who responds too inconsistently (above a T Score of 79) has invalidated the MMPI-2. Since either random responding or a fixed response set could cause an elevation on other validity scales, both VRIN and TRIN should be examined prior to concluding that psychopathology is being overreported (Butcher, Graham, Ben-Porath, Tellegen, Dahlstrom, & Kaemmer, 2001). The True Response Inconsistency Scale (TRIN) consists entirely of paired items that have opposite content. T Scores above 79 indicate a significant tendency to have answered either "true" or "false" without regard to the content of the items, invalidating the test (Butcher et al., 2001).

The L Scale addresses the degree to which the individual tries to appear "perfect" or especially "virtuous," that is, to present him- or herself in an unrealistically positive light. T Scores of 65–69 suggest accentuation of the positive. T Scores of 70 or more suggest blatant exaggeration of positive qualities (Pope et al., 2006). The MMPI-2 profiles are generally invalidated by L Scale T Scores of 80 or more (Butcher et al., 2001).

The F (Infrequency) Scale consists of items among the first 361 on the MMPI-2 that were endorsed by 10% or fewer of the normative population. T Scores below 79 are likely to indicate a valid protocol. T Scores from 80 to 89 generally indicate that exaggerating is likely. T Scores of 90 or greater indicate that a protocol may be invalid (Butcher et al., 2001). T Scores of 110 or more signify a profile that is not interpretable due to extreme responses (Pope et al., 2006). The causes of an invalid score may include malingering, exaggeration of problems (including a cry for help), extreme defensiveness, random responding, and/or significant psychopathology (Groth-Marnat, 2009). Importantly, research indicates that high F Scale scores correlate with histories of trauma, depression, dissociation, PTSD, and traumatic environments in an individual's family of origin (Elhai et al., 2004). People who have been rejected or stigmatized due to posttraumatic changes may respond in a way that draws attention to the pain and injury they feel, to try to ensure that their psychological pain and problems do not get overlooked (Briere, 2004). Thus, the F Scale is much less useful in assessing malingering among trauma victims than among other populations.

The Fb (F Back) Scale consists of items numbered 281 or higher, primarily addressing infrequent responses in the second half of the MMPI-2. High scores may result from fatigue or from any of the factors listed before for the F Scale. The same cutoff scores as for the F Scale may be used (Butcher et al., 2001; Pope et al., 2006). Rogers, Jackson, Sewell, Tillbrook, and Martin's (2003) meta-analysis suggested a cutoff score for Fb that is 12 points higher than the score on the F Scale, to reduce false-positives.

The K Scale addresses a more subtle and sophisticated defensiveness than does the L Scale. A high score does not imply psychopathology. T Scores from 65 to 74 suggest substantial defensiveness, whereas T Scores of 75 or higher suggest "faking good"; that is, the individual is presenting an unrealistically positive impression of self or of life due to conscious or unconscious exaggeration. High K Scale T Scores make it much less likely that psychopathology will be indicated on the clinical scales (Butcher et al., 2001). On the original MMPI, individuals with advanced education and/or high socioeconomic status were relatively likely to produce elevations on the K Scale regardless of whether they were intentionally being defensive. The K Scale on the MMPI-2 is normed on a population with a higher educational level, making it unnecessary to interpret the scale differently for those individuals with substantial education. It should be noted, however, that K may be lower for individuals who have less education than high school (Graham, 2006; Pope et al., 2006).

The S (Superlative Self-Presentation) Scale is similar to the K Scale, but includes items from throughout the test, rather than only the first 370 items. Individuals with high scores may be claiming one or more positive qualities; for example, a belief in human goodness, a feeling of serenity, feeling content with life, denial of negative feelings, and/or denial of moral flaws. T Scores of 69 or less suggest a valid test protocol, 70–74 moderate defensiveness, and 75 or more that the protocol may be invalid due to "faking good"; that is, the individual is presenting an unrealistically positive impression of self or of life due to conscious or unconscious exaggeration. When this is the case, interpretation of the clinical scales may need to be modified to adjust for the unrealistic presentation. If the T Score is 65 or more, the five subscales of the S Scale may be interpreted (Butcher et al., 2001; Pope et al., 2006).

The Fp (Infrequency-Psychopathology) Scale consists of items that were answered in the scored direction by no more than 20% of either the normative sample or a sample of psychiatric inpatients. When the F Scale is elevated and random responding has been ruled out, a T Score of 100 or more on Fp suggests significantly excessive reporting of psychopathology; that is, "faking bad," conscious or unconscious exaggeration of psychopathology. In contrast, if Fp is below 70, it is relatively likely that any severe psychopathology reported is real. T Scores between 70 and 99 suggest either exaggeration of symptoms or a "cry for help" (Butcher et al., 2001; Nichols, 2001). Scores of 100 or more strongly suggest malingering (Graham, 2006). The Fp Scale is the most specific, and most sensitive, measure of overreporting on the MMPI-2 (Nichols, 2001; Polusny & Arbisi, 2006; Pope, Butcher, & Seelen, 2000; Resnick et al., 2008). Rogers, Jackson, Sewell, Tillbrook, and Martin (2003) specify that "Fp appears to be the most effective scale in the assessment of feigning," in part because "these cut scores appear to be effective across disorders and even moderately useful with the problematic diagnosis of PTSD" (p. 173). Rogers, Payne, Berry, and Granacher (2009) indicate that Fp cut scores discriminate well between feigned and legitimate patients in clinical settings, and produce relatively few false-positives in people with PTSD. Even so, automatic application of cutting scores to differentiate groups is seldom appropriate. Numerous variables must be considered in this process. Briere (2004) and Elhai et al. (2004) indicate that Fp appears to be more sensitive than the F Scale in determining whether a PTSD protocol is valid. Greene (2008) indicates that a raw score of 6 or 7 reflects either malingering or inconsistent responding.

The F − K (F minus K) Index, also known as the Dissimulation Index, suggests "faking bad" if the *raw* score for the F Scale is 15 or more points greater than the *raw* score for the K Scale (Butcher et al., 2001). Scores of 25 or more strongly suggest exaggeration of psychopathology (Nichols, 2001; Rogers, Sewell, & Salekin, 1994). Because it is very important to minimize false-positives, high cutoff scores should be used (Greene, 2008). If F − K is equal to or less than −8, it is very unlikely that the person was feigning (Rogers, Sewell, & Salekin, 1994). The F − K Index has been found to be especially good at identifying "motivated faking" (Briere, 2004).

The ODecp (Other Deception) Scale was developed by Nichols and Greene (1997) as a means of identifying highly defensive individuals. A cutoff score of 20 identified 95% of those individuals in the authors' research. This scale (with slightly different content) was known as the Positive Malingering (MP) Scale on the MMPI.

The Gough Dissimulation Scale (Ds, modified as the Dsr for the MMPI-2) was designed to indicate psychopathology, but used items that psychiatric patients did not usually endorse (Graham, 2006). It was found by Rogers, Jackson, Sewell, Tillbrook, and Martin (2003) to be nearly as good as the F and Fp Scales at identifying malingering. Rogers and colleagues recommended utilizing Fp, along with either F or Dsr, based on their meta-analysis of 65 feigning and 11 diagnostic studies. Rogers et al. (2009) indicated that Ds cut scores seldom produce false-positives. Greene (2008) recommends using a cutoff score of 38 or more to minimize false-positives.

Fake Bad Scale (FBS)

Although the Fake Bad Scale (FBS) (Lees-Haley, English, & Glenn, 1991) is derived from the MMPI-2, it is addressed separately because of the degree of controversy surrounding its use. Distinguished scientists and authors fall on both sides of the controversy. In 2007, Pearson Assessments added the FBS to the scored validity scales on the MMPI-2, referring to it as the "FBS (Symptom Validity) Scale" (Butcher, Gass, Cumella, Kally, & Williams, 2008). In a December 2008 statement about the FBS, Ben-Porath and Tellegen (2008) offer an extensive bibliography on the FBS that should be consulted by the reader. The FBS consists of 43 items from the MMPI-2.

Butcher et al. (2008) addressed numerous issues regarding the validity of the FBS. Among their criticisms, they indicate that real physical problems produce high FBS scores, that litigation-related stress may cause elevations on the FBS, that women tend to score higher on the FBS than do men by about two points, that people exposed to severe trauma tend to have higher FBS scores, that there is an excessive percentage of false-positives (people alleged to be malingering who are not), and that there is not a consensus regarding the cutoff point that should be used to indicate probable malingering. The authors offer as an example a study of women with demonstrated eating disorders, 8% of whom would be labeled malingerers because their raw scores exceeded the very conservative cutoff score of 30 on the FBS. At the recommended cutoff point of 29 or more, 11% would have been falsely labeled as malingerers. The authors indicate that "FBS appears to be a measure of general maladjustment and somatic complaints, as opposed to malingering" (p. 197). Further, they indicate that the FBS fails to provide any evidence of the conscious intent to "fake bad" that is necessary if malingering is to be diagnosed, while people with somatoform disorders (who unconsciously express psychological symptoms through physical symptoms) tend to have high FBS scores. They also indicate that there is no manual for the FBS, preventing psychologists from understanding the bases for the scale. Finally, they cite three Florida court cases in which the FBS was excluded on the basis that it was not generally accepted by the psychological community (*Frye v. United States*, 1923).

Ben-Porath, Greve, Bianchini, and Kaufmann (2009) responded to Butcher et al. (2008). They begin by indicating that malingering should not be diagnosed on the basis of any single test or scale: "a formal diagnosis of malingering should be based on the integration of diverse sources of information" (p. 63). They further note that malingering should not be diagnosed without the identification of an external reward. With regard to cutoff scores, Ben-Porath and colleagues indicate that the recommended cut scores have changed based on research, as ought to be the case with any test or scale. With regard to the allegation of too many false positives, the authors cite Greifenstein, Fox, and Lees-Haley (2007), who found that only 1.2% of respondents in 1,052 cases of medical and psychiatric patients without known incentive to overstate symptoms were false positives when a cutoff of 29+ was used. Other cited research ranged from 0 to 2.9%, scoring above a raw score of 29. Further, they indicate that, for patients with mild traumatic brain injuries (Mtbi) or chronic pain, "[n]one of the no-incentive mild TBI patients and only 1.5% of the no-incentive pain patients score 29 or higher. In contrast, 28.9% of the mild TBI patients with incentive and 27.5% of the chronic pain patients with incentive scored higher than 29" (p. 72). They point out that no test provides an unequivocal measure of intent, but that scores above a certain level may indicate that malingering is likely. In addition, the authors indicate, somatization and other disorders can coexist with malingering, but "[o]nly at the higher levels will the score be specific to intentional exaggeration" (p. 75). With regard to gender bias, the authors acknowledge that women tend to score two points higher than men, but indicate that research has found that "women who were diagnosed as malingering independent of their FBS scores were more likely to elevate FBS than similarly diagnosed men" (p. 76), and that "the gender effects disappear at levels of FBS that indicate the possibility of malingering" (p. 77). With regard to court cases, Ben-Porath and colleagues indicate that the FBS has been accepted in many cases, even if excluded from some.

Williams, Butcher, Gass, Cumella, and Kally (2009) responded to Ben-Porath et al. (2009), noting that the FBS was added to the MMPI-2 Extended Score Report without significant guidance regarding avoidance of misuse of the scale. There is still no manual or manual supplement providing comprehensive information regarding the scale. They repeated their concern about gender bias, and about the validity of a cutoff score of 29+ as a basis for serious concern about self-reported symptoms. While these authors concur with Ben-Porath and colleagues that a high score on the FBS is not, in itself, sufficient for a diagnosis of malingering, they note that web-based guidelines do not contain that advice. They indicate concern that Ben-Porath et al. recommend the FBS for any setting in which the MMPI-2 is used, rather than only those with a clear external incentive. They indicate continuing concern that "the FBS is highly correlated with empirically validated scales measuring somatoform disorders and somatic problems" (p. 190), and that there is no consensus regarding the appropriate cutoff score for presumed indication of malingering. They cite research indicating that individuals with traumatic brain injuries may score above standard cutoffs, as well as individuals with somatization disorders. The authors conclude by indicating that "[o]ne can view the FBS only in a highly favorable light by ignoring the methodological problems in the studies underlying its develop or by disregarding a significant body of empirical research that casts doubt on the accuracy of the FBS, even as an adjunct to diagnosing malingering" (p. 196).

Resnick et al. (2008) report that the FBS was not able to successfully differentiate between real and malingered PTSD in their study. "This finding may be due to the relatively high average elevations noted on the FBS scale by genuine PTSD patients (M = 82.00)" (p. 119).

Greene (2008) calculated cutting scores associated with various degrees of false positives. A cutting score of 28 is associated with a 10% false positive rate; 31 with a 5% rate; 34 with a 2% rate; and 35 with a 1% rate.

According to Rubenzer (2009), many studies have found that the FBS is the best MMPI-2 validity scale when addressing psychological injuries or disabilities due to nonpsychotic disorders, while other studies have found it to be nearly useless. A point in its favor is that the FBS correlates highly with performance on cognitive Symptom Validity Testing. Recent reviews of the FBS in the context of compensation cases support its use, Rubenzer reports. However, Rubenzer indicates that, "[w]idely different cutoff scores are maximally effective across studies, and two groups appear prone to elevated scores: females with a prior psychiatric history and patients with severe objectively manifested physical distress, such as drug withdrawal." Further, the FBS has been found to have an excessive number of false-positives. However, Rubenzer indicates, "scores above 28 were rarely found (false-positive rates from .01–.03) in nonlitigating cases" (p. 120). It is in *litigated* cases that the issues related to false-positives and other matters become critical, however, making this a continuing concern.

Personality Assessment Inventory (PAI)

The PAI (Morey, 1991) has some advantages over the MMPI-2, including a lower reading level (fourth rather than sixth grade), a shorter length, scales that do not overlap, and a choice of four rather than only two responses per item. It has been found to be effective in discriminating real from simulated psychiatric patients, but also has a high false-positive rate (Bender, 2008). Its efficacy in identifying feigned TBI or other neurocognitive deficits has not yet been established (Bender, 2008).

> ### CAUTION
>
> The mixed support for and concerns about the Fake Bad Scale require the psychologist to use caution in interpreting the scale. It should never be used alone as an indicator of malingering. If an individual has a raw score of 29 or greater, a careful search should be done for independent evidence of malingering, including a significant external incentive to malinger. Great care should be taken to avoid confirmatory bias. If substantial independent evidence is not identified, malingering should not be diagnosed. The reader should also study the ongoing research on the FBS as it is published, to permit making a decision as to whether use of this instrument can be defended in court.

Resnick et al. (2008) indicate that the PAI has three scales for the detection of malingering: Negative Impression (NIM), Malingering Index (MAL), and Rogers Discriminant Function Index (RDF). The NIM focuses on rare symptoms, while MAL and RDF focus on spurious pathological patterns. They report that NIM successfully differentiates between real and malingered civilian PTSD, but that a study of combat veterans had a 35% false positive rate. The MAL and RDF have not done well at differentiating between real PTSD sufferers and malingerers. They recommend that the MMPI-2 be used rather than the PAI when evaluating feigned PTSD.

Sellbom and Bagby (2008) reviewed the research on the PAI and malingering. They indicate that the PAI shows promise at screening *out* malingering, but that a high degree of false positives prevent the test from being used to screen *in* malingering, especially in forensic settings. Iverson and Lange (2006) indicate that the "literature to date suggests that PTSD can be successfully faked on the PAI" (p. 88). Rogers (2008d), however, indicates that the PAI is effective at addressing malingering.

Trauma Symptom Inventory (TSI)

The TSI (Briere, 1995) is a 100-item questionnaire with three validity scales, with the Atypical Response Scale (ATR) being particularly focused on potential malingering. Using a cutting score of T > 90, false positives were held to 5%. However, the TSI validity scales have been found to be only moderately effective at detecting malingering (Resnick et al., 2008). Sellbom and Bagby (2008) reviewed the research on the TSI and malingering. They conclude that the TSI validity scales, including ATR, were not sufficient to differentiate malingerers from nonmalingerers.

Structured Interview of Reported Symptoms (SIRS)

The SIRS (Rogers, 1992; Rogers, Bagby, & Dickens, 1992) is considered to be the best single instrument for detection of malingering (Melton, Petrila, Poythress, & Slobogin, 2007; Rogers & Bender, 2003). It is a 172-item structured interview designed to evaluate feigning and other response styles. It has been found to successfully differentiate malingerers from clinical groups with substantial accuracy (Resnick et al., 2008). Each of the eight primary scales addresses a specific strategy for detection of feigning.

> [D]etection strategies are organized into two general categories: *unlikely* (i.e., the mere reporting of these test items is indicative of feigning) and *amplified* (i.e., higher-than-expected frequency or intensity of reported symptoms is considered indicative of feigning). Primary scales in the unlikely category include rare symptoms (RS), symptom combinations (SC), improbable and absurd symptoms (IA), and reported versus observed symptoms (RO). Those in the amplified category consist of blatant symptoms (BL), subtle symptoms (SU), selectivity of symptoms (SEL), and severity of symptoms (SEV).... In addition, a defensiveness scale (DS) evaluates defensiveness via the denial of common psychological problems. (Rogers, Payne, Berry, & Granacher, 2009, p. 216)

Rogers et al. (2009) investigated the validity of the SIRS in compensation cases. They obtained data from 569 individuals who had forensic neuropsychiatric evaluations related to workers' compensation, personal injury, or disability determinations. They identified three groups: feigned mental disorders (FMD), feigned cognitive impairment (FCI), and genuine mental and/or cognitive impairments (GEN-Both). Of the 569 individuals, 380 were involved in compensation cases. Sources of referrals included both plaintiffs (35.1%) and defendants (63.4%).

Criterion validity was addressed via comparisons with the Minnesota Multiphasic Personality Inventory, Second Edition (MMPI-2) and several symptom validity tests: the Victoria Symptom Validity Test (VSVT; Slick, Hopp, Strauss, & Thompson, 1997); the Test of Memory Malingering (TOMM; Tombaugh, 1996); and the Letter Memory Test (LMT; Inman et al., 1998). Several tests of intelligence were also administered. The SIRS was found to correlate very well with the MMPI-2's validity scales. Consistent with the test manual, the SIRS was not found to do well at identifying feigned cognitive impairment (FCI). It was also found that intellectual impairment led to patients with real psychopathology appearing similar to those individuals feigning cognitive impairment, so the SIRS should not be used with individuals with low IQs (full scale IQ below 80). The presence of cognitive disorders (e.g., traumatic brain injury), however, did not produce high SIRS profiles. Results for patients referred by plaintiff versus defense attorneys did not significantly differ.

Rogers et al. (2009) note that the National Comorbidity Survey indicated that about two-thirds of people diagnosed with PTSD were also diagnosed with at least two other disorders, making comorbidity the rule. The authors also note that approximately half the people with a diagnosis of PTSD exhibited some psychotic symptoms. Rogers and colleagues found that only patients diagnosed with Major Depression had a single Axis I diagnosis. Rogers et al. (2009) conclude that "the SIRS is a highly reliable measure of FMD [feigned mental disorders] .... The current investigation establishes its effectiveness for compensation and disability cases with common trauma-related diagnoses (PTSD and major depression)" (p. 223).

The SIRS focuses on differentiating malingering from legitimate subjects, but does not work as well regarding a "'partial malingerer'—the individual who experiences genuine symptoms, but who also selectively reports, exaggerates, or fabricates some symptoms depending on the circumstances" (Heilbrun, 2001, pp. 182–183). The SIRS has a false-positive rate of 2 to 3% (Rogers & Shuman, 2005).

Millon Clinical Multiaxial Inventory, Third Edition (MCMI-III)

Sellbom and Bagby (2008) reviewed the research on the use of the MCMI to detect malingering. They conclude that no MCMI-III (Millon, 1997) scale successfully identifies malingering to a sufficient degree, and recommend against its use for that purpose. Melton, Petrila, Poythress, and Slobogin (2007) indicate that the response style scales of the MCMI-II and III "have not been subjected to much research, and the research that has been conducted has been discouraging" (p. 60).

Structured Inventory of Malingered Symptomatology (SIMS)

The SIMS (Widows & Smith, 2005) is a 75-item true-false screening instrument addressing both psychological and neuropsychological symptoms. It requires only a fifth-grade reading level. It has demonstrated efficacy as a screening instrument for malingering. It should not be used with individuals who are severely impaired, since they may produce false-positive protocols (Smith, 2008). If the SIMS suggests that malingering is likely, a more thorough measure (e.g., SIRS, MMPI-2) should be used to make the determination.

Symptom Validity Testing

Cognitive Symptom Validity Testing (SVT) attempts " 'to detect poor effort or intentional failure' using a variety of strategies.... Failure on a performance-based validity test can corroborate feigning in a modality distinct from self-report, in a mode that probably requires intentional poor performance (consciously not attending to the task, purposely answering incorrectly), and weighs against interpreting elevations on self-report validity scales as benign overreporting" (Rubenzer, 2009, p. 127). Scoring below chance has been a primary means of identifying malingerers, but research indicates that that method identifies at most 10% of feigners (Rubenzer, 2009). Interference may come from such things as headaches, emotional distress, or a psychiatric disorder, or any other condition that significantly interferes with the ability to pay attention, process information, and give an appropriate response (Nicholson & Martelli, 2007c). There is also evidence that malingerers tend not to perform significantly below chance on such measures (Nicholson & Martelli, 2007c), with Rogers (2008b) estimating the percentage as at most 25%. Cutting scores on SVTs are generally set at a point at which both healthy and clinical populations tend to score well (Nicholson & Martelli, 2007c). According to Rogers (2008d), "SVT is the only detection strategy that can provide definite evidence of cognitive feigning. However, most feigners do not perform substantially below chance, thereby limiting SVT to demonstrating the presence, but not the absence, of feigned cognitive impairment" (p. 394).

One type of SVT is a forced-choice method involving "presentation of some sensory, cognitive, or other stimuli/test material whereupon the person is subsequently asked to provide a response. Possible responses are limited, usually to an either-or decision, with one response being correct and one wrong. If the person chooses more wrong responses than could be expected on the basis of chance responding, it may be concluded that he or she was intentionally performing below his or her true capacity or deliberately choosing wrong responses in an effort to appear more impaired than he or she actually is" (Nicholson & Martelli, 2007c, p. 429). Rogers (2008b) indicates that it is a strength that "failures significantly below chance provide definitive evidence of feigning" (p. 25), but that few malingerers fail such tests.

The majority of cognitive SVTs use a memory paradigm wherein a task appears difficult, but is performed without great difficulty by both clinical and healthy populations (Nicholson & Martelli, 2007c). Rubenzer (2009) recommends the Word Memory Test (Green, 2003) as perhaps the best of the SVTs in that it has nearly 100% sensitivity, far higher than other SVTs, though it may produce a larger false-positive rate than some other tests. Rubenzer also recommends utilizing "the age-corrected [WAIS] Digit Span scale score, the difference of the Vocabulary and Digit Span age-corrected scale scores [...], and Reliable Digit Span (the number of digits repeated forward and backward, correct for both trials, summed)" (p. 128). Bender (2008) notes that "only 5% of the normative sample (both healthy and clinical samples) score below the 5th percentile on the Digit Span subtest of the WAIS-III," suggesting that it may be useful in assessing effort. Both Digit Span and Reliable Digit Span may be inappropriate for people with borderline IQs, however. Rubenzer indicates that the TOMM (Tombaugh, 1996) is effective at identifying cognitive feigning except when there is dementia or other real cognitive impairment. Rubenzer also recommends that evaluations include the Memory Complaints Inventory (Green, 2004) to identify whether the examinee has memory and/or concentration complaints.

Slick, Sherman, and Iverson (1999) defined malingered neurocognitive deficit as "the volitional exaggeration or fabrication of cognitive dysfunction for the purpose of obtaining substantial material gain, or avoiding or escaping formal duty or responsibility" (p. 552), quoted by Rubenzer (2009). They proposed what have come to be known as the "Slick criteria." If there is an external reward, *and* questionable performance on at least one neuropsychological or self-report test, *and* inconsistent or questionable presentation, the individual may be described as definitely, probably, or possibly malingering. The Slick criteria are fairly well accepted by neuropsychologists. Other authors have suggested that failures on two or three psychiatric or cognitive indicators of validity should be evidence of malingering (Rubenzer, 2009). Bender (2008) notes that "possible" malingering is not useful in a forensic context.

According to Rubenzer (2009), Goldberg, Back-Madruga, and Boone (2007) did a literature survey to identify the affect of psychiatric disorders on SVTs. They conclude that depression did not affect the results of any of 12 SVTs, but that data are lacking regarding the effect of Bipolar Disorder, personality disorders, or PTSD on SVTs. Rubenzer suggests that PTSD should not have an effect on a cognitive SVT unless the individual also has memory complaints.

There are numerous reasons why the results of SVT may not be valid; for example, the patient may read poorly, may have difficulty responding appropriately to the items, the SVT may be culturally inappropriate, the patient may be disinterested or actively resistant for some reason, the patient may have a headache or other problem that interferes with performance, and/or the examiner may make an error (Nicholson & Martelli, 2007a). Further, "poor effort is neither necessary nor sufficient for a determination of malingering to be made in TBI cases" (Bender, 2008, p. 69).

Symptom validity testing should be used cautiously. The general signs of neurocognitive malingering follow:

CAUTION

1. The degree of cognitive is beyond that expected.
2. The degree of impairment is inconsistent with the degree of functional disability.
3. Reported symptoms and/or cognitive profile(s) do not make neurological sense.
4. Test performance does not fit known cognitive profiles.
5. Discrepant performance on tests of similar ability.
6. Frequent near misses.
7. Failing on easy items, and passing more difficult ones.
8. Quick to say, "I don't know."

Source: Bender, 2008, p. 85

Recommended Symptom Validity Tests

A number of SVTs have been found to demonstrate utility in assessing symptom validity:

> Computerized Assessment of Response Bias (CARB)[1]
>
> Digit Memory Test[1]
>
> Digit Span (from WAIS)[1, 2, 4]
>
> Letter Memory Test[1]
>
> Portland Digit Recognition Test (PDRT)[1]
>
> Reliable Digit Span (from WAIS)[1, 4]
>
> Rey Auditory Verbal Learning Test[2]
>
> Rey Memory for 15 Item Test (Rey MFIT)[1, 3]
>
> Rey Word Recognition List[1]
>
> Validity Indicator Profile (VIP)[3, 5]
>
> Victoria Symptom Validity Test (VSVT)[1]
>
> Test of Memory Malingering (TOMM)[1, 3, 4, 5]
>
> Word Memory Test (WMT)[1, 3, 4, 5]

COLLATERAL INFORMATION

The forensic expert needs to review all records that are reasonably likely to shed light upon the status of the individual, both pre- and posttrauma. The pretrauma information identifies a baseline: what the individual was like prior to the traumatic event. The posttrauma data indicate the changes the individual went through as a result of the trauma *or other events in his or her life.* In general, the records reviewed should go back at least five years, and a minimum of three years, prior to the allegedly traumatic event, to try to ensure that nothing important is missed, and to

---

[1] Sweet, Condit, & Nelson, 2008
[2] Berry & Schipper, 2008
[3] Rogers, 2008d
[4] Rubenzer, 2009
[5] Melton, Petrila, Poythress, & Slobogin, 2007

form a substantial baseline of pretrauma functioning. Psychological tests cannot be used in isolation to establish whether there is malingering; they must be considered in the context of the individual's life circumstances, including life history (Drob, Meehan, & Waxman, 2009; Melton, Petrila, Poythress, & Slobogin, 2007; Kane, 2007c).

The records reviewed should include all available medical records (including psychotherapy records), arrest records, school records, employment records, military records, personnel records, and any other records that may shed light on the individual's functional abilities prior to and following the traumatic event (Ackerman & Kane, 1998; Kane, 2007b; LeBourgeois, 2007; Otto, 2008). Interviews of third parties (e.g., family members, friends, co-workers) may be cautiously used, recognizing that the person interviewed may have biases. It is important to evaluate the quality of the information in the records, of course, trying to ensure that only valid information is considered (Otto, 2008). Whenever possible, multiple sources of information that address the same factors should be utilized.

Medication records should identify any direct or side effects that may contribute to the clinical picture. For example, an individual who appears depressed may be heavily medicated (to the degree required by his or her condition), or overmedicated. Although there is strong evidence that Posttraumatic Stress Disorder (PTSD) is likely to cause a work-related disability, other factors (e.g., social support, perceived employment support, satisfaction with work and life) may affect the level of disability, and therefore need to be carefully assessed (Koch, O'Neill, & Douglas, 2005). Without a strong database it will also be difficult, if not impossible, for an expert to testify to a "reasonable degree of psychological (or medical or social work, etc.) certainty," and the record review should be considered to be below the standard of practice (Ackerman & Kane, 1998; Heilbrun, 2001).

> # CAUTION
> ....
> An assessment of malingering that does not include a thorough review of relevant records does not provide an adequate basis for a decision regarding whether the individual is feigning.

Detecting Malingering and Secondary Gain in Pain Patients

The person reporting chronic pain should be able to offer "a detailed and complete description of the pain.... Patients suffering from pain, whether it is primarily due to physiological or emotional factors, should be able to describe in exact detail the origin, direction, intensity, duration and history of the pain. Malingerers are apt to be vague and general, often saying 'It hurts all over.' Additionally, most people do not possess the medical or physiological sophistication to correctly fake the symptoms of pain, which often follows precise and exact neuroanatomical pathways" (Grote, Kaler, & Meyer, 1986, p. 97).

People reporting chronic pain tend to also exhibit symptoms of Posttraumatic Stress Disorder (PTSD), with pain serving as a constant reminder of the trauma that caused the pain (Boccaccini, Boothby, & Overduin, 2006). Unfortunately, there is no specific test for determining the validity of pain complaints. A survey of forensic and pain specialists found that the four tests most frequently used to assess for malingering were the MMPI-2, the Validity Indicator Profile (VIP), the Structured Interview of Reported Symptoms (SIRS), and the Test of Memory Malingering (TOMM) (Boccaccini, Boothby, & Overduin, 2006). The primary methods used to assess the validity of pain symptoms were obtaining medical and other records, examining inconsistencies between reported symptoms and other sources of information (tests, records, interviews of collaterals), and use of specific measures of pain and/or malingering (Boccaccini, Boothby, & Overduin, 2006).

CLINICAL INTERVIEW

When all the testing is done, the primary remaining task is to tie up all of the information from the review of records and other collateral information, the testing, and any other data available to the evaluator. This requires a clinical interview of sufficient length and breadth to permit the evaluator to make a decision regarding the likelihood that the individual is malingering. The primary goal of the interview, beyond the attempt to understand the aforementioned data sources, is to assess the motivation of the evaluatee, to further assess his or her response style, and to address any specific legal issues (Rogers, 2008c). Part of this will have already been accomplished if one has used the SIRS, a structured interview. Additional questioning will still be necessary, however, to address all of the essential issues.

SUMMARY

Although most individuals do not malinger, it is essential to try to identify those who do. The means for doing so is a comprehensive evaluation that utilizes psychological testing, collateral information, and interviews. The evaluator looks for convergence of the data obtained through all methods, as well as hypotheses regarding the reason the individual may have for feigning. It must be kept in mind that malingering requires *conscious* dishonesty, and it must not be diagnosed without evidence of such conscious intent. The two instruments that are most likely to yield useful information are the SIRS and the MMPI-2, but a number of other instruments may be of value in a particular evaluation. When cognitive malingering is at issue, symptom validity testing may provide persuasive evidence of feigning. Because of the great stigma that accompanies an accusation of malingering, the evaluator should reserve that designation for the most blatant cases. Any less significant cases should address feigning in the context of the individual's response style as reflected by the various methods of data gathering. Rogers (2008d, p. 409) offers sample descriptive statements that may be utilized to address degrees of feigning.

TEST YOURSELF

1. **What is the single most important psychological test to administer?**
   (a) Wechsler Adult Intelligence Scale-III or IV (WAIS-III or IV)
   (b) Minnesota Multiphasic Personality Inventory—2 (MMPI-2)
   (c) Wechsler Memory Scale III (WMS-III)
   (d) Test of Memory Malingering (TOMM)
2. **The weight of the professional literature supports the contention that there is a "compensation neurosis," and that patients tend to become free of their symptoms when litigation ends.**
   True or False?
3. **Exaggeration of real symptoms is a good indication that the individual is malingering.**
   True or False?
4. **What kind of test is frequently used as part of a neuropsychological evaluation to assess effort and possible malingering?**
   (a) Sentence completion tests
   (b) Rorschach inkblot test
   (c) Symptom validity tests
   (d) Trail Making Test
5. **Clinical interviews and reviews of records are unimportant if one has administered a number of good psychological tests.**
   True or False?
6. **According to Rogers, the best tests for detecting coaching are:**
   (a) WAIS-III and WMS-III.
   (b) MMPI-2 and SIRS.
   (c) WAIS-III and PAI.
   (d) symptom validity tests.

7. **Research is unanimous that the Fake Bad Scale is the best test for evaluation of malingering.**

   True or False?

8. **An individual who consciously produces or fabricates physical or psychological symptoms in order to be able to take on the sick role is clearly malingering.**

   True or False?

Answers: 1. b; 2. False; 3. False; 4. c; 5. False; 6. b; 7. False; 8. False.

Recommended Readings

Melton, G. B., Petrila, J., Poythress, N. G., & Slobogin, C. (2007). *Psychological evaluations for the courts* (3rd ed.). New York: Guilford.

Rogers, R. (Ed.) (2008). *Clinical Assessment of Malingering and Deception* (3rd ed). New York: Guilford.

Young, G., Kane, A. W., & Nicholson, K. (2007). *Causality of psychological injury: Presenting evidence in court.* New York: Springer Science+Business Media.

Five

ESSENTIALS OF COMPETENCY TO STAND TRIAL ASSESSMENT

Melissa Westendorf

While there has not been tremendous change in the fundamentals of competency or fitness to stand trial assessments in the past 10 years (since the first edition of this book), there have been some modest changes in the law and the addition of two assessment instruments for clinical use. This chapter will begin with a brief legal history of competency to stand trial and relevant psychological research on the issue. In addition, this chapter has been reorganized, detailing each section of a proposed report to provide the reader with a blueprint of how to do a competency evaluation, although some portions will remain predominantly unchanged from the first edition of this chapter. Lastly, this chapter will cover special issues related to competency, including juvenile competency to stand trial, cognitively impaired defendants, malingering, and the "ultimate legal issue" debate.

LEGAL STANDARD

Competency to stand trial is the most frequently adjudicated competency issue addressed by forensic psychologists and the criminal law system (Melton, Petrila, Poythress, & Slobogin, 2007), with an estimated 60,000 (Bonnie & Grisso, 2000) requests made each year, or nearly 5% of all felony defendants (Hoge, Bonnie, Poythress, & Monahan, 1992). Early common law, originating from the seventeenth century, mandated out of fairness that a defendant must be competent to stand trial. The current controlling standard, established in *Dusky v. United States* (1960), is "whether the defendant has: (1) sufficient present ability to consult with his attorney with a reasonable degree of rational understanding; and (2) a rational as well as factual understanding of proceedings against him" (p. 402). In other words, the defendant must have a factual and rational understanding of the proceedings against him and have a sufficient ability to reasonably consult with his attorney. The *Dusky* standard was repeated in *Drope v. Missouri* (1975), which indicated it "has long been accepted that a person whose mental condition is

112

such that he lacks the capacity to understand the nature and object of the proceedings against him, to consult with counsel, and to assist in preparing his defense may not be subjected to a trial" (p. 171). The essential question for a competency evaluator is whether the mental condition deficit "in *this* defendant, facing *these charges, in light of existing* evidence, anticipating the substantial effort of a *particular* attorney with a *relationship of known characteristics*" results in an incompetent defendant (Golding & Roesch, 1988, p. 79). These standards are controlling in the federal legal system, with minor variations employed in state courts. Hence, it is very important to consult your state's specific statutes for the precise controlling language.

> ### DON'T FORGET
> Defendant's PRESENT abilities are evaluated in adjudicatory competence assessments.

> ### CAUTION
> Consult your state's statutes for the competency to stand trial standard.

Since *Dusky*, the Supreme Court has clarified some issues concerning competency to stand trial. For example, the term *competency* has been interpreted in *Swisher v. United States* (1965) to refer not merely to the presence of mental illness but also to the effects of mental illness on functional abilities to fulfill the role of the defendant. In addition, *Jackson v. Indiana* (1972) explicates specific conditions on the treatment of incompetent defendants. *Godinez v. Moran* (1993) held that there is no different or higher standard required for waiving other important rights (pleading guilty or waiving counsel), and that the *Dusky* standard applied to these rights too. However, more recently the Supreme Court in *Indiana v. Edwards* (2008) held that "states may insist upon representation by counsel for those who are competent to stand trial but who still suffer from severe mental illness to the point where they are not competent to conduct trial proceedings by themselves" (p. 2379). *Indiana* appears to indicate that the *Dusky* standards apply to those defendants with counsel, whereas those defendants who want to forgo counsel at trial require a different standard of competency to assure a fair trial.

PSYCHOLEGAL ISSUES RELEVANT TO COMPETENCY

Mental health professionals can approach competency evaluations or most psychological evaluations in one of two ways: ideographically or nomothetically (Poythress & Zapf, 2009). An ideographic approach uses those competency instruments that are most similar to either a semi-structured interview or a self-report measure, permitting the mental health professional the ability to adapt the measure to meet the specific needs of the individual defendant for his or her individual circumstances. Here, these measures assess various domains related to competency, typically requiring a professional judgment of the defendant's ability on a particular domain on a Likert scale. Most often the scores are not summed, averaged, or calculated in any way for comparison to a normative group. In addition, the interview itself is different from one examiner to the next and different examiners may score the same response in different ways, depending on their perspective of the importance of the various abilities for a particular defendant. A nomothetic approach requires the use of structured competency instruments that have a standardized administration protocol on a predetermined set of functional legal abilities. The scores derived from these measures are interpreted in light of offenders who have previously completed these instruments during the development phase of the particular instrument.

Poythress & Zapf (2009) addressed benefits and limitations of the two approaches as applied to competency evaluations. In their view, strengths of the ideographic approach include increased breadth of coverage, permitting the mental health professional to go beyond the particular instrument to circumstances that are less frequent in this context. In addition, this approach supports flexibility in the interview depending on the unique characteristics of each defendant; for example, cognitive impairment and so forth. Lastly, each interview can be tailored to the specific circumstances of the defendant in the particular case before the court. However, with strengths also come limitations of this approach, including potential evaluator variability in "scoring" the measures despite similar responses and interpretations of "scores" that are guided by an evaluator's clinical judgment as opposed to being grounded in research or tied to a previous group.

Benefits to the nomothetic approach to competency evaluations include decisional transparency in rendering clinical judgments (Poythress & Zapf, 2009). This transparency occurs because questions are fixed, scoring is guided by predetermined criteria, and evaluators' biases are reduced due to the structure of the instrument. In addition, the normative data permits the court to better understand the opinion rendered by the evaluator when making its legal determination of competency. One significant limitation of the nomothetic instruments is that the domains assessed are fixed during the test development phase, thereby preventing flexibility for less oft-encountered issues related to competency. For this reason, a nomothetic instrument should not be used in isolation when completing a competency evaluation.

Another psycholegal issue influencing the examination of adjudicatory competence is Bonnie's decisional competency reformulation (Bonnie, 1992). Decisional competence has been articulated by Bonnie (1992, 1993) as an additional component of competency. Bonnie (1993) argues that foundational competence are those abilities any defendant needs to participate in the proceedings, whereas decisional competence focuses on the specific, contextual variables in a defendant's case and the various decisions he or she would be required to make in that particular case. Hence, only those issues that are germane to the particular case (e.g., ability to plead guilty, ability to waive right to self-incrimination, etc.) would be explored and relevant to the defendant's competency. However, it is not clear if this decisional competence goes beyond the *Dusky* criteria or would be incorporated into the current standards set forth by the court.

Tom Grisso, a leading investigator in the field of adjudicatory competence, compiled a list of functional abilities that require assessment in any competency to stand trial assessment (Grisso, 2003). This list is a compilation of previous lists developed by legal analysts and researchers attempting to quantify or enumerate the *Dusky* requirements. In addition, Grisso added the decisional abilities to form a more complete list addressing all the requirements he believes satisfy the *Dusky* standards (see Table 5.1). Therefore, to satisfy the inquiries of this list an

Table 5.1 Grisso's Functional Ability Concepts

Consulting and Assisting Counsel

Understanding that counsel works for defendant

Understanding counsel's inquiries

Capable of responding to counsel's inquiries in a manner that provides relevant information for the defense

Can provide consistent account of events relevant to charges and a defense

Can manage the demands of trial process (stress, maintaining demeanor)

Capable of testifying if necessary

Factual Understanding

That the defendant is accused of a crime

That the court will decide on guilt or innocence

That the trial could result in punishment

Of the various ways that defendants may plead

That certain sentences are possible (their nature and seriousness)

Of the roles of various participants in the trial process

Of the general process of trials

Rational Understanding (Decisional Abilities)

Beliefs about one's own trial process are not distorted by delusional beliefs

Appropriately motivated to further one's defense

Reasoning ability sufficient to process relevant information during decision making

Source: Adapted from Grisso (2003).

evaluator should use a variety of methods for a comprehensive evaluation; for example, nomothetic and ideographic.

In summary, adjudicatory competence is the present ability of the defendant to factually and rationally understand the proceedings against him and to possess a reasonable ability to assist his lawyer. There are two overarching approaches to conducting these evaluations, nomothetic and ideographic; however, any approach should cover the domains in Table 5.1 to ensure a comprehensive evaluation of competence to stand trial.

PROCEDURE

A request for a competency evaluation can occur at any time during the trial process and defendants are presumed competent unless the question is raised. Defense counsel typically requests the evaluation, although the motion can be raised by the defense, the prosecution, or the court, *sua sponte* (on its own motion). It should be noted that even though the prosecution has the power to request an evaluation, several organizations (e.g., American Psychiatric Association, American Bar Association [ABA]) strongly recommend that an evaluator not perform an evaluation until defense counsel is obtained. Furthermore, it is important to be aware that occasionally competency evaluations are requested for reasons other than "actual doubt" about the competency of the defendant (e.g., obtaining immediate treatment for the defendant's behavioral disorder, allowing for additional time to prepare the case, and confusion between insanity and competency). Therefore, a clarification of the referral question is sometimes necessary before proceeding with the interview.

CAUTION

Clarify the referral question.

After the evaluation, the defendant is either found competent (in which case the criminal process continues) or incompetent (in which case the criminal proceedings are suspended). A majority, or nearly 80%, of all defendants evaluated for competency to stand trial are competent (Zapf & Roesch, 2006). If incompetent, the defendant's charges may be dropped in exchange for the defendant's promise to seek treatment (more likely for less severe offenses), or the defendant may be committed to the mental health system for treatment or restoration to competency (more likely in serious offenses). The commitment is limited by the *Jackson v. Indiana* (1972) decision, which held that incompetent defendants committed for mental health treatment can only be confined for a reasonable period of time to determine whether the individual can be restored or whether a substantial probability exists that competency can be restored. If an incompetent defendant is committed, then periodic reviews (typically every six months) must be performed to inform the court whether the defendant is, or is likely to be, restored. Inpatient commitments for competency restoration can be very costly on state budgets; therefore, some programs are developing (such as in Milwaukee, Wisconsin) or have been developed (in Florida) to establish outpatient restoration programs to ease fiscal constraints.

COMPETENCY EVALUATION

This section of the chapter will provide a sample format for the competency report (for other samples, see Melton, Petrila, Poythress, and Slobogin [2007]; Grisso [1988]). Within each section relevant issues will be addressed pertaining to the adjudicatory competence question. The very first paragraph of the report should detail from whom the referral came, the referral question, including charges filed, the name of the defendant, concomitant case number for which competency is being evaluated, and when the interview occurred.

PREVIEW

Sample Report
Database
Notice
Social History
Mental Health Observations
Diagnoses (Optional)
Competency Assessment
Conclusions/Summary

Database

This section should detail the information and documents obtained and reviewed for the evaluation, the dates and length of the interview(s), where the interview occurred, and all collateral contacts. The absolute minimum requirements necessary to complete the evaluation are the criminal complaint or charging document, supporting police records, and mental health records if the defendant is confined in an institutional setting (e.g., mental health facility or jail). This information will provide the examiner with a list of current medications or potential aberrant behavior (or the lack thereof). When a defendant is in the community, mental health information may be more difficult to obtain; however,

CAUTION

Sometimes a second interview is required when defendants fall into a grey area of competency or training is required on some topics during the evaluation.

when setting the initial appointment, the evaluator can request this information be brought to the examination. Furthermore, a brief interview with a reliable collateral contact in the defendant's life may be a source of current mental health information. Finally, it is important to speak with the defense attorneys to ascertain their perceptions of the defendant's interactions in the legal context.

Notice

A competency to stand trial evaluation must begin with a *Notice* or limits of confidentiality discussion with the defendant. Grisso (1986a) recommends per ABA standards that the defendant should be informed of the purpose of the evaluation, potential uses of disclosures made during the evaluation, and the consequences of the defendant's refusal to cooperate in the evaluation. In addition, the defendant should be informed of the potential consequences of the competency decision, specifically if (competent) the court proceedings continue or if (incompetent) the defendant could be committed to a mental health facility for competency restoration while the court proceedings are suspended. It is recommended after an explanation of the constraints of confidentiality, that the examiner should have the defendant recite the information back to the examiner in his or her own words to ensure the defendant understands the limits. Certain defendants will be unable to spontaneously reproduce the notice, therefore the examiner can provide forced choice questions related to confidentiality limits. However, there will be times when a defendant cannot respond to forced choice questions, which may also be dispositive of the defendant's current mental or cognitive health and should be reported to the court or counsel. The examiner can give concrete examples if the defendant has difficulty with the more abstract concepts of limited confidentiality. Defense counsel may be present during the evaluation, although counsel should not be an active participant and videotaping or audiotaping is strongly recommended to produce an evidentiary record (Grisso, 1998).

Relevant History

A brief social history is recommended to provide the examiner some time to build a rapport with the defendant and make observations in the context of the interview. The examiner can make some clinical judgments about the defendant's cognitive, emotional, and behavioral status. In addition, this interview provides some possible indicators of the defendant's ability to interact with the attorney. An in-depth clinical interview is not warranted given that the competency referral question revolves around the person's *present* ability in the courtroom, no matter the mental health history or history of previous competency findings. In addition, most competency evaluations result in a "competent" conclusion, therefore an inordinate amount of time spent during this section is not particularly useful to the evaluation outcome. Nevertheless, it is helpful to obtain at least a brief mental health history to ascertain previous mental health symptoms or diagnoses, current psychotropic medication, and inpatient or outpatient treatment. These may be relevant to the current evaluation and potential restoration if necessary; for example, schizophrenic currently medication noncompliant.

Mental Status Observations

Next, a mental status section should be included to detail the defendant's current presentation during the interview or interviews. Generally, this section is similar to mental status examinations that occur in other forensic or psychological evaluations. Although many psychologists operate off a memorized list of mental status questions, there are mini-mental status measures (e.g., Folstein Mini Mental Status Examination; Folstein, Folstein, & McHugh, 1975) that can be used to assist with this section. Typically, there is little need for psychological testing due to its limited nexus to the psycholegal competency outcome. However, a brief cognitive test may confirm or deny the existence of intellectual deficits and may assist the evaluator's determination whether the defendant can be restored within the statutory time limits delineated in state laws.

Diagnoses (Optional)

Some examiners proffer a mental health diagnosis based on the evidence gathered during the evaluation. Oftentimes this is either "by history" or has been provided by some other form of collateral documentation. Other examiners do not provide a diagnosis and, in any event, this does not change the essence of the competency outcome.

Competency Assessment

This section details the essence of the competency assessment and the discussion will focus on the ideographic and nomothetic approaches to adjudicatory competence. If the examiner is using an ideographic unstructured competency format (or without a competency tool), the interviewer should at least have notes on the abilities to address, for example, Grisso's recommendations in Table 5.1, so as not to forget any significant discussion points as required by the *Dusky* or

≡ Rapid Reference 5.1

Use open-ended questions

Do not assume defendant's involvement in the crime (e.g., "Tell me what the police say you did")

Have specific details of crime to detect for true memory deficits or malingering

Avoid rigid, test-like questions

controlling state standards. In addition, Rapid Reference 5.1 provides additional recommendations as the examiner completes this type of interview.

It is strongly recommended by experts in the field to use a competency instrument (Poythress & Zapf, 2009; Melton, Petrila, Poythress, & Slobogin 2007) so that competency evaluations become more standard across evaluators and all important capacities are assessed. In fact, recent research has revealed preliminary findings that some clinicians opine competency (or incompetency) more than other clinicians (Murrie, Boccaccini, Zapf, Warren, & Henderson, 2008). A standardized approach becomes even more important given that judges more often than not rely solely on the clinician's opinion (Poythress & Zapf, 2009). Following these recommendations, if the examiner is going to use a competency instrument, there are several options available. This section will review screening instruments, semi-structured instruments, and structured instruments, also called second generation instruments (Melton, Petrila, Poythress, & Slobogin, 2007), currently available for clinical use.

SCREENING TOOLS

Competency Screening Test

The Competency Screening Test (CST; Lipsitt, Lelos, & McGarr, 1971) is a 22-item sentence completion instrument that determines whether a more extensive assessment for competency is necessary. (For basic information on the CST and its publisher, see Rapid Reference 5.2; for reliability and validity data, see Rapid Reference 5.3). The authors developed the measure as a screening instrument that, along with a brief psychiatric interview, would divert competent defendants from a possibly lengthy hospitalization required to complete a full competency assessment. Historically, this was how most adjudicatory competency evaluations were completed and still occur in some states. This was viewed as advantageous given that a majority of defendants referred for complete evaluation are competent.

≡ *Rapid Reference 5.2*

Competency Screening Test (CST)

Authors: Lipsitt, P., Lelos, D., & McGarr, A. L.

Affliation: Laboratory of Community Psychiatry, Harvard Medical School

Citations: Laboratory of Community Psychiatry, Harvard Medical School (1973). *Competency to stand trial and mental illness* (DHEW Publication No. ADM 77–103). Rockville, MD: NIMH, Department of Health, Education, and Welfare.

Administration Time: 25 minutes

Conceptually the CST items measure three constructs: (1) the potential for a constructive relationship between client and lawyer; (2) the client's understanding of the court process; and (3) the ability of the client to deal emotionally with the criminal process.

Administration/Scoring/Interpretation

The 22 CST items are unfinished sentences that the defendant must complete. If the defendant cannot read the incomplete sentences, then it is appropriate for the examiner to read the sentence and write the response. On average, a

≡ *Rapid Reference 5.3*

Reliability and Validity Data for the CST

Reliability:	Interrater	.93 (Lipsitt, Lelos, & McGarr 1971)
		.94 (Randolph, Hicks, & Mason, 1981)
		.92 (Randolph, Hicks, Mason, & Cuneo, 1982)
Validity:	Construct	8% CST incompetents, consistent with estimated
		Base rates (Nottingham & Mattson, 1981)
	Factor Analysis	Three factors (Nicholson, Briggs, & Robertson, 1988)

defendant can complete the CST in 25 minutes. The CST items are scored with a 0, 1, or 2, depending on the correspondence between the given response and the examples given in the manual. A score of 2 points is given for a response that appropriately responds to the sentence stem and reflects a high level of legal comprehension. A score of 1 is given for those responses that fall below the standard but are not clearly inappropriate. These responses are characterized by "passive acquiescence, circularity, redundancy, or avoidance of the issue, or are impoverished, though not clearly inappropriate" (Lipsitt, Lelos, & McGarr, 1971, p.106). In addition, scores of 1 should reflect a moderate level of legal comprehension. Finally, a score of 0, reflecting a low level of legal comprehension, is given to those responses that are clearly inappropriate. These responses are characterized by "substantial disorganization in grammatical structure and/or content, expressions of inability to relate or trust, definition of the lawyer's role as punitive or rejecting, extreme concreteness, perseveration, or expressions of self-defeating behavior" (p.106). Furthermore, a 0 should reflect flattened affect or certain thought disorders that would substantially interfere with a legal defense. Definitions and examples are provided in the manual to assist in scoring the CST. The CST can be scored in 15 to 20 minutes. Item scores are summed to find a total CST score, ranging from 0 to 44. A composite score of 20 or below designates a "low score" in which competency to stand trial is questionable. In other words, a score of 20 or below "screens in" those defendants who warrant a more comprehensive evaluation.

Strengths and Weaknesses

Despite the usefulness of a quick screening device for incompetency to stand trial, there are several weaknesses that need to be considered by the examiner. First, some research of the CST finds an undesirably high false positive rate indicating that competent defendants are labeled as not competent and therefore assessed as requiring a comprehensive evaluation where no need exists (Melton, Petrila, Poythress, and Slobogin, 2007). Conversely, Roesch and Golding (1987) found a high false negative rate with the CST. Furthermore, the conceptual framework of the CST is not obviously empirically related to competency to stand trial. Finally, critics posit that the justification for the CST scoring appears questionable or weak at best.

> **DON'T FORGET**
> ....
> Easy to administer
> Good reliability data (Grisso, 2003)
> CST can be used in jail or outpatient setting

Georgia Court Competency Test

The Georgia Court Competency Test (GCCT) was developed at the Forensic Services Division of Central State Hospital in Milledgeville, Georgia, as a competency tool to address the specific needs of that geographical area. (For basic information on the GCCT and its publisher, see Rapid Reference 5.4; for reliability and validity data, see Rapid Reference 5.5). Since then others have utilized the GCCT for clinical and research purposes. A revised version of the GCCT was developed at the Mississippi State Hospital (GCCT-MSH). Both instruments were developed as screening tools to identify clearly competent defendants rather than as comprehensive measures of competency (Melton, Petrila, Poythress, & Slobogin, 2007).

Administration/Scoring/Interpretation

The original authors developed the GCCT on the following conceptual definitions for abilities related to legal competency: (1) knowledge of the charge; (2) knowledge of the possible penalties; (3) some understanding of the courtroom procedure; and (4) the ability to communicate rationally with an attorney in the preparation of a defense. Items were created to reflect the four abilities, with items perceived as more important given additional weight. In the original version, questions were in the following domains: (1) Picture of the court

---

≡ Rapid Reference 5.4

Georgia Court Competency Test (GCCT)
Georgia Court Competency Test—Mississippi State Hospital (GCCT—MSH)

Authors:

(GCCT) Wildman, W., White, P., & Brandenberg, C.

(GCCT-MSH) Nicholson, R., Briggs, S., & Robertson, H.

Citations:

(GCCT) The Georgia Court Competency Test: An attempt to develop a rapid, quantitative measure of fitness for trial. Unpublished manuscript: Forensic Services Division, Central State Hospital, Milledgeville, GA.

(GCCT-MSH) Nicholson, R., Briggs, S., & Robertson, J. (1988). Instruments for assessing competence to stand trial: How do they work? *Professional Psychology: Research and Practice, 19,* 383–394.

Administration time:

10 minutes

≡ Rapid Reference 5.5

Reliability and Validity Data for the GCCT and GCCT-MSH

Reliability:	Internal Consistency	.89 (Ustad, Rogers, Sewell, & Guarnaccia, 1996)
	Interrater	.96 (Melton, Petrila, Poythress, & Slobogin, 1997)
	Test-Retest	.79 (Wildman, White, & Brandenburg, 1990); .84 (Melton, Petrila, Poythress, & Slobogin, 1997)
Validity:	Construct	Three factors: I. General Legal Knowledge
		II. Courtroom Layout
		III. Specific Legal knowledge (Nicholson, Briggs, & Robertson, 1988)
	Predictive	75% hit rate (Wildman, White, & Brandenberg, 1990)

(e.g., Where will the witness testify?); (2) Functions (e.g., What does the judge do?); (3) Charges (e.g., What are you charged with?); (4) Helping the lawyer (e.g., focus on how the defendant will help his lawyer); (5) Alleged crime (e.g., What actually happened about the charge you are here on?); and (6) Consequences (e.g., focuses on what defendant believes might happen if the jury finds him guilty). The administration time is approximately 10 minutes.

The original version is scored by assigning a rating; the maximum score for each item ranges from 1 to 10, depending on the item, with a total sum of 50 possible. For those items that do not have an obvious correct or incorrect response, scoring criteria are available in the manual. The defendant's total score is then multiplied by 2 with a total possible range from 0 to100. Due to the additional four times in the GCCT-MSH, the weights were revised to retain the 0 to 100 range of the original version. Total scores above 70 indicate a competent defendant and scores of 69 or below indicate a need for further competency assessment.

Strengths and Weaknesses

The research investigating either version of the Georgia competency tools appears to have generated a moderate amount of psychometric support for screening purposes (Nicholson, Briggs, & Robertson, 1988). The research has demonstrated a stable three-factor structure underlying the instruments and also that the tools can efficiently screen for competent defendants (Ustad, Rogers, Sewall, & Guarnaccia, 1996). In addition, the research demonstrates that the tools appear

DON'T FORGET

The GCCT and GCCT-MSH are only screeners. They do not cover all facets of adjudicatory competence, so additional information must be obtained before opining on competence.

comparable to other competency instruments in terms of reliability and validity. One significant shortcoming is that the instrument focuses solely on foundational competencies and pays little attention to important decisional competencies found in other competencies tools (Bonnie, 1992).

Fitness Interview Test–Revised

The revised edition of the Fitness Interview Test (FIT-R; Roesch, Zapf, Eaves, & Webster, 1998) is an interview and rating scale designed specifically for use in Canada, but may be applicable in the United States given the similarity in legal and clinical practice. (For basic information on the FIT-R and its publisher, see Rapid Reference 5.6; for reliability and validity data, see Rapid Reference 5.7). However, some authors reason the FIT-R should only be used with Canadian populations given the United States requirement of "rationality" not required by the

≡ Rapid Reference 5.6

Fitness Interview Test–Revised (FIT-R)

Authors:

Roesch, R., Zapf, P., Eaves, D., & Webster, C.

Affiliation:

Mental Health, Law, and Policy Institute, Simon Fraser University

Citation:

Roesch, R., Zapf, P., Eaves, D., & Webster, C. (1998). *The Fitness Interview Test (Revised Edition)*. Burnaby, British Columbia, Canada: Mental Health, Law, and Policy Institute, Simon Fraser University.

Administration time:

30 minutes

≣ *Rapid Reference 5.7*

Reliability and Validity Data for the FIT-R

Reliability:	Interrater	.98 (Viljoen, Roesch, & Zapf, 2002)
Validity:	Predictive	87% (Zapf & Roesch, 1997; Zapf, Roesch, & Viljoen, 2001)
	Construct	kappa = .53 between FIT-R and MacCAT-CA (Zapf & Roesch, 2001)

CAUTION

The FIT-R should only be used with Canadian populations given the United States requirement of "rationality" not required by the Canadian system.

Canadian system (Skeem, Golding, & Emke-Francis, 2004). The FIT-R is a standard semi-structured screening interview that is followed by the completion of a rating scale in which the evaluation assesses the degree of incapacity for each issue. The FIT was originally developed in 1984, with major revisions occurring in 1998 to account for Canada's 1992 criminal code changes. The instrument is designed to reflect the defendant's competency status at the time of the interview, rather than predict his status in the future. Furthermore, the FIT-R is intended to identify those individuals who are clearly competent to stand trial.

Administration/Scoring/Interpretation

The FIT-R is divided into three sections. According to Roesch and colleagues (1998), the objectives are as follows: "(1) understand the nature of the object of the proceedings: *factual knowledge of criminal procedure;* (2) understand the possible consequences of the proceedings: *appreciation of personal involvement in and importance of the proceedings;* and (3) communicate with counsel: *ability to participate in defence*" (p. 21). Section I consists of six items involving, for example, the defendant's understanding of the arrest process, the nature and severity of the current charges, and the role of key participants. Section II consists of three items that focus on the defendant's appreciation of the range and nature of the possible penalties and available defenses. Finally, Section III consists of seven items regarding the defendant's ability to communicate facts, relate to his/her attorney, and plan legal strategy.

Each response is rated on a 3-point scale indicating the degree of impairment. A score of 2 indicates severe impairment, whereas a score of 0 indicates that for the item scored there is little to no impairment of ability to meet the legal criteria. If the defendant responds with an "I don't know" the examiner is permitted to probe with further questions; however, if the examiner is unable to discern the defendant's capabilities then a score of 1 (possible or mild impairment) should be given. It is important to note that it may not be the specific answers per se that guide the scoring of the item; the examiner must also consider whether the defendant has the ability at all that is being examined.

Once the interview is complete the examiner must determine a final judgment of fitness. This final process involves three steps, including determining the presence of a mental disorder, determining the defendant's capacity in each of the three psycholegal abilities, and finally, examining the previous information and arriving at a final fitness determination (Roesch, Zapf, Eaves, & Webster, 1998, p. 24). Further, the process instructs the examiner that the co-occurrence of a mental disorder and a psycholegal impairment is sufficient to recommend further assessment recalling that the FIT-R is only a screening device for unfitness to stand trial.

Strengths and Weaknesses

Research has demonstrated that the FIT-R has excellent utility as a screening instrument (Roesch, Zapf, Eaves, & Webster, 1998; Zapf & Roesch, 1998). More recent research has indicated the FIT-R's interrater reliability (Viljoen, Roesch, & Zapf, 2002), predictive validity (Zapf & Roesch, 1997), and construct validity were good (Zapf & Roesch, 2001). Therefore, research seems to support this instrument as a good screening device for competency.

SEMI-STRUCTURED TOOLS

Competency to Stand Trial Assessment Instrument

The Competency to Stand Trial Assessment Instrument (CAI), a semi-structured interview and rating scale, was developed as the companion test to the CST at the Harvard Laboratory of Community Psychiatry during a project funded by the Center for Studies of Crime and Delinquency, National Institute of Mental Health. (For basic information on the CAI and its publisher, see Rapid Reference 5.8; for reliability and validity data, see Rapid Reference 5.9). The CST was developed as a screening tool, with the CAI used as the complementary full-scale assessment tool. The CAI was developed from a multidisciplinary review of appellate cases and legal literature, actual pretrial competency hearings, and

≡ *Rapid Reference 5.8*

Competency to Stand Trial Assessment Instrument (CAI)

Authors:
McGarry, A. L., and associates

Affiliation:
Nassau County Department of Mental Health (New York)

Citation:
Laboratory of Community Psychiatry, Harvard Medical School (1973). *Competency to stand trial and mental illness* (DHEW Publication No. ADM 77–103). Rockville, MD: NIMH, Department of Health, Education, and Welfare.

Administration Time:
60 minutes with competent defendant

interviews with attorneys and judges. From this review, the authors conceptualized competency to stand trial as an ability to cooperate with one's attorney in one's defense, an awareness and understanding of the nature and object of the proceedings, and an understanding of the consequences of the proceedings.

Administration/Scoring/Interpretation
The CAI consists of 13 functions related to the defendant's "ability to cope with the trial process in an adequately self-protective fashion" (Laboratory of

≡ *Rapid Reference 5.9*

Reliability and Validity Data for the CAI

Reliability:	Interrater	.92 (experienced raters); .87 (inexperienced raters) (Laboratory of Community Psychiatry, 1973)
		Minimal reliability data
Validity:		Appears to be somewhat correlated to other measures designed to test competency to stand trial
		Minimal validity data

Community Psychiatry, 1973, p. 99). In the manual, the 13 functions are conceptually defined in statements, with two to three sample questions given for each function. The 13 functions include:

1. Appraisal of available legal defense
2. Unmanageable behavior
3. Quality of relating to attorney
4. Planning of legal strategy including guilty pleas to lesser charges where pertinent
5. Appraisal of role of persons involved in a trial
6. Understanding of court procedure
7. Appreciation of charges
8. Appreciation of range and nature of possible penalties
9. Appraisal of likely outcome
10. Capacity to disclose to attorney available pertinent facts surrounding the offense
11. Capacity to realistically challenge prosecution witnesses
12. Capacity to testify relevantly
13. Self-defeating versus self-serving motivation (legal sense)

Examples of the functions' contents (and recommended questions) for each item include: for item 1, the defendant's awareness of his possible legal defenses and how consistent these are with the reality of his particular circumstances ("How do you think you can be defended against these charges?"); for item 3, the interpersonal capacity of the accused to relate to the average attorney ("Do you have confidence in your attorney?"); and for item 9, how realistically the accused perceives the likely outcome and the degree to which impaired understanding contributes to a less adequate or inadequate participation in his defense ("How strong a case do they have against you?"). The semi-structured nature of the test mandates clinical flexibility rather than pure recitation of each question. It is expected that the examiner will probe with follow-up questions after the defendant answers initial recommended questions given in the manual; however, there is no additional guidance given in the manual as to the nature of the follow-up. Finally, the authors have estimated that with a competent defendant the interview can be completed in 60 minutes.

The items are rated on a Likert scale from 1 (reflecting total lack of capacity to function) to 5 (reflecting no impairment; defendant can function adequately). A score of 6 is assigned when insufficient information exists to rate the item. The items are neither summed nor weighted; instead the items are intended to stand alone. A score of 1 on any one item does not necessarily indicate a clinical decision with regard to competency. However, an accumulation of items with scores of 3 or less may indicate cause for restoration or inpatient hospitalization. In addition, the authors of the CAI have noted that the test is not a predictor of the defendant's functioning in a future trial because as time passes his score may vary. The manual includes clinical examples of each rating level for each function to assist the rater in scoring the CAI. The process of scoring assumes that the defendant will have adequate counsel and that the administrator of the CAI understands the realities of the criminal justice system. Finally, the scoring is not standardized and norms are unavailable for the CAI.

Strengths and Weaknesses

The CAI has been criticized for lacking empirical support with regard to scoring or interpreting the measure; however, the functions appear to have individual face validity (Melton, Petrila, Poythress, & Slobogin, 2007). The combination of these two circumstances has led examiners to use the CAI as an interview alone, without using the scoring criteria. Professionals who use the CAI in this fashion generally report a favorable impression of the instrument. Others have argued that the CAI holds promise as a screening measure and comprehensive interview, but does lack a nexus between psychopathology and psycholegal impairment (Zapf & Roesch, 2006).

> **DON'T FORGET**
> ....
> Although explicit scoring criteria may be deficient, the CAI is a good tool to guide a competency interview.

Interdisciplinary Fitness Interview

The Interdisciplinary Fitness Interview (IFI) is a competency instrument created to assess various legal and psychopathological characteristics of competency to stand trial (Roesch & Golding, 1987). (For basic information on the IFI and its publisher, see Rapid Reference 5.10; for reliability and validity data, see Rapid Reference 5.11.) The IFI was developed by Golding and Roesch after they evaluated the item content and structure of the CAI, interviewed individuals who used the CAI, and completed a literature review and analyses on the competency construct. The authors believe the IFI improves upon the existing competency measures (e.g., the CAI) by addressing both legal and psychopathological issues, providing an instrument that utilizes two evaluators, including an attorney, and allowing the evaluator to assign a weight or importance rating to each item. Overall, the IFI is intended to address three overarching conceptual principles: functional memory, appropriate relationship with attorney, and appreciating the legal system.

≡ Rapid Reference 5.10

Interdisciplinary Fitness Interview (IFI)

Authors:

Golding, S., Roesch, R., & Schreiber, J.

Affiliations:

University of Utah (Golding) and Simon Fraser University (Roesch)

Citation:

Golding, S., Roesch, R., & Schreiber, J. (1984). Assessment and conceptualization of competency to stand trial: Preliminary data on the Interdisciplinary Fitness Interview. *Law and Human Behavior, 8,* 321–334.

Administration Time:

45–60 minutes

Administration/Scoring/Interpretation

The IFI is a semi-structured interview, which has three major sections: (1) legal items; (2) psychopathological items; and (3) an overall evaluation. A fourth section—consensual judgment—consists of items that reflect post-assessment resolution of differences between evaluators. An outline of all four sections appears in Table 5.2.

≡ Rapid Reference 5.11

Reliability and Validity Data for the IFI (Golding, Roesch, & Schreiber, 1984)

Reliability:	Interrater	.40 to .90, with less agreement on legal items than psychopathological items
		97% agreement—Fitness/ Unfitness
Validity:	Construct	76% agreement between IFI assessments and hospital decisions of competency
		.14 to .50 correlations between items and final fitness determination

Table 5.2 Interdisciplinary Fitness Interview Items

Section A: Legal Items

1. Capacity to appreciate the nature of the alleged crime, and to disclose pertinent facts, events, and motives
2. Quality of relationship with one's current attorney
3. Quality of relationship with attorneys in general
4. Anticipated courtroom demeanor and trial conduct
5. Appreciating the consequences of various legal options

Section B: Psychopathological Items

1. Primary disturbance of thought
2. Primary disturbance of communication
3. Secondary disturbance of communication
4. Delusional processes
5. Hallucinations
6. Unmanageable or disturbing behavior
7. Affective disturbances
8. Disturbances of consciousness/orientation
9. Disturbances of memory/amnesia
10. Severe mental retardation
11. General impairment of judgment/insight

Section C: Overall Evaluation

1. Overall fitness of judgment
2. Rating of confidence in judgment
3. Comment on basis for decision about defendant
4. Other factors taken into account in reaching decisions

Section D: Consensual Judgment

1. Fitness judgment after conferring with partner
2. Changes in rating of individual items after conferring
3. Reasons for changes

Note: Adapted from Roesch and Golding (1987).

The manual more fully describes each of the three main sections, including the items and the subsections for each item. The authors note that it is not possible to enumerate all the subareas: rather, the subareas provide only a general "lay of the land" (Roesch & Golding, 1987, p. 325), which allows the rater flexibility for individual evaluations. To facilitate the interview, the manual gives a set of suggested questions and follow-up probes designed to maintain rapport throughout the interview. The manual also proffers clinical guidance for difficulties encountered during the interview.

The items in Section A are rated from 0 (no incapacity) to 2 (substantial incapacity). After a rating of 0 to 2 is given, the items are then assigned a weight, which indicates the influence of that item on the rater's overall decision for incompetence. Roesch and Golding (1987) have indicated this weighting system comports with their understanding of the competency construct by allowing the evaluator to determine when a particular deficit may or may not influence competence. Next, the rater determines the presence or absence of the 11 items or symptoms listed in Section B. If the symptom is present the rater must ascertain whether the presence of the symptoms has any relation to the competency issues. Finally, Section C of the IFI addresses specific judgment, assigns a confidence rating to that judgment, and indicates the various factors that influenced their judgment but were not addressed by the standard rating scales.

Strengths and Weaknesses

The IFI is an attempt to incorporate legal and psychopathological concepts into a comprehensive assessment of competency to stand trial. Unfortunately, because there is little reliability and validity data on the instrument, the IFI's applicability in competency evaluations is weakened. However, the IFI appears to assess a more complete picture of incompetency by evaluating additional relevant dimensions of competency than traditional measures.

> **DON'T FORGET**
> ....
> More cumbersome tool due to use of two evaluators (mental health professional and attorney); however, the complement adds structural strength to the tool.

Interdisciplinary Fitness Interview—Revised

The IFI has been updated with the Interdisciplinary Fitness Interview-Revised (IFI-R), authored by Stephen Golding (1993), one of the coauthors of the original measure. The approach of the IFI-R is "a functional one, in which the ultimate criterion is based on how the defendant will behave in the judicial process" (p. 28). The IFI-R represents a substantive revision based upon Golding's research and clinical experience using the instrument. The IFI-R involves a semi-structured interview and rating format. There are two sections of the IFI-R: current clinical condition and psycholegal abilities. Under the former section, there are several subsections that describe the major domains of disturbance that should be assessed in an interview. They include attention/

consciousness, delusions, hallucinations, thought disorders—impaired reasoning and judgment, cognitive impairment—impaired memory, and mood and affect. Ratings range from 0 (absent or does not bear on defendant's fitness) to 2 (symptoms are likely to significantly impair the defendant's fitness). There are four general sections included in the assessment of psycholegal abilities, including (1) capacity to appreciate charges and to disclose pertinent facts, events, and motives; (2) courtroom demeanor and capacity to understand the adversarial nature of proceedings; (3) quality of relationship with attorney; and (4) appreciation of, and reasoned choice with respect to legal options and consequences. Rating range from 0 (no or minimal capacity) to 2 (substantial capacity).

Evaluators must be experienced mental health professionals skilled in the clinical evaluation of mental disorders and forensic psychology. An attorney is no longer required to complete the evaluation. Golding (1993) has recommended that evaluators should prepare for the fitness evaluation by interviewing the defendant's attorney and prior mental health contacts, reading available mental health records and police reports or prior arrest records, and finally, speaking with jail personnel. With this level of preparation an evaluation can be conducted efficiently and comprehensively. Golding has further recommended recording the interviews. For people interested in the IFI format it is recommended that the IFI-R be requested as well (see Rapid Reference 5.12).

≡ *Rapid Reference 5.12*

Interdisciplinary Fitness Interview–Revised (IFI-R)

Author:

Golding, S.

Affiliation:

University of Utah

Citation:

Golding, S. (1993). *Training manual: Interdisciplinary Fitness Interview revised.* Department of Psychology, University of Utah.

Obtain:

Copies of the IFI-R and manual may be obtained from Stephen L. Golding, PhD, Psychology Office, 390 S. 1530 E., Room 52, Salt Lake City, UT 84112.

User Requirements:

Must be licensed psychologist, psychiatrist, or social worker

STRUCTURED TOOLS

MacArthur Competence Assessment Tool—Criminal Adjudication

The MacArthur Competence Assessment Tool—Criminal Adjudication (MacCAT-CA; Poythress et al., 1999) is a 22-item measure that assesses three competence related abilities: Understanding (Items 1–8), Reasoning (Items 9–16), and Appreciation (Items 17–22). (For basic information on the MacCAT-CA and its publisher see Rapid Reference 5.13; for reliability and validity data see Rapid Reference 5.14.) The MacCAT-CA (nomolithic tool) was developed to improve the field of competence assessment by creating a standardized, normed tool for adjudicative competence. It was reasoned that although the first generation or ideographic tools had been immensely helpful in improving competence assessments, there was a clear need for a standardized tool (Grisso, 1992).

The MacArthur Foundation Research Network on Mental Health and the Law first created the MacArthur Structured Assessment of Competence—Criminal Defendants (MacSAC-CD; Hoge, Bonnie, Poythress, & Monahan, 1992). After piloting the MacSAC-CD, the tool was eventually restructured, becoming the MacCAT-CA. A large normative study was funded by the National Institute of Mental Health between 1996 and 1998, resulting in the MacCAT-CA availability for clinical use by 2000. Important features incorporated into the MacCAT-CA were:

1. Item content was derived from an initial consideration of a comprehensive theory of legal competence.

≡ Rapid Reference 5.13

MacArthur Competence Assessment Tool—Criminal Adjudication (MacCAT-CA)

Authors:
Poythress, N., Nicholson, R., Otto, R., Edens, J., Bonnie, R., Monahan, J., & Hoge, S.

Affiliation:
Florida Mental Health Institute, University of South Florida, Tampa, FL

Citations:
The MacArthur Competence Assessment Tool—Criminal Adjudication: Professional manual. Odessa, FL: Psychological Assessment Resources.

Administration Time:
25–45 minutes

≣ Rapid Reference 5.14

Reliability and Validity Data for the MacCAT-CA

Reliability:	Interrater	icc = .75 to .90 (Otto et al., 1998)
	Internal Consistency	.81 to .88 (Poythress et al., 1999; Poythress, Bonnie, Monahan, Otto, & Hoge, 2002)
Validity:	Construct	.36 to .49 with clinician's global ratings of competency (Otto et al., 1998)

2. Administration is standardized, and scoring for most items is in reference to explicit criteria.
3. Both present knowledge about the legal system and the capacity to assimilate new information are assessed.
4. Multiple psycholegal abilities (i.e., understanding, reasoning, and appreciation) are assessed.
5. Quantitative indices of these abilities are interpreted in reference to national norming samples (Poythress et al., 1999, p. 6).

Conceptually, the three competence-related abilities (understanding, reasoning, and appreciation) were derived from the literature on competency to consent to treatment, with each ability related to the *Dusky* criteria (Melton, Petrila, Poythress, & Slobogin, 2007). Furthermore, the Bonnie division between foundational and decisional competence was integrated in the MacCAT-CA competence-related abilities. Lastly, defendant on training various competence-related constructs has been integrated into format of the MacCAT-CA as a capacity check.

Administration/Scoring/Interpretation

The MacCAT-CA is a 22-item measure that begins with a brief vignette about a bar fight between "Fred" and "Reggie," which establishes the context for the first 16 items. The vignette can be reread (verbatim) to the defendant to ensure comprehension of the vignette. The last six items (17–22) are based on the defendant's appreciation of his specific circumstances rather than on the vignette. Item content is provided in Table 5.3.

Each MacCAT-CA item is scored on a 0, 1, or 2-point scale using the test's *Professional Manual* for item interpretation. Total scores for each of the competence-related abilities can then be compared to various large groups of

Table 5.3 Item Content for MacCAT-CA

Understanding
1. Roles of defense attorney and prosecutor
2. Elements of an offense
3. Elements of a lesser included offense
4. Role of the jury
5. Role of the judge at trial
6. Consequences of conviction
7. Pleading guilty
8. Rights waived in making a guilty plea

Reasoning
9. Self-defense
10. Mitigating the prosecution's evidence of intent
11. Possible provocation
12. Fear as a motivator for one's behavior
13. Possible mitigating effects of intoxication
14. Seeing information: A defendant's ability to identify information that might inform Fred's choice
15. Weighing consequences: A defendant's ability to infer or think through the implications of a chosen course of action
16. Making comparisons: A defendant's ability to verbalize features (advantages/disadvantages) of a chosen option in contrast or comparison to features of the other option

Appreciation
17. Likelihood of being treated fairly
18. Likelihood of being assisted by defense counsel
19. Likelihood of fully disclosing case information to the defense attorney
20. Likelihood of being found guilty
21. Likelihood of punishment if convicted
22. Likelihood of pleading guilty

Source: Reproduced by special permission of the Publisher, Psychological Assessment Resources, Inc., 16204 North Florida Avenue, Lutz, FL 33549, from the *MacCAT-CA Professional Manual* by Norman G. Poythress, PhD, Robert Nicholson, PhD, Randy K. Otto, PhD, John F. Edens, PhD, Richard J. Bonnie, LLB, John Monahan, PhD, and Steven K. Hoge, MD. Copyright 1999 by PAR, Inc. Further reproduction is prohibited without permission of PAR, Inc.

incompetent and competent examinees who underwent evaluation during the development of the MacCAT-CA. The three scores are not combined to form a total score of competence or incompetence. The authors assert the tool can be completed within 25–45 minutes.

Strengths and Weaknesses

Strengths of the MacCAT-CA include the standardized administration, the ability to compare a particular defendant's results with various groups of other individuals who have completed the tool, and the analogous validity and reliability data to other measures of adjudicative competency. In addition, the literature, previous research, and fundamental psycholegal theory have driven the development of this tool (Mossman et al., 2007). However, there have also been concerns about certain aspects of the MacCAT-CA. First, some argue the vignette approach to competency does not permit exploration into the individual's unique case characteristics. In addition, there is a concern that the verbal demands of the MacCAT-CA may be too challenging for those with low-average intelligence and may lead to poor performance despite their ability to be conversant about their case and their ability to work with their attorney. These shortcomings are overcome with the recommendation that the MacCAT-CA is not a stand-alone "test" of competency; rather, it is one piece of a competency assessment (Poythress et al., 1999).

DON'T FORGET

The MacCAT-CA is only one piece of a comprehensive adjudicatory competency assessment.

Evaluation of Competency to Stand Trial–Revised

The Evaluation of Competency to Stand Trial–Revised (ECST-R) is a recently published competency tool (Rogers, Tillbrook, & Sewell, 2004) that has been added to the field of adjudicative competency assessment (for basic information about the ECST-R and its publisher see Rapid Reference 5.15; for information about reliability and validity data see Rapid Reference 5.16). The conceptual development of the tool came from a panel of mental health and legal experts.

≡ Rapid Reference 5.15

Evaluation of Competency to Stand Trial–Revised (ECST-R)

Authors:

Rogers, R., Tillbrook, C. E., & Sewell, K. W.

Citation:

Rogers, R., Tillbrook, C. E., & Sewell, K. W. (2004). *Professional Manual for the ECST-R: Evaluation of Competency to Stand Trial–Revised.* Lutz, FL: Psychological Assessment Resources.

≡ *Rapid Reference 5.16*

Reliability and Validity Data for the ECST-R

Reliability:	Interrater	.98 to .99 (Rogers, Jackson, Sewell, Tillbrook, & Martin, 2003)
	Internal Consistency	.83 to .89 (Rogers, Jackson, Sewell, Tillbrook, & Martin, 2003)
Validity:	Construct	Significant positive associations with MacCAT-CA and clinical judgments of experienced clinicians (Rogers, Jackson, & Sewell, 2004)

Administration/Scoring/Interpretation

The ECST-R includes three scales that represent the *Dusky* criteria: (1) Consult with Counsel, 6 items; (2) Factual Understanding of the Courtroom Proceedings, 6 items; and (3) Rational Understanding of the Courtroom Proceedings, 7 items. Furthermore, there are an additional 28 items that form the Atypical Presentation scale, specifically developed to screen for possible feigning. The three ECST-R scales are rated on a 5-point scale, although the meanings for each number vary for each of the scales. For all three scales, item ratings are then summed to produce a scale score, which is then converted to a T-score and used for comparison to the normed offender groups. The ranges of T-scores are then categorized into specific ranges from normal to mild impairment, moderate impairment, severe impairment, extreme impairment, and very extreme impairment. Lastly, ECST-R produces Certitude scores, indicating the confidence level in the classification of impairment for the three scales. (For discussion of confidence standards in competency assessments, see Buchanan [2006]).

Strengths and Weaknesses

The strengths of the ECST-R mirror those of the MacCAT-CA in that the tool provides a standardized, albeit more flexible than the MacCAT-CA, approach to competency assessment, including the ability to compare the defendant with normed offender groups. In addition, the ECST-R's three scales relate to the specific *Dusky* criteria. Lastly, the Atypical Presentation Scale is the first scale in a competency tool to address possible feigning, an issue that must always be contemplated in any forensic evaluation. Researchers have criticized the ECST-R for only considering the presence of psychotic disorders for interfering with competency as opposed to anxiety disorders or mental retardation (Melton, Petrila, Poythress, & Slobogin, 2007), for example. In addition, Melton and collegues are concerned about the internal validity problems of the ECST-R. They argue that a defendant can achieve a "no impairment" on each of the six items in the Consult with Counsel scale, yet when summed and converted to a T-score the defendant would be considered to have "severe" or "very severe" impairment for that scale. Melton and associates reason that cross-examination on "how scale interpretation can be so different from the sum of its parts" could be very difficult for the clinician utilizing the ECST-R (p.155).

SPECIAL POPULATIONS

Special tools have been developed for two specific populations; that is, the cognitively impaired and juvenile delinquents, for which adjudicative competency is also at issue.

Competence Assessment for Standing Trial for Defendants with Mental Retardation

It has been estimated that 2% to 7% of the referrals for competency to stand trial assessments are for defendants with mental retardation, with approximately one-half of cognitively impaired defendants not referred for evaluation (Bonnie, 1990). The Competence for Standing Trial for Defendants with Mental Retardation (CAST-MR) is primarily a multiple-choice questionnaire designed to assess competence to stand trial in mentally retarded defendants (Everington & Luckasson, 1992). (For basic information on the CAST-MR and its publisher, see Rapid Reference 5.17; for reliability and validity data, see Rapid Reference 5.18.) The test items were derived from competency case law, competence assessments for mentally ill defendants, and the psychological literature on competence to stand trial. Everington and Luckasson (1992) developed the CAST-MR because of the absence of reliability and validity data for mentally retarded defendants on the available competency to stand trial instruments (e.g., CST, CAI, IFI). The researchers criticized these tools because of the open-ended questions, inappropriate syntax and vocabulary for defendants with lower abilities, and the heavy focus on mental illness rather than legal criteria necessary to make decisions regarding competency. Therefore, the authors developed the CAST-MR to remedy the weaknesses in assessment tools when defendants are diagnosed with mental retardation.

≡ Rapid Reference 5.17

Competence Assessment for Standing Trial for Defendants with Mental Retardation (CAST-MR)

Authors:

Everington, C. T., & Luckasson, R.

Affiliation:

Miami University (Everington) and University of New Mexico (Luckasson)

Citation:

Everington, C. T., & Luckasson, R. (1992). *Competence assessment for standing trial for defendants with mental retardation.* Worthington, OH: International Diagnostics Systems.

Administration Time:

30–45 minutes

≡ Rapid Reference 5.18

Reliability and Validity Data for the CAST-MR

Reliability:	Interrater	Sections I and II–100%
		Section III–80%
		Total Score–98%
	Test-Retest	.89 and .90
	Internal Consistency	.87 to .90
Validity:	Construct	Discriminates between MR and non-MR defendants and between groups of MR defendants (MR—competent; MR—incompetent)
	Criterion-related	Hit rate with forensic evaluators was 70% face valid according to criminal disability attorneys

Note: Adapted from Everington (1990); Everington & Dunn (1995); Everington & Luckasson (1992).

Administration/Scoring/Interpretation

The CAST-MR was developed for use by forensic evaluators as one part of an overall assessment and should only be considered in the context of all available information. Interviews and observations of the defendant alone and with his attorney, intellectual assessments, and a social history should supplement the CAST-MR. In complex legal cases (i.e., capital murder versus theft), it may be appropriate for additional questions to be formulated by the attorney and the forensic examiner. Information from the CAST-MR may also be used to help delineate an individualized training program for those individuals who are found incompetent but are candidates for restoration (Everington, 1990; Everington & Luckasson, 1992). (See Rapid Reference 5.19.) Finally, the authors have encouraged use of the CAST-MR for research purposes.

The CAST-MR questions are read aloud to the defendant. The examiner may repeat items up to three times or may use prompts given in the manual to elicit more information from the defendant. Short breaks should be given to defendants who demonstrate signs of fatigue. There are two booklets—the Examiner Form and the Subject Form—for the CAST-MR. The Examiner Form contains all the questions with the correct response for each item marked with an asterisk. The examiner records the answers while the Subject Form permits the defendant to follow along.

There are three sections of the CAST-MR: Section I, "Basic Legal Concepts," 25 questions; Section II, "Skills to Assist Defense," 15 questions; and Section III, "Understanding Case Events," 10 open-ended questions. For Sections I and II the examiner should circle the correct response on the Examiner Form and assign 1 point for each correct answer. No points are assigned for incorrect answers and no answers. The total score for each section is the sum of all the points assigned for that section. For Section III the examiner assigns either 0, 0.5, or 1 credit for each question. The manual provides examples and general indicators for each credit category. Again the total score for this section is the sum of the points assigned for the section. If the defendant refuses to answer any Section III questions for legal reasons, the question is treated as missing data. For such a question, the average score for the section is assigned to that question.

Strengths and Weaknesses

Preliminary data on the CAST-MR appear very promising in their own right and are comparable or better than data available on other competency instruments for defendants without mental retardation. However, the data to date are based on a limited number of subjects and further projects should involve long-term investigation to achieve adequate samples of defendants. One criticism of the CAST-MR initial research is that community residents with mental retardation were subjects

≡ *Rapid Reference 5.19*

Suitable Examinees for the CAST-MR

The CAST-MR is designed for those who:	function in the range of mild to moderate mental retardation
	have WAIS IQ scores of approximately 35 to 75
	meet the classification guidelines of the American Association of Mental Retardation

The CAST-MR may be administered to but is not designed for individuals with severe mental retardation.

rather than criminal defendants (Melton, Petrila, Poythress, & Slobogin, 2007). In addition, those with mental retardation who are judged to be clinically competent tend to score significantly below defendants with no mental retardation on the CAST-MR (Everington & Luckasson, 1992), suggesting that perhaps these individuals still do not have the competence-related requirements of *Dusky* despite a "competent" finding on the measure (Melton, Petrila, Poythress, & Slobogin, 2007). Lastly, criticism has been leveraged at the multiple-choice format of the measure because it does not realistically portray the challenges a defendant will face in "real world" criminal proceedings.

Juveniles

Juvenile competence to stand trial was largely ignored by courts during the first half century of the juvenile justice system. This was primarily due to the rehabilitative purposes of the juvenile justice system rather than the adversarial nature of adult criminal courts (Grisso, 1998). However, in the 1960s, *In re Gault* (1967) required that juvenile courts provide the same due process rights (e.g., right to counsel, to avoid self-incrimination, to challenge evidence in court) to juveniles as afforded to adults in criminal proceedings. These rights have extended to competence to stand trial in a majority of the states (Grisso, 1998). This right in juvenile court has been interpreted by some appellate courts and states to apply the *Dusky* standard to juveniles; however, there are some opinions that permit immaturity to be a basis for incompetency, in addition to mental illness (e.g., *In re Causey*, 1978). Complicating the matter for juveniles is the increased use of direct filing or waiving juveniles into adult court. (See Table 5.4 for Grisso's recommendations for when to at least consider adjudicatory competency in a particular juvenile.)

Table 5.4 Conditions Suggesting Evaluating Juvenile's Competency

1. Age 12 years or younger
2. Prior diagnosis/treatment for mental illness or mental retardation
3. "Borderline" level of intellectual functioning, or record of "learning disability"
4. Observations of others at pretrial event suggest deficits in memory, attention, or interpretation of reality

Note: Adapted from Grisso (1998).

Research has investigated whether competency to stand trial adult measures would be applicable to juvenile delinquents. Studies investigating the applicability of the MacCAT-CA to juvenile defendants, aged 16–17 years old, indicate that these juvenile offenders demonstrated comparable competence-related abilities as adult defendants (Poythress, Lexcen, Grisso, & Steinberg, 2006; Otto et al., 1998). Studies evaluating whether the MacCAT-CA could be used with a variety of age groups have demonstrated that the measure may not capture the differences between early adolescent defendants and adult defendants (Woolard & Harvell, 2005).

CAUTION

Concerns about MacCAT-CA applicability to juveniles

No age-appropriate norms

Some items less relevant to juveniles (e.g., role of jury)

Mental illness emphasis may misclassify adolescents

Source: Poythress, Bonnie, Monahan, Otto, & Hoge, 2002.

In addition to the MacCAT-CA, the FIT-R has also been investigated for its applicability to juvenile defendants. The benefits of the FIT-R demonstrated in preliminary studies indicate good interrater reliability and moderate correlation between age and intelligence and judgment of competence-related abilities (Viljoen, Vincent, & Roesch, 2006; Viljoen & Roesch, 2005). Despite the MacCAT-CA's and FIT-R's promising future with adolescents, it is more advantageous to have a specific juvenile tool.

Therefore, to better address juvenile special adjudicatory needs or potential deficits, Grisso has developed the Juvenile Adjudicative Competence Interview (JACI; Grisso, 2005). The benefit of the JACI is that while an examiner is inquiring about competence-related abilities (e.g., nature and seriousness of offense, nature and purpose of the juvenile court trial, possible pleas, etc.), developmental issues are taken into consideration (Melton, Petrila, Poythress, & Slobogin, 2007).

No scores are tallied for the JACI; rather, it provides a guideline for areas of inquiry and capacity checks on teachable topics relevant to competency. There are no norms or validity studies published to date for the JACI. However, the JACI is a useful guide when completing a juvenile adjudicatory competence evaluation.

SUMMARY AND CONCLUSIONS

This section of the report integrates the findings from the interview, collateral contacts, and competency interview and/or tool used during the evaluation to provide an opinion on the defendant's *present* functioning. The examiner should clearly delineate the nexus between any mental condition found and the direct impact on the defendant's competence-related abilities. In addition, if the examiner opines the defendant is incompetent, this section should discuss whether restoration is possible within any statutory time limits.

Reporting the Results

Disseminating the results of the evaluation should also follow a certain procedure to ensure proper treatment of the defendant (Grisso, 1988). First, for a privately requested evaluation (i.e., one that has not been ordered by the court), the results should be reported only to the requesting attorney prior to providing a written report. It is the defense attorney's responsibility to release the information to other parties. The results should be communicated prior to a written report because a private attorney may decide to withhold the information (results support competency finding) from the court, thereby saving the time and expense of generating a written report. This meeting also provides an opportunity for the attorney to understand how to better work with the defendant and it allows the attorney to inform the examiner of special problems that may need to be addressed in a written report.

An examiner may also relate the findings directly to the defendant with the attorney's permission. This allows the examiner to present and explain the findings tactfully, which may not be possible when the examiner testifies. For a court-ordered evaluation, a written report must be prepared for the court, with copies disseminated to each party by the court. Finally, sometimes a generous amount of time passes between when a competency evaluation and report are generated for the court

> **CAUTION**
>
> When an "insanity" referral accompanies a competency referral, write two reports to preserve the defendant's rights at later stages of the criminal proceedings (Zapf & Roesch, 2006).

and when possible testimony occurs. For example, in a personal experience, nine months lagged between the two events. If this should occur, the defendant should be reevaluated to determine whether the previous finding still stands, as present functioning is at issue, and whether an addendum should be provided to the court (if court ordered).

Special Issues

Feigning or Malingering Incompetency
One systematic weakness of most (except ECST-R) competency to stand trial measures is that they are vulnerable to the feigning or malingering defendant. Recent research has begun evaluating standard malingering measures and specialized scales in competency tools in the context of adjudicatory competence evaluations (Jackson, Rogers, & Sewell, 2005; Rogers, Jackson, & Sewell, 2004; Rogers, Sewell, Grandjean, & Vitacco, 2002). Vitacco, Rogers, Gabel, & Munizza (2007) reported that the M-FAST, SIMS, and ECST-R ATP Scale were all good at identifying possible malingerers, with the ECST-R ATP Scale having good scale homogeneity and excellent discriminant validity.

Ultimate Legal Issue
There is debate in the literature as to whether the forensic evaluators should answer the "ultimate legal issue" question; here, whether the defendant is or is not competent to stand trial. Research has demonstrated that judges and forensic examiners agree up to 90% of the time in adjudicative competency cases (Zapf, Hubbard, Cooper, Wheeles, & Ronan, 2004), indicating that judges most often rely solely upon the opinion of the examiner, sometimes even without a hearing (Roesch & Golding, 1980). Research has demonstrated fairly good agreement on competency assessments overall (Poythress & Stock, 1980); however, it is not surprising given that the base rate of competency is estimated to be upwards of 80% (Zapf & Roesch, 2006). Agreement significantly deteriorates when the specific functional abilities that comprise the competency opinion are investigated (Skeem, Golding, Cohn, & Berge, 1998) and sometimes interrater agreement become very poor (Morris, Haroun, & Naimark, 2004) for the components of competency. For these reasons (among others), Melton and colleagues (2007) argue clinicians should avoid offering legal conclusions about competency; rather, that they should include in their reports descriptive details about the defendant's functioning that permits the court to form its own opinions on the issue. Unfortunately, research and academic pursuits do not match up to the actual courtroom in this circumstance given that most often judges want the final determination of

competency provided in the report and may even order the examiner to answer the "ultimate legal" conclusion. If this occurs, Melton recommends providing a cautionary opinion to the court. Conversely, Federal Rule of Evidence 704 allows mental health experts to testify to the ultimate legal question of a defendant's pretrial status, or competency to stand trial.

SUMMARY

This chapter outlined the legal standard of competency to stand trial and the concomitant psycholegal issues. The reader has been provided with a general outline of how to prepare for, evaluate, and write an adjudicatory competency evaluation. General information on several competency to stand trial tools available for clinical use were discussed, explicating each tool's strengths and weaknesses that should be considered when a tool is used for the assessment. Important to recognize is that all adjudicatory competency assessments require more than just the use of any one of these competency tools. A comprehensive measure of competency to stand trial requires an interview, collateral contacts, and a competency interview, with a competency tool. Skeem, Golding, and Emke-Francis (2004) enumerate five recommendations to improve competency assessment procedures (see Table 5.5).

Table 5.5 Recommendations for Improving Adjudicatory Competency Evaluations

Recommendation	Reasoning
Use the Right Tools	Use those tools that directly target adjudicatory competence rather than traditional psychological assessment measures
Get the Right Information	Supplement the correct psycholegal tool with additional information, from the defendant and collateral sources
Take Context Seriously	"Competent for What?" (p. 203) Need to know the challenges facing the particular defendant
Test and Substantiate Your Conclusions	Substantiate conclusions with clear data and reasoning, must describe how a particular competency deficit is related to symptoms of psychopathology or intellectual impairment
Obtain Specialized Forensic Training	To remain abreast of new legal and technological developments in the field

Note: Adapted from Skeem, Golding, and Emke-Francis(2004).

Lastly, additional resources should be reviewed for a more thorough understanding of adjudicatory competency, including tools and other issues not addressed in this chapter; for example, amnestic defendant, restoration with medication, and so forth.

🔖 TEST YOURSELF 🔖

1. What is the *Dusky* Standard for competency to stand trial? (see p. 113)

2. What is the difference between the ideographic approach and the nomothetic approach? What are the advantages and disadvantages? (see pp. 113–114)

3. List two screening tools, two semi-structured tools, and two structured tools. (see pp. 120–140)

4. What are the different sections of a competency to stand trial report? (see pp. 117–120)

5. List the tools developed for defendants with mental retardation and juvenile offenders. (see pp. 140–145)

Six

ESSENTIALS OF INVOLUNTARY CIVIL COMMITMENT ASSESSMENT

Andrew W. Kane

The state can impose itself upon individuals' freedoms under either or both of two doctrines: *police power* or *parens patriae* (Parry, 1998; Simon & Shuman, 2007). The former involves regulations and laws to protect public health, safety, and welfare, using police or other authorities to protect individuals from themselves or someone else. Most persons detained by the police are processed within the criminal justice system. Many, however, are taken to hospitals for assessment and possible treatment on the basis that they are mentally ill or otherwise dysfunctional and, as a result, are seen as needing help—voluntarily or not. If the individual is also considered to be dangerous to self or others, the statutes of every state permit holding the individual for possible involuntary commitment or other involuntary services. Most involuntary commitment processes are initiated through a police detention (Meyer, Landis, & Hay, 1988). In the modern era, this "preventive detention" has been used almost exclusively with the mentally ill (La Fond & Durham, 1992). The latter term, *parens patriae*, literally "father of the country," permits hospitalization based on a need to be cared for. People cannot generally be forced to accept treatment for a physical illness, even a serious or contagious one, in most states, but can be forced to accept mental health treatment (Stefan, 2001).

EFFECT OF INVOLUNTARY CIVIL COMMITMENT ON THE INDIVIDUAL

The person who becomes the subject of an involuntary commitment proceeding is accused of being mentally ill and dangerous. Competency to make decisions in one's own best interests is questioned. One may lose control over many decisions of daily life, such as what to eat, where to eat or sleep, when to go out and where to go, and what to do with one's money. One acquires the stigma of being deviant and possibly dangerous. One's employment, credit, reputation, and dignity may be harmed (Preparation and Trial, 1981). Some people will become dependent on the hospital, fostering helplessness that interferes with essential furthering of independence. Hospitalization may also foster regression, hindering the process of recovery (Shuman, 2005).

Clinicians must be constantly aware that commitment candidates are under great stress from the legal process, in addition to stress from their problems. The combination almost guarantees that disturbed behavior will be elicited. Attempts should be made to minimize the impact of stress at the time of interview, and one must take into consideration the fact that it cannot be reduced entirely (Melton, Petrila, Poythress, & Slobogin, 2007).

CAUTION

The anger, anxiety, and depression you note may be the product of the involuntary hospitalization, not the independent mental state of the individual. You must try to separate the individual's mental condition from hospitalization-induced (iatrogenic) conditions.

MENTAL HOSPITALIZATION AS A DANGER IN ITSELF

Concern has been stated by various critics that involuntary commitment involves an increased risk of institutionalizing people, making them dependent on the hospital and less capable of functioning outside of the institution (Melton, Petrila, Poythress, & Slobogin, 2007). Lengthy hospitalization reduces patients' ability to make their own decisions, as most significant decisions are made for them in the hospital, making adjustment to living in the community difficult for most long-term patients (Durham & La Fond, 1988). Further, research indicates that the best predictor of future hospitalization is past hospitalization. Hospitalization is also rarely the least restrictive alternative (Melton, Petrila, Poythress, & Slobogin, 2007). Increasing the length of hospitalization does not reduce the probability of future hospitalization, and does not consistently improve social adjustment or reduce psychopathology. Aftercare is more important than length of hospitalization in determining whether an individual will successfully adjust to life in the community (Durham & La Fond, 1988).

CAUTION

Hospitalization may produce dependency and interfere with functioning outside of the hospital. Involuntary commitment should be a last resort.

WHAT IS MENTAL ILLNESS?

Although each individual statute contains its own definition, the minimum requirement for mental illness is usually that the individual be acutely psychotic, though that term may not be used. The major exception is for suicidal people. The Wisconsin statute defines "'[m]ental illness', for purposes of involuntary commitment," as "a substantial disorder of thought, mood, perception, orientation, or memory which grossly impairs judgment, behavior, capacity to recognize reality, or ability to meet the ordinary demands of life" (Wis. Stat. § 51.01(13)(b)). Nearly all state statutes refer to "mental illness," though some use a similar term such as "mental disorder" (Parry, 1998). Some states specifically include, while others specifically exclude, conditions such as developmental disability and alcohol or other drug abuse (Parry, 1998). It should be noted that "civil commitment cannot under the [Americans with Disabilities Act] be justified by reference to disability or need for treatment alone" (Stefan, 2001, p. 131).

CAUTION

You must use your state's statutory definition of "mental illness." Does it allow any exceptions to the general rule that the individual must be psychotic or suicidal?

INDICATIONS FOR HOSPITALIZATION

Katz (1989) offers guidelines for assessing whether inpatient hospitalization is necessary. These guidelines are outlined in Rapid Reference 6.1.

LEGAL STANDARDS FOR CIVIL COMMITMENT

Every state has some process for involuntarily hospitalizing persons who are considered to be seriously mentally ill and dangerous to themselves or to others, utilizing either or both of the state's police power or *parens patriae* authority (Parry, 1994; Shuman, 1994). No state law permits involuntary commitment solely based on the presence of a mental illness and a need for treatment (Melton, Petrila, Poythress, & Slobogin, 2007).

Types of Commitment

According to Parry (1994), there are eight basic types of involuntary commitment:

≡ Rapid Reference 6.1

Indications for Acute Inpatient Care

- A psychiatric disorder severe enough that it would be very difficult to treat on an outpatient basis
- Evidence that the individual's condition is unlikely to improve unless he or she is temporarily in a low-stress inpatient environment
- Indications (serious threats or behavior) of being a danger to self or others
- Behavior that is highly disruptive to the individual's environment and is due to a severe psychiatric condition
- The individual is withdrawing from abusive levels of alcohol or other drugs, especially if there is a physical withdrawal syndrome
- Presence of a physical illness that requires inpatient treatment, together with psychiatric symptoms severe enough that the physical treatment cannot be accomplished on a medical ward
- Failure of psychiatric treatment on an outpatient basis, with serious psychiatric symptoms persisting
- Lack of availability of community-based services adequate to address the individual's needs
- Need for short-term crisis management

1. *Informal commitment*, which may also be called voluntary commitment, in which the person signs himself or herself into a hospital but is free to sign out at will.
2. *Voluntary commitment*, in which a competent person is admitted voluntarily, but the individual must satisfy certain bureaucratic criteria before being discharged, and/or the facility has a right to initiate involuntary commitment proceedings rather than discharging the individual.
3. *Third-party commitment*, in which someone other than the potential patient (e.g., a guardian) who has legal authority over that person can sign the individual into a hospital.
4. *Short-term or observational commitment*, in which an individual is either released after a specified period of time or is held over for a possible extended commitment. About half of the states have formal observational commitment statutes, but all states have functional equivalents (Simon & Shuman, 2007). Most states limit this period to 24–72 hours (Simon & Shuman, 2007).

At this point initial screening is normally conducted. The individual is usually evaluated by a hospital psychologist or psychiatrist, who makes an initial recommendation in a probable cause hearing in court regarding involuntary commitment for treatment. If probable cause is found—that is, the judicial officer rules that there is sufficient evidence that the individual may be both mentally ill and dangerous—the individual may be held for a final hearing on the question of involuntary civil commitment (Simon & Shuman, 2007).

During the period between the probable cause and final hearings, the alleged mentally ill individual is typically examined by experts appointed by the court (for example, two psychiatrists, or one psychiatrist and one clinical psychologist). These experts evaluate the individual in the context of the statutory requirements and make independent reports to the court. Unless the individual is discharged by the ward psychiatrist prior to the final hearing date, or a stipulation is entered into between the attorneys for the individual and the county prior to the final hearing date, a hearing is held with a judge presiding. The alleged mentally ill individual may have a right to a jury trial. On the basis of testimony, the factfinder determines whether the individual is both mentally ill and dangerous. While commitments are normally for a period of months, most individuals stay in the hospital at most a few weeks.

5. *Extended commitment*, in which persons are held for long-term, and possibly indefinite, treatment in inpatient facilities, "but only after the most rigorous substantive and procedural due process requirements are met" (Parry, 1994, p. 321).

6. *Outpatient commitment*, in which the commitment is to an outpatient, rather than inpatient, facility. This may be a form of preventive detention in some cases, or it may be seen as a less restrictive alternative to inpatient care. In some cases, fewer due process protections are afforded to outpatient committees, given the lesser loss of liberty. Those who fail to comply with outpatient treatment may find themselves the subject of proceedings for inpatient commitment. Outpatient commitment can work to prevent hospitalization when the program is properly structured (La Fond & Durham, 1992). See the following for further discussion of outpatient commitment.

7. *Criminal commitment*, in which an individual alleged or adjudicated incompetent to stand trial, or who has been adjudicated "not guilty by reason of insanity," is treated involuntarily.

8. *Recommitment*, referring to the procedure for renewal of a period of involuntary commitment. In most cases, the same standards apply as during the initial commitment, though the burden of proof may shift to the committed individual. Recommitments constitute about one-third of the 500,000-plus commitment hearings in this country annually (Parry, Turkheimer, & Hundley, 1992). The number of involuntary commitments has not changed substantially in many years. As requirements for commitments became more stringent, the "slack" was taken up by commitment of patients as "gravely disabled" (Simon, 1992). Only informal commitment is truly voluntary (Parry, 1994). Each of the others involves some coercion.

Specific Requirements

Every jurisdiction requires some type of mental disorder and some type of dangerousness in order for the involuntary commitment statute to apply (Simon & Shuman, 2007). Although some states exclude individuals with developmental disabilities from involuntary commitment statutes, most states have similar provisions for the involuntary hospitalization of these individuals as well (Shuman, 2005). Title II of the Americans with Disabilities Act permits discrimination against individuals with disabilities if that individual poses "a significant risk to the health or safety of others..." (Stefan, 2001).

The U.S. Supreme Court indicated in *O'Connor v. Donaldson* (1975) and *Foucha v. Louisiana* (1992), among others, that an individual may not be involuntarily hospitalized without both mental illness and dangerousness (Appelbaum, 1993; Melton, Petrila, Poythress, & Slobogin, 2007; Parry, 1998; Perlin, Champine, Dlugacz, & Connell, 2008; Shuman, 2005; Wrightsman, Nietzel, & Fortune, 1998; Zander, 2005). Even if incapable of giving informed consent, the Supreme Court has indicated, the mentally ill individual will not meet the criteria for involuntary placement unless dangerous to self or others (*O'Connor v. Donaldson*, 1975; Parry, 1990, 1995; Simon & Shuman, 2007; Zander, 2005; *Zinermon v. Burch*, 1990).

Involuntary civil commitment requires some type of judicial hearing in every state. The patient must receive formal notice of the hearing and its purpose, must be represented by an attorney, and must be found to be both mentally ill and dangerous on the basis of at least "clear and convincing" evidence (*Addington v. Texas*, 1979; Perlin, Champine, Dlugacz, & Connell, 2008; Simon & Shuman, 2007). Clinicians are permitted to recommend commitment, and to present their reasoning, but only a judicial officer may make a decision to involuntarily commit an individual (Simon & Shuman, 2007).

Some states require that the evidence of dangerousness be shown by a recent overt threat or act, and that there is an imminent danger to the patient or someone else (Shuman, 2005; Simon & Shuman, 2007). "Recent" is interpreted many ways, however, referring to days in some jurisdictions and a month or more in others.

DON'T FORGET

Check your state law to determine the required criteria in your jurisdiction.

In summary, Parry (1994) indicates, the involuntary commitment is typically of persons who have "(1) severe, significant, gross, or substantial mental illnesses who because of their mental illnesses (2) pose a danger to self or others, or are gravely disabled, and for whom (3) inpatient hospitalization is the least restrictive viable alternative" (p. 323). It should be noted that a distinction is generally made between "dangerous to self" and "inability to care for self" or "gravely disabled." The former includes persons who are suicidal or who self-mutilate, whereas the latter includes persons who are unable to independently conduct the activities of daily living (providing for their own food, clothing, shelter, etc.) necessary for survival. Those who are dangerous to themselves are generally committed on the basis of the state's police power; those unable to care for themselves are committed on the basis of the *parens patriae* doctrine (Perlin, vol. 1, 1989; Perlin, Champine, Dlugacz, & Connell, 2008; Simon & Shuman, 2007).

Assessment of "grave disability" involves a careful analysis of the facts of a case and the context in which the individual was living when brought into the hospital. Being mentally ill is not sufficient; there must be evidence that the mental illness caused the individual to be unable to meet his or her basic needs. Further, there must be an assessment of the individual's responsibility for the context in which he or she was living, and of the potential solutions, keeping in mind that the individual has a right to live in the least-restrictive alternative consistent with his or her needs (Perlin, Champine, Dlugacz, & Connell, 2008).

Despite the requirement for dangerousness, researchers have found that a substantial proportion of involuntarily committed individuals have not behaved in a dangerous manner in

DON'T FORGET

You must determine what your state requires with regard to dangerousness, and ensure that you follow the statutory criteria in doing your evaluation.

any way, let alone committed a violent act. Many adjudications of dangerousness are based on an individual's perceived level of functioning rather than on objective data regarding his or her behavior, particularly annoying or bizarre behavior (La Fond & Durham, 1992).

LEAST RESTRICTIVE ALTERNATIVE

Most states, either through statute or case law, recognize a right to treatment in the least restrictive setting (La Fond, 1994; Melton, Petrila, Poythress, & Slobogin, 2007; Parry, 1994; Parry, 1998; Perlin, Champine, Dlugacz, & Connell, 2008), though a general lack of appropriate facilities in the community often makes fulfilling this requirement difficult. The top priority, Parry (1994) indicates, should be to make available the least restrictive alternative favored by the individual or a legal guardian, or, if that is not

> **CAUTION**
>
> You must determine what your state requires regarding the least-restrictive alternative consistent with the needs of the person. If possible, recommend specific institutions (hospitals, group homes, etc.) that would provide the least-restrictive alternative.

possible, then base it on the individual's best interests while incorporating as many as possible of the individual's preferences.

COMPETENCY AND INFORMED CONSENT

Involuntary commitment, in itself, carries no implications regarding an individual's ability to make willing, voluntary, and knowing choices, whether regarding treatment or anything else (*Lessard v. Schmidt*, 1974; "Mental Patients," 1985; National Center for State Courts, 1986; Perlin, Champine, Dlugacz, & Connell, 2008). An adjudication regarding one area of competency does not imply that an individual is incompetent in any other area (Melton, Petrila, Poythress, & Slobogin, 2007; Perlin, 1995). Although there is a legal presumption that an individual who has not been adjudicated incompetent is competent, if an individual is applying for admission to a hospital, that assumption must be tested by an agent of that facility, per the Supreme Court ruling in *Zinermon v. Burch* (Parry, 1994). Melton, Petrila, Poythress, & Slobogin, (2007) indicate that children age 9 and up can often make competent treatment decisions. With specific regard to medication, Perlin, Champine, Dlugacz, and Connell (2008) wrote that, "Predicated on due process and right to privacy grounds, an institutionalized person retains, absent an emergency, a qualified right to refuse unwanted medication."

Consent to treatment, Grisso (1986) indicates, requires "(1) Knowledge of information relevant for a treatment decision; (2) that the decision is Voluntary; and (3) that the patient is (was) Competent to make the decision." Unfortunately, the law does not provide a generally accepted definition of competence. It is essential that there not be confusion between an individual's ability to make/communicate competent choices due to mental illness, and the fact that differences in values may lead to different choices (Shuman, 1986). Much of the research on patients' understanding of their treatment, including medication, did not control for whether patients were in fact given a substantial amount of information, nor whether it was given in a clear and understandable manner (Grisso, 2003). Evaluation of a patient's decision-making capacity also needs to consider how complex the circumstances are, how serious potential consequences are, and whether any individual deficits can be compensated for by having family, friends, or other support people assist with the decision-making process (Grisso, 2003).

MacArthur Treatment Competence Study

The best-designed and most thorough study to date of the ability of mental patients to give informed consent (Appelbaum & Grisso, 1995; Appelbaum & Grisso, 1998; Grisso, 2003; Grisso & Appelbaum, 1995; Grisso & Appelbaum, 1998; Grisso, Mulvey, & Fletcher, 1995) was conducted with funding from the MacArthur Foundation. Informed consent requires:

> [I]nformation regarding the nature and purpose of the recommended procedure, probable benefits, likely risks, and the alternatives to the proposed treatment—including the option of forgoing treatment altogether—along with […] benefits and risks.… [P]atients must have the opportunity to make decisions in the absence of coercion by those providing their care.… (Appelbaum & Grisso, 1995)

Appelbaum and Grisso (1995) suggested that four criteria be accepted as basic to a determination of competence:

1. Ability to communicate a choice is the first, and least stringent, standard.
2. The second and most common component of judicial standards for competence is the ability to understand relevant information.

3. A third legal standard is the ability to appreciate the nature of the situation and its likely consequences. This standard requires that patients be able to apply the information abstractly understood to their own situation.

4. Finally, courts also have applied the standard of ability to manipulate information rationally in determining decision-making competence. This standard emphasizes patients' abilities to employ logical processes to compare the benefits and risks of treatment options. A decision sometimes has been called irrational merely because the patient's choice was unconventional (which is not a sufficient basis by itself to consider the decision maker incompetent). In contrast, the "irrationality" to which this standard properly refers pertains to illogic in the processing of information, not the choice that eventually is made.

Perlin, Champine, Dlugacz, and Connell (2008) indicate that

> The MacCATT-T focuses on the examinee's understanding of the diagnosed disorder; his or her appreciation that the diagnosis is, in fact, correct, or his or her nondelusional explication of why he or she disagrees with it; her understanding of the needed treatment and its benefits and risks; her appreciation that the treatment may provide benefit, or her nondelusional explanation for why she doubts it; her understanding of alternative treatments; the reasoning employed to make a treatment choice; and her appreciation of the consequences that might flow from or the benefits and risks that treatment may provide in her everyday life. Finally, the examinee is asked to make a treatment choice. (p. 163)

A court will be particularly interested in whether the individual has taken a proposed medication before, whether it was effective, whether there were significant side effects, whether the current and past situations are similar, and how the evaluator weighed these data (Perlin, Dlugacz, Champine, & Connell, 2008).

Grisso and Appelbaum (1995) concluded that "opponents of allowing persons with mental illness equal decision-making rights no longer can maintain that all persons who are in need of hospitalization for mental disorder lack the requisite abilities to make decisions regarding their treatment. Nearly one half of the Schizophrenia group and 76% of the Depression group performed in the 'adequate' range...." They recommended that patients who seem to have difficulty understanding information be given further explanations to reduce the number who may initially appear incompetent to make treatment decisions. Only the relative few who do not respond to the teaching would become candidates for a hearing to determine their competence to refuse treatment.

Slobogin (1996) disagrees in part with some of the aforementioned conclusions. He indicates that "a person should be found competent as long as he or she understands the relevant facts and holds no patently false beliefs about them. . . . Only a person who does not understand the relevant facts, or who understands them but holds a belief about them for which there is no evidence, is incompetent" (pp. 21–22). Further, a patient who believes that the side effects of a proposed medication outweighs the benefits could also be considered incompetent by the MacArthur criteria. Slobogin believes that "the focal point of the evaluation should be the reasons for the person's stance," (pp. 21–22) which could include a wish to avoid unwanted treatment.

Explanations should generally use simple language and brief sentences. Each decision the patient needs to make should be discussed separately, with alternatives, and the advantages and disadvantages of each should be expressly discussed. Patients should be asked to paraphrase the important things said, so that there can be an evaluation of how well he or she understands. Ask what choices could be made, and what the potential consequences of each decision are. The patient who only repeats what is said,

> # DON'T FORGET
> ....
> - Mental patients are generally presumed to be competent unless adjudicated incompetent.
> - Children can competently make some decisions by age 9, and most decisions by age 14.
> - It is not generally the individual's choice that is at issue, it is whether that individual possesses the evaluative capacity to make a knowing and voluntary decision.

or who states a conclusion but is unable to discuss it, may have been coerced to come to that decision. The patient who can discuss the advantages and disadvantages of each of several possible decisions and why each is being chosen is relatively likely to be making an independent decision.

PREDICTION OF DANGEROUSNESS

Mental illness, in and of itself, does not suggest a greater likelihood of violence. In fact, the data indicate the opposite: without additional conditions, mental illness suggests a *lower* probability of violence (Elbogen & Johnson, 2009; Monahan et al., 2001). The more additional predictive factors that are present, and the seriousness of those additional predictive factors, the greater the risk that an individual will do something violent.

Prediction of behavior is difficult to do with any degree of accuracy, especially prediction of dangerousness, in part because dangerousness is a state, a temporary condition, rather than a trait inherent to the individual. A given individual may do something dangerous in one situation but show no potential for danger in any other situation. Part of the difficulty is that the "harm" and "risk" implied by the term dangerousness is generally treated as a dichotomous variable (either present or absent), rather than as the continuum each really is. "Violence is also the product of the unique interaction between the individual and the environment and, as such, defies predictability" (Simon & Shuman, 2007, p. 124–125).

Rather than predicting "dangerousness," the clinician is asked to assess short-term *risk* of behavior that is dangerous to self or others. While clinicians do not do well at assessing long-term risk, assessment of short-term risk is much more readily accomplished (Melton, Petrila, Poythress, & Slobogin, 2007; Simon & Shuman, 2007). "[B]ecause dangerousness for civil commitment purposes usually must be imminent, clinicians can limit their assessments to the 'short term, rather than long-term,' which can help increase the accuracy of the assessment" (Parry, 1998).

Until recently, nearly all the published research shows that mental health professionals have a strong tendency to overestimate dangerousness. In fact, relatively few people who are expected to become violent actually do (Menzies, Webster, McMain, Staley, & Scaglione, 1994). With the use of actuarial methods, however, clinicians have become much better at predicting dangerousness, including reduction of the rates of false-positives (people predicted to do something dangerous who do not) and false-negatives (people predicted to not do anything dangerous who do something dangerous) (Gardner, Lidz, Mulvey, & Shaw, 1996). According to Monahan (quoted in Edwards [1996]), "the research would indicate that clinicians are [now] better than chance, but worse than perfection" at predicting violent behavior.

Using data from the National Institute of Mental Health (NIMH) Epidemiological Catchment Area study, researchers found that persons with no psychiatric diagnosis evidenced a 2.1% rate of violence, those with mania or bipolar disorder 11.0%, those with Major Depression 11.7%, those with Schizophrenia 12.7%, those with alcohol abuse or dependence 24.6%, and those with other drug abuse or dependence 34.7% (Monahan, 1992). McNeil and Binder (1987) found that by the end of the third day in the hospital there was no longer a difference between patients initially alleged to be dangerous to others and those not so alleged. A similar study by Beck and Bonnar (1988) had comparable results. Wrightsman, Nietzel, and Fortune (1998) indicate that predictions can be reasonably accurate if "(1) the predictions are for the short-term future [and]

(2) they are made for environmental settings for which the clinician has data about the person's past behavior." The clinician is advised to "describe factors present in the individual shown in studies to correlate with increased risk of violence" (Shuman, 2005, p. 16–8).

Monahan et al. (2001) published the results of the most major study to date of risk assessment, conducted under the sponsorship of the MacArthur Study of Mental Disorder and Violence. Their multiyear, multisite study of more than 1,000 patients found that a number of factors correlated with risk of violence. The authors provide a table of risk factors (Appendix B, pp. 163–168) for violence/aggression during the first year post-hospitalization. One of the columns is an "odds ratio" in which the number indicates the degree of increase in probability for a given factor. Thus, the odds ratio for "male gender" is 1.51; that is, males are 51% more likely to be violent/aggressive than females, when other factors are statistically removed. Actual violence, of course, depends on many factors related to both the person and the situation. Selected data (including some from other studies they list) indicate the following information shown in Table 6.1.

Table 6.1 Risk Factors For Violence Post-Hospitalization

Hare PCL: SV > 12	4.05
Chart diagnosis of Antisocial Pty. Dis.	3.11
Violent fantasies about escalating harm	2.80
Substance disorder, no major disorder	2.47
Father ever used illegal drugs	2.40
Recent violent behavior	2.32
Frequent violent fantasies	2.23
Any arrest for a crime against a person	2.11
Violent fantasies while with target	2.08
Serious adult arrest	2.04
Substance abuse at time of admission	2.01
Violence at time of admission	1.97
Violent fantasies	1.94
Violent fantasies focused on 1 person	1.91
Father ever intoxicated (alcohol)	1.87
Any arrest besides crime against person	1.80
Father ever arrested	1.79

(continued)

Table 6.1 (Continued)

Involuntary hospitalization	1.78
Any head injury with loss of consciousness	1.69
Homelessness	1.66
Frequency of adult arrests	1.60
Mother ever used illegal drugs	1.54
Perceived stress	1.54
Seriousness of physical child abuse	1.51
Male gender	1.51
Major disorder and substance abuse	1.47
Personality disorder only	1.46
Nonviolent aggression at admission	1.44
Command hallucinations	1.43
Any head injury without loss of consciousness	1.43
Mother ever intoxicated (alcohol)	1.41
Suicide attempt	1.31
Unable to care for self	1.29
Frequency of abuse as a child	1.25
Diagnosis of "other psychosis"	1.00
Diagnosis of depression	0.92
Any delusions	0.74
Diagnosis of Mania	0.74
Diagnosis of Schizophrenia	0.38

Monahan and his colleagues developed an iterative classification tree (ICT) to foster the assessment of risk of a given individual. Because of the great complexity of the classification tree, which asks progressive questions based on the answers received from the patient, the ICT was placed on a CD and made commercially available under the name "Classification of Violence Risk" (COVR) through Psychological Assessment Resources (www.parinc.com). In a follow-up study, Monahan et al. (2005) found that the instrument correctly classified 91% of 102 patients predicted to be low risk, and 49% of those predicted to be high risk. Overall, 76% of the patients were correctly classified. Monahan et al. (2006) discussed the development of the software. A review of the data on the COVR by McCusker (2007) suggested caution in using the COVR for violence risk assessment until additional research more strongly supports its conclusions, particularly for individuals predicted to be at high risk of post-hospitalization violence.

Fazel, Gulati, Linsell, Geddes, and Grann (2009) did a meta-analysis of the 20 studies they identified between January, 1970, and February, 2009, that assessed the risk of violence of 18,423 individuals with Schizophrenia or other psychoses, which they compared with the level of violence in the general population of 1,714,904. Eleven of the studies reported on the affect of comorbid substance abuse. The authors found that there was no significant difference between people with Schizophrenia and those with other psychotic disorders. People with psychoses were slightly more likely to exhibit violence than the general population, and significantly more likely to commit homicides, though the homicide probability was only 0.3% for either psychosis or substance abuse. However, "the increased risk of violence in schizophrenia and the psychoses comorbid with substance abuse was not different than the risk of violence in individuals with diagnoses of substance use disorders. In other words, schizophrenia and other psychoses did not appear to add any additional risk to that conferred by the substance abuse alone" (pp. 7–8). Further, substance abuse markedly increased the risk of violence for people with comorbid psychotic and substance abuse disorders. These findings are consistent with those of the MacArthur violence risk assessment research, particularly the finding that people with psychoses but without substance abuse do not have a high level of violence, while those who abuse alcohol or other drugs do have a significantly higher risk of violence. According to Martin Grann, PhD, one author of the 2009 study, "people with schizophrenia are not dangerous.... If a person is an alcoholic or a drug addict, he is less likely to be violent if he also has schizophrenia. So, in this context, you could say schizophrenia is actually protective" (quoted in Cassels, C. [2009] August 31). For more information, see also the article entitled "Substance abuse main driver of violence in Schizophrenia, psychoses" *Medscape Medical News* (retrieved from www.medscape.com, September 10, 2009).

Even utilizing such empirical data, one must be aware that it is more likely than not that a given mentally ill individual will not be dangerous (Grisso & Appelbaum, 1992; Melton, Petrila, Poythress, & Slobogin, 2007; Mericle & Havassy, 2008), that 90% of the mentally ill are not dangerous to themselves or others at any time (Monahan, 1992; Steadman & Robbins, 1998), and that dangerous patients rarely remain dangerous for more than three days (Beck & Bonnar, 1988; McNeil & Binder, 1987).

As difficult as dangerousness is to predict, it will continue to be a substantial factor in involuntary commitment cases. Courts have nearly always ruled that mentally ill individuals must be dangerous if they are to be deprived of liberty.

Unless required to state a conclusion regarding perceived dangerousness, experts should limit themselves to statements regarding factors that enhance or reduce the probability of violence (Melton, Petrila, Poythress, & Slobogin, 2007). Rapid Reference 6.2 outlines factors that make violence relatively likely.

> # DON'T FORGET
>
> Few mentally ill individuals are dangerous. If you believe that the person you are evaluating is, indicate the nature of the danger and the reason(s) for your belief.

DUTY TO WARN OR PROTECT

The duty to warn or protect, also known as the Tarasoff duty, has been interpreted by many courts and mental health professionals as an indication that the professional must not discharge patients who seem dangerous to themselves or others, even if maximum hospital benefit has been achieved. Many professionals believe they are less likely to be sued for holding a nondangerous patient than for releasing a potentially dangerous one. Accordingly, involuntary commitment sometimes functions as a means of avoiding potential tort liability rather than as the therapeutic process it is meant to be. Even if the professional does not believe the individual is mentally ill, he or she may be held for a hearing so that it is the judge, not the mental health professional, who has the responsibility for any dangerous behavior after discharge. Furthermore, patients who are both mentally ill and dangerous who get committed may be held longer than necessary in an attempt by the hospital staff to ensure that they avoid potential liability for negligent release (La Fond, 1994).

THE ROLE OF COERCION

Although involuntary commitment is obviously coercive, most aspects of hospitalization are usually considered benign or even helpful. Both hospitalization and the defense attorney may, however, prove to be coercive.

> # CAUTION
>
> Court-appointed evaluators are generally given quasi-judicial immunity; that is, they are immune from being sued on the basis of a decision or recommendation they make as part of a forensic case. Your ethical obligation is to make decisions and recommendations based on your evaluation, whether consistent with or different from those of hospital staff. Quasi-judicial immunity gives you freedom to do so. Find out how your state handles quasi-judicial immunity for evaluators in commitment cases.

≡ Rapid Reference 6.2

The factors that make violence relatively likely (other than the first three, not necessarily in order of importance) are:

1 A history of violence—the single most predictive factor (Borum, Swartz, & Swanson, 1996; chf46edit@comcast.net; Harris & Rice, 1997; Melton, Petrila, Poythress, & Slobogin, 2007; Monahan, 1992; Monahan & Steadman, 1994; Monahan et al., 2001; Mossman, 1994; Mulvey, 1994; Simon, 1992; Steadman & Torrey, 1994; Wrightsman, Nietzel, & Fortune, 1998).

2 Substance abuse—the second most predictive factor (Borum, Swartz, & Swanson, 1996; Elbogen & Johnson, 2009; Fulwiler, Grossman, Forbes, & Ruthazer, 1997; Harris & Rice, 1997; Marzuk, 1996; Melton, Petrila, Poythress, & Slobogin, 2007; Mericle & Havassy, 2008; Monahan & Steadman, 1994; Monahan et al, 2001; Mulvey, 1994; Simon, 1992; Steadman & Robbins, 1998; Steadman et al., 1998; Tardiff, Marzuk, Leon, Portera, & Weiner, 1997; Torrey, 1994).

3 Diagnosis of Antisocial Personality Disorder (psychopathy) (Borum, Swartz, & Swanson, 1996; Harris & Rice, 1997; Melton, Petrila, Poythress, & Slobogin, 2007; Monahan et al., 2001; Tardiff, Marzuk, Leon, Portera, & Weiner, 1997).

4 Active psychotic process (active hallucinations, especially command hallucinations; prominent delusions, especially regarding being threatened)—not a chronic psychosis nor a history of psychosis (Borum, Swartz, & Swanson, 1996; Harris & Rice, 1997; Marzuk, 1996; Melton, Petrila, Poythress, & Slobogin, 2007; Monahan, 1992; Monahan et al., 2001; Mulvey, 1994; Torrey, 1994).

5 Young age (under 30 or so) (Borum, Swartz, & Swanson, 1996; Melton, Petrila, Poythress, & Slobogin, 2007; Monahan, 1992; Monahan & Steadman, 1994; Monahan et al., 2001; Simon, 1992).

6 Family factors (Monahan et al., 2001).

7 Personality factors (Monahan et al., 2001).

8 Danger to self (suicidal ideation, gravely disabled, etc.) (Monahan et al., 2001).

9 History of legal violations (Monahan et al., 2001).

10 Post-discharge, the quality of aftercare arrangements and the degree of compliance with treatment, especially psychotropic medication (Monahan & Steadman, 1994; Torrey, 1994).

The patient who has an urgent wish to get out of the hospital, or the one who just wants to please, may accept encouragement to become a "voluntary" patient. Such patients may also be open to bribery (e.g., an open ward rather than a closed one if "voluntarily" hospitalized). A patient may agree to almost anything he or she believes the staff wants, rather than carefully considering available choices. This is particularly true if the explanation the patient receives is too long, complex, or technical (Hiday, 1992; Mayers, 1994). Research on coercion in treatment by the MacArthur Network for Mental Health and the Law indicates that treatment was harmed when the patient viewed it as coercive, but helped when the patient viewed it as noncoercive. Factors that patients saw as coercive included threats or use of force, and the use of deception. Factors that patients saw as indications of noncoercion included the degree to which people in the treatment system appeared to act out of concern for the patient, whether the patient felt respected by the treatment provider, whether the patient felt he or she was permitted to state opinions and beliefs regarding the proposed treatment, whether the patient's statements were seriously considered, and the patient's perception of fairness in the treatment process. Stanhope, Marcus, and Solomon (2009) found that patients who reported good relationships with their case managers did not feel coerced, while those who reported poor relationships with case managers did feel coerced. Winnick (1997) concludes that coercive means should be minimal, as they are antitherapeutic. Noncoercive means, particularly persuasion and involving patients in the decision-making process, facilitate treatment and should always be emphasized (Kallert, 2008; Mulvey & Monahan, 1998; Simon & Shuman, 2007; Winnick, 1997).

Monahan et al. (2005; see also Monahan [2008]) assessed the use of several types of leverage, with more than 1,000 outpatients evenly divided among five states. The types of leverage assessed included money, housing, criminal justice, and outpatient commitments. They found that between 44 and 59% of the patients in the five sites experienced at least one type of leverage. Leverage was most frequently used with younger patients, patients with the worst psychopathology, patients with repeated hospital admissions, and patients most heavily using intensive outpatient services. Money (usually in the form of requiring representative payees) was used for 7 to 19%; outpatient commitment was used for 12 to 20%; threats of criminal sanctions were used for 15 to 30%; and housing assistance was used for 23 to 40%. Substance abuse increased the likelihood that at least one type of leverage would be used. The authors indicate that sites in different states tended to differ in which forms of leverage were used. While outpatient commitment has received the most publicity and discussion, it was the least frequent form of leverage used in these five sites, the authors indicate. They suggest that attention be paid to all forms of leverage when discussing the facilitation of treatment compliance.

Bonnie and Monahan (2005) suggest changing the dialogue regarding coercion by dealing with issues of contracting rather than force. They argue that most mentally ill individuals are competent to make decisions

> **CAUTION**
>
> If it appears that the individual you are evaluating is responding to perceived coercion, try to get the person to discuss what he or she would do if the coercion did not exist. Coerced decisions to take medication, utilize aftercare, and so forth are usually not stable decisions.

regarding what services to accept, including what sorts of leverage to accept as a trade-off for receiving those services. Patients should, they indicate, be permitted to make choices regarding forms of treatment in return for access to money and services that they wish to obtain, or to avoid consequences (criminal sanctions) they wish to avoid. They stop short of advocating that this be a general policy, calling instead for research on such contracting regarding its appropriateness.

ACCURACY OF HOSPITAL STAFF AND RECORDS

Hospital staff are trained to view patients as suffering from illnesses that can be treated and (it is hoped) cured (or at least significantly improved). Most view medication and hospitalization as central to this process when the individual is psychotic, whether acutely or chronically. Consciously or unconsciously, diagnoses, chart notes, and staff discussions may be skewed in this direction. Further, if the physician is reticent to release a given patient, either because of a belief that more care is needed or because of concern about potential dangerousness, the patient may be held for a court hearing (Preparation and Trial, 1981). The independent evaluator must not get caught up in this process. Opinions should take staff statements and notes into consideration, understanding that they may be biased in favor of hospitalization.

EVALUATING THE CANDIDATE FOR COMMITMENT

The validity of the information from the client depends on a number of factors, including the degree to which he or she is in touch with reality, his or her honesty, and how much attention he or she has paid to the process of hospitalization. The information received should be contrasted with information from the hospital chart and other records.

Personal Interview

The *Ethical Principles of Psychologists and Code of Conduct* (2002), the *Specialty Guidelines for Forensic Psychologists* (APA, 1991), and the *Guidelines of the American Academy of Psychiatry and Law* require that the expert conduct a personal examination of the patient. Many states require a personal examination as well (Parry, 1998). The Americans with Disabilities Act requires that threat assessment "may not be based on generalizations or stereotypes about the effects of a particular disability," but that it must be based upon "individualized assessment, based on reasonable judgment that relies on current medical evidence or on the best available objective evidence" (Stefan, 2001, p. 129).

Review of Records

Prior to interviewing the client the evaluator should be familiar with allegations in police reports, a commitment petition, or other documents (including the medical chart) associated with the commitment process. Compare the story obtained from the client with the statements in hospital records and other documents, and evaluate the meaning of any discrepancies between the client's statements and other data sources (Mental Health Division, 1996).

Medication

Note what medication the individual is on at the time of the interview. If the patient appears depressed or drowsy, is it likely that the condition is caused by excess medication? Is the medication prescribed consistent with the tentative diagnosis? If the patient is refusing medication, is it for a logical reason (e.g., past experience with the medication's side-effects) or not (e.g., a belief that the medication contains poison).

The Patient Interview

The interview is critical to the evaluation process. Determine the following:

- What is the patient's understanding of why he/she was brought to the hospital?
- What is the patient's explanation of the allegations in the police detention report or the petition for commitment? Does the patient's explanation make sense, or does it appear to be the product of a psychotic process?
- If allegedly suicidal, does the patient confirm suicidal thinking? Was there a plan? What was the lethality of the plan? How suicidal is the

patient now? Is there a history of suicide attempts? Does the patient communicate hopelessness?

- Can you corroborate allegations in the court papers and/or medical chart regarding thought processes, mood, difficulty taking care of him/herself?
- If medication is being taken, are there any significant problems with the medication?
- If medication is being refused, does the patient have a cogent reason for refusing?
- In addition, a complete mental status examination should be done. A form, following (Kane Involuntary Civil Commitment Inventory worksheet), may be adapted to fit the criteria for commitment in the evaluator's jurisdiction.

Psychological Testing

The questions addressed in an involuntary civil commitment evaluation rarely require psychological testing, with the possible exception of intelligence tests for patients with developmental disabilities. If there is a significant possibility of an organic basis for psychopathology, a neuropsychological screening may be appropriate. Psychological tests are rarely used in commitment evaluations (Parry, 1998).

Need for Privacy

Interviews should be conducted in a reasonably private and quiet setting. If private rooms are not available, meet in the area of the ward with the most privacy and quiet. If the setting for the interview appears to have had an adverse affect on the patient, note that in your report.

Communication

Most people who are mentally ill can communicate quite adequately. The largest obstacle is likely to be the fact that most people who become candidates for involuntary commitment are lower or lower middle class and are not well educated (Hiday, 1988). It is therefore necessary for the evaluator to proceed slowly, explaining each step fully, in simple language. Do not become condescending or parental (Preparation and Trial, 1981).

Like any individual, the allegedly mentally ill person may say he or she understands what has been said when that is untrue, to try to give a good impression. It may therefore be essential that the evaluator ask the client to repeat important points in his or her own words.

When the Client's Words and Behavior Are Inconsistent

Some patients will say that they want to fight being committed, but their behavior will indicate otherwise. For example, assume that a patient has been advised that commitment is less likely if he or she behaves well, cooperates with staff, avoids confrontations, and so forth. The patient proceeds to pick fights with other patients, argues with staff, and tries to escape from the unit. The patient is told that this behavior makes commitment more likely. The patient's behavior does not change. Like the cliché that "actions speak louder than words," the patient is likely to be indicating that he or she does not wish to fight the commitment.

Suicidal Patients

Suicidal patients must be given special attention. Most persons who are acutely or imminently suicidal (ready to make an attempt) are in that most dangerous state of mind for only a matter of hours or, at most, days. Suicide is rarely a first choice for an individual; rather, it is perceived as the only choice at the time. Once the person sees that there are other options, there is normally a marked reduction in suicidality. It is common for patients admitted to the hospital after a suicide gesture or attempt to be on "suicide watch" for only a few days, and to have few remaining suicidal thoughts within a week or two. The evaluator needs to assess what alternatives the patient now sees and how he or she will pursue those alternatives. Expressions of hopelessness should be minimal or absent, given the strong correlation between hopelessness and suicide attempts.

Staff Interviews

The evaluator needs to decide whether staff interviews are necessary. If there is a great deal of information in the chart, interviews may be superfluous.

Least-Restrictive Alternative

It is essential for the evaluator to consider what community-based treatment and other resources may be available as alternatives to hospitalization. The evaluator should be familiar with community-based resources. If not adequately familiar, information may be available through the local public defender's office or mental health association. The ward social worker may also be of assistance. The evaluator should be able to specify both the level of treatment needed by the patient and, ideally, a specific example of an appropriate facility. If possible, indicate what services may be important to the patient's community adjustment; for example, a community support program, visiting nurse, and/or a membership or drop-in program for chronic mental patients.

THE RECORDS

Review of the patient's records provides necessary data regarding the patient's adjustment to the hospital and other factors. In most cases, the current medical chart will contain all the information necessary for a commitment evaluation to be completed.

The chart will give information regarding the staff's understanding of the reasons for detention, the results of psychiatric and/or psychological evaluations, treatment history, abnormalities found on the medical examination, the nature of the treatment plan (which should be concrete, objective, measurable, and feasible), results of lab tests, and medication orders. Some of the most important information will come from progress notes, which should be added each shift and which give an ongoing record of the client's behavior and progress. There should be a correlation between information in the progress notes and any changes in medication. Appropriate reasons for changes include the patient becoming more psychotic, suicidal, violent, or withdrawn, or showing evidence of medication-related side effects.

Although hospital staff are generally conscientious regarding entries in the chart, it must be kept in mind that errors can be made. A staff member may have misheard a patient, or the staff member who makes an entry in the chart may be reporting what he or she heard from another staff member (which may or may not be accurate). Staff also have a habit of writing things like "patient was delusional," or that "he appeared to be internally preoccupied" as evidence of hallucinations. Both are meaningless statements, since their accuracy cannot be determined by the evaluator.

THE PRELIMINARY HEARING

Sometimes called a probable cause hearing, this is the patient's initial chance to challenge the allegations of mental illness and dangerousness in a court or administrative hearing. If probable cause is found, the patient will be held for a final hearing. The evaluation discussed in this chapter normally occurs after probable cause is found but before a final hearing.

JURY TRIALS

While most hearings are conducted before a judge or court commissioner, most states have provision for a jury trial when requested by the patient or his or her attorney. If the evaluator must testify at that hearing, it is important to remember to address many answers, especially those involving relatively long explanations, to the jury rather than to the attorney asking the question.

THE INDEPENDENT EXPERT

Conceptually, the independent expert has little or no conflict of interest, unlike the hospital staff whose jobs may depend on keeping beds occupied. If the independent expert is court-appointed and paid, rather than retained by the defense attorney, the case for true independence (and credibility) is furthered. Many states permit the defense to request that a specific psychologist or psychiatrist be appointed, at court expense.

The amount of time spent by the expert will be contingent in part on the custom in the jurisdiction, in part on the nature of the case, in part on the length of the report expected, and in part on the amount paid to the expert for the evaluation. An expert should not put in less time than is considered the norm in the jurisdiction. The "nature of the case" includes how usual or unusual the particular patient and situation are, whether the expert needs to interview anyone other than the patient and selected staff, and whether any other investigation must be done. In some jurisdictions, written reports are rather brief; in others, quite substantial. The expert should follow the norm.

Finally, there is a wide range of payments made to court-appointed experts. If the rate paid is well below usual and customary rates for psychotherapy and forensic services, the expert cannot be expected to review old charts, conduct extensive interviews, and so forth, for that token payment. On average, the present author has spent a little over an hour for each of his 3,000-plus evaluations, excluding travel, writing time, and consultation with the attorney. That typically includes 30 to 45 minutes with the chart, 0 to 5 minutes with staff, and 15 to 40 minutes with the patient. Those times meet or exceed the norm for this jurisdiction.

CLINICAL INTERVIEW BY EXPERT

The expert needs to be aware that he or she is seeing the patient under difficult circumstances, particularly if it is a first admission. The person is therefore relatively likely to feel and act disturbed, and may be suspicious of the expert's impartiality. For the assessment to be valid, the expert needs to consider these factors (Melton, Petrila, Poythress, & Slobogin, 2007).

Some jurisdictions have standard forms or formats that are to be used by experts who conduct commitment evaluations. Others permit the expert to use a narrative format, describing in a few paragraphs the content of the evaluation. The Kane Involuntary Civil Commitment Inventory form, shown on the following pages, was devised by the present author in order to ensure that all relevant questions are answered. Comments on the nature and purpose of various items are in brackets. Readers are invited to adapt this form to reflect the statutory requirements in their respective state. Wisconsin statutes will be used as a representative example.

TREATMENT VERSUS CARE AND CUSTODY

Many state statutes distinguish between "treatment" and "care and custody." Involuntary civil commitment requires that the individual be treatable, while an individual who is not treatable may be considered for a guardianship and protective placement. A state appellate court differentiated between the terms by discussing "rehabilitation" versus "habilitation": "Habilitation means the maximizing of an individual's functioning and the maintenance of the individual at that maximum level. Rehabilitation means returning an individual to a previous level of functioning which had decreased because of an acute disorder" (*In re: Athans*, 1982, p. 334).

Most states similarly require evidence of treatability for involuntary commitment, and that appropriate treatment can be obtained at the facility at which the patient will be held (Stromberg et al., 1988). The evaluator needs to be aware of how one's state addresses "treatability/rehabilitation" versus "habilitation/care and custody." If a patient is held under a treatability standard but has organic brain damage or is otherwise not rehabilitatable, the wrong standard is being applied.

CAUTION

If the individual is not treatable, involuntary civil commitment is not the proper mechanism for institutionalizing the individual in most states. Find out what your state requirement is.

Kane Involuntary Civil Commitment Inventory

Date of examination: _____   Time spent with subject: _____

Date of birth: _____   Date of admission: _____

Place of examination: _____

Ethnicity: Cauc. Af.Am. Hisp. Am.Indian Asian Other: _____

Preliminary Questions

["Prior to the examination the subject individual shall be informed that his or her statements can be used as a basis for commitment and that he or she has the right to remain silent, and that the examiner is required to make a report to the court even if the subject individual remains silent." Wis. Stat. §51.20(9)(a).]

(1) Did you inform the subject as to the nature of and reason for the examination, that it was ordered by the Court, and that your findings would be made available to the Court?   **YES NO**

(2) Did you inform the subject that any information volunteered could form part of the basis for his/her involuntary commitment, and that, therefore, he/she had a right to remain silent?   **YES NO**

(3) Did the subject appear to understand your instructions?   **YES NO**

(4) Is the subject presently under medication, and, if so, what is the medication and dosage?   **YES NO**

_____

(5) In your opinion, does the medication affect the subject's ability to understand these instructions, and, if yes, how?   **YES NO**

_____

Mental Status Examination

(6) Description of the subject's interview status (circle or write in):

   (a) The subject's reaction to the interview: _____

   (b) General appearance: **GOOD FAIR POOR**

   (c) Motor behavior: Appropriate or: _____

   (d) Facial expressions, voice, and speech: Appropriate and/or: _____

   (e) Affect and mood: Appropriate or: _____

(7) Description of the subject's thought content and thought processes:

(a) Suicidal ideation:	**Evident**	**Not evident**
(b) Depressive or manic trends:	**Evident**	**Not evident**
(c) Hallucinations:	**Evident**	**Not evident**
(d) Delusions:	**Evident**	**Not evident**
(e) Grandiosity:	**Evident**	**Not evident**
(f) Persecutory trends:	**Evident**	**Not evident**
(g) Conceptual disorganization:		
Tangentiality:	**Evident**	**Not evident**
Loose associations:	**Evident**	**Not evident**
Flight of ideas:	**Evident**	**Not evident**

[The questions in #7 largely define whether the individual is a proper subject for commitment. If all answers are "not evident," the person is not likely to meet the statutory criteria for involuntary commitment. See #10 for those criteria.]

(h) Organic signs:	**Evident**	**Not evident**

[If organic signs are evident, the individual may not be a proper subject for treatment (versus care and custody), and would therefore not fall under an involuntary commitment statute, which is for treatable mental illnesses.]

    1. Orientation: **Oriented** or **Not oriented to:**

        Time   Place   Person   Situation

    2. Memory: Reflex:
                 Recent:
                 Remote:

    3. Cognition: [Administration of selected items from the Wechsler Adult Intelligence Scale-III or IV (WAIS-III/IV)—IF there is a question re: organicity.]

(i) Insight:	**GOOD**	**FAIR**	**POOR**
(j) Judgment:	**GOOD**	**FAIR**	**POOR**

Subject's Statements to the Examiner

(8) Summary of incidents leading to detention and pertaining to past history and present events:

[A full page is allotted for writing down significant statements made to the examiner, preferably verbatim. Of particular interest are statements that suggest psychosis or suicidality (e.g., admission of hallucinations, statements of delusions, or a stated wish to hurt oneself or die).]

(9) Based solely on your examination, can you render an opinion to a reasonable degree of psychological certainty as to the mental condition of the subject: **YES NO**

[If the answer is "no," the examiner is obviously not in a position to testify regarding commitment. The most common reason for saying "no" is if the subject with not speak with the examiner. Psychologists are ethically prohibited from having opinions "to a reasonable degree of psychological/scientific certainty" if they cannot interview an individual (*Ethical Principles of Psychologists and Code of Conduct* (APA, 2002), Standards 9.01, 9.06; *Specialty Guidelines for Forensic Psychologists* (Committee on Ethical Guidelines for Forensic Psychologists, 1991) Guideline VI(H). Similarly, the *Principles of Medical Ethics with Annotations Especially Applicable to Psychiatry* (2008) indicates that "The psychiatrist may permit his or her certification to be used for the involuntary treatment of any person only following his or her personal examination of that person." (Section 7(4).)]

(10) If yes:

(a) The subject   **IS   IS NOT**   acutely psychotic;

[If not acutely psychotic or suicidal, the individual is not likely to be a proper subject for treatment, and, therefore, not a proper subject for involuntary commitment, which requires treatability.]

(b) The subject **IS   IS NOT**   acutely suicidal;

(c) The subject **IS   IS NOT**   developmentally disabled;

(d) The subject **IS   IS NOT**   capable of benefiting from treatment (as defined by statute) if he/she were to participate in such treatment;

[If not capable of benefiting from treatment, the subject is not appropriate for involuntary commitment; he or she may, however, be appropriate for guardianship and protective placement, i.e., care and custody.]

(e) The subject **CAN   CANNOT**   function adequately outside of a hospital setting, even with community support (e.g., counseling/psychotherapy, homemaker services, a group home of halfway house, or a Day Hospital program);

[That is, what is the least-restrictive environment appropriate to the needs of the individual?]

   (f) The subject's disorder **IS IS NOT** so extensive that he/she requires care and treatment for his or her own welfare, or the welfare of others, or of the community;

[This is the first of two definitions of "mental illness" in this statute (Wis. Stat. §51.01(13)(a). This one is *not* for purposes of involuntary commitment. The next section, Wis. Stat. §51.01(13(b) states that "'Mental illness' for purposes of involuntary commitment means a substantial disorder of thought, mood, perception, orientation, or memory which grossly impairs judgment, behavior, capacity to recognize reality, or ability to meet the ordinary demands of life."]

   (g) The subject **DOES DOES NOT** have a SUBSTANTIAL disorder of thought, mood, perception, orientation, or memory;

   (h) If he/she DOES have a substantial disorder, this disorder **DOES DOES NOT** GROSSLY impair judgment, behavior, capacity to recognize reality, or ability to meet the ordinary demands of life.

[By addressing the two requirements of the statute separately, it is clear whether the subject fails either part of the test for "mental illness for purposes of involuntary commitment."]

(11) Did you consult the patient chart or other records: **YES NO**

If yes, did that collateral information **SUPPORT** or **CONFLICT WITH** your opinion, and how: _____

(12) What is your opinion regarding the dangerousness of the subject:
   (a) No risk _____
   (b) Mild risk _____
   (c) Moderate risk _____
   (d) Substantial risk _____

[Knowing from research that professionals tend to overestimate dangerousness, four choices are offered. Only the fourth meets the statutory requirement for "[a] substantial probability of physical harm to himself or herself" (Wis. Stat. §51.15(a)(1) or "[a] substantial probability of physical harm to other persons" (Wis. Stat. §51.15(a)(2) or "[a] substantial probability of physical impairment or injury to himself or herself due to impaired judgment" (Wis. Stat. §51.15(a)(3). There is also a "gravely disabled" section (Wis. Stat. §51.15(a)(4). These four choices are consistent with the recommendation of Melton et al. (2007) that clinicians state their conclusions in terms of relative risk.]

(13) The above opinion is supported by the **PRESENCE ABSENCE** of significant evidence of dangerous behavior on the ward (specify): _____

(14) Did the subject express any interest in any form of mental health treatment or social services:

YES NO

If YES: Inpatient hospitalization / Medication / Group home / Outpatient counseling Job counseling / Case manager / Other, or specifics:
_____

(15) In your opinion, the subject **IS IS NOT** capable of *expressing or applying* an understanding of the advantages and disadvantages of accepting treatment and the alternatives to accepting the particular treatment offered, after the advantages, disadvantages, and alternatives have been explained to him/her.

[This is the definition of "competence to refuse medication" found in Wis. Stat. §51.61(1)(g)(4). "Expressing" would typically be in the form of paraphrasing what he or she has been told. "Applying" refers to the individual being able to indicate that he or she does have a mental illness, if that is the case. Because many patients who refuse medication have hearings regarding their competence to refuse, it is efficacious to explore this area during the commitment evaluation.]

(16) What would you recommend as an OPTIMAL treatment program for the subject at this time:
Inpatient hospitalization / Medication / Group home / Outpatient counseling / Job counseling / Case manager / Other, or specifics:
_____

(17) Additional comments:

(a) Re: hospital chart or discussion with staff: _____

(b) Re: interview of subject: _____

[These two open-ended questions provide a place to add anything important that has not been covered in another part of the form.]

I, the undersigned examiner, certify that I HAVE / HAVE NOT, by personal examination and inquiry, satisfied myself as to the mental condition of _____, the subject of this proceeding, and that the results of said evaluation are contained in my answers to the foregoing questions, which answers are true to a reasonable degree of psychological certainty, and, if called upon to do so, I would so testify under oath.

Andrew W. Kane, PhD, ABAP

Licensed Psychologist

Board-Certified Assessment Psychologist

Professor, Wisconsin School of Professional Psychology

Adjunct Clinical Professor, Department of Psychology, University of Wisconsin-Milwaukee

Associate Clinical Professor, Department of Psychiatry and Behavioral Medicine, Medical College of Wisconsin

2815 North Summit Avenue, Milwaukee, WI 53211-3439

PRIVILEGE AGAINST SELF-INCRIMINATION

Although candidates for involuntary civil commitment in some states have a privilege against self-incrimination, this is not true in many other states. Most courts have found that the right to assert the privilege against self-incrimination is not applicable in involuntary civil commitment proceedings. Following the lead of *French v. Blackburn* (1977), courts have generally held that, because clinical interviews are essential to the process of determining an individual's mental status, it would thwart the entire process—and require release of potentially dangerous persons who remained silent—to permit patients to assert the privilege (Melton, Petrila, Poythress, & Slobogin, 2007; Perlin, 1989, Vol. 1; Perlin, Champine, Dlugacz, & Connell, 2008).

> **DON'T FORGET**
>
> If your state offers the candidate for commitment the right to remain silent, do not assume that silence means that the individual is hiding something or must be psychotic. The exercising of one's rights must not be used against the individual.

PSYCHOTROPIC MEDICATION AND ITS SIDE EFFECTS

While psychotropic medications have made it possible for many patients to be discharged from hospitals into the community, these same drugs often have major negative side effects, including dry mouth, difficulty eliminating, drowsiness, blurred vision, and various involuntary movement disorders (e.g., muscle spasms, grimacing, tongue movements, Parkinson-like movements). They have often been found to be employed both for treatment and as chemical straitjackets, either to make the patients easier for staff to control or for punishment (Melton, Petrila, Poythress, & Slobogin, 2007; Simon, 1992). A patient who is aware of these problems, especially from personal experience, may have a legitimate reason for refusal.

OUTPATIENT COMMITMENT

In accord with the movement toward treatment in the least restrictive setting appropriate to the needs of the individual, all states allow some form of outpatient commitment (Swartz et al., 1997). Involuntary outpatient commitment may take any of three forms: (1) conditional release from an inpatient facility; (2) commitment to an outpatient program as a less-restrictive alternative; or (3) commitment to outpatient treatment on the basis of less-strict criteria than for inpatient commitment. The typical statute applies to individuals who need treatment in order to prevent "disability or deterioration" that is likely to result in the individual becoming dangerous to self or others and who can function safely in the community when medicated, but who are adjudicated to be incompetent to refuse medication (Perlin, 1993, cumulative supplement). There is some concern, however, that outpatient commitments will be used to maintain control over individuals who do not meet the statutory requirements for an inpatient civil commitment (Perlin, 1989, Vol. 1).

Research on the effectiveness of outpatient commitment is mixed. Burgess, Bindman, Leese, Henderson, and Szmukler (2006) found that "community treatment orders used on discharge from a first admission to hospital were associated with a higher risk of readmission, but CTOs following subsequent admissions were associated with lower readmission risk" (p. 574). Frank, Perry, Kean, Sigman, and Geagea (2005) found that mandated community treatment was associated with a decrease in time the patients in their study were hospitalized. Zanni and Stavis (2007) found that patients who had an outpatient commitment were likely to have fewer hospitalizations, decreased stays, fewer episodes and less time in seclusion, and fewer episodes and hours in restraints. Swartz and Swanson (2004) found that outpatient commitment is primarily effective if patients are under commitment for at least six months. Petrila, Ridgely, and Borum (2003) report that methodological errors limit conclusions from all but two studies, one in New York and one in North Carolina. Neither study provides definitive evidence in the effectiveness of outpatient commitments, but both suggest that it may be effective under some circumstances—particularly if over six months, and if substantial community-based resources are available to the committed outpatients. Kisely, Campbell, and Preston (2005) wrote, in an article in the prestigious Cochrane Database of Systematic Reviews, that there is minimal evidence that compulsory treatment in the community has a significant positive effect on use of health services, costs, social functioning, mental status, life quality, or satisfaction with the receipt of care. Kisely, Campbell, Scott, Preston, and Xiao (2007) reviewed eight papers covering five studies. They concluded that "the evidence for involuntary out-patient treatment in reducing either admissions or bed-days is very limited. It therefore cannot be seen as a less restrictive alternative to admission" (p. 3). Finally, there is substantial evidence that the success of outpatient treatment, with or without commitment, is highly dependent on the quality and quantity of outpatient services available to people needing those services. Without a major commitment to a comprehensive range of mental health services, neither outpatient commitment nor outpatient treatment in general can be successful (Harvard Mental Health Letter, 2008; Swartz, 2007).

SEXUAL OFFENDER COMMITMENTS

According to Zander (2005), states began to pass laws for the involuntary civil commitment of sexual offenders in the late 1930s, and by 1960 the majority of states had civil commitment statutes for "sexual psychopaths" or "sexual deviates." Many of these laws were repealed in the 1970s, however, in the face of evidence that treatment was not effective, the inability of psychiatrists to diagnose sexual psychopathology, and public opinion favoring punishment over treatment. In the 1990s, however, many states began adopting legislation to address offenders who had completed prison terms and were therefore to be released, or who had completed treatment related to an insanity commitment and were to be released. As of 2005, there were 17 states that had adopted "sexual predator" or "sexually violent person" (or a similar title) laws. Discussion of these laws and practices are beyond the scope of this chapter.

CAUTION

The information in this chapter is, of necessity, generic rather than specific to your state. Psychologists are ethically required to become familiar with the applicable statutes prior to undertaking highly technical tasks such as involuntary civil commitment evaluations. Copies of the relevant statutes may generally be obtained from courts, from attorneys, from libraries, and on the Internet. It is also strongly recommended that the psychologist consult with a knowledgeable colleague and/or attorney familiar with this type of case.

 TEST YOURSELF

1. **In what ways may hospitalization be dangerous for an individual?**
   - (a) Increases risk of institutionalizing people
   - (b) Makes people dependent on the hospital
   - (c) Makes people less capable of functioning outside the hospital
   - (d) Reduces people's ability to make independent decisions
   - (e) Makes future hospitalizations significantly more likely
   - (f) All of the above

2. **Which of the following is not a specific indication for inpatient hospitalization?**
   - (a) Thoughts or behaviors that pose a threat to self or others
   - (b) The failure of outpatient treatment, with the expectation that inpatient treatment will reverse the process

(c) A psychiatric condition for which diagnostic evaluation, treatment, or both should be initiated in an inpatient setting

(d) The patient disagrees with the psychiatrist about which medication the patient should take

(e) Removal from the patient's environment is seen as essential to reversing the illness process

(f) Withdrawal from alcohol or other drugs

(g) Physical illness complicated by psychiatric symptomatology that makes treatment untenable on a medical unit

3. Which of the following is not a type of involuntary civil commitment?

(a) Informal commitment

(b) Voluntary commitment

(c) Third-party commitment

(d) Least-restrictive commitment

(e) Extended commitment

(f) Outpatient commitment

4. How is "mental illness" defined by nearly all involuntary civil commitment statutes?

(a) A significant, severe, substantial, or gross impairment

(b) Any diagnosis in DSM-IV

(c) Any diagnosis in ICD-9-CM

(d) Danger to self or others

5. What factor other than mental illness is required in nearly every state to be present if an individual is to be involuntarily committed?

(a) Suicidal ideation

(b) Incompetence

(c) Dangerousness to self or others

(d) Possession of a knife or gun

6. The "least-restrictive alternative" is

(a) the setting that offers the greatest freedom while still being appropriate to the needs of the individual, based in part on the wishes of the person or, if necessary, his or her best interests.

(b) any setting in the community.

(c) a ward without a locked door.

(d) the setting that makes it least likely that the individual will become a candidate for involuntary civil commitment again.

7. What factors permit clinicians to predict violence with a reasonable degree of certainty?

(a) A history of violence

(b) Substance abuse

(continued)

(c) Active psychotic process

(d) Young age (under about 30)

(e) Diagnosis of Antisocial Personality Disorder

(f) Post-discharge, the quality of aftercare arrangements, and the degree of compliance with treatment

(g) All of the above

8. Quasi-judicial immunity means that court-appointed experts

(a) are equivalent to judges.

(b) are generally immune from being sued on the basis of a decision or recommendation they make.

(c) cannot be convicted of a crime.

(d) cannot be involuntarily committed.

9. Which of the following is not a common form of coercion in hospitalizations?

(a) Bribery (e.g., open vs. closed ward)

(b) The patient doing what he or she believes the staff wants done

(c) Force or the threat of force

(d) Use of deception

(e) Arresting the individual

Answers: 1. f; 2. d; 3. d; 4. a; 5. c; 6. a; 7. g; 8. b; 9. e

Seven

ESSENTIALS OF JUVENILE ASSESSMENT

Sheryl Dolezal and Marc J. Ackerman

SETTING THE CONTEXT OF THE JUVENILE JUSTICE SYSTEM

The juvenile justice system has been around for a little over 100 years—the first juvenile code was developed in 1899. Prior to that time, a juvenile's actions were addressed within the general scope of criminal law. At about the turn of the twentieth century, the juvenile court system was developed. In the juvenile court, as opposed to the criminal court, the court acted on behalf of the juvenile and provided treatment in order to assist them in overcoming the behaviors that brought them to the court in the first place. Therefore, the overriding philosophy was rehabilitation rather than punishment, the belief being that the juveniles were developmentally immature and not fully accountable for their behavior. Juvenile proceedings were not adversarial and the court did not have a need for protection of due process. Aside from the judge, the key players within the juvenile court system were mental health professionals and probation officers.

This philosophy continued for a number of years and then two United States Supreme Court cases, *Kent v. United States* (1966) and *In re Gault* (1967), had a profound effect on the juvenile justice system. These cases recognized the constitutional rights of minors, including due process (e.g., the right to an attorney, notice of charges, and against self-incrimination). Proceedings have become more adversarial. There is conflict within the juvenile justice system between punishment for offenses committed and support for rehabilitation.

The perception of many is that juvenile crime is on the rise. In response to this perception, legislators in every state in the early 1990s amended their juvenile justice codes "to get tough" on juvenile crime. Despite this, rehabilitation continues to play an important role in the juvenile justice system, and intervention and treatment remain priorities. Therefore, clinicians must be familiar with the juvenile justice system to ensure that their evaluations are legally relevant and beneficial to the Court.

FORENSIC ASSESSMENT IN DELINQUENCY CASES

Examiners who perform evaluations should have familiarity with developmental psychology, theories of delinquency, adolescent psychopathology, risk assessment, forensic interviewing and assessment instruments, malingering, suggestibility, and standards of forensic practice. Moffitt (1993) identified two pathways of juvenile offending that remain in use today: *life course persistent* and *adolescence limited*:

Life Course Persistent
- Early onset—before age 13
- Behavior disorder diagnosis—Oppositional Defiant Disorder, Conduct Disorder, Attention Deficit/Hyperactivity Disorder
- Poor attachments
- Violence history—for their own gain, not reactive/emotional
- Lack of guilt
- Lack of empathy

Adolescence Limited
- Later onset—age 13 or older
- No behavior disorder diagnosis
- Adequate attachments
- Little violence history
- Lack of predatory violence
- Capable of guilt and empathy

The prevalence of mental disorders is high among youth involved with the juvenile justice system, affecting approximately 60–70% who are in detention facilities (Teplin, Abram, McClelland, Dulcan, & Mericle, 2002). Some of these juveniles experience problems with depression, suicidal ideation, aggressive behaviors, educational problems, physical, sexual, and emotional abuse, and substance abuse. Both behavioral and environmental factors need to be examined and addressed when assessing juveniles.

Cauffman and Steinberg (2000) also stressed the importance of addressing a juvenile's psychosocial maturity as it relates to decision making. They identified four developmental capacities of particular importance: responsibility, time perspective, interpersonal perspective, and temperance. Responsibility relates to the juvenile's ability to be self-reliant, independent, and also to the degree to which he is influenced by external pressures. Time perspective relates to the juvenile's ability to consider both long- and short-term consequences to his behavior. The interpersonal perspective assesses the juvenile's ability to understand the perspectives of others. Temperance addresses the juvenile's emotional and behavioral controls and his ability to control his impulses.

Juveniles need to be interviewed within a developmentally appropriate context, based on their age as well as emotional, cognitive, and verbal development. Abstract concepts may also need to be explained more clearly. More time is often needed to focus on rapport building and to allow for extended interviewing. It is also important to warn juveniles about the possible uses of self-incriminating information obtained through the evaluation process. Prior to being evaluated, the juvenile should be informed of the purpose, nature, and potential implications of the evaluation.

Based on the nature and purpose of the evaluation, both clinical and forensic tests are used to assess juveniles. Many of the forensic instruments available that are typically used to assess adults have not been standardized on juveniles.

Forensic juvenile assessments address the legal standard related to the referral and are used to assist the judge/trier of fact in resolving the ultimate legal question/ issue. Many experts are in disagreement as to whether or not clinicians should provide a direct answer to the ultimate issue. Melton, Petrila, Poythress, and Slobogin (2007) believe that clinicians should be discouraged from offering opinions or conclusions related to the ultimate legal issue. They suggest that clinicians provide relevant information related to the referral but that conclusions regarding the ultimate issue are the responsibility of the judge and/or jury. Despite this, clinicians are often encouraged, and at times required, to address ultimate legal issues.

Melton, Petrila, Poythress, and Slobogin (2007) suggest that several guidelines are applicable for forensic reports despite the context. They note that it is important to separate facts from inferences, to stay within the scope of the referral question, to avoid information overkill and underkill and to minimize clinical jargon. It is also important to formulate clear and concise conclusions and recommendations.

In summary, Steffen and Ackerman (1999, p. 169–170), note that when developing a framework for juvenile evaluations the following guidelines should be considered:

1. Understand the legal standard related to the referral (know your local statutes).
2. Determine psychological constructs from the legal standard.
3. Choose psychological tests, interview formats, collateral sources, and other techniques aimed at eliciting relevant information.
4. Inform the juvenile of the reasons for the evaluation and the limits of confidentiality.

5. Evaluate the juvenile based on the constructs.

6. Communicate the results so that they provide utility for the court.

DON'T FORGET

Forensic juvenile assessments should:

- Be specific to the individual
- Be based on the construct from the legal standard
- Utilize appropriate forensic and clinical assessment measures
- Include interviews of the juvenile and collateral resources
- Include appropriate review of all relevant records obtained
- Provide a rationale for the conclusions presented
- Provide information relevant to the ultimate legal question
- Provide clear and concise recommendations

COMPETENCY TO WAIVE *MIRANDA* RIGHTS

In *Miranda v. Arizona* (1966), the United States Supreme Court ruled that any confessions made by defendants and used against them in criminal proceedings must be preceded by warnings informing them of their constitutional rights. Confessions would be considered invalid if the police failed to inform individuals of their rights prior to eliciting a confession from them. The individual's rights include notification of the right to remain silent, the potential use of his statements in future court proceedings, the right to be represented by an attorney and have the attorney present during questioning, and to have an attorney appointed by the state if they could not afford one. Most police departments have *Miranda* rights printed on paper in various formats for the defendant to sign. Many jurisdictions also audiotape or videotape police interviews that can later be reviewed by examiners. The protections of *Miranda*, an adult case, were soon extended to juveniles by state courts in *Kent v. U.S.* (1966) and *In re Gault* (1967). These cases affirmed that these constitutional rights also applied to juveniles at all stages in delinquency proceedings. Statements made by the defendant are not admissible unless they waive their *Miranda* rights knowingly, intelligently, and voluntarily. *People v. Lara* (1967), *West v. U.S.* (1968), and *Fare v. Michael C.* (1979) ruled that adolescent status does not automatically invalidate a juvenile's waiver of *Miranda* rights, but recognized that adolescents are at greater risk than adults for deficits in intelligence and functioning relevant to their ability to waive their rights. Juveniles are also more suggestible than adults, which can lead to false confessions (Richardson, Gudjonsson, & Kelly, 1995).

The question to evaluate a juvenile's capacity to waive *Miranda* rights is usually raised by the defense attorney, but it may also come from the court itself. A referral for these evaluations are often received months after the juvenile has waived his rights and confessed. Therefore, the evaluation is retrospective in nature. Unfortunately, because the evaluation may take place months after the confession, the juvenile's performance and presentation at the time of the evaluation may not be indicative of what his cognitive and emotional state was at the time he waived his rights.

Waiver of *Miranda* Rights

Steffen and Ackerman (1999) suggest that examiners ask the following questions to assess the validity of the juvenile's waiver (p. 171):

- Was the juvenile aware of the consequences of the waiver? Did the juvenile understand that he or she was waiving his or her rights?
- Did the juvenile have the capacity to understand the choices, weigh the consequences, demonstrate a rational reasoning process, and make decisions in his best interest?
- Was the juvenile tricked, coerced, or subjected to any improper interrogation techniques? Is the juvenile highly suggestible? How does the juvenile respond to authority?
- What time was the juvenile apprehended? What time was he questioned? How long was the juvenile held? Was the juvenile tired, hungry, or ill? Were the parents or guardian present? Who read the *Miranda* rights, and how were they presented?
- What is the juvenile's intellectual ability? Are there personality characteristics that are relevant? What current stressors exist? What was the mental/emotional state of the juvenile at the time of questioning? Was the juvenile under the influence of alcohol or drugs? What were the expectations of the parents? What are the developmental characteristics of the juvenile? Is the juvenile malingering?

Framework of the *Miranda* Evaluation

The following factors should be addressed by the examiner when evaluating the juvenile.

Obtaining and Reviewing Records

The examiner should obtain any and all records available to them when performing *Miranda* waiver evaluations. Records should include current police reports including all documentation of the interrogation, as well as any audio or videotapes; any legal or police reports from any previous arrests including dispositions, medical records, and mental health records from all treatment sources, including previous psychological evaluations; and academic records including academic testing, grades, and Individual Education Plans (IEPs).

Interviewing the Juvenile

After reviewing the records, the examiner must interview the juvenile. Initially, the clinical interview is similar to other evaluations, with the examiner obtaining psychosocial/background information. During the interview, the examiner also assesses the juvenile's current mental status and makes behavioral observations. The juvenile is also interviewed about the events regarding his arrest, questioning, and police investigation. The examiner should have the juvenile go through step-by-step his recollection of the interrogation process, his understanding of the options that he had, how he came to the conclusion of signing the waiver, and what he thought would happen afterward. It is also important to obtain the juvenile's interpretation of what happened before, during, and after the interrogation. Assessment of his comprehension of *Miranda* rights is also important. The possibility of malingering should always be assessed.

Psychological Testing

The specific need for psychological testing often depends on background information obtained. Often standardized measures of intellectual and academic functioning are administered; as reasoning, intellectual ability, comprehension, problem solving, and reading are areas to be addressed. Generally, the examiner will choose one standardized IQ measure and one standardized academic measure. In addition, standardized personality tests are often administered. The examiner should include one personality test that measures psychopathology, emotional and behavioral symptoms, reality testing, emotional maturity, and perceptual accuracy. A standardized forensic instrument should also be administered to assess the juvenile's understanding and appreciation of *Miranda* rights. See Rapid Reference 7.1 for a selection of appropriate cognitive, personality, and forensic instruments available.

Interviewing Parents or Guardians

The examiner should interview all pertinent individuals who can provide information about the arrest and interrogation; often this is the parent or guardian. Interviewing the parent or guardian is important in obtaining information related to the juvenile's history, mental status/behavioral observations, current legal issues, and about the days prior to the arrest. Interviews with all collateral individuals should be conducted without the juvenile present, in order to provide independent reports in an attempt to determine corroborating information.

Instruments for Assessing Understanding and Appreciation of *Miranda* Rights

These instruments are an integral part of any juvenile or adult evaluation related to waiver of *Miranda* rights. Objective scoring criteria allow the examiner to compare the performance of the individual being assessed to a large normative sample of adult and juvenile offenders. Four instruments were developed for evaluating, understanding, and appreciating *Miranda* rights: Comprehension of Miranda Rights (CMR), Comprehension of Miranda Rights-Recognition (CMR-R), Comprehension of Miranda Vocabulary (CMV), and Function of Rights in Interrogation (FRI).

Administration/Scoring/Interpretation
The CMR can be administered in less than 15 minutes and requires the defendant to paraphrase each element of the *Miranda* warning to assess their comprehension of each of the statements. The juvenile's responses are then scored as "adequate," "questionable," or "inadequate," based on the scoring criteria provided to the examiner. A total CMR score is then obtained, which ranges from 0–8. This is the primary measure of understanding *Miranda* Rights.

The CMR-R can be administered in 5 to 10 minutes. It does not require the juvenile to paraphrase the warnings but assesses his ability to understand the warnings even if he does not have the verbal ability to express his knowledge. The CMR-R has the defendant identify statements that are the "same" or "different" from the warning. Three statements are presented for each *Miranda* warning to determine if the defendants can recognize the meaning of their rights. A total score from 0 to 12 is calculated.

The CMV is a vocabulary test that can be administered in 10 minutes. It is made up of six words used in the *Miranda* warning and the juvenile's definitions are scored using objective scoring criteria. A total score ranging from 0 to 12 is then calculated.

The FRI assesses the juvenile's ability to grasp the significance of *Miranda* rights in the context of arrest and interrogation. It uses hypothetical brief vignettes that are accompanied by drawings, as well as a series of questions regarding each scenario. The situations include the following:

- A juvenile about to be questioned by police after arrest: Questions focus on whether or not the juvenile appreciates the adversarial nature of the encounter with the police officers.
- A juvenile consulting with defense counsel: Questions focus on the juvenile's appreciation of the role and nature of his relationship with the defense attorney as an advocate for him.
- A juvenile being pressured by police officers to make a statement: Questions focus on the juvenile's appreciation of the protective nature of the "right to silence" despite the authority of police officers.
- A juvenile in a hearing before a juvenile court judge: Questions focus on the juvenile's appreciation of the role of a prior confession or assertion of the right to silence in a later court hearing.

Each instrument provides a norm-based assessment of the juvenile's capacity for understanding and appreciating the *Miranda* warning at various levels of intelligence. These instruments have been cited as scientific authority by a number of state appellate courts throughout the country and are admitted as evidence (Grisso, 1998).

The Miranda Comprehension Study (Grisso, 1981) compiled the following results on the capacities of juveniles compared with adults:

- Juveniles age 14 and under demonstrated significant impairment compared to older adolescents and young adults.
- Juveniles ages 15 to 16 did not perform significantly worse than young adults.
- Juveniles ages 15 to 16 with lower IQ scores (below 80) demonstrated significant impairment compared to young adults with similar IQ scores. The understanding of *Miranda* rights was equivalent for juveniles ages 15 to 16 with lower IQ scores and juveniles age 14 and under.

These instruments are currently being revised as the Miranda Rights Comprehension Instruments-II (MRCI-II) and are scheduled to be released in the near future. In the revision a fifth warning is being added, informing individuals that they have a right to stop the interrogation process at any time and ask for an attorney. Simplified wording to better reflect warnings read to juveniles will also be used. Norms for the revised instrument will exist for adolescents 10 to 17 years old. The Perceptions of Coercion during Holding and Interrogation Procedures (P-CHIP) was also developed to assess "voluntary" confessions (Grisso, Vincent, and Seagrave, 2005).

Outline for a Sample Report for *Miranda* Evaluation

Identifying Data:

Name: _____

Date of Birth: _____

Court Case Number: _____

Reason for Referral: Who requested the evaluation and what is the reason for the referral?

Data Base: The current charges and when the *Miranda* rights were waived. Dates interviewed and where interviews took place, names of tests administered, collateral contacts, records reviewed, and any other information used as part of the evaluation

Statement of Nonconfidentiality: Documenting defendant's understanding of the purpose of the evaluation and the limits of confidentiality

Relevant History: Basic demographics/social history as well as information relevant to the case

Current Mental Status and Behavioral Observations: Mental status, rapport, level of effort, and behavioral observations

Waiver of *Miranda* Assessment:

Clinical Interview: Results from the interview

Psychological Testing: Results of cognitive and personality tests: IQ, comprehension, reasoning, vocabulary, problem solving, decision making, sequencing, reading ability, relevant personality/emotional features, reality testing, thought process, and perceptions/distortions

Results of *Miranda* Instruments: (CMR, CMV, CMR-R, FRI) Ability to understand *Miranda* rights and their legal relevance and the reasons for any deficits (mental retardation, cognitive deficiencies, poor/limitations in reasoning, and emotional factors). Malingering should also be assessed.

Context of the Waiver of *Miranda*: The circumstances surrounding the arrest, conditions under which he was held, where he was held, police interactions, admission, length of time he was held incommunicado, opportunities for the juvenile to contact an attorney or other support person, time of day, fatigue, sleep, illness, how the rights were given and by whom, and the juvenile's level of stress.

Analysis and Opinion: Summary and integration of the data, noting strengths and weaknesses, offering opinions to a reasonable degree of psychological certainty about the juvenile's capacities that are relevant for deciding the validity of the *Miranda* waiver and offering clinical recommendations, if appropriate, that may be helpful to the Court.

COMPETENCY TO STAND TRIAL

The premise that individuals accused of an offense must be competent to participate in legal proceedings against them can be traced back to seventeenth century
Common Law, and is rooted in American Law (Melton, Petrila, Poythress, &
Slobogin, 2007; Stafford 2003). Today, the standard for raising the question of
competence is quite liberal. Any possible doubt based on the juvenile's behavior
or history, such as a history of a mental disorder or concern regarding the juvenile's behavior while interacting with his attorney, which may suggest a mental
health problem that might interfere with trial competence, can result in the request for an evaluation to assess the juvenile's competence.

The prevailing standard for determining competence to stand trial was stated
in *Dusky v. United States* (1960). Most states have employed the same *Dusky* standard for competence in juvenile court as is applied in criminal court. Several appellate courts (*In re Causey*, 1978) have ruled that immaturity, not just the presence
of a mental disorder, can be the basis for a finding of incompetency in juvenile
court (Grisso, 1998). Because rates of violent offenses have increased, including
a greater likelihood of waiver to adult court, the issues of a juvenile's competence
to stand trial has increasingly been raised since the mid-1990s (Grisso, 1998). The
juvenile justice system has responded to this by affirmining a juvenile's right to be
competent to stand trial in juvenile court (*In the Interest of S.H.*, 1996).

There are a number of challenges that forensic psychologists face in performing evaluations for juvenile court. To address competency, most juvenile
courts have adopted a test identical or similar to the *Dusky* test. The *Dusky*
standard sets the federal and state standard for trial competence and is based
upon whether the defendant "has sufficient present ability to consult with
his lawyer with a reasonable degree of rational understanding—and whether
he has a rational, as well as factual understanding of the proceedings against
him" (*Dusky v. United States*, 1960). Goldstein (2004) noted that this requires
the following:

- Comprehension of the nature of the charges
- Understanding courtroom proceedings
- The ability to assist in one's own defense
- Distinction between capacity and willingness
- Distinction between reasonable and perfect comprehension
- Emphasis on present ability

Grisso (2005, p. 52), noted the following list of items relevant for competency
to stand trial evaluation:

- To understand the nature and purpose of the trial process
- To understand the nature and seriousness of the charges
- To understand possible pleas
- To understand possible penalties (sentences)
- To understand the roles of various participants in the trial process
- To understand the nature of plea agreements
- The ability to reason about waivers of rights
- The ability to consult with counsel
- The ability to maintain appropriate demeanor during trial and testify if necessary

Psychologists can use these criteria when performing a competency evaluation to assist them in formulating questions for interview and in determining other relevant assessment measures that may be beneficial to use. These criteria are also beneficial when assessing the two prongs of *Dusky*: whether the defendant has sufficient ability to consult with his attorney with a reasonable degree of rational understanding and to determine whether the defendant has a rational and factual understanding of the proceedings against him.

The issue of competency regarding juvenile offenders has been increasingly raised. It is often raised because the defendant's attorney has observed behavior by the defendant that would be suggestive of a cognitive or mental disorder that would interfere with the juvenile's ability to understand the court process or to adequately communicate with his attorney. Based on clinical and developmental research on children and adolescents, Grisso (1998, p. 88) recommended that the question of a juvenile's competence be assessed in cases involving any of the following conditions:

- The client is 12 years old or younger.
- There has been a prior diagnosis or treatment of a mental illness or mental retardation.
- There is evidence of borderline intellectual functioning or a record of a learning disability.
- There have been observations of others at pretrial events that suggest deficits in memory, attention, or the interpretation of reality.

It is important to note that the presence of any of these conditions does not mean that the defendant is incompetent, but rather that there could be a potential need to raise the issue of competency. Otto and

DON'T FORGET

The test of competence is one of capacity rather than simply knowledge or willingness.

Goldstein (2005) note that the test of competence is one of capacity rather than simply knowledge or willingness. Juveniles who simply do not know their charges, the possible penalties, or the process of the legal system are not incompetent to proceed, provided that they have the ability to incorporate and utilize such information in their decision making when it is available to them.

Otto et al. (1998, p. 443) outlined the following abilities required by juveniles to participate in legal proceedings:

1. Understanding
   - The ability to understand the nature of the charges
   - The ability to understand the consequences of various pleas
   - Rights waived in pleading guilty
   - The roles of various courtroom participants (judge, defense attorney, prosecutor)
   - Sentencing based on the severity of the offense
2. Reasoning
   - The ability to develop a defense (self-defense, criminal intent)
   - Understand the motivation for their behavior
   - The capacity to weigh options and consequences
   - The ability to understand and process information and make important decisions
3. Appreciation
   - Beliefs about being treated fairly
   - The ability to work collaboratively with their attorney (trust/disclosure)
   - Beliefs about the likelihood of being found guilty and the consequences
   - Belief about plea bargaining
   - Ability to manage the stress of the proceedings

CAUTION

It is important to remember that incompetence is not synonymous with having a mental disorder. A defendant may have a serious mental disorder and still be competent to stand trial. Their mental illness or symptoms need to interfere with their present abilities as outlined previously for competency.

Framework of the Competency Evaluation

Obtaining and Reviewing Records

The examiner should obtain all records related to mental health, education, and legal history. Current police reports and legal information should also be carefully reviewed. Collateral contacts with mental health professionals, teachers, and parents can also be beneficial. It may also be appropriate for one or more of these contacts to complete a structured inventory regarding the juvenile's emotional and behavioral functioning. An important third-party source is generally the defense attorney. Therefore, as part of the competency evaluation, the defense attorney should be interviewed to obtain information about the juvenile's abilities.

Interviewing the Juvenile

Examiners should begin with a brief social history first. Beginning in this manner tends to reduce the defensiveness of the juvenile and the juvenile may provide information that collateral resources and records do not have. The examiner should also interview the juvenile about past legal experiences with the police and the court system. The adolescent's account of his current legal circumstances can also be discussed; however, a detailed description is not necessary. The examiner is primarily interested in the juvenile's ability to relay his version of what occurred in such a manner that others are able to understand and follow. The examiner then can embark on asking juvenile competency-related questions. The content of these questions should be guided by the categories of information developed by Otto and colleagues (1998) that were previously outlined. Often it is beneficial to prepare questions in advance or to modify one of the structured interviews used with adults. Generally, questions are fairly direct and open-ended and may include some of the following:

- What does the judge do in a trial?
- What is the role of your attorney (prosecutor/witnesses)?
- What is your attorney's name and when was the last time you saw her?
- What happened the last time you went to court?
- Do you feel that you can talk to your attorney?
- Do you think that your attorney is trying to help you?
- What does it mean to plead guilty (not guilty)?
- What do you think is likely to happen if you are found guilty?
- What will you do while you are in court?

The examiner should also assess the juvenile's ability to reason and problem solve. Hypothetical scenarios can also be used to assess these areas.

If a juvenile does poorly in demonstrating his understanding of concepts, the examiner can pick several of the concepts, teach them to the juvenile, and then later during the interview, the examiner can return to these points to assess the juvenile's retention and understanding. This allows the examiner to determine the juvenile's ability to learn basic concepts.

Psychological Testing

To assess cognitive and academic ability, the examiner generally chooses one standardized IQ measure and one standardized academic measure. Standardized personality tests generally measure psychopathology, emotional and behavioral symptoms, reality testing, thought processes, and perceptual accuracy. Examiners have a number of instruments available to them; however, unless there are additional concerns, one self-report inventory and the Rorschach are generally appropriate.

A number of instruments have also been developed that assess the abilities of adults who are undergoing evaluation of their competency to stand trial. Unfortunately, these instruments only have adult norms, which limit their use with an adolescent population. Although these instruments are not intended for use with juveniles, they may be used as a guide to assist the examiner during the competency interview. Instruments should not be scored if they were not normed on a juvenile population. A number of competency assessment instruments have been developed for use with adults but their overall utility for use with juveniles is still undetermined (see Grisso, 2003; Roesch et al., 1999; and Melton, Petrila, Poythress, & Slobogin, 2007 for reviews on various instruments). Grisso (1998) has recommended the Competency Assessment to Stand Trial-Mental Retardation (CAST-MR) instrument for use with juveniles, as its format is concrete and it uses elementary vocabulary and an uncomplicated sentence structure. The Mac-Arthur Competence Assessment Tool-Criminal Adjudication (MacCAT-CA; Poythress et al., 1999) was normed for adult defendants to assess competency. Grisso and colleagues (2003) conducted a study on juvenile performance using the MacArthur Judgment Evaluation assessing their choices and reasoning. Some of the results indicated the following:

- On the MacCAT-CA juveniles under age 15 performed more poorly on average than young adults, with a greater number manifesting impairment consistent with adults who had been found incompetent to stand trial. One-third of the juveniles aged 13 or younger demonstrated this significant level of impairment, while 16- to 17-year-olds on average were no different than adults in their performance.
- Measured intelligence was strongly related to performance on the MacCAT-CA. For example, among the younger juveniles assessed, approximately one-half with IQs below 75 were as impaired on the MacCAT-CA, as are seriously mentally ill adults who were considered incompetent.
- Accepting a plea was inversely related to age—the younger the participant, the more likely they were to accept the plea and make other decisions complying with authority.
- Many juveniles, more often than adults, have deficits related to trial preparation that are similar to adults who are determined to be

incompetent to stand trial due to mental disorders. The juveniles' deficits were not related to a mental disorder, but to the fact that they are operating with cognitive and psychological abilities that are still developing, as a consequence of their relative immaturity in relation to adults.

Presently, competence assessment instruments that simply structure the inquiry, such as the Fitness Interview Test-Revised (FIT-R; Golding, 1993) and the Competence to Stand Trial Assessment Instrument (Laboratory for Community Psychiatry, 1973) may be beneficial to use if examiners maintain awareness of the differences in terminology and processes between criminal and delinquency proceedings.

Another instrument useful to assess juvenile competency is Grisso's Juvenile Adjudicative Competence Interview (JACI). The JACI provides a structured set of questions that the clinician can use to assess the juvenile's understanding, appreciation, and reasoning. Its purpose is to ensure that examiners are obtaining relevant information to accurately assess the juvenile's competence. Scores are not produced for the juvenile's responses. Grisso (2005, p.74–75) provides an overview of the JACI. It begins with questions pertaining to the juvenile's Experience and Legal Context. The main section provides interview questions for 12 content areas:

The Juvenile Court Trial and Its Consequences
  1. Nature and Seriousness of the Offense
  2. Nature and Purpose of the Juvenile Court Trial
  3. Possible Pleas
  4. Guilt and Punishment/Penalties

Roles of the Participants
  5. Role of the Prosecutor
  6. Role of the Juvenile Defense Lawyer
  7. Role of the Probation Officer
  8. Role of the Juvenile Court Judge

Assisting Counsel and Decision Making
  9. Assisting the Defense Lawyer
  10. Plea Bargains/Agreements
  11. Reasoning and Decision Making

Item 11 uses a vignette to assess the juveniles' ability to apply what they know to four problems:

  1. Deciding About Having a Defense Lawyer
  2. Deciding How to Assist Your Lawyer

3. Deciding How to Plead
4. Deciding About a Plea Bargain

The twelfth and final area, Participating at a Juvenile Court Hearing, allows the examiner to note impressions, based on observation of the juvenile during the assessment process regarding:

- Ability to Attend (to events in the hearing)
- Ability to Maintain Self-Control (during the hearing)
- Ability to Testify (at a hearing)

(See Selected Instruments at the end of this chapter for a selection of appropriate intelligence, achievement, personality, and forensic tests that are available for competency evaluations.) The examiner should also always assess for the possibility of malingering.

DON'T FORGET

When assessing competence:
- The focus is on capacity
- The focus is on present ability and not past or future abilities
- The focus is on cognitive functioning and not one of mental illness
- The requirement is a reasonable degree of understanding

CAUTION

Most competency instruments were developed and normed on adults and not juveniles; therefore, caution needs to be exercised when using competency instruments with juveniles.

MENTAL STATE AT THE TIME OF THE OFFENSE

Little has been written about the insanity defense as it applies to juveniles. However, a more adversarial juvenile system will likely prompt statutes that address this issue. The premise of the insanity defense is that most criminal offenders choose to commit crimes for rational reasons, of their own "free will," and are deserving of punishment; some mentally disturbed offenders have behavior that is so irrational and/or uncontrollable that we feel uncomfortable imposing criminal liability on them (Melton,et al 2007). With the exception of strict liability offenses, every crime has at least two elements: *mens rea*, or the mental state or level of intent associated with the crime, as well as *actus reus*, which is the physical conduct associated with the crime. To convict an individual of a particular crime, the state must prove that the individual committed the *actus reus* with the requisite *mens rea*. An individual's intent to commit the crime can be significantly impacted by one or more mental disorders.

The legal standards employed to evaluate insanity defenses vary across jurisdictions. Melton, Petrila, Poythress, and Slobogin (2007) have noted that most jurisdictions employ a combination of the following standards.

Outline for a Sample Report for Competency Evaluation

Identifying Data:

Name: _____

Date of Birth: _____

Court Case Number: _____

Reason for Referral: Who requested the evaluation and what is the reason for the referral?

Data Base: Dates interviewed and where interviews took place, names of tests administered, collateral contacts, records reviewed, and any other information used as part of the evaluation

Statement of Nonconfidentiality: Documenting defendant's understanding of the purpose of the evaluation and the limits of confidentiality

Relevant History: Basic demographics/social history as well as information relevant to the case

Current Mental Status and Behavioral Observations: Mental status, rapport, level of effort, and behavioral observations

Competency Assessment:

Clinical Interview: Results from competency interview assessing the juvenile's understanding of the legal process and its adversarial nature, the understanding and appreciation of the charges and allegations, the understanding and appreciation of possible sanctions and dispositions, the capacity to work with his attorney and provide relevant information, the ability to testify relevantly, and the ability to display appropriate courtroom behavior

Psychological Testing: Results of cognitive and personality tests: IQ, comprehension, reasoning, vocabulary, problem solving, decision making, relevant personality/emotional features, reality testing, thought process, and perceptions/distortions. Malingering should also be assessed

Analysis and Opinion: Summary and integration of the data noting strengths and weaknesses, provide opinion to a reasonable degree of psychological certainty about the juvenile's competency to proceed, provide any recommendations that may be helpful to the Court, and if the juvenile is not competent to proceed, provide recommendations for restoration and the estimated length of time required for the juvenile to be restored to competency

- *M'Naghten Standard.* Established in the mid-1800s, it indicated that at the time of committing the act, the defendant was under such a defect of reason, from disease of the mind, as to not know the nature and quality of the act he was doing; or, if he did know it, that he was unaware what he was doing was wrong.
- *Irresistible Impulse.* This adds a volitional component to the previously established cognitive component of the M'Naghten standard. It indicates that the defendant is not legally responsible even if he knew what he was doing was wrong if he was unable to restrain himself from committing the act because of mental disease or defect.
- *American Law Institute Standard.* This standard combines the concepts of both M'Naghten and "irresistible impulse" but makes it clear that a defendant's cognitive and/or volitional impairment at the time of the offense need only be substantial rather than total to merit an insanity defense. It was designed to exclude an abnormality manifested only by repeated criminal or antisocial conduct. It indicates that a defendant is not responsible for criminal conduct if at the time of such conduct the defendant, because of mental disease or defect, lacked substantial capacity either to appreciate the wrongfulness of the criminal conduct, or was unable to conform his conduct to the requirements of the law.
- *American Bar Association Standard.* Problems stemming from the volitional prong prompted the formulation of a modified proposal, which indicated that a defendant is not responsible for criminal conduct if at the time of such conduct and as a result of mental disease or defect, that person was unable to appreciate the wrongfulness of such conduct. A concern was that if any mistakes were to be made, it would most likely stem from utilizing the volitional standard.

Assessment of juveniles is similar in format and structure to evaluations conducted on adults within the criminal justice system (see Rogers & Shuman, 2000; Borum, 2003; Goldstein, Morse, & Shapiro, 2002; and Otto & Borum, 2004). Otto and Borum (2004) note that in conducting such evaluations the forensic psychologist must consider how the defendant's behavior might be related to adolescent development and psychopathology.

The standards for insanity defenses are broad and vary across states. Melton, Petrila, Poythress, and Slobogin (2007) delineated several trends in these cases:

- The most successful cases are those that involve diagnoses of psychosis or mental retardation.

- Substance abuse, personality disorders, disorders of impulse control (e.g., pathological gambling, kleptomania, and pyromania), pedophilia, and crimes of passion do not exculpate defendants. Legal definitions of disease or defect are vague and vary from jurisdiction to jurisdiction; therefore, it cannot be assumed whether a particular diagnosis can be equated with insanity or its threshold.
- Every test of insanity requires that the mental disease or defect "cause" the offense itself. The evidence must show that "but for" the disorder, the criminal act would not have occurred.
- The burden of proof varies across jurisdictions. Most states place the burden of proof on the defendant to show that by a "preponderance of evidence" (51% certainty) they were insane at the time of the offense. Arizona and the federal court system require the defendant to prove insanity by "clear and convincing evidence" (75% certainty). The remainder of states requires the prosecution to prove the defendant's sanity "beyond a reasonable doubt" (90–95% certainty). If the trier of fact is not convinced beyond a reasonable doubt that the defendant was sane at the time of the offense, the prosecution loses.

In most jurisdictions both the cognitive and volitional approaches need to be assessed when conducting these types of evaluations. Did the juvenile have a mental disorder/defect that caused a cognitive impairment at the time of the offense? Did the mental disorder/defect cause the juvenile to have a loss of control over his behavior at the time of the offense? The mental state at the time of the offense evaluation is one of the more challenging evaluations that examiners face. The focus of the evaluation is the defendant's mental state at the time of the offense, often having to determine what their mental state was weeks and often months earlier. It can also be more difficult to obtain accurate collateral/third-party information. Often, examiners take on the role of detective attempting to put together pieces of a puzzle while looking for consistencies and inconsistencies in the information they obtain. Melton, Petrila, Poythress, & Slobogin (2007) believe that three broad domains need to be investigated. These include: third-party information, phases and tone of the defendant interview, and psychological testing, hypothesis, and other special procedures. Eventually the data obtained is integrated for the examiner to generate an opinion as to whether the individual's mental state at the time of the offense impaired their ability to appreciate the wrongfulness of the act and whether he or she had the ability to behave within the requirements of the law.

Framework of the Mental State at the Time of the Offense Evaluation

Obtaining and Reviewing Records

The examiner should obtain and review all mental health, educational, and legal records pertaining to the juvenile, as well as current police reports and legal records. Interviewing collateral contacts is also beneficial to gain information as to the defendant's mental state before, during, and after the alleged offense. Collateral contacts could take the form of witnesses, codefendants, complainants, family, friends, or others who can assist in reconstructing the defendant's mental state at the time of the offense. Attention should be paid to any inconsistencies as well as determining consistency between information obtained. Records and collateral contacts can be used to corroborate information obtained by the juvenile.

Interviewing the Juvenile

At the present time there is no widely standard interview procedure for mental state at the time of offense evaluations. These evaluations generally take more than one session of interviewing the defendant. The defendant's own words when describing the offense should be transcribed and used as a basis for addressing this topic in the report. Open-ended questions should be asked to elicit information from the defendant. The examiner should also investigate what the defendant's thoughts, feelings, and perceptions were at the time of the offense. Further, it is also beneficial to interview the defendant with regard to his functioning to assess his mental state both the week before and the week after the commission of the crime. The initial interview with the defendant should cover psychosocial/background information such as family history, education, employment, medical, mental health, legal, and substance use. The examiner should also obtain a detailed account of the alleged criminal act and the defendant's thoughts, feelings, and perceptions at that time, as well as any responses or reactions afterward. One or more subsequent interviews can be used to clarify information and address any areas of inconsistency.

Psychological Testing

To assess cognitive and academic ability, the examiner should generally choose one standardized IQ measure and one standardized academic measure. Standardized personality tests that measure psychopathology, emotional and behavioral symptoms, reality testing, thought processes, and perceptual accuracy are also used. Generally, the examiner should administer one self-report measure and the Rorschach. The examiner should also consider using a modified forensic instrument (e.g., the Rogers Criminal Responsibility Assessment Scales, or R-CRAS) to measure psychological and situational variables pertinent to insanity evaluations.

≡ *Rapid Reference 7.1*

The following psychological tests can be used as part of a battery for conducting *Miranda* and competency evaluations:

Standardized Cognitive/Achievement Tests

- Wechsler Intelligence Scale for Children-IV
- Wechsler Adult Intelligence Scale-IV
- Wide Range Achievement Test 4
- Kaufman Adolescent and Adult Intelligence Test
- Kaufman Assessment Battery for Children, Second Edition
- Kaufman Test of Educational Achievement
- Wechsler Individual Achievement Test, Second Edition
- Woodcock-Johnson III NU-Complete Cognitive/Achievement

Note: When selecting standardized cognitive tests, examiners should choose one intelligence test and one achievement test to administer.

Standardized Personality Tests

- Adolescent Psychopathology Scale
- Millon Adolescent Clinical Inventory
- Minnesota Multiphasic Personality Inventory-Adolescent
- Personality Assessment Inventory-Adolescent
- Rorschach Psychodiagnostic Series
- Behavior Rating Scales
- Behavior Assessment System for Children, Second Edition

Standardized Forensic Test: Instrument for Assessing Understanding and Appreciation of *Miranda* Rights

- Comprehension of *Miranda* Rights
- Comprehension of Miranda Rights-Recognition
- Comprehension of Miranda-Vocabulary
- Function of Rights in Interrogation

Standardized Forensic Instruments for Assessing Understanding of Charges and Ability to Assist Counsel

- Competency Assessment to Stand Trial-Mental Retardation
- MacArthur Competence Assessment Tool-Criminal Adjudication
- Juvenile Adjudicative Competence Interview

Standardized Forensic Instrument for Assessing Variables Relating to Legal Sanity

- Rogers Criminal Assessment Scales

Rapid Reference 7.1 provides a listing of some of the tests that are appropriate to assess cognitive, personality, and legal insanity components of mental state at the time of the offense evaluations. The possibility of malingering should also be assessed.

Rogers Criminal Responsibility Assessment Scales

The Rogers Criminal Responsibility Assessment Scales (R-CRAS) were developed as a method for standardizing data/information pertinent to legal insanity evaluations. The mental state at the time of the offense is a retrospective evaluation and the R-CRAS allows the examiner to quantify the defendant's impairment at the time of the offense, conceptualize the impairment, and render an opinion with respect to the appropriate legal standard. It assists the examiner in rendering an accurate opinion on criminal responsibility using the ALI standard, the most widely used standard in the United States, but also includes experimental decision models for "guilty but mentally ill" and M'Naghten standards.

Administration/Scoring/Interpretation

The administration of the R-CRAS follows a standardized approach. The examiner should first review all available clinical records and police reports pertinent to the case prior to examining the defendant. Next, the examiner should conduct one, but preferably several, clinical interviews with the defendant. Clinical interviews should focus on the defendant's thoughts, feelings, perceptions, and behaviors at the time of the crime as well as the period of time immediately preceding and following the commission of the alleged crime. Finally, the examiner should complete the R-CRAS immediately following the final clinical interview.

All of the information available to the examiner is used to score each of the items on the R-CRAS. Multiple sources of information are important, including corroborating data. The R-CRAS is divided into two parts; Part I establishes the degree of impairment on psychological variables relative to the determination of insanity. Each variable is rated on a 4- to 6-point scale that assesses the relative severity of the criteria being evaluated. The examiner selects the single most accurate rating with 0 for "no information," and then 1 to 5 or 6, with each progressive number suggesting increasing severity of symptoms, more severe pathology, or greater disorganization. The 0 "no information" category should only be used in unusual situations when information is unable to be obtained. Detailed information regarding administration and scoring are outlined in the manual. Specific items in Part I address:

- Reliability of the defendant's self-report
- Substance use

- Organicity
- Mental retardation
- Delusions
- Amnesia
- Thought disturbance
- Mood-related symptoms/affect
- Anxiety
- Planning and preparation
- Awareness
- Self-control

Part II assists the examiner in rendering an opinion based on the ALI standard, and also includes the M'Naghten and "guilty but mentally ill" standards. The examiner must score a "yes," "no," or "no opinion" response for each of the criteria in Part II. If all of the specified criteria are met, the conclusion can be reached that the legal standard is met. Criteria in Part II include:

- Malingering
- Organicity
- Major psychiatric disorder
- Loss of cognitive control
- Loss of behavioral control

CAUTION

- Several scores of 0 should alert the examiner to the possibility that the evaluation for criminal responsibility is not complete and further information needs to be obtained. If the examiner is unable to obtain critical information they must render a "no opinion" on the R-CRAS.
- It is important the examiner use multiple sources of data to corroborate the defendant's reports.

The R-CRAS, when used as part of a thorough assessment of a defendant's mental state at the time of the offense, can provide additional information for the examiner to use when formulating an opinion. The R-CRAS presents factors that should be considered in insanity evaluations in an orderly fashion and can assist examiners in organizing their interviews and thoughts. Criticisms have also arisen regarding the instrument. Melton, Petrila, Poythress, and Slobogin (2007) suggest that there is a misplaced emphasis on addressing the ultimate issue question, that claims to quantify areas of

CAUTION

The R-CRAS was developed and normed on adult offenders. Juvenile norms are not known to be available for this measure. This measure should only be used as an interview guide to assess essential factors pertinent to mental state at the time of the offense evaluations.

Outline for a Sample Report for a Mental State at the Time of the Offense Evaluation

Identifying Data:

Name: _____

Date of Birth: _____

Court Case Number: _____

Reason for Referral: Who requested the evaluation and what is the reason for the referral?

Data Base: Dates interviewed, where interviews took place, current charges, names of tests administered, collateral contacts, records reviewed, and any other information used as part of the evaluation

Statement of Nonconfidentiality: Documenting defendant's understanding of the purpose of the evaluation and the limits of confidentiality

Relevant History: Basic demographics/social history as well as information relevant to the case

Collateral Contacts: Information obtained from collateral contacts as to the defendant's mental state at and surrounding the time of the offense.

Current Mental Status and Behavioral Observations: Mental status, rapport, level of effort, and behavioral observations

NGI Assessment:

   Clinical Interview: Detailed account of the criminal act including results of standardized interview (R-CRAS), detailed account of the defendant's emotional/ psychological and behavioral functioning at and surrounding the alleged offense.

   Psychological Testing: Results of cognitive and personality tests: IQ, cognitive functioning, relevant personality/emotional features, reality testing, thought process, and perceptions/distortions. Malingering should also be assessed.

Analysis and Opinion: Summary and integration of the data noting consistencies and inconsistencies, description of symptoms of mental disorder and their interference with functioning. Assist the Judge/Trier of Fact in understanding the defendant's mental condition. Provide opinion to a reasonable degree of psychological certainty relevant to legal insanity and offer recommendations to the Court regarding treatment if it is determined that the defendant is legally insane.

judgment are logical or intuitive, and that the claims related to scientific rigor are exaggerated. According to Melton, the major risk is that examiners or courts may attribute undeserved scientific status to judgments that remain logical and commonsense in nature (p. 256).

AMENABILITY TO TREATMENT AND RECOMMENDATIONS FOR DISPOSITION

To assist with determining and addressing mental health needs, several multidimensional brief screening instruments have been developed. Screening tools should be used with all youth at the point of entry into the juvenile justice system, to identify those individuals that need immediate mental health services or immediate attention for further assessment. Screening tools are just that; they are not intended to acquire information for permanent decision making about long-range treatment. These screening tools can assist in identifying individuals that may need more detailed assessment for dispositional planning.

The Massachusetts Youth Screening Instrument-Version 2 (MAYSI-2; Grisso & Barnum) is a brief, self-report measure, that is designed to identify juveniles with emotional and behavioral difficulties that may be a result of a mental disorder or emotional difficulties that require immediate attention. Accurate identification of emotional and behavioral problems is essential for youth entering the juvenile justice system. Oftentimes, identification of these problems is difficult as parents, guardians, or caretakers are unavailable at intake.

The MAYSI-2 is appropriate for juveniles aged 12–17 and administration and scoring takes about 10–15 minutes. It is a 52-question self-report inventory. It assesses six primary areas: Alcohol/Drug Use, Angry-Irritable, Depressed-Anxious, Somatic Complaints, Suicide Ideation, and Thought Disturbance. There is also a seventh scale that assesses Traumatic Experiences. Scores above the "Caution" cutoff indicate a "clinical level of significance," and scores in the "Warning" cutoff suggest that the individual scored higher than 90% of the normative sample at juvenile justice intake. The MAYSI-2 does not have built-in mechanisms for judging underreporting or overreporting, nor a Thought Disturbance scale for girls. Individuals need a fifth grade reading ability to complete the test on their own, otherwise it can be orally administered. The MAYSI-2 can be administered by juvenile justice workers with only brief in-service training. This instrument is also available in Spanish (Grisso & Quinlan, 2005).

The Problem-Oriented Screening Instrument for Teenagers (POSIT; Rahdert, 1991) is a youth self-report screening instrument that identifies potential problems in 10 areas, which can then be more thoroughly assessed. The instrument was developed to assess youth entering the juvenile justice system. It contains 139 "yes/no" questions and is designed for individuals 12–19 years old. It has 10 scales that include: Substance Abuse/Use, Physical Health, Mental Health, Family Relations, Peer Relations, Educational Status, Vocational Status, Social Skills, Leisure/Recreation, and Aggressive Behavior/Delinquency. Individuals need a fifth grade reading level to complete the instrument, which takes 20–30 minutes. It is also available in Spanish. No special qualifications are needed to administer the measure.

Scott (2002) notes that an individual's amenability to treatment is important to consider and statutes definitions can often be vague. Many juveniles involved with the juvenile justice system agree to treatment but fail to follow through. Schetky (2003) notes that some useful topics to consider when addressing this area are: diagnoses, prior treatment record and compliance, motivation for treatment, willingness to accept responsibility for their crimes, and effectiveness of available treatments. Further, Schetky (2003) states that treatment recommendations should be geared to underlying mental health problems and substance abuse using evidence-based data. Also, educational needs should be considered, as many individuals in the juvenile justice system have learning disorders, special education needs, and attention deficit/hyperactivity disorder.

Dangerousness

Assessments of dangerousness in children and adolescents within the juvenile justice system generally occur to assist in determining whether a defendant can be released into the community while pending a hearing, at sentencing or disposition to assist in determining the level of security needed, or to aid in planning for supervision within the community if they are sentenced and placed back into the community. Grisso (1998) notes that assessing risk is different from that of adults, as patterns related to personality and behavior in juveniles are in a state of transition due to developmental factors.

Assessing dangerousness requires that the examiner be familiar with the factors that affect the level of risk, such as prior history of violence, exposure to violence, mental health disorders, history of victimization, impulsivity, need for arousal, access to weapons, family role models, capacity for empathy, presence of cognitive impairment, substance abuse, alienation, and conduct disorders. Positive influences such as engagement in school and with family should also be factored in as these tend to be associated with a better prognosis (Schetky, 2003).

Schetky (2003) noted that juveniles who are the most worrisome are those with a callous, unemotional interpersonal style, restricted behavioral repertoires, high levels of defiance, predisposition to acting out behaviors, impulsivity, early onset of delinquency, and lack of internal conflict over their asocial or antisocial behavior. Positive mitigating factors include low intelligence, developmental delay, crimes committed in self-defense, history of being abused, mental illness, response to medication, and peer coercion.

Grisso (1998) notes that areas to be assessed are as follows.

- Past Behavior: Chronicity, recency, frequency, severity, and context.
- School Problems: Truancy, dropout, and so forth. This is more critical the earlier school problems began.
- Substance Use: The use of substances by juveniles who have engaged in violent behaviors increases the risk of future violence.
- Peers and Community: Violent peer groups provide a social norm that encourages violence, increases the likelihood the youth will find themselves in violent situations, and provides greater access to weapons.
- Family Conflict and Aggression: This creates present and future stress, makes violence more acceptable, contributes to an antisocial attitude, and increases the likelihood that children from these families will engage in aggressive and violent behavior.
- Social Stressors and Supports: Divorce, serious illness, and financial stress tax coping abilities and increase feelings of insecurity, threat, and loss that can in turn lead to aggressive behavior
- Personality Traits: Anger, impulsivity, and lack of empathy increase the risk of future violence.
- Mental Disorders: Individuals with past aggressive behavior are at greater risk of future aggression if they have certain mental disorders (depression, attentional and hyperactivity disorders, Schizophrenia, other psychotic disorders, trauma disorders, and brain syndromes).
- Opportunity: Availability of victims and weapons.
- Future Residence: Secure, nonsecure, or community.

Whenever possible it is suggested that clinicians attempt to gain collateral information by reviewing available records and interviewing collateral contacts. The more sources of information available to the clinician the better they may be at determining risk/dangerousness. There are also two instruments that clinicians can use to assist them in assessing children and adolescents as well: the Early Assessment Risk List (EARL) and the Structured Assessment of Violence Risk in Youth (SAVRY).

The EARL-20B (Early Assessment Risk List for Boys, Version 2; Augimeri, Koegl, Webster, & Levene, 2001) aids clinicians in making judgments about future violence and antisocial behavior among boys under 12 years old, especially those who demonstrate behavior problems and are considered to be high risk. The instrument contains 20 risk items divided into three categories: Family Items, Child Items, and Responsivity Items. Each item is given a score of 0, 1, or 2 depending on the certainty and severity of that variable's presence. The EARL-21G (Early Assessment Risk List for Girls, Version 1, Consultation Edition; Levene et al., 2001) is a parallel instrument for assessing risk in girls. The domains are the same but the risk factors are different. The EARL-20B and the EARL-21G were modeled after the HCR-20 (Webster et al., 1997), a measure used for assessing the risk of violence in adults. Thus far the EARL has demonstrated good interrater reliability and validity.

The SAVRY (Structured Assessment of Violence Risk in Youth; Bartel, Borum, & Forth, 2000; Borum, Bartel, & Forth, 2003) focuses on violence risk in adolescents. It is designed for youth between the ages of 12 and 18 who have been detained or referred for an assessment of risk violence. It is composed of 24 risk items, divided into three categories—Historical, Individual, and Social/Contextual—and it has six Protective factors. It uses a three-level coding structure to assess risk items as "high," "moderate," or "low." The Protective factors are rated either "absent" or "present." Specific coding guidelines are provided for the levels. The form prompts evaluators to make a final "summary risk rating" of low, moderate, or high. The summary risk rating is a professional judgment based on the overall results of the SAVRY risk and protective factors. McEachran (2001) found relatively high reliability for total scores of .83 and moderate coefficients of .72 for summary risk ratings. Validity studies have been promising (Borum, Bartel, & Forth, 2005).

Psychopathy

Researchers do not believe that psychopathy begins to develop in adulthood; instead the foundation for such characteristics are manifested early in life (Johnstone & Cooke, 2004; Lynam, 2002; Saltaris, 2002). Measures such as the Hare Psychopathy Checklist: Youth Version (PCL: YV; Forth, Kosson, & Hare, 2003) have been developed to assess psychopathic traits in adolescents using a structured clinical rating system. The Hare Psychopathy Checklist: Youth Version (PCL-YV) uses semi-structured and collateral information to assess interpersonal, emotional, and behavioral features of psychopathy. It assists in identifying patterns of cheating, fighting, bullying, and other antisocial behaviors. The length of time it takes to complete it varies due to a number of factors such as length of interview, collateral contacts, records to be reviewed, and knowledge of the case. The examiner rates items on a scale of 0 to 2 (Yes, No, and Maybe). It can be used with individuals ages 12–18, male and female. The test has sound psychometric properties and provides a reliable and valid measure of psychopathy in adolescents. It has internal consistency ratings of .85 to .94 across settings (Forth, Kosson, & Hare, 2003).

Edens, Skeem, Cruise, and Cauffman (2001) and Seagrave and Grisso (2002) note serious concerns about placing the label of "psychopathy" on juveniles whose personality and emotions are still developing. Their concerns include:

- Personality disorders should only be diagnosed in adulthood.
- Psychopathy cannot be reliably assessed in juveniles because of developmental overlap.
- Labeling a juvenile as "psychopathic" is ethically problematic.

WAIVER INTO ADULT COURT

One of the hotly debated areas related to juvenile justice is the option to waive juvenile defendants to adult court. The trend in most states over the last several decades is to make it easier to waive juveniles into adult court. Prior to the 1960s, standards regarding the transfer of juveniles were vague. *Kent v. U.S.* (1966) addressed the transfer of juveniles on waiver to criminal court. In this case the court determined that in waiver hearings juveniles have the right to be represented by counsel, to avoid self-incrimination, and to confront and cross-examine opposing witnesses. Within a few years of *Kent v. U.S.*, almost all states had legislated "danger" and "amenability to rehabilitation" standards and most states required that both be applied (Grisso, 1998).

Two of the main evaluation questions pertain to whether there is a risk of harm to others and whether there is likelihood that the juvenile can be successfully rehabilitated in the juvenile justice system. Youth cannot be waived to criminal court unless they present a serious risk of harm to others, which is referred to as the "Danger" standard. The "Amenability" standard addresses not whether the juvenile can modify their behavior but whether they are appropriate to do so within the state's system of rehabilitation for delinquent offenders. A third factor to consider and assess in the evaluation is the juvenile's maturity. The adolescent's continuing development needs to be taken into consideration and may affect the evaluation process.

Prior to beginning any evaluation it is important to clarify the legal issue at hand and the questions that the court wants addressed. In waiver evaluations, the issues typically of concern are the seriousness of the alleged crime, the risks posed by the juvenile, characteristics of the youth, the needs of the juvenile, amenability to treatment/rehabilitation, and dispositional alternatives (Schetky, 2003). As with any evaluation it is important to obtain available discovery materials such as police reports, mental health records, previous evaluations, and school records. It is also important to interview collateral contacts that would have information pertinent to the evaluation. It is important to take a detailed psychosocial history, which includes addressing any history related to trauma, developmental problems, the use of alcohol or other drugs, and mental health problems. Addressing the Danger and Amenability standards require the same concepts, data collection, and clinical expertise as described in the preceding sections.

Unfortunately, it is often the case that adult correctional facilities are unable to meet the needs of juvenile offenders. Other problems include: higher rates of recidivism by juveniles upon release from adult facilities, poorly trained staff, inappropriate use of restraints and harsher punitive practices, and higher rates of victimization and suicide rates (Schetky, 2003).

Schetky (2003, p. 4) notes that there are a number of ethical dilemmas for examiners who perform waiver evaluations:

- Does a recommendation for waiver amount to writing off youths and causing recapitulation of their abusive childhood?
- How do we balance the need to help the youth with the need to protect society?
- How do we weigh short-term results against long-term needs?

DON'T FORGET

Melton, Petrila, Poythress, and Slobogin (2007, p. 491) suggest several points to remember when assessing status offenders.

- Status offenses are not a stepping-stone to delinquency.
- Adolescent girls who have been victims of sexual abuse enter the juvenile justice system often under status offenses and have harsher dispositions than males.
- Many runaways have been thrown out of their homes or have left due to the abuse they have been subjected to at home.
- They often come from homes where there is serious family dysfunction.
- Many status offenders are incarcerated because alternative emergency placements are unavailable.
- Status offense petitions are often misused as a means of obtaining services for troubled youth and families.
- Status offense petitions are often signs of failure or dissatisfaction with services available rather than indicators of culpable behavior of the juvenile.

STATUS OFFENDERS

The most common status offenses are truancy, running away from home, and habitually disobeying parents. These "status offenses" are set apart in the sense that although legal proceedings are similar to delinquency proceedings "status offenses" cannot result in a finding of delinquency. This has limited what juvenile courts can do when arriving at treatment/rehabilitative options for "status offenders"—as they cannot be sent to certain types of secure facilities, rehabilitation programs have been developed for delinquent youths. Psychologists working in the juvenile justice system are frequently asked to evaluate status offenders and to provide the court with treatment recommendations. The Don't Forget section notes several facts to consider when conducting evaluations and writing reports.

CHILDREN AS WITNESSES

There are times that children or juveniles are required to testify in court in their own cases or as witnesses in the cases of others.

In recent years, there has been a growing controversy about whether children should be subjected to live court testimony. One side of the argument addresses the issue of how victimizing in-court testimony can be to children, while the other side of the argument addresses the defendant's constitutional rights. Many alternatives to live testimony have been suggested, including in-camera testimony, videotaped testimony, audiotaped testimony, and the use of screens in court. All of these approaches have advantages and disadvantages. Assuming that children will be required to testify in some cases, many issues must be addressed when considering their testimony.

Dent (1992) has addressed the issue of the effects of age and intelligence on a child's ability to be an effective witness. A number of studies have been performed that suggest that children as young as 6 years of age can be as reliable as adults when answering questions. Research has also demonstrated that retarded children and children with learning disabilities provide less complete and less accurate responses. In addition, they are more susceptible to suggestion than are children of normal intelligence. Dent has reported that female children tend to give more complete and accurate reports than do male children. She also noted that "if child witnesses are allowed to relate their report with minimal prompting, either as free recall or response to general, open-ended questions, then the results of the present research suggest they would not be significantly less accurate than adult witnesses" (p. 8). Dent has further indicated that the results of some of her research suggest that children's

[M]emory deteriorates sharply over a period of two weeks and then more gradually, up to two months, after witnessing the event. Reduced accuracy has been found in the recall of children aged five to nine years after a five month delay.... [This] would suggest that evidence from witnesses would be obtained as early as possible. A video recording of the interview could fulfill the dual purpose of being a record of the witnesses' earliest and most vivid and complete memory and showing how the recall was elicited. (p. 9)

In conclusion, Dent (1992) stated, "The results indicated quite clearly that, though increased completeness could be obtained by use of specific questions, this was at the expense of accuracy, particularly for the two child groups" (p. 10).

Schwartz-Kenney, Bottoms, Goodman, and Wilson's (1992) research on the competency of children as witnesses shows that the younger the child, the greater the number of errors that are made and the smaller the percentage of correct responses. She compared the two groups of young children on free recall and police lineup conditions. She found that there are significantly more correct responses on lineup (52%) as compared with free recall (34%). There was also a decrease in the number of "do not know" responses in lineup (1%) versus free recall (26%). In all, younger children had more commission errors, fewer correct responses, and more "do not know" responses.

Children Testifying

"The competency of the child to testify in court about sexual abuse is often a question evaluated forensically. So, too, are issues that bear not unto competency as such, but on the reliability and accuracy of a child's report of sexual abuse" (Clark in Kuehnle & Connell, 2009, p. 70).

The issue of whether children should be required to testify in courts of law requires a balance between concern about the children's rights and recognizing that testifying places children in a powerful position. Goodman (1991) has pointed out that if children are required to testify, it is most likely to take place in child sexual abuse allegation cases. When Goodman refers to children's testimony, she is talking about not only testifying in court but also the reports of events to police, social service workers, psychologists, and other people related to these cases.

There are three important components to memory. They include encoding (entry into the memory system), storage, and retrieval. Memory is influenced by semantic knowledge, awareness, and utilization of mnemonic strategies and understanding which strategies work best in a given situation (Klemfuss & Cici, 2009).

There are a number of inappropriate assumptions that are made about children's eyewitness testimony. Klemfuss & Cici (2002) list the following as the most important:

- If a child has been repeatedly and painfully sexually abused as an infant (0–12 months old), she can remember it when she is older.
- Does repeatedly asking children open-ended questions, such as "What happened? What else happened?" usually lead them to making false claims of sexual abuse?
- Does asking children to use sexually anatomically detailed dolls (dolls with genitalia) to show "what bad things happened" lead to false reports of sexual abuse?
- Can a psychologist tell whether a child's description of an event has been influenced by another adult? (pp. 166–171).
- It is rare, if not impossible, for a person to remember anything from the first year of life. This includes even repeated, painful abuse.
- While repeated closed-ended questions may make children susceptible to false memories, repeated open-ended questions generally either have no effect on children's reports or strengthen their reports through rehearsal.
- There is no reliable research evidence indicating that using anatomically detailed dolls aids children's reports of abuse. However, there is evidence that the use of anatomical dolls may lead children to make false claims of sexual abuse.
- There is no reliable measure that professionals or laypersons can use to determine which children's reports have been tampered with. This is especially true if the child has been influenced by suggestive interviews (p. 173).

In summary, children remember less and are more vulnerable to memory tainting than adults. Older children and adults are never able to remember things that happened to them before one year of age, and usually cannot remember things that happened to them before three or four (p. 174).

Rapid Reference 7.2 outlines factors that affect suggestibility.

SUGGESTIBILITY

A child's susceptibility to suggestibility is perhaps one of the most important factors to be addressed when evaluating children's reports about abuse and determining whether they should testify or not.

===== *Rapid Reference 7.2*

Factors That Affect Suggestibility

- The more intelligent the child, the less suggestible.
- The greater the child's executive functioning, the less suggestible.
- Higher socioeconomic status (SES) children are less suggestible than lower SES children.
- The more self-confident the child, the less suggestible.
- The greater the attachment security, the less suggestible.
- Posttraumatic Stress Disorder (PTSD) does not have an effect on suggestibility.

Note: Adapted from Harris et al. (2002, pp. 198–199).

"Empirical evidence suggests that children incorporate parental suggestions into their memory for events. One may also be concerned about one parent coaching a child to lie about the actions of the other parent" (McAuliff, Kovera, & Gilstrap, 2009, p. 133).

"Without preparation, child witnesses may not understand their role in court, may not know how courts generally work, and may misunderstand the judges' and attorneys' language" (p. 135).

In spite of court rulings and desires to the contrary, at times children will be required to testify in courts. When this occurs, a number of steps should be taken to aid the child, most of which involve preparing the child. Dezwirek-Sas (1992) participated in the London Family Court Clinic project on helping children prepare for testimony in court. Nine criminal justice system stressors were identified (see Rapid Reference 7.3).

Dezwirek-Sas also identified factors related to the child's ability to testify. They include the child's level of cognitive social functioning, the child's level of anxiety and fear, the child's overall temperament and premorbid history, and the child's emotional sequelae related to the sexual abuse.

Preparing the Child for Testimony

In preparing a child for testimony, Saywitz (1991) was most concerned that the assessor develop sensitivity toward the child's overall functioning. Three areas are addressed with respect to these issues.

≡ Rapid Reference 7.3

Common Stressors in the Criminal Justice System

Dezwirek-Sas (1992, p. 184) has identified the following nine stressors:

1. *Delays.* Numerous unforeseen adjournments and lengthy delays that span many months, even years in a child's life.

2. *Public exposure.* Having to recount embarrassing and frightening incidents in a public room at an age when speaking publicly about oneself is difficult.

3. *Facing the accused.* Having to face the accused person when on the stand despite intense fear for personal safety.

4. *Understanding complex procedures.* Being exposed to court procedures that are foreign and easily misunderstood by children who do not know the legal terminology for the adversarial context.

5. *Change of Crown Attorneys.* Having changes in Crown Attorneys on their case just prior to or on the day of court, which undermines their sense of security and self-confidence. The lack of supportive/comfortable relationship when entering into court with their counsel because insufficient time had been spent together.

6. *Cross-examination.* Being cross-examined by a defense lawyer, who can be very aggressive. At times withstanding cross-examination that can be downright harassing in that it exploits the child's sensitivity and vulnerability.

7. *Exclusion of witnesses.* Being "alone" in court because of the removal of witnesses results in the child finding himself or herself in court on the stand without significant adult figures in his or her life (family) present as support.

8. *Apprehension and placement outside the home.* Being removed for safety reasons from one's home while the accused is allowed to stay. Children are often the ones to leave and are then stripped of their extended family support while the accused remains home.

9. *Lack of preparation for the role of witness.* Not being aware of the expectations of them because they are child witnesses. Most children are totally unprepared to give testimony and do not understand the adversarial system.

1. *Observe and assess the child's developmental status.* It is important that the assessor have a measure of the child's level of cognitive functioning, so it is necessary to use appropriate language when communicating with a child. The assessor must look at communication skills and cognitive academic skills, as well as social and emotional skills. Examples of inappropriate vocabulary include typical legal language that a child may

not understand. For example, the phrase *point to* should be used instead of *identify*. Children often interpret the word *charges* to mean something having to do with a credit card, the word *court* to mean something involved with basketball or tennis, and the word *date* to mean a social engagement with someone. A child should not be asked "how many times" if the child does not know how to count.

2. *Match the task with the child's skill level.* For a child to be appropriately interviewed in a sexual abuse allegation situation, the child will need to know a number of concepts. For example, the child must understand height, distance, weight, age, time, body parts, colors, location, and kinship terms. In addition, the basic concepts of first, last, never, always, even, before, after, above, and below must be understood. Therefore, the assessor must determine whether the child understands these basic concepts. If not, the completeness of the interview may be in question.

3. *Prepare the child for questioning.* Sass and Wolfe (1991) have addressed the issue of preparing the child for questioning and indicated that there was a tenfold increase in abuse allegations in the 20 years between 1970 and 1990. Testimony utilizing closed-circuit television and videotape has taken the place of live testimony in many courtrooms. Unfortunately, many courts remain adult-oriented places. Sass and Wolfe also pointed out that one of the areas a child does not understand is why lengthy delays can occur when objections are made, when sidebar conferences occur, or when the judge or attorneys are reviewing legal documents. The child must be prepared to understand that these delays can occur and that they have nothing to do with the child's own performance or competence. Secondary victimization can result from the need for the child to testify, the length of time before the trial commences, and the need for the child to recall the trauma long after completing significant therapeutic work toward resolving it.

 TEST YOURSELF

1. **During a competency evaluation, the examiner must address and include statements about the alleged offense.**
   True or False?

2. **Forensic instruments can be used interchangeably with adults and juveniles.**
   True or False?

3. Which type of evaluation is most frequently requested?
(a) Mental state at the time of the offense
(b) Competency
(c) Dangerousness
(d) Amenability to treatment

4. When assessing competence the focus is on capacity, present ability, cognitive functioning, and a reasonable degree of understanding.
True or False?

5. Collateral resources do not need to be interviewed in mental state at the time of offense evaluations.
True or False?

6. All of the following are factors that affect suggestibility except:
(a) the more intelligent the child, the less suggestible the child is.
(b) the better the child's executive functioning, the less suggestible the child is.
(c) lower socioeconomic (SES) children are less suggestible than higher SES children.
(d) the more confident the child, the less suggestible the child is.
(e) the higher the attachment security of the child, the less suggestible the child is.

Answers: 1. False; 2. False; 3. d; 4. True; 5. False; 6. c

SELECTED INSTRUMENTS

Adolescent Psychopathology Scale. Available from Psychological Assessment Resources. (800–331–8378)

Behavior Assessment System for Children, Second Edition. Available from Pearson Assessments. (800–627–7271)

Competence Assessment for Standing Trial for Defendants with Mental Retardation. Available from IDS Publishing Corporation. (614–885–2323)

Early Assessment Risk List. Available from the Child Development Institute, Toronto. (http;//www.childdevelop.ca)

Hare Psychopathy Checklist: Youth Version. Available from Psychological Assessment Resources. (800–331–8378)

(continued)

Instruments for Assessing Understanding and Appreciation of *Miranda* Rights. Available from Professional Resource Press. (800–443–3364)

Juvenile Adjudicative Competency Interview. Available from Professional Resource Press. (800–443–3364)

Kaufman Adolescent and Adult Intelligence Test. Available from Pearson Assessments. (800–627–7271)

Kaufman Assessment Battery for Children (2nd Ed.). Available from Pearson Assessments. (800–627–7271)

Kaufman Test of Educational Achievement (2nd Ed.). Available from Pearson Assessments. (800–627–7271)

MacArthur Competence Assessment Tool-Criminal Adjudication. Available from Psychological Assessment Resources. (800–331–8378)

Massachusetts Youth Screening Instrument-Version 2. Available from Professional Resource Press. (800–443–3364)

Millon Adolescent Personality Inventory. Available from Pearson Assessments. (800–627–7271)

Minnesota Multiphasic Personality Inventory-Adolescent. Available from Pearson Assessments. (800–627–7271)

Personality Assessment Inventory-Adolescent. Available from Psychological Assessment Resources. (800–331–8378)

Problem-Oriented Screening Instrument for Teenagers. Available from the National Clearinghouse for Alcohol and Drug Information. (http://ncadi.samhsa.gov/)

Rogers Criminal Responsibility Assessment Scales. Available from Psychological Assessment Resources. (800–331–8378)

Rorschach Psychodiagnostic Series. Available from Psychological Assessment Resources. (800–331–8378)

Structured Assessment of Violence Risk in Youth. Available from Specialized Training Services. (858–675–0860)

Wechsler Adult Intelligence Scale (4th Ed.). Available from Pearson Assessments. (800–627–7271)

Wechsler Individual Achievement Test (2nd Ed.). Available from Pearson Assessments. (800–627–7271)

Wechsler Intelligence Scale for Children (4th Ed.). Available from Pearson Assessments. (800–627–7271)

Wide Range Achievement Test (4th Ed.). Available from Psychological Assessment Resources. (800–331–8378)

Woodcock-Johnson Normative Update Complete III. Available from Riverside Publishing. (800–323–9540)

Eight

ESSENTIALS OF SUBSTANCE ABUSE ASSESSMENT

Edward M. Rubin

FACTS AND FIGURES

According to the Annual Report (2003) of the Arrestee Drug Abuse Monitoring program of the National Institute of Justice (http://www.ojp.usdoj.gov/nij/topics/drugs/adam.htm), there is exhaustive evidence of the powerful relationship between drug use and crime. In 2008, the Home Office of the United Kingdom reports, "There is a strong association between crime and drugs. Evidence suggests that amongst offenders, drug use is much higher than in the general population. There is also evidence that some types of crime are carried out in order to feed drug habits or would not have been carried out if individuals were not under the influence of drugs" (http://www.homeoffice.gov.uk/rds/drug-offending.html).

- Drug users report greater involvement in crime.
- Drug users are more likely than nonusers to have criminal records.
- People with criminal records are much more likely than others without records to report being drug users.
- Crime rates increase proportionately with increases in drug use.

Regarding those who have been arrested (not necessarily convicted or sentenced), it is also reported that in most cities where urine drug screens were used to screen arrestees, more than 50% of those tested were found to have used drugs recently.

The Bureau of Justice Statistics reports that, in 2004, "17% of state prisoners and 18% of federal inmates said they committed their current offense to obtain money for drugs" (www.ojp.usdoj.gov/bjs/dcf/duc.htm).

"In the 2004 Survey of Inmates in State and Federal Correctional Facilities, 32% of state prisoners and 26% of federal prisoners said they had committed their current offense while under the influence of drugs. Among state prisoners, drug offenders (44%) and property offenders (39%) reported the highest incidence of drug use at the time of the offense. Among federal prisoners, drug offenders (32%) and violent offenders (24%) were the most likely to report drug use at the time of their crimes" (http://www.ojp.usdoj.gov/bjs/dcf/duc.htm#to).

The Bureau of Justice Statistics reports that two-thirds of victims who suffered violence by an intimate (a current or former spouse, boyfriend, or girlfriend) reported that alcohol had been a factor. Among spouse victims, three out of four incidents were reported to have involved an offender who had been drinking. By contrast, an estimated 31% of stranger victimizations where the victim could determine the absence or presence of alcohol was perceived to be alcohol-related (http://www.ojp.usdoj.gov/bjs/cvict_c.htm). Of cases concluded in Federal district court since 1989, drug cases have increased at the greatest rate (http://www.ojp.usdoj.gov/bjs/glance.htm#outcomes).

(For those interested in more criminal justice information, consult the Office of National Drug Control Policy at http://www.whitehousedrugpolicy.gov/ or the U. S. Department of Justice, Office of Justice Programs, Bureau of Justice Statistics at http://www.ojp.usdoj.gov/bjs/.)

Despite the fact that psychologists have been able to obtain state credentials as certified alcohol or drug counselors for over 30 years and the emergence of the APA Professional College certification over 10 years ago in the specialty of substance abuse, relatively few psychologists have adequate training and knowledge in the area of substance abuse evaluation or treatment. There are even fewer psychologists who believe that it is within their area of expertise to evaluate, testify, consult, or provide other substance abuse information to the criminal or civil courts. In addition, when considering the criminal justice system, despite evidence that substance abuse has a serious impact on crime and criminality in the United States, it is not a well-received issue when raised in the context of a criminal trial. With the possible exception of involuntary intoxication, being under the influence of alcohol or some other drug prior to or during the commission of a crime is not exculpatory. Neither is it exculpatory to have an extensive history of substance abuse or multiple treatment episodes, as many criminal defendants have. Thus, when a request for a criminal forensic substance abuse evaluation is made, most often by the defense, it is often because there is little else in the record and few other facts of the case that the attorney believes can be helpful.

A more recent consideration and opportunity with regard to the role of providing forensic psychological assessment is in the field of drug treatment courts. There are over 2,000 drug treatment courts operating in the United States today. As defined by the National Drug Court Institute on their home page, at http://www.ndci.org/courtfacts.htm:

Drug courts represent the coordinated efforts of the judiciary, prosecution, defense bar, probation, law enforcement, mental health, social service, and treatment communities to actively and forcefully intervene and break the cycle of substance abuse, addiction, and crime. As an alternative to less effective interventions, drug courts quickly identify substance abusing offenders and place them under strict court monitoring and community supervision, coupled with effective, long-term treatment services.

As stated in the previous quote, drug treatment courts can offer many defendants alternatives to incarceration, once they qualify. Each jurisdiction can set its own standards and qualifications, but each defendant will need an evaluation or assessment to see if he or she meets the appropriate criteria. Psychologists can provide a pivotal role by learning about substance abuse and being able to provide the assessments needed by each drug treatment court.

SOURCES OF REFERRALS AND TYPES OF INFORMATION REQUESTED

In general, requests for forensic services related to substance abuse questions come from only a few sources, although a majority of referrals in the criminal justice system, at least in my experience, originate with defense attorneys. Other requests may come from the office of the state public defender, private defense attorneys, the office of the district attorney, divorce attorneys, and other psychologists or mental health professionals. A judge can also appoint a psychologist to perform the forensic substance abuse evaluation.

One of three types of information is most often requested by defense counsel in these situations.

1. *Information or testimony specifically about the effect of substance abuse and/or intoxication on a particular defendant.* The questions then become, what was the impact of the intoxication on the defendant's capacity to think, and was it related to an *intent* to commit the particular crime?
2. *General information or testimony about the effects of substances on affect, cognition, and behavior.* This may then allow the defense attorney to argue about the specific influence of the alcohol or other drugs in this particular case of his or her client and to convince the trier of fact (judge or jury) to include deliberations for a less severe crime than the one charged. The judge would then need to include instructions to the jury before deliberation that the jury consider not only the original crime charged by the district attorney but a lesser offense as well. For example, this

might mean the jury, in its deliberations, would consider not only a charge of second-degree intentional homicide, but also a charge of manslaughter.

3. *Information to be included in a presentence report.* Though this information may not necessarily have an impact on the charges brought, or on the trial, it might aid the attorney in arguing for, and the judge in deciding upon, an appropriate sentence. Most often, at least in my experience, there are clearly psychological factors involved in the case, and quite often treatment needs to be exposed during the evaluation process.

In providing testimony or other information to the court in the first two situations described, either implied or explicit, is the legal issue of diminished capacity. This particular defense "recognizes that a defendant may have had a mental or other impairment at the time of the alleged crime which does not rise to the level of insanity but may affect *mens rea* sufficiently to reduce the degree of the crime" (Kaplan & Miller, 1996, p. 288). This defense allows the introduction of expert testimony on this issue of *mens rea*, or a "culpable mental state" (Kaplan & Miller, 1996, p. 285). Substance abuse and intoxication, at least in many states, is seen as having the potential to negatively affect the individual's mental state such that it may reduce or eliminate criminal intent. Thus, the argument that many defense attorneys try to make is that the defendant was so intoxicated or impaired by the addiction that he or she lacked the capacity to form the intent to commit the crime. Of course, except for alcohol, level of intoxication with other drugs is quite difficult to substantiate.

Other requests for forensic substance abuse evaluation services may come from prosecutors through the office of the district attorney. An example is a case in Milwaukee in which a deputy sheriff was struck and killed on the side of an expressway while aiding a motorist. The attorney defending the driver of the car that struck and killed the officer was arguing that the driver suffered from a form of narcolepsy. A psychologist consultant to the prosecutor provided information about the effect of alcohol on behavior, particularly driving behavior. He was also asked to provide potential questions to the district attorney that would counter the defense's esoteric argument. This line of questioning would raise the more likely probability that the alcohol consumed by the driver just prior to the accident influenced the driver's judgment, depth perception, reflexes, and so on, suggesting to the jury that it was likely that intoxication led to the accident. No testimony was required in this case by the psychologist, but the consultant was asked to sit in court to listen to the direct and cross-examination of several of the defense witnesses. This provided a context within which to formulate questions to provide the district attorney for his examination of the witnesses. Other requests from prosecutors can stem from their desire to *rule out* intoxication as a possible defense.

Requests for forensic services from the civil court require other considerations. In child custody evaluations, it is not unusual that requests for a specific substance abuse evaluation of one or both parents be made as part of the custodial evaluations. These requests generally come from one of two sources. The first is from the attorney for one of the spouses. Most often, he or she is asking for a substance use evaluation of the *other* spouse. This may be due to a history of past substance abuse on the part of the spouse who is asked to be evaluated to rule out present problems or because of a present concern about drinking or other drug use. Another source of the evaluation requests may be from the psychologist who is doing a full custody evaluation because of concerns she or he may have. Less often, the guardian ad litem—the attorney appointed by the court in these cases to represent the best interests of the child(ren)—will request the substance abuse evaluation.

The information that is most often requested in these cases is the formulation of a substance use diagnosis, if appropriate. If there is a substance use diagnosis present, subsequent issues to be addressed in the evaluation focus on the impact the chemical dependency might have on parenting abilities. In addition, treatment recommendations are often requested.

ETHICAL CONSIDERATIONS

Prior to beginning any evaluation, it is vital to provide fully informed consent to the client. In addition, a clear understanding on the part of the psychologist about who has hired her or him and for what purpose is essential (Bersoff, 2008). Despite clinical training in objectivity, there may well be subtle (and maybe not so subtle) pressure from the referring attorney to find certain things or present the findings in a particular light. (See Chapter 1 for a more detailed discussion of this and other ethical concerns.)

When substance abuse issues are involved, there are some additional, unique ethical and confidentiality considerations. Federal law (42 U.S.C. §§ 290dd.–2 [1992]) and the Federal regulations that implement it (42 C.F.R. Part 2) guarantee the strict confidentiality of information about all people who receive any substance abuse prevention and/or treatment services. These particular regulations are more restrictive of communication than are those governing the doctor-client relationship or the attorney-client privilege and are much more strict than confidentiality addressed in the HIPAA (Health Insurance Portability and Accountability Act of 1996) regulations (see http://www.hhs.gov/ocr/privacysummary.pdf).

The regulations cover provision of specialized treatment, counseling, and assessment and referral services for clients with alcohol or other drug problems. The regulations are designed to cover "programs" that receive any sort of Federal assistance. An individual who provides any of the aforementioned services may be considered a program, and the definition of "Federal assistance" is broadly interpreted to "include indirect forms of Federal aid such as tax-exempt status or State or local funding that is derived, in whole or in part, from the Federal government" (Substance Abuse and Mental Health Services Administration, 1997, pp. 95–96). This means that a psychologist must carefully consider his or her particular situation to see if it meets the federal criteria such that extra care must be taken with regard to confidentiality. For example, if a psychologist's office bills Medicaid or Medicare, they are deemed to fall under these Federal guidelines for confidentiality.

Because criminal forensic evaluations frequently take place in the prison or jail where the defendant is incarcerated, both the coercive environment and the motives of the defendant in agreeing to participate in the assessment process must be considered in the interpretation of the clinical and testing material. Unless the evaluation is court ordered, the defendant's freedom to not participate or to selectively participate in the evaluation must be clearly stated and understood. In substance use evaluations, not only are the circumstances surrounding the alleged criminal act explored vis-à-vis the defendant's use of alcohol or other drugs, but other criminal activities may be explored as well. Fully informed consent is vital as these potential admissions may well be against the individual's penal interest. Therefore, written releases should always be executed. Even with a written release, an accompanying full explanation of how the information included in the psychological report may become a matter of public record if used in court should be included prior to proceeding with the evaluation.

In some civil cases (e.g., custody evaluations), the picture is somewhat different and often not as clear as in criminal cases. In general, although on first consideration it may seem counterintuitive, family court cases tend to be *more* antagonistic than criminal cases. Recall that in these circumstances, there may well be two contentious sides, often vying for leverage or advantage to help develop a particular case. Also, there are often three attorneys involved. Not only does each of the parents have an attorney, but a guardian ad litem is generally appointed to advocate solely for the interests of the child(ren). The initiation of the referral for an assessment may come from any of the attorneys or from the judge in the matter. An evaluation may be ordered on one or both of the parties who may or may not be willing participants in the entire process. Also, if an evaluation is performed and then not released for some reason, it is more likely that the court will order the release of the results. As in all situations, careful documentation of informed consent as well as the process of evaluation and how the conclusions and recommendations (if any) were reached is imperative.

ASSESSMENT FOR SUBSTANCE USE DISORDERS

Information used in making a substance use disorder assessment can come from a number of sources. Rapid Reference 8.1 lists the four primary areas from which such information can be gathered.

Records

In most circumstances, before meeting the individual to be evaluated, a number of records should be provided to the psychologist doing the evaluation. Whether the referral is from the criminal justice or the civil court system, before agreeing to complete the evaluation, a discussion should take place with the referring attorney about what other records or documentation are already available or should be requested. (See Rapid Reference 8.2.)

From the criminal court, this typically includes information obtained as part of the "discovery" process—the release from opposing counsel of the information and evidence from which they have built their case. This most often will include any arrest or investigation records and/or supplemental reports filed by the police. These records describe the entire police involvement from the time of their initial awareness of the crime (e.g., radio dispatch to a crime scene) through the interviews with victims and witnesses to the circumstances of the arrest of the defendant. There may also be transcripts, or more often now, CD audio files of interviews and interrogations with the defendant, or his or her confession. There

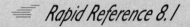

Rapid Reference 8.1

Four Domains from Which Assessment Information Can Be Drawn

- Records
- Clinical interview
- Collateral information
- Objective test data

≡ *Rapid Reference 8.2*

Examples of Records to Review Prior to Forensic Evaluation

Arrest records

Records of previous substance abuse treatment

Supplemental police reports or mental health treatment victim and witness statements

Hospital records

Defendant statements

Previous evaluations

Preliminary hearing transcripts

Relevant depositions

may also be video or pictures of the scene available, as well. Included may also be lists of evidence collected. This information can aid in assessing the role of substance use and any possible mitigating impact that substance use or intoxication might have had in the circumstances. At times, a transcript from the preliminary hearing may also be useful. The preliminary hearing takes place in a courtroom. It is at this point that a decision was made by a judge or court commissioner that it is likely that a crime has been committed and that the defendant may well have committed it. It will contain some actual testimony of the arresting police officer(s) and perhaps a witness or two. This particular information is not always necessary or even available, but if it is, it may provide information about the defendant's appearance and behavior at the time of the arrest that can be helpful in the assessment process.

Of course, any relevant previous hospital or other treatment records should be requested and reviewed as well. This may well include emergency room admissions. Also, if a blood alcohol concentration or urine or blood drug screen was determined at some point after the arrest, that is vital information for the forensic psychologist to have. Testimony from other witnesses about quantity, frequency, and history of drinking or other substance use may also be included in the court proceedings or witness statements. In addition, a request can be made of the referring attorney for any other *relevant* material. Generally, it is not necessary to review the entire file; leave to the discretion of the referring attorney what might be necessary for review after discussion with the forensic psychologist.

In some civil cases, as in custody disputes, it may also be necessary to request and review any depositions, if these have been made. These are interviews conducted under oath and recorded by a court reporter. They are conducted prior to any actual court proceedings. In reviewing depositions, the perspective on the substance abuse issues from both parties will be presented through the questions and answers during the interviews. It can help clarify how each parent views the impact of substance abuse on the issues of custody and parenting of the child(ren).

Clinical Interview

The best source of information is a thorough clinical interview. When done properly, the interview may take one-and-a-half to three hours. The time is well spent, however, as it contributes to the establishment of rapport, which in turn enhances the reliability of the information that is being gathered. A review of the scientific literature concludes, as reported by Connors and Volk (2003), that "many others believe these [self]-reports can be valid and useful in the screening as well as assessment and treatment of alcohol abusers"(p. 25). This is especially true when information is collected in multiple modalities, as is done in this sort of evaluation. Even in circumstances in which there may be significant negative consequences, clinical information can be obtained in a way that is relatively free of distortion or deception. In fact, the validity of self-reported drug use in patients with alcohol use disorders has been shown to be relatively high (Staines et al. 2001).

A good clinical interview should minimally include inquiry into the areas noted in Rapid Reference 8.3. Information about the material that various sections of a clinical interview should include is available elsewhere (e.g., Zuckerman, 2005). However, some detail about garnering substance abuse history is provided here. It should also be noted that, according to the National Institute on Drug Abuse (TIP 42, p. 4), "National surveys suggest [co-occurring disorders] are common in the adult population." It should come as no surprise, then, that when assessing substance abuse issues in a forensic population, one might rather commonly find a variety of other concurrent mental health issues.

The practitioner who does substance abuse evaluations must generally be familiar with the various substances of abuse, regional variations in popularity and availability, the effects and pharmacology of various drugs, costs, and mode of administration. This permits a more detailed interview and gives the psychologist a general framework in which to begin to assess the veracity of the information being provided.

≣ *Rapid Reference 8.3*

....

Topics to Cover in the Clinical Interview

- General client information
- Chief complaints
- History of problem
- Medical history
- Substance abuse history
- Psychiatric history
- Social history
- Family history
- Legal history
- Mental status exam
- DSM-IV-TR multiaxial diagnoses

Drugs of Abuse

A. Central nervous system stimulants

This includes drugs such as amphetamines and cocaine; caffeine and nicotine, but also 3,4-methylenedioxymethamphetamine, or ecstasy ("XTC").

B. Central nervous system depressants

This includes drugs such as barbiturates, non-barbiturates, tranquilizers, alcohol, and narcotics. The latter category includes "OC's", or oxycontin, frequently diverted and used illicitly.

C. Hallucinogens

This includes such drugs as LSD, psilocybin, peyote, and marijuana.[a]

D. Inhalants

This includes such things as nitrous oxide, amyl nitrite, glue, toluene, and paint thinner.

Note: This list is not exhaustive, but merely provides examples.

[a]Falls into two categories, depending on potency—central nervous system depressants or hallucinogens.

E. Club drugs

This includes drugs such as GHB (Gamma hydroxy butyrate), ket-amine, Rohypnol (a drug related to the tranquilizers), and steroids.

Information that should be gathered during this part of the clinical interview includes a description of the circumstance of initial use of alcohol and other psychoactive substances as well as a description of the first intoxication. This should be followed by a description of any changes in the pattern of drinking or dug use over time. Included in this is a description of both quantity and frequency of use, as well as the circumstances of any use (e.g., drinking only on weekends, at parties, solitary use, etc.). The most recent patterns of use should be described, as well, using various time frames such as between the last 6 and 12 months, in the past month, or prior to incarceration. The phenomenology of the drinking or drug experience should also be explored. This means that the individual is asked to describe what the specific effect of the alcohol or other drug has on him or her. Assumptions are often made about the particular effect of a drug on an individual based on one's own experiences or academic knowledge. Even though the basic pharmacological effects of a drug are understood, the unique experience or expected effect of the drug on that particular individual being evaluated is well worth understanding. This specific information can provide clues to a possible co-occurring psychiatric disorder or other factors motivating the substance use. (See Rapid Reference 8.4.)

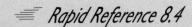

≡ Rapid Reference 8.4

Information to Be Gathered for the History for Each Drug Used

First Use

First intoxication

Changes in pattern of use over time

Quantity/frequency information

Recent use

Circumstances of use

  Cost

  Method of ingestion

  Effect of the drug(s)

Drug phenomenology

In most of the circumstances in which one may be called on to provide a forensic assessment for substance abuse, the individual being evaluated will want to present himself or herself in a particular light. Thus, the possibility for distortion in this particular environment is not nearly so subtle as one may encounter where legal issues are not at stake.

Collateral Information

To do a comprehensive evaluation, psychologists must be prepared to gather additional information from other sources where possible (Jacobson, 1989). As Maisto & Connors (1992) described, collateral individual reports possess several properties that make them valuable second measures, including being flexible in content and time period addressed. Also, currently, there are no strong alternatives to subject and collateral reports when assessing drinking patterns of more than a month or so ago.

Collateral information can be invaluable in performing the forensic substance abuse evaluation. It can provide the evaluator with information that is congruous and consistent vis-à-vis the clinical information gathered in the interview, or it may provide information that calls the clinical interview material into question. Thus, it may contribute strikingly to one's confidence in the material that is being gathered and may suggest areas for further exploration. Collateral information can be gathered from any number of other sources, including a spouse or partner, other family members, supervisor or employer, coworkers, and others. Obviously, the collection of the collateral information often takes the form of additional interviews. Although not necessary, there are instruments designed to aid in the collection of collateral information. The Center on Alcoholism, Substance Abuse, and Addictions has a wide variety of assessment instruments available for free on their web site (http://casaa.unm.edu/inst.html), including several specifically for obtaining information from significant others (e.g., Form 90 AC).

One question specifically related to drinking is often asked in criminal justice system referrals. This is about the actual level of intoxication of the defendant at the time of the commission of the alleged criminal act. A second question, previously mentioned, is regarding the possible impact or effect that intoxication may (or may not) have had on the commission of the crime. Specifically, the questions, at least as they are posed under some state statutes, ask if the defendant was in fact intoxicated and, if so, whether the intoxication was such that the defendant lacked substantial capacity to form the intent (*mens rea*) to commit the crime with which he or she is charged.

With regard to the first question, there are formulas available to help determine the blood alcohol concentration at the time of a crime (see Rapid Reference 8.5). The blood alcohol concentration is the proportion of alcohol to blood in the body. It is often expressed as the percentage of alcohol in deciliters of blood; for example, 0.10 percent refers to 0.10 grams of alcohol per deciliter of blood. In most states, 0.08 is considered the legal limit for "driving while intoxicated."

The resultant blood alcohol concentration estimate must be adjusted for elimination of alcohol over time. This is done by multiplying the number of hours from the beginning of drinking to the time of the commission of the crime (or whenever the defendant stopped drinking) by .015 and subtracting that result from Step 3 in Rapid Reference 8.5. This result is the approximate blood alcohol concentration at the time of the commission of the crime, but it is important to understand that this yields *only* an estimation. Information gathered about the kind of alcohol (e.g., its proof, or concentration) and how quickly and how much alcohol was consumed has generally been provided only by the defendant unless corroborated by collateral sources. In the eyes of the court, this may well make the information suspect.

At this point, an estimate of the level of alcohol concentration in the defendant's blood at the time of the crime has been derived. The second question noted previously may also need to be addressed; that is, what impact did this level of intoxication have on the defendant? This is a difficult question to answer and often can only be addressed in general terms. Prior history with alcohol, tolerance, expectations, and learned experience regarding the effects of alcohol all influence the specific effects alcohol will have on any one individual on any specific occasion. To help with this, some general guidelines have been published that give the approximate effect of varying amounts of alcohol on human behavior and cognition.

According to the National Institute on Alcohol Abuse and Alcoholism (1995), investigators have found no blood alcohol concentration threshold below which there is no impairment of any kind. There is always some impact of even small amounts of alcohol.

The guidelines for blood alcohol levels that appear in the following Don't Forget do not exist for other drugs of abuse. It is much more difficult to ascertain amounts, potency, purity, and so on, and therefore specific statements about intoxication and effect are even more difficult to make. Because of this, most often, the request made by the defense attorney is that the expert describes for the judge or jury the general pharmacological effects of the drug(s) used and leaves it to the attorneys to relate those effects to the specific case at hand during the closing arguments.

≡ *Rapid Reference 8.5*

. . . .

Determining Blood Alcohol Concentration

One formula for estimating probable blood alcohol concentration from a given number of drinks is provided by Fitzgerald and Hume (1987).

1. Convert "beverage ounces" to fluid ounces of alcohol (multiply number of ounces by alcohol percent as decimal).

   Examples:

   1 shot of 86 proof[a] = 1 oz. × 0.43 = 0.43 fl. oz

   1 12 oz. beer (4.5%) = 12 oz. × 0.045 = 0.54 fl. oz

   1 4 oz. glass wine (12%) = 4 oz. × 0.12 = 0.48 fl. oz

   [a] Proof indicates the alcohol content of distilled beverages. The percentage of alcohol by volume is one-half the proof number; in this example, 86 proof is 43% alcohol.

2. Multiply body weight times the numerical constant (for average r, then for high and low to get range). Note product.

   Examples:

   150 [lbs.] × 0.125 [Average r N.C.[a]] = 18.75

   150 [lbs.] × 0.096 [Low r N.C.] = 14.40

   150 [lbs.] × 0.158 [High r N.C.] = 23.70

   [a] N.C. = numerical constant.

3. Divide (Step 1) by (Step 2) to get estimated probable blood alcohol concentration.

   There are also sites on the Web that allow one to enter demographic and quantity/frequency information to then derive estimates of blood alcohol concentration. One site is available through the Centre for Addiction and Mental Health in Canada, which also provides an evaluation of the risk of individual's drinking:

   http://www.alcoholhelpcenter.net/Program/BAC_Standalone.aspx

   Other sites are:

   http://www.intox.com/wheel/drinkwheel.asp

   http://www.ou.edu/oupd/bac.htm

   Finally, there is a computer program available that will estimate blood alcohol concentration for you. A full description and manual are available at: http://casaa.unm.edu/download/baccus.pdf.

DON'T FORGET

Blood Alcohol Level and Behavioral Effects

Blood Alcohol Level Percentage	Behavioral Effects
0.02–0.03	Few obvious effects; slight intensification of mood.
0.05–0.06	Feeling of warmth, relaxation, mild sedation; exaggeration of emotion and behavior; slight decrease in reaction time and in fine-muscle coordination; impaired judgment about continued drinking.
0.07–0.09	More noticeable speech impairment and disturbance of balance; impaired motor coordination, hearing, and vision; feeling of elation or depression; increased confidence; may not recognize impairment.
0.11–0.12	Coordination and balance becoming difficult; distinct impairment of mental faculties and judgment.
0.14–0.15	Major impairment of mental and physical control; slurred speech, blurred vision, and lack of motor skills; needs medical evaluation.
0.20	Loss of motor control; must have assistance moving about; mental confusion; needs medical assistance.
0.30	Severe intoxication; minimum conscious control of mind and body; needs hospitalization.
0.30–0.60	This level of alcohol has been measured in people who have died of alcohol intoxication.
0.40	Unconsciousness; coma; needs hospitalization; about the LD 50 (the dose at which half of those with this level of intoxication will die).

In civil cases where there are custody disputes, different questions are raised. The issue most often to be addressed is to determine whether the parent in question has a substance use disorder, and if so, what implications that poses for parenting and custody arrangements. In other civil cases referred from state departments of regulation and licensing, there is a question about substance abuse on the part of the licensed, referred professional. In these latter cases, in addition to addressing the questions of chemical dependency and ability to practice, recommendations are often requested regarding potential treatment interventions.

Objective Test Data

As in the application of all psychological testing, there are a number of instruments that can be used in a forensic substance abuse assessment. Selection depends on what questions are being addressed. Also, there are a multitude of instruments available to meet these specific needs of a forensic psychologist. Those included here are merely examples of what is available; by no means is the list of Selected Instruments (pp. 246–247) exhaustive. These instruments have had significant acceptance in this field. For a comprehensive review of relevant instruments, the reader is referred to *Assessing Alcohol Problems: A Guide for Clinicians and Researchers, Second Edition* (National Institute on Alcohol Abuse and Alcoholism, 2003). Miller, Westerberg, and Waldron (2003) pointed out that there are six functions of evaluation. Four of those six may apply directly to forensic assessment issues: screening, diagnosis, assessment, and treatment planning.

Screening is one of the tasks most often required in a criminal or civil forensic context. The task is to first identify if in fact there exists a substance abuse problem for the individual being evaluated. Screening measures are not designed to do more than provide the evaluator with a heightened index of suspicion. In criminal justice populations, screening often leads to the conclusion that there may be a substance abuse problem. Screens are generally quite brief and adaptable to a variety of settings. Often, since they are so easily administered, it may be useful to administer more than one. This can contribute significantly to one's confidence that a problem may exist. Most popular are the CAGE Questionnaire (or CAGE-AID, adapted to include drugs), the TWEAK for women, and the Alcohol Use Disorders Identification Test (AUDIT).

The CAGE-AID Questionnaire consists of four questions:

1. [*C*ut] Have you ever felt you should cut down on your drinking (or drug use)?
2. [*A*nnoyed] Have people annoyed you by criticizing your drinking (or drug use)?
3. [*G*uilty] Have you ever felt bad or guilty about your drinking (or drug use)?
4. [*E*ye-opener] Have you ever had a drink (or used drugs) first thing in the morning?

Items are scored either 0 or 1, with a higher score suggestive of alcohol (or drug) problems. A total score of 2 or more is considered significant, and thus should lead to further evaluation or assessment. The CAGE is designed for use with people 16 years or older and takes less than one minute to administer in the course of an interview.

The AUDIT was developed by the World Health Organization. It consists of 10 questions scored on a Likert-type scale ranging from 0 to 4. It has several questions about amount and frequency of drinking, three questions about alcohol dependence symptoms, and four questions addressing life problems caused by alcohol. It is targeted for adults and requires about two minutes to administer. It can easily be incorporated into the clinical interview. Scoring is quite simple and takes only a minute.

Another very popular screening instrument is the Michigan Alcohol Screening Test (MAST). It has a number of incarnations and may be the most widely used screening instrument for lifetime alcohol problems. In its original form, it is a 25-item list of common signs and symptoms of alcohol problems. It requires about 10 minutes to take and can be self-administered or included in a clinical interview. The full version of the MAST takes five minutes to score. There are also a variety of briefer versions available (e.g., Brief MAST and Short MAST), and a geriatric version has been developed as well (MAST-G).

In the full version of the MAST, a cutoff score of 5 is strongly suggestive of alcohol problems, although Jacobson (1989) has recommended a higher cutoff score (e.g., 12). This reduced the sensitivity of the test somewhat, "but increased specificity dramatically" (p. 23).

The TWEAK is a five-item scale that has been specifically developed and validated to screen women for at-risk drinking during pregnancy. It is very brief, taking less than two minutes to administer. Consisting of five questions, it can be self-administered or included in a clinical interview.

1. [*T*olerance] How many drinks can you hold?
2. [*W*orried] Have close friends or relatives worried or complained about your drinking in the past year?
3. [*E*ye-opener] Do you sometimes take a drink in the morning when you first get up?
4. [*A*mnesia, blackouts] Has a friend or family member ever told you about things you said or did while you were drinking that you could not remember?
5. [*K*ut] Do you sometimes feel the need to cut down on your drinking?

Researchers found that this five-item screening instrument "appears to be the optimal screening questionnaire for identifying women with heavy drinking or alcohol abuse and dependence in racially mixed populations" (Bradley, Boyd-Wickizer, Powell, & Burman, 1998, p. 170).

Another instrument that has also been developed specifically for screening pregnant women is the T-ACE. It consists of the following four items:

1. [*T*olerance] How many drinks does it take to make you feel high?
2. [*A*nnoyed] Have people annoyed you by criticizing your drinking?
3. [*C*ut] Have you felt you ought to cut down on your drinking?
4. [*E*ye-opener] Have you ever had a drink first thing in the morning to steady your nerves or get rid of a hangover?

Two scales on the MMPI-2 may be of use in the forensic evaluation of substance abuse. These are the Addiction Admission Scale, which detects acknowledgment of alcohol/drug problems, and the Addiction Potential Scale, which attempts to measure personality factors underlying the development of addictive disorders.

Greene, Weed, Butcher, Arredondo, and Davis (1992) found that "both scales discriminate between psychiatric and substance abuse samples, and do so more effectively than other substance abuse scales designed for use with the MMPI" (p. 405). It should be noted, however, that in the latest National Institute on Alcohol Abuse and Alcoholism (NIAAA) review (2003) of Assessing Alcohol Problems, neither the MMPI as a whole, or any of its subscales except the MacAndrew Alcoholism Scale are noted as being of value in this rather narrow arena of forensic substance abuse assessment.

One other indirect instrument is the third edition of the Substance Abuse Subtle Screening Inventory (SASSI-3). It is a brief self-report with separate versions targeted at both adults and adolescents. It can be objectively and easily scored and has decision criteria to classify people who have a high probability of having a substance dependence disorder. The SASSI-3 has both face valid and subtle items that have no apparent relationship to substance use. These items are included to identify some individuals with alcohol and other drug problems who are unwilling or unable to acknowledge substance misuse or symptoms associated with it. There is, however, debate about the utility of the subtle items, with some (Feldstein & Miller, 2007) asserting that there is no empirical evidence that the indirect scales of the SASSI-3 add anything to its face valid items in screening for alcohol problems.

The next task of forensic assessment of substance abuse is to provide a diagnosis, where appropriate. A number of instruments are available to help with this task (see Selected Instruments, pp. 246–247), one of which is the Diagnostic Interview Schedule for DSM-IV Alcohol Module (DIS). It is a fully structured interview based on diagnostic criteria of the DSM-IV and is targeted to adults. It is useful in diagnosing respondents of various cultural and educational backgrounds. The DIS takes about 10 to 20 minutes to administer and requires some training for administration.

In this same format, the Structured Clinical Interview for the DSM may be the most widely used of the DSM interviews. The substance abuse questions take about 10–20 minutes to complete, and a diagnosis of substance abuse or dependence can then be determined. One can also add appropriate DSM qualifiers (e.g., mild, moderate, severe, in partial or full remission) at the completion of the interview.

Another structured interview using a booklet and scoring sheet and taking between 30 to 45 minutes to administer, the Substance Use Disorder Diagnostic Schedule (SUDDS-IV) yields information for the lifetime and current diagnosis of alcohol or other drug abuse according to the DSM-IV/DSM IV-TR. It also gathers information about mood and anxiety disorders.

Falling under the rubric of multidimensional assessment measures, both the Personality Assessment Inventory and the Minnesota Multiphasic Personality Inventory (MMPI-2) are worth mentioning. Although neither is designed solely for the purpose of assessing substance abuse difficulties, the former instrument does have scales designed to assess alcohol and drug problems as well as to assess malingering. More about this instrument can be read in Chapter 2 of this book. They are both noteworthy for aiding clinicians in detecting personality characteristics that may suggest the presence of a personality disorder, which may contribute to the likelihood of developing potential addiction problems. They can both be used in forensic settings contributing to a more global perspective about the individual being evaluated. This permits the evaluator to place the substance abuse questions within a broader context of general individual functioning and provides a framework in which to understand the substance abuse. The information gleaned from these instruments can also help frame recommendations regarding treatment, incarceration, or other related issues that the court may want addressed. Despite this, however, both are notably absent from the most recent edition of *Assessing Alcohol Problems: A Guide for Clinicians and Researchers (2003)*.

The third function of evaluation is assessment. Screening and diagnosis both yield conclusions that are categorical in nature; that is, at the end of the process the screen is positive or negative, and the individual either meets criteria for a diagnosis of substance abuse or dependence or does not. In the domain of assessment, there is an attempt to gather information that will describe the unique situation and qualities of the individual in a more continuous manner. In this regard, drinking or drug-using information is descriptive, with both quantity and frequency information being relevant (see Selected Instruments, pp. 246–247 for a list of assessment instruments). In addition, the unique phenomenological experience of the person being evaluated is important. The particular impact that the person's drinking or drug use has had on her or his life is also part of the assessment. The Drinker Inventory of Consequences or its drug use version, the Inventory of Drug Use Consequences, developed through Project MATCH, is quite useful for this part of the evaluation. A public domain instrument, it has been used in a wide variety of settings, and requires only about 10 minutes for its self-administration. It provides information about drinking or drug use consequences in a variety of domains of an individual's life.

Another instrument, and one of the most well known for substance abuse assessment, particularly in the research realm, is the Addiction Severity Index (ASI). A semi-structured interview targeted at adults, it addresses seven potential problem areas for individuals who may be abusing psychoactive substances: medical status, employment or support, alcohol and/or drug use, legal status, family/social status, and psychiatric status. Additionally, the ASI is quite adept at discerning individuals with co-occurring mental health difficulties. "It has been repeatedly demonstrated that [the psychiatric status] portion of the ASI may be the best predictor of treatment outcome" (Jacobson, 1989, pp. 30–31). Primary drawbacks of the ASI include the fact that it may take an hour or so to administer the interview, and administration does require some training to maintain the instrument integrity.

Another comprehensive instrument useful for assessment is the Alcohol Use Inventory (AUI), which is also effective in treatment planning. It comprises a set of 24 scales designed to measure different aspects of an individual's involvement with alcohol. It directly addresses the unique experience of the individual's drinking in that it assesses individually perceived benefits and styles of drinking, as well as the individual's perceptions about the consequences of their use. The AUI is targeted at adults and adolescents over 16 years of age. It is self-administered and consists of 228 items, requiring between 30 and 60 minutes to complete. It can be scored by hand or computer and it provides a profile of scales as well as interpretive information.

The 88-item Comprehensive Drinker Profile is another structured interview requiring about two hours to complete and about 30 minutes to score. A shorter version (the Brief Drinker Profile) is also available. It is targeted toward adults and does require training for the administration of the instrument. An empathic, nonjudgmental, nonconfrontive attitude is also recommended by the authors for successful use of this instrument. It is designed to treat the person being evaluated as a unique individual, and gathers demographic information, as well as information on quantity and frequency of drinking, motivation, and sense of self-efficacy.

Neuropsychological Considerations

Although rarely part of a forensic assessment for substance abuse, occasionally neuropsychological impairment may need to be addressed. Heavy use of alcohol and some other psychoactive drugs can certainly lead to neuropsychological compromise. Most of the deficits created by heavy drinking are subtle and difficult to identify. Hester and Miller (2003) have pointed out that "Deficits in neurocognitive functioning may be among the earliest and most sensitive indicators of alcohol-related impairment. . ." (p. 95). There is evidence that adult alcoholics perform less competently than controls in four domains: executive functioning, memory, visual-spatial, and motor performance. Therefore, they suggest that certain of the Performance subscales of the WAIS seem to be able to detect early alcohol-related deficits. Relevant data for the new version of the Wechsler (WAIS-IV) are not yet available. On the new instrument, however, subtests that may be useful in this regard include coding, visual puzzles, and symbol search.

Although this instrument is not frequently used any longer, several subtests of the Halstead-Reitan Neuropsychological Test Battery also seem to be quite sensitive to alcohol-related difficulties. These include the Categories Test, the Tactual Performance Test, the Trail Making Test (especially section B), and the Finger-Tapping Test.

Biomedical Data

These data, when available, generally come by way of breath, blood, or urine testing done after arrest, or they are available from the medical records of previous treatment experiences reviewed as part of the evaluation process. In addition to any blood alcohol concentration measures taken after arrest, one may have the opportunity to review other data. Urine toxicology assays can reveal the presence or absence of a wide variety of psychoactive substances. Particular blood markers worthy of note include mean corpuscular volume. This is an indication of the size of the individual's red blood cells, which tends to be elevated in one who drinks heavily. The most commonly used biochemical markers are enzymes found in the liver (among other places in the body). The activity of these enzymes has a tendency to increase as a result of heavy drinking. Although serum glutamic-oxaloacetic transaminase along with other liver functions is often assessed, the most specific enzyme elevation found for alcohol abuse is gamma glutamyl transferase. A fairly new marker is carbohydrate-deficient transferrin. An abnormality occurs after regular drinking of about five to seven standard drinks a day for about a week. All of these markers are useful as corroborating data, but none is accurate enough to replace self-report or to make a definitive diagnosis.

Other Test Data

In the course of a forensic evaluation, one needs to gather information beyond that specifically related to drinking or drug use. In addition to performing a mental status exam as part of a clinical interview, administration of a brief instrument that also assesses mental status can serve to increase the examiner's confidence in the other information collected. Using either a Folstein Mini-Mental State Exam or Short Test of Mental Status serves that purpose quite well. Both instruments take only 5 to 10 minutes to administer and score and can provide a gross estimate of cognitive functioning. A brief assessment of intellectual capacity can also be useful in providing data to enhance confidence in the clinical material and that the informed consent was understood. The Shipley Institute of Living Scale is short, easy to administer, and can provide a general assessment of intellectual capacity. Alternatively, two WAIS-IV subtests can also serve to provide a general measure of cognitive potential (Vocabulary and Block Design). If one desires to add a brief neuropsychological screen, the Brief Neuropsychological Cognitive Examination (BNCE) may be considered. As previously mentioned, the clinician may also choose to administer an objective personality measure (e.g., PAI or MMPI-2) to help increase the understanding of the clinical context for the forensic questions being asked. To add to those data, a brief projective test such as Incomplete Sentences may be helpful. Although this instrument can give information about a number of important areas in the examinee's life (depending on time constraints and the examinee's reading level, of course), it should be noted that this instrument may not meet the Daubert standard in states where this rule has been accepted and adopted into the court's considerations.

Time constraints and location are often an issue in forensic assessments, particularly if the individual is incarcerated. Access often becomes a significant issue at that point. When an evaluation is not done in your office, but rather in a jail or prison, all test instruments must be taken to the facility, where they are always subject to search and justification to the prison authorities. Also, depending on both the examiner's time and availability and the cooperation of the criminal justice system, it may be difficult to have multiple visits with the person being evaluated. At times, it can be difficult to even *locate* the individual who is to be evaluated.

It is both intriguing and challenging to provide substance abuse evaluations for forensic purposes. Because the requests can come from criminal or civil courts, the clinician will be exposed to a variety of psychological and legal issues. Being able to cope with some ambiguity and anxiety is clearly a strength for psychologists who wish to practice in this field.

SELECTED INSTRUMENTS

Addiction Severity Index. No commercial source; public domain.

Alcohol Use Disorders Identification Test. Available from Programme on Substance Abuse, World Health Organization, 1211 Geneva, Switzerland, or from Thomas F. Babor, Alcohol Research Center, University of Connecticut, Farmington, CT 06030.

Alcohol Use Inventory. Available from National Computer Systems, P.O. Box 1416, Minneapolis, MN 55440.

CAGE. No commercial source; public domain.

Comprehensive Drinker Profile. Available from Psychological Assessment Resources, P.O. Box 998, Odessa, FL 33556. Software available from William Miller, Ph.D., Department of Psychology, University of New Mexico, Albuquerque, NM 87131.

Diagnostic Interview Schedule. Available from Department of Psychiatry, Box 8134, Washington University School of Medicine, 4940 Children's Place, St. Louis, MO 63110. Computerized version available from Dr. J.H. Greist, Department of Psychiatry, University of Wisconsin, 600 Highland Ave., Madison, WI 53792.

Drinker Inventory of Consequences (DrInc). In Project MATCH Monograph series, volume 4. Write to NIAAA, 5600 Fishers Lane, Rockville, MD 20857.

Folstein Mini-Mental Status Exam. See Folstein, M. F., Folstein, S. E., & McHugh, P. R. (1975). Mini-mental state: A practical method for grading the cognitive state of outpatients for the clinician. *Journal of Psychiatric Research, 12,* 189–198.

MacAndrew Alcoholism Scale-Revised. Available from Pearson Education, Inc., Upper Saddle River, NJ 07458.

Michigan Alcoholism Screening Test. Available from Melvin L. Selzer, MD, 6967 Paseo Laredo, La Jolla, CA 92037.

Personality Assessment Inventory. Available from Psychological Assessment Resources, Inc., Lutz, FL 33549.

Minnesota Multiphasic Personality Inventory-2. Available from Pearson Education, Inc., Upper Saddle River, NJ 07458.

Brief Neuropsychological Cognitive Examination. Available from Western Psychological Services, Los Angeles, CA 90025.

Short Test of Mental Status. See Kokmen, E., Naessens, J., & Offord, K. (1987). A short test of mental status. Description and preliminary results. *Mayo Clinic Procedures, 62,* 281–288.

Structured Clinical Interview for DSM-IV. Available from New York State Psychiatric Institute, New York, NY 10032.

Substance Abuse Subtle Screening Inventory-3. Available from The SASSI Institute, Springville, IN 47462.

Substance Use Disorders Diagnostic Schedule. Available from Evince Clinical Assessments, Smithfield, RI 02917.

T-ACE. Available from S. Martier, Ob/Gyn, 4707 Saint Antoine, Detroit, MI 48201.

TWEAK. Available from Marcia Russell, Ph.D., Prevention Research Center, Berkeley, CA 94704.

Wechsler Adult Intelligence Scale-IV. Available from Pearson Education, Inc., Upper Saddle River, NJ 07458.

Nine

ESSENTIALS OF MALTREATMENT ASSESSMENT

PHYSICAL ABUSE, SEXUAL ABUSE, PSYCHOLOGICAL ABUSE, AND DOMESTIC VIOLENCE

Marc J. Ackerman

Have abusive situations been increasing in recent years, or has society become more aware and less tolerant of abuse generally with the result of it being reported more frequently? Clearly, the latter is true, but in addition, society has widened the range of acts that are defined as abusive. For example, a generation ago what was considered "reasonable punishment" for a child is now deemed to be child abuse in many jurisdictions. This chapter focuses on four major areas of abusive behaviors, although there is some overlap. They are: (1) physical abuse, (2) domestic violence, (3) psychological or emotional abuse, and (4) sexual abuse.

The Children Abuse Prevention Treatment Act (Public Law No. 100–294) defines child abuse and neglect as physical or mental injury (sexual abuse or exploitation, negligent treatment, or maltreatment)

> [O]f a child (a person under the age of 18, unless the child protection law of that State in which the child resides specifies a younger age for cases not involving sexual abuse) by a person (including any employee of a residential facility or any staff personnel providing out-of-home care) who is responsible for the child's welfare under circumstances which indicate that the child's health or welfare is harmed or threatened thereby...

Physical abuse is characterized by inflicting physical injury by punching, beating, kicking, biting, burning, or otherwise harming a child. Although the injury is not an accident, the parent or caregiver may not have intended to hurt the child. The injury may have resulted from over-discipline or physical punishment that is inappropriate to the child's age.

Additionally, the U.S. Department of Health and Human Services (1992) noted:

> Child neglect is characterized by failure to provide the child's basic needs. Neglect can by physical, education or emotional. The latest incidence study

defines these three types of neglect as follows: Physical neglect includes refusal of or delay in seeking health care, abandonment, expulsion from home, or not allowing a runaway to return, and inadequate supervision. Education neglect is permission for chronic truancy, failure to enroll a child of mandatory school age, and inattention to a special educational need. (p. 2)

LONG-TERM EFFECTS OF ABUSE

There is extensive professional literature on the long-term effects of physical abuse. What follows is a summary of what the literature has reported.

Adolescents who exhibit aggressive and violent behaviors, including extrafamilial and dating violence, demonstrate higher rates of maltreatment than the general population (Malinosky-Rummell & Hansen, 1993, p. 70). Violent adolescents in residential facilities and violent inmates and outpatients demonstrate higher rates of physical abuse than do less violent or nonviolent comparison groups (p. 70). Of the men whose parents did not hit each other, those who had been physically abused as teenagers had twice the rates of violence toward their wives than nonabused men (p. 71–72). Physically abused children demonstrate significantly more noncompliance and nonaggressive conduct disorders (p. 72).

Evidence exists to support a relationship between childhood physical abuse and substance abuse as an adolescent, in addition to a higher rate of parental substance abuse (p. 73). Studies have also demonstrated that maltreatment has been linked to adolescent, female college student, and male and female inpatient self-injurious and suicidal behaviors (p. 73). Physically abused youths between 6 and 16 years of age have more emotional problems—including anxiety, depression, somatization, hostility, and paranoid ideation—than nonabused children. There is a relationship between childhood physical abuse and effectiveness of interpersonal relationships during adulthood (p. 74). All of these aforementioned related concerns affect academic and vocational abilities of physically abused children entering adulthood (p. 74).

Children who have been physically abused have poor emotional regulation and make errors interpreting cues from their environment (Teisl & Cicchetti, 2007) and have a higher fear of intimacy in adulthood (Repic, 2007, p. 49). Physically abused children overattend to relevant visual and auditory anger cues and attend more to task-irrelevant auditory anger cues (Shackman, Shackman, & Pollak, 2007, p. 838). Rapid Reference 9.1 lists some traits of physical abuse perpetrators.

Downs, Smyth, and Miller (1996) studied the relationship between childhood violence and alcohol problems among men who batter. They concluded:

Experiences of childhood violence are associated with (a) mediator variables, including anti-social behaviors and depressive symptomatology,

≡ *Rapid Reference 9.1*

Traits of Physical Abuse Perpetrators

Miner and Chilamkurti (1991, p. 356) found that physical abuse perpetrators:

- Show more physiological reactivity to child-related stimuli than do nonperpetrators.
- Have more physical symptom-related complaints than do nonabusive parents.
- Have a greater external locus of control, which suggests that they look for control from outside themselves as opposed to from within.
- Are more likely to see their children as being intentionally disruptive or disobedient.
- Have a greater expectation for the children to engage in appropriate behavior.
- Experience greater stress, greater depression, and greater levels of anxiety than do nonabusing parents.

that are themselves associated with development of alcohol problems and perpetration of partner violence for men in adulthood; (b) experiences of childhood violence, more strongly, observation of interparental violence during childhood predict perpetration of partner violence in adulthood for males; and (c) presence of partner violence associated with certain types of alcohol problems for men. (p. 327)

Egami, Ford, Grenfield, and Crum (1996) reported that 58.5% of adults who reported abuse of children and 69.3% of those who have neglected a child had a lifetime diagnosis of mental disorder. They also reported that low socioeconomic status was a risk factor for neglecting, but not abusing behavior (p. 921).

An interesting study conducted by Herrenkohl, Egolf, and Herrenkohl (1997) was a 16-year longitudinal study following preschool children who had been maltreated and those who had not, in an effort to determine how this would affect adolescent assaultive behavior. The researchers found that "severity of physical discipline, negative quality of the mother's interaction with the child, and the experience of sexual abuse were related to adolescent assaultive behavior" (p. 422).

Zuravin, McMillen, DePanifils, and Risley-Curtiss (1996) addressed intergenerational cycles of maltreatment. They found that the more severe forms of sexual abuse (those involving intercourse) increase the probability that the maltreatment will be passed on to the second generation but that less severe forms do not (p. 315).

DOMESTIC/FAMILY VIOLENCE

Family violence can take the form of spouse abuse and is sometimes referred to as domestic violence. The U.S. Department of Health and Human Services (1991) has defined it as

> [T]he use or threat of physical violence by the abuser to gain control and power over the victim. It occurs in households of both married and cohabiting couples. Although either party may be the victim, most victims are women. The three types of spouse abuse (physical abuse, sexual violence, and psychological/emotional abuse) often occur in combination.
>
> [. . .] Physical abuse can take many forms including kicking, hitting, biting, choking, pushing, and assaults with weapons. Sometimes particular areas are targeted, such as the abdomen of a pregnant woman. (p. 3)

Cascardi, O'Leary, Lawrence, and Schlee (1995) discussed the characteristics of women physically abused by their spouse.

> Abused women reported significantly more fear of their spouse, and reported their spouses were significantly more coercive and psychologically aggressive than women in the two match nonabused groups. Abused women did not report higher rates of abuse as a child, nor did they report higher rates of past psychopathology than women in the nonabused groups. However, abused women and nonabused discordant women reported higher rates of emotional abuse in childhood than maritally satisfied nonabused women. (p. 616)

Children Who Witness Violence

A considerable amount of research has been performed in recent years about the effects of children observing domestic violence. In summary, the results state:

- Memory for violent events witnessed in childhood may last a lifetime (Goodman & Rosenberg, 1991, p. 97).
- These children tend to feel worthless, mistrust intimate relationships, exhibit aggression themselves, and may be delayed intellectually (Goodman & Rosenberg, 1991, p. 104).
- Children who witnessed domestic violence are at increased risk for maladaption (Kolbo, Blakely, & Engleman, 1996, p. 281).
- Preschool children exposed to parental violence had many more behavior problems, exhibited significantly more negative effect, responded less appropriately to situations, were more aggressive

with peers, and had more ambivalent relationships with their care-givers than those from nonviolent families (Graham-Bermann & Levendosky, 1998, pp. 59–60).

- More than 80% of the children who observed violence between parents were also physically abused by one or both parents (Pagelow, 1990, p. 347).
- Small children have nightmares, insomnia, bedwetting, headaches, stomachaches, asthma, and encopresis. Older children often feel guilty that they cannot prevent the violence. Boys may tend to act out, showing aggression and disruptive behavior, while girls are more likely to become clinging, withdrawn, passive, and anxious (Pagelow, 1990, p. 348).
- Reynolds, Wallace, Hill, Weist, and Nebors (2001) report higher levels of symptoms of posttraumatic stress disorder, greater numbers of depressive symptoms, and lower self-esteem for boys who have witnessed domestic violence (p. 1201). They report that these were not evident in girls and that boys exhibit a stronger emotional reaction to domestic violence than girls.
- Girls who witnessed domestic violence were at risk for internalizing anxiety and more likely to display externalizing behavior and socialized aggression (Spilsbury et al., 2007, p. 495).
- Perceived threat and control were associated with greater clinically significant levels of trauma symptoms (Spilsbury et al., p. 487).
- Support has been found for the theory of learned helplessness, whereby children maltreated or witness to violence during childhood are more likely to be victimized during adulthood (Renner & Slack, 2006, p. 599).

Some Facts about Domestic Violence

Although studies on domestic violence are not complete, here are some important facts. According to the American Medical Association, 25% of the women in the United States, or 12 million women, will be abused by a current or former partner during their lives. The incidence of domestic violence is estimated at 4 million cases annually, or one assault every 15 seconds. Women in the United States are more likely to be victimized by a current or former male partner than by all other assailants combined. Over 50% of all women murdered are killed by male partners, and 12% of murdered men are killed by female partners.

Over half of the defendants accused of murdering their spouse had been drinking alcohol at the time of the offense. Nonfamily murder defendants were even more likely to have been drinking. Also, almost half of the victims of spousal murder had been drinking alcohol at the time of the offense—about the same proportion as for victims of nonfamily murder. Conditions associated with domestic violence include miscarriages, drug and alcohol abuse, attempted suicide and other forms of mental illness, low birth weight babies, pain, injuries, and permanent physical impairment. Of men who beat their wives, 47% do so three or more times a year. Battering may start or become worse during pregnancy; more than 23% of pregnant women are abused during pregnancy. Of all women who use hospital emergency and surgical services, 21% are battered. One in four married couples experience one or more incidents of domestic violence, and repeated severe episodes occur in one marriage out of every four (Sattler, 1998, p. 698).

Psychological Abuse

Psychological abuse can take many forms. In adults, it is often referred to as intimate partner abuse. As few as 1% of abused women experience physical violence without physical abuse. On the other hand, psychological abuse/intimate partner abuse commonly occurs without physical violence. Psychological abuse/intimate partner abuse has been shown to be related to depression, alcoholism, and problem drinking (Arias, Street & Brody, 1996); chronic illness (Marshall, 1996); and PTSD (Jones, Hughes, & Unterstaller, 2001).

It has been widely reported for decades that psychological abuse/intimate partner abuse has a greater negative impact on emotional well-being than does physical abuse (Babcock, Roseman, Green, & Ross, 2008, p. 809). "As expected, both physical and psychological abuse were related to PTSD symptomotology; however, psychological abuse did not predict PTSD symptoms over and over that are attributable to physical violence" (p. 814).

A child is considered to be emotionally or psychologically abused when he or she is the subject of acts or omissions by the parents or other persons responsible for the child's care that have caused, or could cause, a serious behavioral, cognitive, emotional, or mental disorder. In some cases of emotional or psychological abuse, the acts of the parents or other caretakers alone, without any harm to the child's behavior or condition, are sufficient to warrant intervention by a child protective services agency. An example would be if the parents or caretakers used extreme or bizarre forms of punishment, such as habitual scapegoating, belittling, or rejecting treatment. Demonstrable harm to the child is often required before a child protective services agency is able to intervene (U.S. Department of Health and Human Services, 1992, p. 3).

The accepted definition of child maltreatment reported in Garbarino, Guttman, and Seeley (1987) came from the *Interdisciplinary Glossary on Child Abuse and Neglect*:

"The definitions of emotional abuse include verbal or emotional assault, close confinement and threatened harm. The definitions of emotional neglect include inadequate nurturance/affection, knowingly permitting maladaptive behavior (for example, delinquency) and other refusal to provide essential care" (pp. 4–5).

Hart, Binggeli, and Brassard (1998, pp. 32–33) have pointed out that psychological maltreatment not only stands alone but is often embedded in other forms of maltreatment. They identified six major types of psychological maltreatment:

1. *Spurning,* which includes belittling, shaming, and public humiliation.
2. *Terrorizing,* which includes caretaker behavior that threatens or is likely to physically hurt, kill, abandon, or place the child in a dangerous situation.
3. *Isolating,* which generally involves placing unreasonable limitations on the child's freedom of movement.
4. *Exploiting/corrupting,* which includes modeling, permitting, or encouraging antisocial behavior, or developmentally inappropriate behavior.
5. *Denying emotional responsiveness,* which is generally considered to be ignoring the child's needs.
6. *Mental health, medical, and educational neglect,* which involves ignoring the need for, or failing or refusing to allow or provide treatment for serious emotional/behavioral problems, physical health problems, and/or educational problems.

SEXUAL ABUSE

"The evaluation of children suspected of having been sexually abused is one of the most challenging endeavors in clinical and forensic practice" (Kuehnle & Connell, 2009, p. xi).

"Child sexual abuse is an event or a series of events, it is not a disorder as such, and it does not constitute a diagnosis" (Kuehnle, 2003).

In spite of the fact that there are many behaviors that can be found in sexually abused children, there is no single symptom that characterizes sexually abused children. "The view of sexual abuse as a trigger that sets off an internal process in the child that surfaces as predicable behavioral and emotional symptoms, does not have an empirically based foundation" (Kuehnle, 2002, p. 439).

The U.S. Department of Health and Human Services (1992) defined sexual abuse as

[F]ondling a child's genitals, intercourse, incest, rape, sodomy, exhibitionism, and sexual exploitation. To be considered child abuse, these have to be committed by a person responsible for the care of the child (for example, a parent, baby sitter, or a day care provider). If a stranger commits these acts, it would be considered sexual assault and handled solely by the police and criminal courts. (p. 2–3)

"No professional license or degree necessarily indicates qualification to perform a CSA evaluation. Similarly, having completed education and training in the distant past does not assure present or future competence; one must remain abreast of developments in the subspecialty area of CSA assessment... most experts agree that mental health professionals interested in conducting evaluations or other interventions in CSA cases, should have, at minimum, core competencies... " (Koocher, 2009, p. 84 and 90).

Rapid Reference 9.2 lists ethical considerations for mental health professionals dealing with such evaluations.

Core competencies to conducting evaluations or other interventions in CSA cases are described in the following list (see Rapid Reference 9.3).

- Didactic content and supervised experience in the psychodiagnostic assessment of children and adults.
- Solid familiarity with forensic assessment of adults and children (e.g., philosophical issues, legal terminology, relevant case law, application of psychological skills to legal problems, testimony to ultimate legal issues, and ethical standards).
- Supervised experience in conducting CSA assessments (Koocher. 2009, p. 90).

≡ Rapid Reference 9.2

Ethical Considerations

Mental health professionals must:

1 Recognize and respect their obligations to vulnerable parties, both alleged victims and alleged perpetrators.
2 Strive for neutrality, avoiding bias and role conflicts as they do their work.
3 Create a careful record of what they do in the most transparent manner possible, and willingly subject their work to appropriate scrutiny.
4 See, evaluate, and consider all relevant data and rival hypotheses.
5 Seek reliable and valid data from which to draw well-founded conclusions.
6 Fairly and honestly present their findings, clearly indicating the limits of certainty and the significance of their findings (Koocher, 2009, p. 83).

≋ Rapid Reference 9.3

Before Beginning the Assessment

- Do I have the requisite professional license, educational background, and clinical experience to competently conduct such an evaluation?
- Do I have the best scientifically derived knowledge necessary to conduct a CSA evaluation in general?
- Do the assessment tools I plan to use meet all appropriate professional standards (American Psychological Association, American Educational Research Association, and National Council on Measurement in Education [APA, AERA, and NCME, 1999])?
- Do I need any specialized knowledge, data, or assistance related to age, gender, race, ethnicity, culture, language, or other such factors to work competently on this particular case?
- Do I know enough about the law, including judicial and administrative rules, in the applicable jurisdiction to proceed in this case?
- Are there any potential conflicts, such as multiple relationships, that might pose an actual conflict or the perception of one?
- Do I have any personal issues that might compromise my professional boundaries or ability to conduct an unbiased evaluation? (Koocher, 2009, p. 83)

"A large body of empirical research strongly supports the assertion that structured forensic interviews with alleged child victims of sexual abuse that are conducted with the NICHD protocol reduce the impact of interviewer biases and elicit more accurate and more detailed information from children than unstructured interviews" (Herman, 2009, p. 260). As a result, there is a significant reduction in false negative errors. The NICHD interview protocol is considered the gold standard for interviews in cases of alleged child sexual abuse.

Testimony that supports the validity of a child sexual abuse allegation based on psychosocial evidence is not reliable and should be barred from civil and criminal proceedings. Testimony that discusses high false positive error rates and how false memories can be unintentionally created through suggestive questioning have a firm basis in science and meet the Daubert standard.

"There currently is no good reason to believe that legal fact finders, gatekeepers, and law enforcement investigators will be more accurate than mental health professionals in judging the validity of uncorroborated allegations of child sexual abuse" (Herman, 2009, p. 261).

≣ *Rapid Reference 9.4*

Guidelines for Conducting Forensic Evaluations in Cases of Alleged Child Sexual Abuse

- Children should be interviewed no more than three times, and the interviewer should be the same person across interviews.
- All contacts between forensic interviewers and children should be electronically recorded from start to finish.
- If possible, forensic child interviews should be conducted by—or at least supervised by—an advanced mental health professional with specialized training in interviewing children, preferably using the NICHD protocol.
- The roles of therapists and forensic interviewers should be separate and should *never* [emphasis added] be performed by the same individual.
- Practitioners should be familiar with the vast empirical research literature.
- If possible, evaluations should be conducted by multidisciplinary teams including advanced forensic mental health professionals, medical professionals, and possibly CPS caseworkers and law enforcement personnel.
- Evaluators should keep an open mind about the validity of abuse allegations during the entire course of the investigation.
- The most frequent reason that a child sexual abuse allegation is made is the child has not been sexually abused, and the allegation is based on a sincere misunderstanding of the child's verbal or nonverbal behavior by a concerned or mentally ill adult (Kuehnle, 2006).

Note: Adapted from Herman (2009, p. 262).

Rapid Reference 9.4 lists a number of recommended guidelines that have been suggested by Herman (2005).

Repeated Interviews

A number of studies have been performed about repeated interviewing. Some studies suggest that repeated interviews may increase the amount of information obtained. Advantages of repeated interviews are greater after short delays than long delays. Long delays between interviews typically reduce the advantage of repeated interviewing (La Rooy, Lamb, & Pipe, 2009, p. 341). "It is clear that outright skepticism about repeated interviewing is unjustified because there are some conditions in which repeated interviews seem advantageous" (p. 352). (See Rapid Reference 9.5.)

≡ *Rapid Reference 9.5*

- Within the legal system, children are frequently interviewed about their experiences more than once, with different information elicited in different interviews.
- New information provided in repeated interviews is most likely to be accurate when the repeated interviews occur close together.
- Repeated interviews are not inherently suggestive, but can maximize the effects of suggestive interviewing.
- There are no published developmentally appropriate protocols and/or guidelines for repeated interviewing.
- The experimental literature is not yet sufficient to support strong conclusions about the risks or benefits of repeated interviews.

Note: Adapted from La Rooy, Lamb, and Pipe (2009, p. 355).

There are a number of factors that should be considered when addressing the reliability of children's memory and suggestibility (see Rapid Reference 9.6).

Rapid Reference 9.7 lists a number of areas of controversy that have clouded the evaluation process in child sexual abuse allegations. Among those are topics of repeated interviews, inconsistencies, and recantation.

≡ *Rapid Reference 9.6*

Children's Memory and Suggestibility

- The most reliable factor that affects children's memory and suggestibility is age.
- In general, young children cannot remember events, even those that were traumatic, if they occurred before the children were aged 3 or 4 years.
- Younger children tend to provide less information and make more errors.
- Free-recall reports are considered most accurate—and are more accurate than children's responses to direct questions.
- The most suggestive questions include those with tag endings (e.g., "Wasn't he?") or embedded assumptions.
- Biased interview statements, pressure, and the general style or demeanor of questioning can increase children's suggestibility and decrease their ability to provide accurate and complete eyewitness reports, regardless of the actual interview questions posed.

Note: Adapted from Malloy and Quas (2009, p. 290).

≡ Rapid Reference 9.7

Areas of Controversy in CSA Cases

- Repeated interviews do not inherently cause false reports or lead to dramatic inaccuracies.
- Inconsistencies in children's reports should be distinguished from report contradictions.
- Inconsistent and inaccurate are not interchangeable terms.
- Recantation of child sexual abuse does occur among substantiated cases that have corroborative evidence of abuse. Thus, recantation alone should not be taken as evidence that abuse did not occur.

Note: Adapted from Malloy and Quas (2009, p. 290).

There is no doubt that sexual abuse adversely affects children and can have a lifelong negative impact on their psychological functioning. Sexually abused children have poor mental health because of their victimization as well as preexisting or co-occurring family problems (McCrae, Chapman, & Christ, 2006, p. 468).

Kendall-Tackett, Williams, and Finkelhor (1993) provided an exhaustive review of 45 studies that had been performed to examine the psychological effects of sexual abuse. They reported that the most commonly studied symptom was sexualized behavior. This included sexual play with dolls, placing objects in anuses or vaginas, excessive or public masturbation, seductive behavior, requesting sexual stimulation from adults or other children, and age-inappropriate sexual knowledge. Tharinger (1990) indicated that 16% to 41% of children who had been sexually abused manifested overt sexual behavior problems (p. 335).

Individuals of different ages exhibit varying symptomotology. For preschoolers, the most common symptoms were anxiety, nightmares, general PTSD, internalizing, externalizing, and inappropriate sexual behavior. For school-age children, the most common symptoms include, fear, neurotic and general mental illness, aggression, nightmares, school problems, hyperactivity, and regressive behavior. For adolescents, the most common behaviors were depression; withdrawn, suicidal, or self-injurious behavior; somatic complaints; illegal acts; running away; and substance abuse. Leifer, Shapiro, Martone, and Kassem (1991) add that Rorschach protocols of sexually abused girls indicated marked problems in ego functioning and more disturbances in their thinking (p. 23).

Some symptoms appear prominently for more than one age group and include nightmares, depression, withdrawn behavior, neurotic mental illness, and aggressive and regressive behavior (Kendall-Tackett, Williams, & Finkelhor, 1993, p.167). Furthermore, the authors concluded that depression, school and learning problems, and behavior problems were the most prevalent symptoms across ages.

The studies reviewed concluded that from 21% to 49% of those studied were asymptomatic. These individuals may have been symptomatic in ways that were not measured, they may not have yet manifested symptoms, or they may simply have been asymptomatic.

Some factors were found to lead to increased symptomotology in victims. Individuals experiencing molestations that included a close perpetrator; a high frequency of sexual contact; a long duration of sexual contact; the use of force during the contact; and sexual acts that included oral, anal, or vaginal penetration were found to experience more symptoms. Also, individuals who had a lack of maternal support at the time of disclosure and a victim's negative outlook or coping style also led to increased symptoms. The influence of age at the time of assessment, age at onset, number of perpetrators, and time elapsed between the end of abuse and assessment is somewhat unclear at the present time and should be examined in future studies on the impact of intervening variables (p.171).

A child's disclosure of the abuse can also be impacted by some individual factors. Delayed disclosure can be a function of accommodation, guilt, self-blame, helplessness, emotional attachment to the perpetrator, idealized self-identity, mistrust of others, dissociation, burden of the secret, or successful/ego-strengthening experiences (Somer & Szwarcberg, 2001, pp 333–334). Children's age, type of abuse, fear of negative consequences, and perceived responsibility for the abuse all contributed to predicting the time of disclosure. The fear of negative consequences was more influential for older children than for younger children. Children whose abuse was intrafamilial took longer to disclose than children whose abuse was extrafamilial. They took longer to report if they felt there were negative consequences associated with reporting (Goodman, Edelstein, Goodman, Jones, & Gordon, 2003, pp. 536–537).

Kendall-Tackett, Williams, and Finkelhor (1993) also reported that resolution of the abuse varies. As time progressed, symptoms abated or improved in 55% to 65% of children. However, depending on the study, from 10% to 24% of the children appeared to have symptoms that worsened. Children involved in court proceedings demonstrated less resolution and a longer time to reach resolution. It has long been felt that children required to testify in court suffer the adverse effects of these proceedings. Williams (1992) indicates that testimony provided by children in protected settings can mitigate the trauma, with children who testified via closed-circuit television, videotape testimony, or closed courtrooms demonstrating fewer symp-toms than children who were required to testify in open court.

Many survivors of sexual abuse continue to exhibit symptomology into adult-hood. Stigmatization (abuse-specific shame and self-blame) and internalizing symptoms (PTSD and depression) explain sexual difficulties and dating aggres-sion more than abuse severity. It serves as a predictor for subsequent sexual dif-ficulties (Feiring, Simon, & Cleland, 2009). Abused women not only have lower ratings on measures of body satisfaction than nonabused women (Sexton, Grant, & Nash, 1990), but also have an increase in suicidality, eating disorders, and self-mutilation (Briere & Runtz, 1993, pp. 320–321). Histories of physical and espe-cially sexual abuse are associated with severe psychological disturbances in adults; in particular, borderline personality disorder (Polusny & Follette, 1995; Weston, Ludolph, Misile, Ruffins, & Block, 1990; Zlotnick, Mattia, & Zeimmerman, 2001). Furthermore, women with histories of sexual abuse have higher anxiety and de-pression scores, greater life stressors, and greater difficulty recovering from post-partum depression than those who did not have histories of sexual abuse and failed to improve as much as the nonabused group (Buist & Janson, 2001, p. 909). The abuse can also impact individuals other than the victim, as it has been found that nonoffending mothers of child sexual abuse victims had heightened levels of depression and anxiety and diminished maternal attachment behaviors (Lew & Bergin, 2001, p. 365).

Interestingly, some survivors of sexual abuse are able to find some positive aspects of their abuse, with almost half of low-income child abuse survivors

≣ Rapid Reference 9.8

- The majority of sexually abused children do not exhibit sexual behavior problems.
- Research is robust in showing that preschool-age sexually abused children have a higher rate of sexualized behavior than nonsexually abused children, but the duration of the behavior difference is unknown.
- A substantial number of male school-age children with sexual behavior prob-lems are not victims of sexual abuse, but instead are victims of other forms of family violence (e.g., physical abuse, witness to domestic violence).
- The majority of children with sexual behavior problems do not develop into adolescent or adult sex offenders.

Note: Adapted from Gurley, Kuehnle, & Kirkpatrick, (2009, p. 146).

perceiving benefit from having been sexually abused in the form of protecting children from abuse, self-protection, increased knowledge of child sexual abuse, and having a stronger personality (McMillen, Zuravin, & Rideout, 1995, p. 1037). It is important that survivors of sexual victimization be aware that, without an understanding of the effects of past experiences, "They are at risk for being victimized again" (Wyatt, Guthrie, & Notgrass, 1992, p. 51; Polusny & Follette, 1995).

"A look at what books and Internet resources have to say about indicators of sexual abuse explains why it is easy to become primed to suspect abuse whenever a child's behavior takes a turn for the worse: These lists are remarkably long" (Poole & Wolfe, 2009, p. 101).

"Parents' description of their children's behavioral changes are not always complete or accurate. One reason it is misleading to rely too heavily on parental reports, is that children do not behave the same in all environments, so behavior at home does not always forecast the same behavior elsewhere" (p.103).

It is helpful to know what the developmentally expected sexual behaviors are in children. Rapid Reference 9.9 provides a list of such behaviors.

≡ Rapid Reference 9.9

Developmentally Related Sexual Behaviors

Early Childhood (2 to 6 years)
- Kisses nonfamily members
- Tries to look at people undressing/in the nude
- Undresses in front of others
- Sits with crotch exposed
- Touches sex parts at home
- Masturbates or stimulates self in other ways
- Touches breasts
- Touches sex parts in public
- Shows sex parts to adults
- Shows sex parts to another child

Middle Childhood (7 to 10 years)
- Tries to look at people undressing/in the nude
- Touches sex parts at home

- Masturbates (rates > 20% for boys)
- Fondles nongenital areas (e.g., back, stomach)
- Shows sex parts to another child

Late Childhood (11 to 12 years)

- Is very interested in the opposite sex
- Masturbates
- Fondles nongenital areas (e.g., back, stomach)
- Shows sex parts to another child (boys)

Note: Adapted from Table 6.1, Poole & Wolfe (2009). Used with permission.

Evaluating the Extent of Psychological Harm Stemming from Sexual Abuse

Veltkamp and Miller (1995, p. 28) have identified several factors that are useful in determining the extent of psychological harm associated with sexual abuse.

The Age of the Child

The younger child may not actually realize what is going on but may experience physical pain, which makes the initial sexual experience an emotionally and physically painful one and contributes to an overall negative attitude regarding sex. More confusion is seen in the older child, who is bewildered, angry, depressed, and guilt-ridden.

Duration

The longer the abuse continues, the more traumatic it becomes.

Aggression

The greater the level of aggression, the more physically and psychologically traumatic its effects become.

Threat

The abusing parent often threatens the child. The greater the threat, the more traumatic the event is to the child. Examples include threat of removal of the child from the family, physical abuse to the child, or the parent being imprisoned.

The Kind of Adult

If the perpetrator is known to the child, the child is more confused and guilt-ridden than if the perpetrator is a stranger. In addition, knowing the perpetrator has a profound impact on the child's ability to trust.

Degree of Activity

The more frequent the activity, the more psychologically traumatic it is to the child.

Lack of Adult Support

If adults do not believe or protect the child, the experience of abuse becomes more traumatic. If the parent overreacts, the child may feel guilty and responsible for the abuse (Veltkamp & Miller, 1995, p. 28).

Children between 18 and 22 months of age engage in brief and sparse statements that usually include only noun and verb content words. Preschool children often cannot answer why, when, or how questions, have difficulty with yes-or-no questions, and have limited understanding of auxiliary verbs. Children between 5 and 10 years of age are basically conversational. However, prior to 10 years of age use of legal terms may be misinterpreted by the children (e.g., the word *court* to a child may represent something in a basketball game or tennis match) (Kuehnle, 1996, pp. 129–130).

DON'T FORGET

When sexual abuse of a young child is alleged, Kuehnle (1996, p. 4) has suggested several possibilities that must be taken into consideration. They are:

- The child is a victim of sexual abuse, and the allegation is credible and accurate.
- The child is a victim of sexual abuse but due to age or cognitive deficits does not have the verbal skills to provide a credible description of his or her abuse.
- The child is a victim of sexual abuse but due to fear will not disclose his or her abuse.
- The child is a victim of sexual abuse but due to misguided loyalty will not disclose his or her abuse.
- The child is not a victim of sexual abuse and is credible but has misperceived an innocent interaction.
- The child is not a victim of sexual abuse but has been *unintentionally* contaminated by a concerned or hypervigilant caretaker or authority figure.
- The child is not a victim of sexual abuse but has been *intentionally* manipulated by a caretaker or authority figure into believing that he or she has been abused.
- The child is not a victim of sexual abuse but knowingly falsely accuses someone of sexual abuse for reasons of personal aggrandizement or revenge.

Because children prior to 6 or 7 years of age have not mastered time, calendar dates, or rote counting, they will have difficulty with details surrounding the allegations. They will also have difficulty answering "why" questions and will be unable to generalize effectively. These children also may not have developed the ability to use pronouns effectively. They will also be more likely to fill in information when their knowledge is incomplete (Kuehnle, 1996).

By 8 years of age children can identify time. However, since auditory discrimination is not fully developed, errors may occur that lead to misinformation (e.g., the word *jury* may be heard as *jewelry*, or *allegation* may be heard as *alligator*) (Kuehnle, 1996).

DON'T FORGET

Factors that affect the accuracy of children's statements during the interview include:

• Age of the child
• Verbal rehearsal of the event
• Specificity of details
• The amount of information that a child has about an event
• Interviewer's position of authority and interviewer's style
• Structure of questions
• Socioeconomic influences
• Personality factors

Note: Adapted from Ceci and Bruck (1993, p. 403–439) and Saywitz (1995, pp. 113–140).

In 1993, Karen Saywitz developed an interviewing technique referred to as narrative elaboration (see Rapid Reference 9.10). Since that time, there have been a number of accepted interview techniques developed for interviewing children in child sexual abuse allegations. The gold standard is the National Institute of Child Health and Human Development (NICHD) interview protocol. There is considerable research to support the use of the NICHD protocol (Lamb, Orbach, Hershkowitz, Horowitz, & Abbot (in press); Hershkowitz, Horowitz, & Lamb (2005, 2007); Pipe, Lamb, Orbach, & Stewart (2007); Michel, Gordon, Ornstein, & Simpson, 2000; Agnew & Powell (2004); Adams, Fields, & Verheve, 1999).

☰ *Rapid Reference 9.10*

- Before beginning the interview, preparation is necessary with respect to (a) developmentally appropriate language, (b) timing and duration of the interview session, (c) types of prompts that might be used, and (d) techniques and topics on which to focus when establishing rapport.
- The outset of the interview should establish ground rules (e.g., correcting interviewer, responding "I don't know").
- Children should have the opportunity to practice recalling a recent, past event in detail through a process like narrative elaboration.
- Interviewers should subject themselves to ongoing peer review and continuing education about interview techniques.
- No single technique is suitable for all children.

Note: Adapted from Brown and Lamb (2009, p. 317).

The RATAC protocol (Rapport, Anatomy identification, Touch inquiry, Abuse, and Closure) was developed by Walters et al., 2003. "Unfortunately, however, there has been no research on what RATAC-trained interviewers actually do when interviewing children" (Brown & Lamb, 2009, p. 305).

A third approach, referred to as the Criterion-Based Content Analysis (CBCA), is a checklist that has been developed in an effort to discriminate between truthful and untruthful accounts. This procedure has been sharply criticized.

In summary, there are a number of concepts that need to be considered in performing these interviews.

Kuehnle (1996) points out that if further studies of narrative elaboration continue to demonstrate its efficacy, perhaps the accuracy and detail of school-aged children's reports can be improved and meritorious cases of abuse more effectively investigated and prosecuted. A technique such as narrative elaboration reduces the need for leading and potentially misleading questions, because more information is initially provided by children themselves, and follow-up

CAUTION

Saywitz (1997) has indicated that there are three dilemmas with regard to child sexual abuse allegations:

1. When open-ended questions fail to give the information needed, there are few guidelines on how to proceed.
2. With regard to establishing rapport, moderate rapport is considered appropriate. However, no studies on rapport exist.
3. The research is also silent on overcoming factors of anxiety, fear, and avoidance on the part of the child.

questions focus on clarifying children's statements rather than adult supposition. This could result in fewer false allegations. Obtaining more competent testimony from children earlier in the process could reduce the number of interviews children undergo (p. 211).

Testing Children Who Have Experienced Sexual Abuse

Few tests have been developed specifically for measuring problems associated with child sexual abuse. However, a number of instruments in the standard battery can be used effectively and productively with children who have been sexually abused. The Child Behavior Checklist (CBCL), sometimes referred to as the Achenbach (and developed by Achenbach [1991]), addresses a number of symptoms that children who have been sexually abused have. The Personality Inventory for Children (PIC) can also be used for the same purpose.

The Children's Impact of Teach Events Scale-Revised (CITES-R) (Wolfe, Wolfe, Gentile, & LaRose, 1997) is a 54-item child self-report instrument. It is designed to look at the traumatogenic factors of betrayal, guilt, sexualization, and stigmatization. In addition, it looks at the PTSD model of intrusive thoughts and numbing responses.

The Trauma Symptom Checklist for Children, developed by Briere (1996), is discussed in detail in Chapter 3.

Kuehnle (1996) states that "since the differences between sexually abused and nonsexually abused children's stories are unknown, conclusions about sexual abuse from the projective data (TAT/CAT) cannot be drawn. Therefore, the use of these tests to *identify* [italics added] children who have been sexually abused is not indicated given the absence of reliability and validity data" (p. 237).

The studies using the Rorschach to differentiate sexually abused from nonsexually abused children have provided inconsistent information. However, research has demonstrated that broad-based psychological dysfunction as measured by the Rorschach is found in children who have been sexually abused (Kuehnle, 1996, p. 241).

Sexually Anatomically Correct Dolls

"Anatomically detailed dolls have been the most controversial of the nonverbal techniques that have been used in investigative interviews with children" (Pipe & Salmon, 2009, p. 369).

Everson and Boat (1997) published a seminal study about the use of dolls and other aids. They discussed the use of anatomical models, demonstration aids

CAUTION

Kuehnle (1996, p. 257) provides a number of cautions and considerations that should be utilized when testing sexually abused children.

- Professionals who formulate diagnostic conclusions based on data from assessment tools that are not reliable and valid instruments are at a higher risk to make false-positive errors (identifying a child as sexually abused who is not) and false-negative errors (identifying a child as not sexually abused who is).

- Many assessment instruments have age limits. Very few standardized measurements are available to directly assess very young children. Thus the assessment of very young children will primarily rely on the reports and observations of caregivers (e.g., parents, teachers, etc.) and observations of the evaluator.

- Nomothetic methods focus on statistical probabilities and compare the child's responses to normative data. Idiographic methods focus on the child's common themes and compare the child's responses for consistencies.

- Standardized observation systems, rather than subjective clinical observations, may be useful in collecting objective data involving parent-child interactions.

- Standardized behavior rating scales have utility in providing the evaluator with information from family members and individuals outside of the family, which can then be compared.

- Because items on behavior rating scales are face valid, respondents can deny or exaggerate the presence of behaviors.

- In a review of the recent empirical studies on the impact of sexual abuse on children, over one-fourth of the sexually abused children were found to show no significant behavior problems on broad-based child behavior rating scales.

- Research suggests that family disruption and stress confound the difference between sexually abused and nonsexually abused children on behavioral measures.

- Behavior rating scales assessing dissociation do not show specificity to behaviors or cognitions exhibited by sexually abused children and therefore do not have predictive diagnostic validity.

- Projective tests (standardized or nonstandardized) cannot be used to determine whether the child has been sexually abused but can be used to understand the personality functioning of the child.

- Children's artwork used as a projective tool cannot be used to identify sexually abused children based on the presence of sexual symbolism.

- Attempts to standardize children's drawings as a projective instrument, used in the assessment of underlying psychological dynamics, have failed to satisfy the standards required of psychometric tests. Furthermore, neither an empirical or clinical consensus has been reached regarding the identification of features in drawings that are mutually exclusive "markers" for sexually abused children.

- Genitals drawn on human figures by children cannot be used as a sole criterion to diagnose sexual abuse.
- Overinterpretation of children's behaviors, test results, or artwork can lead to faulty conclusions.

(showing where something is), and screening tools. The problems with these techniques are that they are inherently suggestive and can demand abilities that the child may not have.

"A specific concern that arises with respect to very young children, for whom dolls would potentially be most useful, is that they may not have the requisite cognitive abilities to use them appropriately. To use dolls and other toys to show as well as tell what happened, children must be able to use them as representatives of themselves, other people, or of objects. Children younger than age 3 have difficulty appreciating that a model can be an object in its own right and also a symbol" (Pipe & Salmon, p. 371).

"Salmon (2001) concluded that toys and dolls do not help children under approximately five years of age to report information about an event or about touch" (Pipe & Salmon, p. 372).

The use of toys in play therapy settings has been advocated for decades. "Studies show that when toys are used to *reenact* what happened, the accuracy of information elicited may be compromised compared to an unaided verbal interview" (p. 376).

Interviewers have often chosen to use two-dimensional body diagrams to aid the interview process instead of anatomically correct dolls. They offer an alternative to dolls to help children recount abusive experiences

CAUTION

"Use of SAC dolls has been mischaracterized as a "test" for sexual abuse, rather than a means for children to clarify their verbalizations through demonstration. The former conceptualization, which is based on a misunderstanding of the proper role of the clinicians in the fact-finding process, leads to exclusion of interview material altogether because of reliance on a scientifically unproven technique" (Melton & Limber, 1989, p. 1231).

and may be especially useful for eliciting or clarifying very specific information relating to touch and establishing the meaning of idiosyncratic body labels. They are also beneficial because they are not as strongly associated with play activities. Most studies have found body diagrams to be helpful (p. 379).

When a child has limited recall of an event, the event is not logically structured, and/or the interviewer's instructions are not clarified, errors may result.

The issue of the use of sexually anatomically correct dolls was addressed at a panel at the 1993 American Psychological Association convention in Toronto, Ontario. The panel raised many of the concerns addressed in this chapter.

Skinner and Berry (1993) reviewed concerns about the use of sexually anatomically correct dolls in child sexual abuse allegation cases. The authors pointed out that the users of anatomically detailed dolls must be cognizant of the psychometric properties of such dolls. They also noted that in one survey, 92% of evaluating professionals used the anatomically detailed dolls. They identified two problem areas in using dolls to validate child sexual abuse allegations.

> The first of these areas focuses on the inappropriate substitution of personal data for scientific data. With the lack of standardized materials, administration procedures, and scoring, and the absence of normative doll-play patterns, each doll user is apt to develop personal administration and scoring guidelines and norms that not only may not generalize across practitioners, but may also reveal more about the practitioner than the child being addressed.... Secondly, given the equivocal evidence for the validity of the dolls, mental health professionals may need to rethink the proposition that sexual play or knowledge in young children is an indicator of sexual abuse. The lack of discriminative validity evidence is not restricted to the analysis of AD [anatomically detailed] doll play patterns. (pp. 417–418)

The authors concluded:

> The lack of sufficient evidence supporting the psychometric properties of AD dolls calls into question the use of those dolls in the validation of child sexual abuse allegations. Being ethically responsible for ensuring the tests employed meet adequate psychometric standard, it appears that a psychologist who uses AD dolls in sexual abuse validation interview is operating in a professionally risky and, perhaps, indefensible manner. Moreover, given that validity is the principal issue underlying the admissibility of psychological evidence in the courtroom ... and the inadequate evidence for the construct and criterion-related validity of AD dolls, evidence collected using AD dolls should not be admitted in court in child sexual abuse

cases at this time. Presently, the use of dolls in validation interviews fails to meet scientific test criteria and, consequently, it can only be concluded that AD dolls should not be used as the basis for expert opinions or conclusions. (p. 417)

The use of sexually anatomically correct dolls in forensic evaluations has raised quite a controversy. As a result, the American Psychological Association Council of Representatives adopted a statement on February 8, 1991, with regard to the use of anatomically detailed dolls. The statement adopted is as follows:

Statement on the Use of Anatomically Detailed Dolls in Forensic Evaluation

Anatomically detailed dolls are widely used in conducting assessments in cases of alleged child sexual abuse. In general, such dolls may be useful in helping children to communicate when their language skills or emotional concerns include direct verbal responses. These dolls may also be useful communication props to help older children who may have difficulty expressing themselves verbally on sexual topics.

These dolls are available from a variety of vendors and are readily sold to anyone who wishes to purchase. The design, detail, and the nature of the dolls vary considerably across manufacturers. Neither the dolls, nor their use, are standardized or accompanied by normative data. There are currently no uniform standards for conducting interviews with the dolls.

We urge continued research in quest of more and better data regarding the stimulus properties of such dolls and normative behavior of abused and nonabused children. Nevertheless, doll-centered assessment of children, when used as part of a psychological evaluation, and interpreted by experienced and competent examiners, may be the best available practical solution for a pressing and frequent clinical problem (i.e., investigation of the possible presence of sexual abuse of a child).

Therefore, in conformity with the *Ethical Principles of Psychologists and Code of Conduct*, psychologists who undertake the doll-centered assessment of sexual abuse should be competent to use these techniques. We recommend that psychologists document by videotape (whenever possible), audiotape, or in writing the procedures used for each administration. Psychologists should be prepared to provide clinical and empirical rationale (i.e., published studies, clinical experiences, etc.) for procedures employed and for interpretation of results derived from using ADDs [anatomically detailed dolls]. (APA, 1991)

UNSUPPORTED CHILD SEXUAL ABUSE ALLEGATION ASSESSMENT TECHNIQUES

Over the decades, well-meaning practitioners have continued to attempt to find various means of assessing child sexual abuse allegations. Among these techniques are play therapy, sand play, and projective drawings. Especially in the post-*Daubert* era and the "evidence based" era in psychology, we must be ever vigilant in using only techniques that are scientifically supported. Those techniques that do not have adequate empirical research, including reliability and validity data, should not be used in forensic evaluations in general, and child sexual abuse allegations specifically. "Experts who also teach or train clinicians should foster a culture of scientific inquiry that emphasizes the importance of empirical support underlying assessment approaches" (Murrie, Martindale, & Epstein, 2009, p. 414). (See Rapid Reference 9.11.)

Children's Drawings

"Drawing initially showed considerable promise as a means of eliciting full accounts of children's experiences without simultaneously increasing their errors. However, the strength of drawing, its reliance on children to provide their own retrieval cues via the drawing process is also a significant limitation and as with other nonverbal techniques, drawing as an interview strategy may involve risks" (Pipe & Salmon, 2009, p. 385).

Presenting information about abuse allegations in the legal arena can be difficult and must be precise (see Rapid Reference 9.12).

≡ *Rapid Reference 9.11*

Concerns about Unsupported Assessment Techniques

- There is virtually no empirical evidence to support the use of sand tray or sand play techniques in assessments related to allegations of child sexual abuse (Murrie, Martindale, & Epstein, 2009, p. 404).
- There is little validity data to support the use of projective drawing techniques in forensic or clinical assessment (p. 407).
- There is very little research to support the argument that projective drawings reveal signs of sexual abuse, and the meager support of research is marked with methodological flaws (p. 413).
- Clinicians have (inappropriately) introduced projective drawings and projective play into evaluations of alleged CSA, but these unsupported assessment techniques fall far short of legal admissibility standards (p. 414).

CAUTION

- Innocuous touches are not reliably reported by young children whether or not body diagrams are used.
- Errors of omission are far more common than errors of commission.
- It is not known whether questioning associated with the use of body diagrams is more or less likely to introduce errors.
- When nonverbal responses are given about touch, they should be followed up with open-ended questioning so that the nature of the contact can be clarified (Pipe & Salmon, 2009).

Rapid Reference 9.12

Presenting Information about Abuse Allegations in the Legal Arena

- Research indicates that jurors are not familiar with factors that influence children's memories and accuracy.
- Expert testimony on the following topics would be helpful for jurors: the effects of suggestive questions, open-ended questions, anatomical dolls, repeated questions, praising abuse-specific reports, witness participation in events, and the prestige of the interviewer.
- Jurors need to be educated about the research, indicating that rarely is physical evidence present in CSA cases and that there are no "typical" behavioral indicators of abuse.
- Extant research indicates that professionals involved in the legal system (e.g., interviewers, public defenders, and investigators) do not adequately understand what interview techniques influence children's accuracy.

Note: Adapted from Buck and Warren (2009, p. 529).

TEST YOURSELF

1. **What are the long-term effects of sexual abuse? (see pp. 259–260)**
2. **How does witnessing domestic violence affect children? (see pp. 251–252)**
3. **Which is a factor that should be considered when assessing children's memory and suggestibility?**
   (a) The most reliable factor that affects children's memory and suggestibility is age.

(continued)

(b) In general, young children cannot remember events, even those that were traumatic.

(c) Free-recall reports are considered most accurate.

(d) The most suggestive questions include embedded assumptions.

(e) All of the above.

4. **Children between 2 and 6 years of age engage in all of the following sexual behaviors except:**

(a) undresses in front of others

(b) is very interested in the opposite sex

(c) masturbates

(d) shows sex parts to another child

5. **The most frequent reason a sexual abuse allegation is made is:**

(a) The child is not a victim of sexual abuse but has been unintentionally affected by a hypervigilant caretaker or authority figure.

(b) The child is not a victim of sexual abuse and is credible, but an innocent interaction has been misperceived.

(c) The child is a victim of sexual abuse, but due to cognitive deficits cannot provide a credible description.

(d) The child is not a victim of sexual abuse, but knowingly, falsely accuses someone.

Answers: 1. see pp. 259–260; 2. see pp. 251–252 ; 3. e; 4. b; 5. b

SELECTED TESTS INSTRUMENTS

Behavioral Assessment Scales for Children—2nd Edition (BASC 2)
Pearson Assessments: http://www.pearsonassessments.com
1–800–627–7271

Personality Inventory for Children
PAR: www.parinc.com
1–800–331–8378

Trauma Symptom Checklist for Children
Western Psychological Services: http://www.wpspublish.com
1–800–648–8857

Child Abuse Potential Inventory
PAR: www.parinc.com
1–800–331–8378

Ten

ESSENTIALS OF VIOLENCE AND RISK ASSESSMENT

Elizabeth Waisanen and Marc J. Ackerman

HISTORICAL OVERVIEW OF RISK ASSESSMENT

Individuals who appeared to be at risk to the community have always been identified within societies. It was not until the late nineteenth century, however, that scientists began to assess dangerousness. Criminologist Cesare Lombroso and his colleagues developed the theory of atavism, which suggested that violent criminals could be identified by their physical features, as they were merely throwbacks to primitive humans. Once caught for their actions, these criminals would be punished based on the individual, not the crime committed. Lombroso often suggested that these individuals should be permanently contained, as they would forever be a danger to the community (Conroy & Murrie, 2007).

The twentieth century saw a shift from containment to rehabilitation. It was thought that perhaps criminals could be treated, though it would take lengthy sentences. The 1930s began the trend of looking to the medical community for explanations of and solutions to criminal behavior. "Moral insanity" was a term used by Dr. James Pritchard to explain otherwise well-functioning individuals with inadequately formed consciences. At this same time, Hervey Cleckley published *The Mask of Insanity*, which suggested that "psychopaths" were intelligent, well-functioning people with little empathy or remorse (Conroy & Murrie, 2007).

The 1960s began the movement toward community treatment. The medical community was chastised for giving merely deviant individuals diagnoses and confining them for indefinite periods of time. Society began to fear this was an infringement upon civil liberties and created unnecessary taxes.

In the late 1960s and 1970s, a series of events called into question professionals' ability to accurately predict whether a violent offender would offend again. In U.S. Supreme Court *Baxgtrom v. Herald* (1966), numerous psychiatric patients whom clinicians had predicted to be dangerous were released. A four-year follow-up study showed that only 20% had been assaultive (Steadman & Cocozza, 1974). A study following individuals released from Bridgewater State Hospital in Massachusetts found that the false-positive rate of patients predicted to be dangerous was over 65% (Kozol, Boucher, & Garofolo, 1972). Steadman and Cocozza followed 257 felons in New York, finding only 14% of those predicted to be dangerous were rearrested for violence (1976). These studies, among many others, gave the appearance that clinicians were apt to label individuals to be dangerous, when in fact they were not likely to reoffend, and a new generation of research was born to find a better way to assess risk of danger.

Though there are many different techniques utilized to assess the risk of offender recidivism, they tend to fall into three main categories: clinical, actuarial, and anamnestic. Clinical risk assessment involves a trained mental health professional making a judgment about future criminal behavior. The professional's intuition and subjective evaluation of the individual are combined with assessing factors identified in the professional literature to be associated with recidivism. Collins and Smail (2007) identify that clinical risk assessment has both strengths and weaknesses. The biggest strength of this method is that it is highly individualized. No two offenders evaluated are viewed as exactly alike, and the clinician assessing the individual includes all dispositional, historical, contextual, and clinical risk factors that are unique to that specific offender. Weaknesses of clinical risk assessment include the lack of empirical basis, the lack of standardized procedures,

≡ Rapid Reference 10.1

Weaknesses of Clinical Assessments

Clinical assessments can be

- Conducted by untrained or inexperienced clinicians
- Subject to inappropriate clinician bias based on prior expectations, uninformed or incorrect data, or clinician attitude and values
- Based on variables that are meaningless or without empirical support
- Unreliable and inconsistent when administered by different clinicans or even the same clinician over time
- Vaguely designed, unstructured, or poorly constructed
- Idiosyncratic and incapable of replication
- Incomplete or lacking in detail
- Unproven and inaccurate
- Confusing and lacking in clear formulation

Note: Adapted from P. Rich, Understanding, Assessing, and Rehabilitating Juvenile Sexual Offenders (p. 115). Copyright © 2003 John Wiley & Sons, Inc. This material is used by permission of John Wiley & Sons, Inc.

and inconsistency of inter- and intra-evaluator reliability. Rapid Reference 10.1 outlines some weaknesses of clinical assessments.

Conversely, actuarial risk assessment connects the relationship between an outcome, such as sexual offending, with measurable, objective variables. This method of risk assessment utilizes empirical research and data to link these variables with the specific outcome, and consideration is given to the strength of the correlation. Many actuarial scales specify static factors to consider and also describe the relative importance of each item in determining the risk of recidivism (Hanson & Thornton, 2002). Strengths of actuarial risk assessment include empirical/atheoretical basis, standardization, and research support that they predict violent behavior better than chance. Some weaknesses identified are that some of the variables examined still require clinical judgment, essential components of individualized evaluation may be missed, and there may be a lack of research or inadequate training (Collins & Smail, 2007). Rapid Reference 10.2 discusses some

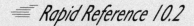

Rapid Reference 10.2

Weaknesses of Actuarial Assessments

- Although sometimes based on objective facts, in many instances actuarial assessment depends on clinical judgment or interpretation to produce pseudo-facts (clinical variables that have the appearance of fact but actually have no objective or consistent existence).

- Actuarial assessments are limited in scope to facts or pseudofacts and are unable to infer or search out important data that do not fit into the structure of the assessment or do not take the form of fact or pseudofact.

- Actuarial assessments are rigid and lack the ability to provide meaning or render judgments about data.

- Actuarial assessments lack the ability to formulate and are thus able to present only a simple picture without any explanation.

- In the case of risk for sexual reoffense, actuarial assessments are not based on truly valid variables, as there is no clear profile of either adult or adolescent sexual offenders or the variables that unequivocally contribute or lead to sexual offending, and this results in the selection of variables that in themselves are the product of judgment and not fact.

- The ability to determine the effectiveness and utility of an actuarial assessment is based entirely on its predictive power, which cannot be fully evaluated without adequate and meaningful recidivism studies.

Note: Adapted from P. Rich, *Understanding, Assessing, and Rehabilitating Juvenile Sexual Offenders* (pp. 114–115). Copyright © 2003 John Wiley & Sons, Inc. This material is used by permission of John Wiley & Sons, Inc.

≣ *Rapid Reference 10.3*

Test Usage Ratings for Evaluations of Risk Assessment/Psychopathy

1 Psychopathy Checklists (PCL; PCL-R: Hare, 2003; PCL-Screening Version: Hart, Cox, & Hare, 1995)
2 Historical Clinical Risk – 20 (Webster, Douglas, Eaves, & Hart, 1997)
3 Violence Risk Appraisal Guide (Harris, Rice, & Quinsey, 1993)
4 Level of Service Inventory (Andrews & Bonta, 1995)*

Note: Adapted from Archer, Buffington-Vollum, Stredny, & Handel, (2006, p. 90).

*There is a newer version of the LSI, which is the LS/CMI, or the Level of Service/Case Management Inventory (Andrews, Bonta, & Wormith, 2004), which has largely taken the place of both the LSI and the LSI-R

weaknesses of actuarial assessments. Rapid Reference 10.3 lists test usage ratings for evaluations of risk assessment/psychopathy.

A third predictive scheme, anamnestic assessment, involves the examiner studying each incidence of an individual's violent behavior. Upon close examination, patterns, common precipitating factors, and antecedents are identified. By gaining this insight, protective measures can be determined and implemented (Conroy & Murrie, 2007).

GENERAL VIOLENCE PREDICTION

Historical Clinical Risk Scheme

The Historical Clinical Risk Scheme (HCR-20) is a structured risk assessment guide that addresses risk from the perspectives of the past, present, and future. The ten Historical factors obviously concern past behaviors (previous violence, young age at first violent incident, relationship instability, employment problems, substance use problems, major mental illness, psychopathy, early maladjustment, personality disorder, and prior supervision failure). The five Clinical items reflect present, dynamic correlates of violent behavior (impulsivity, negative attitude, active symptoms of major mental illness, unresponsive to treatment, and lack of insight). The five Risk Management items look at the future, or what factors may mitigate violent behavior (plans lack feasibility, exposure to destabilizers, lack of personal support, noncompliance with remediation attempts, and stress).

The Historical, Clinical, and Risk Management items are coded on a 3-point scale according to the evaluator's confidence that the risk factor is present. A 0 indicates that the risk factor is not applicable or is not present. A 1 indicates that the risk factor is possibly or partially present, and a 3 indicates that the risk factor is definitely present. Scores on the *HCR-20* do seem to predict violent behavior in both retrospective and predictive studies. Douglas, Ogloff, Nicholls, & Grant (1999) found that patients scoring above the median on the instrument were 6 to 13 times more likely to be violent two years after discharge than those scoring below the median (Goldstein & Weiner, 2003).

The HCR-20 is not meant to be a stand-alone measure and should only be used in conjunction with other tests. Several studies have been performed since the publication of the manual which suggest that the instrument has promise; however, this information is not in the manual, and much of this data was obtained using the Swedish version of the HCR-20 (Arbisi, 2003). It is designed solely for the purpose of assessing the risk of violent behavior in a psychiatric or correctional setting (Cooper, 2003) and should be used in that context only.

C A U T I O N

The HCR-20 should be used in conjunction with other tests to conduct a risk assessment.

Violence Risk Appraisal Guide

The Violence Risk Appraisal Guide (VRAG) was developed in 1993 to determine risk for violent recidivism among offenders. The sample consisted of over 600 men from a maximum-security hospital who had been charged with a serious offense. Institutional files were used to identify 50 predictor variables, and a series of regression models identified 12 static factors that cover a variety of life situations, offending behaviors, and diagnostic characteristics. Huebner, Valentine, Stokes, Cobbina, and Berg (2006) identify the 12 areas as follows:

1. Whether or not the offender lived with both parents until the age of 18
2. Maladjustment in elementary school
3. History of alcohol abuse
4. Marital status
5. Nonviolent offense history
6. Failure on prior conditional release
7. Age at the time of the index offense
8. Injury sustained by the index victim

≡ Rapid Reference 10.4

Probability of Recidivism as a Function of Risk Score

Category	Risk Score Range	Probability of Violent Recidivism within 10 Years
1	−22 or lower	0.08
2	−21 to −15	0.10
3	−14 to −8	0.24
4	−7 to −1	0.31
5	0 to 6	0.48
6	7 to 13	0.58
7	14 to 20	0.64
8	21 to 27	0.82
9	28 or higher	1.00

Quinsey et al. (2006) describe the probability of recidivism as follows:

9. The gender of the index victim
10. The presence of personality disorders
11. Diagnosis of schizophrenia
12. Diagnoses suggested by Psychopathology Checklist-Revised (PCL-R)

Rapid Reference 10.4 outlines the cutoff scores and probability rates for the VRAG.

Rice & Harris (1997) conducted a study of 159 child molesters and rapists to evaluate the ability of VRAG to predict subsequent violence. The men in the sample were all serious sexual offenders with criminal histories, maladjusted childhoods, and poor social adjustment in adulthood. The researchers identified sexual recidivism as an individual being charged with another sexual offense within the ten years following their release. Results indicated that the VRAG performed well

DON'T FORGET

The best predictor of violence recidivism on the VRAG is psychopathy, as measured on the PCL-R.

in predicting violence among high-risk offenders. The study also suggested that offenders who perpetrated against women were at greater risk of committing additional nonsexual violent crimes, while child molesters were at greater risk of sexual recidivism.

Psychopathy Checklist–Revised (PCL-R)

The best predictor of violence recidivism on the VRAG is psychopathy, measured by an individual's score on the PCL-R (Wrightsman & Fulero, 2005). Psychopathy is often related to repeat criminality and violent behavior, and refers to people who repeatedly act in a criminal fashion with little or no remorse. Psychopaths are superficial in interpersonal relationships, lack empathy toward others, but appear charming despite their manipulative manner.

Hare (1991) developed the Hare Psychopathy Checklist-Revised: 2nd Edition (PCL-R) to measure psychopathy, and it has become the most widely used instrument of its kind. Interview, record review, and collateral information are used to answer 20 items, scored in the following manner: 0 = No; 1 = Maybe; 2 = Yes. Factor 1 scores measure interpersonal and affective traits and Factor 2 scores reflect social deviance. Facet Scores, a construct new to the revised edition of the PCL-R, reflect interpersonal traits, affective traits, lifestyle, and antisocial behavior. Reliability and Validity are both extensively established, and it continues to be one of the most widely researched instruments in forensic settings. The twenty traits assessed by the PCL-R score are:

1. Glib and superficial charm
2. Grandiose (exaggeratedly high) estimation of self
3. Need for stimulation
4. Pathological lying
5. Cunning and manipulativeness
6. Lack of remorse or guilt
7. Shallow affect
8. Callousness and lack of empathy
9. Parasitic lifestyle
10. Poor behavioral controls
11. Sexual promiscuity
12. Early behavior problems
13. Lack of realistic long-term goals
14. Impulsivity
15. Irresponsibility

≡ *Rapid Reference 10.5*

Test Usage Ratings for Evaluations of Sex Offender Risk Assessment

1 Static 99 (Hanson & Thornton, 1999)
2 Sexual Violence Risk— 20 (Boer, Hart, Kropp, & Webster, 1997)
3 Minnesota Sex Offender Screening Tool—Revised (Epperson, Kaul, Huot, Hesselton, Alexander & Goldman, 1998)
4 Rapid Risk Assessment for Sex Offense Recidivism (Hanson, 1997)
5 Sex Offender Risk Appraisal Guide (Quinsey, Harris, Rice, & Cornier, 1998)

Note: Adapted from Archer, Buffinton-Vollum, Stredny, and Handel (2006, p. 90).

16. Failure to accept responsibility for own actions
17. Many short-term marital and/or sexual relationships
18. Juvenile delinquency
19. Revocation of conditional release
20. Criminal versatility

The PCL-R is the gold standard for measuring psychopathy and should be considered in any such assessment. There is no other psychopathy instrument that has as much empirical support from an ever-growing research base (Acheson, 2005). The PCL-R requires hours of specialized training to administer, unlike the HCR-20/SORAG/VRAG. All the aforementioned instruments depend on outside sources for verification of truth.

Rapid Reference 10.5 lists the most commonly used risk assessment/psychopathy in forensic evaluations of adults.

SEXUAL OFFENDERS

The past two decades have found consistently increasing numbers of individuals incarcerated for sexual offenses. The Center for Sex Offender Management (CSOM, 2001) indicates that the number of individuals imprisoned for sex offenses has grown by over 7% per year since 1980, and that in 1997 10% of state prisoners were incarcerated for committing a sex offense. Because these offenders more often than not are released back into the community after serving their time, typically under some form of conditional supervision, assessing their risk of committing more sexual crimes becomes an important issue. The central objective of assessing risk is to develop strategies to manage and reduce subsequent violent behavior.

Sex Offender Recidivism

When examining recidivism, it is important to note that the way one defines the word significantly impacts study results and research statistics. The Center for Sex Offender Management (2001) explains that though it is commonly accepted that recidivism is to perpetrate subsequent offenses, there are many different ways to view this. For example, one may look at an individual's subsequent arrest record. This may be problematic because the recidivism rate will be higher than perhaps accurate, as many people are charged with crimes but never convicted. Another way to look at recidivism is by examining subsequent incarceration. This involves committing another sex crime, being tried, convicted, and sent back to prison. This method may be difficult, as the perpetrator may have committed a nonsexual crime and gone back to prison on a parole violation. One could also examine later convictions. This criterion results in a lower recidivism rate, though it may reflect more accurate numbers and eliminates "false positives," or people who were falsely arrested for sex crimes and never charged. Though the recidivism rate may be lower than accurate, this tends to be the preferred method for defining recidivism.

Langan, Schmitt, & Durose (2003) report that 5.3% of sex offenders released from prison in 1994 were arrested for another sex crime within three years of release. Of these re-offenders, 40% committed their subsequent crime within their first year out of prison. Hanson & Morton-Bourgon (2005) indicate that the typical sexual recidivism rate is 10% to 15% after a five-year period. These statistics suggest that, although the majority of released sex offenders do not continue to perpetrate, re-offending does occur, making risk assessment a vital tool in public safety.

Beech, Fisher, and Thornton (2003) identify four categories of risk factors that may be indicative of deviant sexual re-offending. These factors are listed in Rapid Reference 10.6. The first category consists of dispositional factors. These are traits inherent to the individual, such as temperament and personality. The second category entails historical factors, including a history of violent behavior and instability in the early childhood environment. The next classification is of contextual factors. These include poor social supports, perceived stress levels, and the presence of a deviant peer group. Last are clinical factors. Substance abuse and dependence, mental health diagnoses, and an inadequate level of social and emotional functioning all fall into this category.

≡ *Rapid Reference 10.6*

The four categories of risk factors for sexual re-offending are:

1 Dispositional Factors
2 Historical Factors
3 Contextual Factors
4 Clinical Factors

The Center for Sex Offender Management (2001) further categorizes these factors into static and dynamic features. Static factors are those that cannot be changed, such as the aforementioned dispositional and historical aspects of an individual. Dynamic factors can change throughout one's life. For example, an addict can stop using drugs, and an individual with a poor relationship history can learn to better relate to others. Stable dynamic factors can change over time but tend to be lasting qualities. An individual with deviant sexual practices and preferences

DON'T FORGET

Static factors are those that cannot be changed, while dynamic factors can change throughout one's life.

can theoretically change these aspects of himself, but it is not very likely. Acute dynamic factors (e.g., substance intoxication, sexual arousal) can change quickly over a short period of time, and are often present directly prior to the offense.

Methods of Assessing Risk

The prevention of sexual violence is of great concern to the safety and protection of the public. Though the prevention of any crime is important, preventing sexual crimes is especially important, as these offenses are particularly traumatizing to victims and instill significant fear in the community. When practitioners are assessing how sex offenders should be managed, especially in a community setting, it is important that they consider the following: how likely it is that the sex offender will commit more sex crimes, and under what circumstances this offender is most likely and/or least likely to offend (CSOM, 2001).

Sex Offender Risk Appraisal Guide

The Sex Offender Risk Appraisal Guide (SORAG) is a variation of the VRAG. Similarly, it was initially designed to assess for risk of both nonsexual violent and sexual recidivism (Hanson & Thornton, 2002). The SORAG has 14 total items,

10 of which are the same as items on the VRAG. The additional items on the SORAG are as follows:

1. Offender had victims other than girls under 14 years old.
2. Offender has failed on previous releases.
3. Offender was young at the time of the index offense.
4. Offender had deviant sexual interests in phallometric testing (the measurement of changes in penile circumference in response to both sexual and nonsexual stimuli) (Huebner, Valentine, Stokes, Cobbina, & Berg, 2006).

Emerging research suggests that the SORAG is effective in accurately predicting the risk of recidivism. In particular, it has high accuracy in predicting violent recidivism and moderate accuracy in predicting sexual offenses (Harris, Rice, Quinsey, Lalumiere, Boer, & Lang, 2003). It is also considered advantageous when working with sex offender populations where personality disorders are present and "strong deviant sexual preferences vary independently of prior sexual convictions" (Beech, Fisher, & Thornton, 2003, p. 341).

Rapid Risk Assessment for Sexual Offense Recidivism

Hanson and Thornton (2002) state that the goal of the Rapid Risk Assessment for Sexual Offense Recidivism (RRASOR) is to predict sex offender recidivism using a small number of variables that are easily scored. The initial seven items were:

1. Prior sex offenses
2. Prior nonsex offenses
3. Male victims
4. Stranger victims
5. Unrelated victims
6. Never married
7. Younger than 25 years old

Of these original seven variables, only four were deemed to statistically contribute to accurately predicting recidivism. They were: prior sex offenses, any unrelated victims, any male victims, and age under 25 years (Hanson & Thornton, 2002). Despite its relative simplicity, the RRASOR shows predictive accuracy in sample populations.

Static-99

The Static-99 was developed in 1999 by a Canadian research team hoping to create an objective actuarial tool to be used in determining the risk of convicted sex offenders for committing sexual crimes, as well as other, nonsexual crimes that are violent in nature (Huebner, Valentine, Stokes, Cobbina, & Berg, 2006). It was developed for and should be used exclusively on adult, male offenders who perpetrated on an identifiable victim and were tried and convicted for the offense.

The Static-99 is based solely on static factors (Beech, Fisher, & Thornton, 2003), four of which comprise the RRASOR. These factors are examined through a case-file review and are, as identified by Huebner, Valentine, Stokes, Cobbina, & Berg (2006):

1. History of prior sexual offenses
2. Prior sentencing dates
3. Convictions for nonsex offenses
4. Index nonsexual violence
5. Prior nonsexual violence
6. Presence of unrelated victims
7. Presence of victims who were strangers to the offender
8. Presence of male victims
9. Offender is under 25 years old
10. Offender is single

The Static-99 shows reasonable accuracy in the prediction of both sexual and nonsexual recidivism, though it may be limited due to the lack of consideration for dynamic factors. Because of this deficit, Hanson and Thornton (2002) indicate that it cannot be used to "select treatment targets, measure change, evaluate whether offenders have benefited from treatment, or predict when (or under what circumstances) sex offenders are likely to recidivate" (p.18).

DOMESTIC VIOLENCE

Assessments of risk in regards to domestic violence are necessary in a variety of contexts: restraining orders, custody arrangements, sentencing decisions, treatment planning, and so forth. Wrightsman and Fulero (2005) explain that this is still not an exact science, but that risk factors are present. First, individuals who batter their spouses tend to have experienced family violence in their childhoods. Second, though spousal abuse occurs across all socioeconomic, racial, and ethnic lines, individuals with less education and lower income are more prone to engage in this behavior (Hotaling & Sugarman, 1986, as cited in Wrightsman & Fulero, 2005). Third, high levels of alcohol use or abuse also increase the risk of domestic violence. Fourth, about 50% of men who abuse their wives also abuse their children, so it is important to assess for child abuse as well as spousal abuse. The following instruments may be useful tools in making these determinations.

Domestic Violence Screening Inventory

The Domestic Violence Screening Inventory (DVSI) was developed by the Colorado Department of Probation Services to be a brief risk assessment tool that can be used by reviewing criminal history. The authors (Williams & Houghton, 2004) reviewed literature and consulted with judges, lawyers, victim advocates, and law enforcement officers to determine 12 social and behavior factors that are found to be statistically related to domestic violence recidivism. These 12 factors are primarily related to prior criminal history of domestic violence and other violent offenses such as arrests, convictions, and violation of restraining orders. Employment status, recent separation from the victim, and the presence of children during the violent incident are also examined. Clinical judgment is not necessary for this measure.

Child Abuse Potential Inventory, Form VI

The Child Abuse Potential Inventory, Form VI (CAPI) was originally designed to assist child protection workers in screening for physical abuse. It is a self-administered screener composed of 160 items to which the respondent replies "Agree" or "Disagree." The CAPI contains a total of 10 scales. The primary clinical scale (Abuse) can be divided into six factor scales: Distress, Rigidity, Unhappiness, Problems with Child and Self, Problems with Family, and Problems with Others. The

CAUTION

The CAPI should be used alone in determining whether intrusive interventions are necessary, as the possibility of false positives creates an ethical concern.

Abuse scale has a cutoff of 215. In addition, the CAP Inventory contains three validity scales: Lie, Random Response, and Inconsistency.

This test is to be used only in a high-base rate population and only in conjunction with collateral materials, as the initial validation sample consisted of an equally matched number of known abusers and nonabusers. Validity and Reliability are strong. This instrument should be used alone in determining whether intrusive interventions are necessary, as the possibility of false positives creates an ethical concern (Hart, 1989).

Spousal Assault Risk Assessment Guide

The Spousal Assault Risk Assessment Guide (SARA) is a screener for spousal assault and violence risk factors. It should be viewed as a checklist rather than a test, as there are no cutoff scores or norms, and research continues to address psychometric properties. Five sections quickly gain information. The first section looks at Criminal History, specifically three factors: Past assault of family members, past assault of strangers or acquaintances, and past violation of conditional release or community supervision. The second section looks at Psychosocial adjustment. The third addresses spousal Assault History. Included in this section are past physcial assault, past sexual assault/sexual jealousy, past use of weapons and/or credible threats of death, recent escalation in frequency or severity of assaults, past violations of "No Contact" orders, extreme minimization or denial of spousal assault history, and attitudes that support or condone spousal assault. The fourth section discusses alleged/most recent offense, or the index offense. It looks at the severity of the assault, the use of weapons or credible threats of death, and a violation of a restraining order. The last section is for the evaluator to include risk factors not included in the checklist that may be particular to the individual case and may pose risk. This may include stalking, sexual sadism, and so forth.

The SARA is not a controlled psychological test and can be used by many kinds of evaluators. Factor analysis to understand the constructs being measured would be helpful, but there is adequate reliability and validity.

RISK ASSESSMENT IN JUVENILES

Risk assessment appears to be important, particularly to the juvenile justice system. There have been three major ways identified that the juvenile justice system tries to differentiate between juveniles at high and low risk of reoffending. First, laws generally require that the juvenile's level of risk be considered when determining punishment. Second, level of risk may be a factor in considering which type of setting is most appropriate for rehabilitation. Lastly, clinicians form opinions of risk level based on the child's personal history and characteristics (Mulvey, 2005; Conroy & Murrie, 2007). An evaluator who conducts risk assessments on children and adolescents should, of course, be familiar with working with this particular population. Base rates with this population are different than those of adults, as some delinquent behavior, even violent behavior, is so common among youth that it is statistically typical (Conroy & Murrie, 2007). Delinquent behavior by the vast majority of youth also tapers off significantly by adulthood, posing no long-term threat to the community.

Psychometrically sound actuarial instruments for juvenile risk assessment are not as plentiful as what is available for adults. However, there are some empirically supported risk factors. Previous offending and a history of aggressive behavior are particularly strong indicators of subsequent violence. The severity of prior offenses is not necessarily correlated with that of future offenses (e.g., minor delinquency such as shoplifting and vandalism is associated with increased risk of adolescent violence, but studies of juvenile homicide offenders found a very low number with prior offenses), so it is important to consider the chronicity and recency of prior offenses, rather than severity (Hawkins et al., 1998; Grisso, 1998; Conroy & Murrie, 2007).

Early age of first offense is also an important risk factor. In the Pittsburgh Youth Study of over 1,500 urban males, onset of first delinquency before 10 years of age was one of the strongest predictors of violence in later youth and adulthood (Loeber et al., 2005, as cited in Conroy & Murrie, 2007).

Substance abuse has often been considered a major factor in offending by youth, as many youth report being under the influence during the time of the offense. It is a strong predictor of reoffending in children ages 6 to 11, but not for children 12 to 14. This is a complicated concept that may simply mean that substance abuse is so commonplace among children and adolescents with a history of offenses, that perhaps it is of little predictive use (Conroy & Murrie, 2007).

Impulsive children and adolescents may grow up to become impulsive adults, increasing the chances of criminal reoffending. Engaging in sensation-seeking behaviors during middle adolescence tripled the risk of violence (Hawkins et al., 2000). Similarly, psychiatric illness (particularly comorbid ADHD and Conduct Disorder) has been linked with aggression throughout adolescence and adulthood. This may be a function of the diagnostic criteria for many youth psychiatric disorders requiring some sort of acting out or impulsive behavior.

> **DON'T FORGET**
>
> The onset of first delinquency before 10 years of age is one of the strongest predictors of violence in later youth and adulthood.

Adolescent Psychopathology Scale–Short Form

Psychopathic personality features should also be considered. The Adolescent Psychopathology Scale-Short Form (APS-SF) is used to assess the presence or frequency of adolescent problem behavior and symptomology. One hundred fifteen questions or statements about behaviors, thoughts, and feelings that the adolescent may have had over a period of time make up this measure. This is a paper-and-pencil, self-report inventory. The author advises that this is an instrument to be used with other sources of information, and is not to be used as a diagnostic instrument. The APS-SF is particularly useful for school-based professions, as it is both brief and psychometrically sound. Because it is a self-report instrument, the APS-SF has the typical shortcomings of such measures. Validity scales assist in looking for blatant faking. Also, the standardization scale showed ethnic differences for 10 of the 12 clinical sales. Therefore, it is important to exercise caution when interpreting this data for diverse ethnic groups (Pfeiffer, 2003).

Attributing psychopathic traits to adolescents must be done with caution; however, some symptoms of psychopathy among adults are considered developmentally normal for adolescents (e.g., impulsivity, egocentrism, and irresponsibility) (Seagrave & Grisso, 2002).

Aside from individual characteristics, contextual factors must be considered as well when assessing risk in juveniles (Conroy & Murrie, 2007). Aggressive parental discipline, poor supervision, and a high-conflict family environment have all also been shown to correlate with increased violence among youth. Crime-laden neighborhoods also expose individuals to violence at an early age. Negative peer interactions, in the form of rejection, ostracization, and delinquent peer groups, can lead to aggressive behavior.

CAUTION

Most of the work on sex offender recidivism assessment and risk factors relates to adult males (Beech, Fisher, & Thornton, 2003). This means that caution should be exercised when using these tools and literature to assess risk in a juvenile, a woman, or an individual with special needs.

When assessing the recidivism risk of a female sex offender, Beech, Fisher, and Thornton (2003) indicate that it is important to also assess her risk as an individual offender, and also to assess her ability to resist pressure from other individuals. This is due to literature that indicates that many female sex offenders co-offend with male perpetrators, often under coercion (Williams & Nicholaichuck, 2001).

There are two empirical risk assessment tools available for juvenile sexual offenders, though neither has yet to be validated (Beech, Fisher, & Thornton, 2003). The first is the Juvenile Sex Offender Assessment Protocol (JSOAP), which is comprised of four factors. First is sexual drive/preoccupation, which examines prior sex charges, sexual obsessions, level of planning the criminal act, and "gratuitous sexual exploitation of the victim" (Beech, Fisher, & Thornton, 2003, p. 347). The second factor is impulsive/antisocial behavior, which looks at consistency of the caregiver, anger history, history of behavioral problems in school, diagnosis of conduct disorder, early arrest records, variability of offenses, impulsivity, substance abuse, and parental history of alcohol abuse. The third factor is intervention. Items related to this factor include the offender's level of accepted responsibility, desire to change, evidence of empathy and remorse, and absence of cognitive distortions. Lastly, community stability/adjustment looks at the juvenile's ability to manage anger within the community, examines the stability of the home environment and support systems, and the quality of peer relationships (Beech, Fisher, & Thornton, 2003).

The authors also describe the Estimate of Risk of Adolescent Sexual Offender Recidivism (ERASOR). It was designed to examine risk in 12- to 18-year-old sexual offenders, but is still not validated. "Items assess static variables related to past sexual offenses and the dynamic domains of sexual interests, pro-offending attitudes, socioaffective problems, and self-management" (Beech, Fisher, & Thornton, 2003, p. 347). Additionally, items involving the family environment and parental relationships are included. Regardless of the assessment instrument used in assessing juvenile sex offenders for recidivism risk, collateral contacts and family assessments are always of vital importance.

ASSESSING INDIVIDUALS WITH DEVELOPMENTAL DISABILITIES

Individuals with developmental disabilities make up another group that may need to be assessed for sex offense recidivism. It is difficult to use actuarial assessment tools with this population, as there is "significant underreporting of the offenses in file information, because individuals with developmental disabilities are not generally prosecuted for sexual offenses" (Beech, Fisher, & Thornton, 2003, p. 347). Gathering information from individuals within this group may also be difficult, as they may struggle to understand the concepts with which they are presented. They may appear to understand the questions, but may only be trying to please the evaluator. It is also important to note that individuals with developmental disabilities may have no understanding of the severity of their offense, nor may they be able to differentiate between sexually appropriate and sexually inappropriate behavior. Beech, Fisher, and Thornton (2003) discuss an alternative method of assessing dynamic aspects of risk with this population. Pictures of various activities and scenarios can be presented to the individual, and questions may be asked to evaluate that person's attitudes and understanding. Again, when working with this population it is important to gather information from collateral sources, as the individuals themselves may be poor reporters and historians.

🖋 TEST YOURSELF 🖋

1. **The HCR-20 can be used all alone in conducting a risk assessment.**
   True or False?

2. **The best predictor of violence recidivism on the VRAG is**
   (a) history of violent behavior.
   (b) psychopathy (as measured on the PCL-R).
   (c) mental illness.
   (d) none of the above.

3. **The CAPI should be used alone in determining whether intrusive interventions are necessary, as the possibility of false positives creates an ethical concern.**
   True or False?

4. **The onset of first delinquency in middle adolescence is one of the strongest predictors of violence in adulthood.**
   True or False?

5. **All risk assessment instruments are appropriate for use with males, females, and juveniles.**
   True or False?

Answers: 1. False; 2. b; 3. True; 4. False; 5. False

References

Academy of Family Mediators. (1998). *Standards or practice for family and divorce mediation.* Portland, OR: Author.

Academy of Family Mediators. (2001). *Standards or practice for family and divorce mediation.* Portland, OR: Author.

Acheson, S. K. (2005). Review of the Hare Psychopathy Checklist-Revised, 2nd ed.). In R. A. Spies & B. S. Plake (eds.) (2005). *The Sixteenth Mental Measurements Yearbook* (pp. 429–431). Lincoln: University of Nebraska Press.

Ackerman, M. J. (2008). *Does Wednesday mean mom's house or dad's?* (2nd ed.). New York: Wiley.

Ackerman, M. J. (2006). *Clinician's guide to child custody evaluations* (3rd ed.). Hoboken, NJ: Wiley

Ackerman, M. J., & Ackerman, M. C. (1997). Child custody evaluation practices: A survey of experienced professionals (revisited). *Professional Psychology: Research and Practice, 28,* 137–145.

Ackerman, M. J., & Ackerman, S. D. (1992). *Comparison of different subgroups on the MMPI-2 of parents involved in custody litigation.* Unpublished manuscript.

Ackerman, M. J., & Brey, T. R. (in press). Child custody evaluation practices: A survey of psychologists. *Family Court Review.*

Ackerman, M. J., & Kane, A. W. (1998). *Psychological experts in divorce actions* (3rd Ed.). New York: Aspen Law & Business.

Ackerman, M. J., & Kane, A. W. (2005). *Psychological experts in divorce actions* (4th ed.). New York: Aspen Law & Business.

Ackerman, M. J., & Kane, A.W. (2008). *Psychological experts in divorce actions* (4th ed.). 2008 Cumulative Supplement. New York: Aspen Law & Business.

Ackerman, M. J., & Kravit, A. (in preparation). Commonly elevated scales on the Minnesota Multiphasic Personality Inventory, Second Edition in a contested custody evaluation.

Ackerman, M. J., & O'Leary, U. (1995, August). *Comparison of different subgroups on the MMPI-2 of parents involved in custody litigation.* Paper presented at the 103rd annual convention of the American Psychological Association, New York.

Ackerman, M. J., & Schoendorf, K. (1992). *The Ackerman-Schoendorf scales for parent evaluation of custody (ASPECT).* Los Angeles, CA: Western Psychological Services.

Ackerman, M. J., & Waisanen, E. L. (in preparation). Commonly elevated scales on the Minnesota Multiphasic Personality Inventory, Second Edition–Restructured Form in a contested custody evaluation.

Adams, B. J., Field, L., & Verhave, T. (1999). Effects of unreinforced conditional selection training, multiple negative comparison training, and feedback on equivalence class formation. *Psychological Record, 49,* 685–702.

Addington v. Texas, 441 U.S. 418, 426 (1979)

Agnew, S. E. & Powell, M. B. (2004). The effect of intellectual disability on children's recall of an event across different question types. *Law and Human Behavior, 28*(3), 273–294

Allen, L. M., Conder, R. L., Green, P., & Cox, D. R. (1997). *CARB '97 Manual for the computerized assessment of response bias.* Durham, NC: CogniSyst.American.

American Academy of Child and Adolescent Psychiatry (AACAP). (1997). Practice parameters for the forensic evaluation of children and adolescents who may have been physically or sexually abused. *Journal of American Academy of Child and Adolescent Psychiatry, 36* (Suppl.), 37s–56s.

American Academy of Matrimonial Lawyers' Guidelines (in press).

American Professional Society on the Abuse of Children (1997). *Psychosocial Evaluation of Suspected Sexual Abuse in Children* (2nd ed.). Chicago: American Professional Society on the Abuse of Children.

American Psychiatric Association. (2000). *Diagnostic and statistical manual of mental disorders* (4th ed.). Washington, DC: Author.

American Psychiatric Association (2008). *The principles of medical ethics with annotations especially applicable to psychiatry*. Washington DC.: Author.

American Psychological Association. (1992). Ethical principles of psychologists and code of conduct. *American Psychologist, 47,* 1597–1611.

American Psychological Association. (1987). General guidelines for providers of psychological services. *American Psychologist, 42,* 1–12.

American Psychological Association. (1991). Specialty guidelines for forensic psychologists. *APA Monitor, 22,* 22.

American Psychological Association. (1995). Twenty-four questions (and answers) about professional practice in the area of child abuse. *Professional psychology: Research and Practice, 26,* 377–385.

American Psychological Association. (1997). *Patient's bill of rights*. Washington, DC: Author.

American Psychological Association. (1998). *Guidelines for Psychological Evaluations in Child Protection Matters*. Retrieved October 17, 2009, from http://www.apa.org/practice/childprotection.html

American Psychological Association. (2002). Ethical principles of psychologists and code of conduct. *American Psychologist, 57,* 1060–1073.

American Psychological Association. (2007). Record keeping guidelines. *American Psychologist, 62,* 993–1004.

American Psychological Association. (2009). *Guidelines for Child Custody Evaluations in Family Law Proceedings*. Retrieved October 17, 2009, from www.apa.org

American Psychological Association Council of Representatives. (1991). *Statement of the use of anatomically detailed dolls in forensic evaluation*.

American Psychology-Law Society (in press). *Specialty Guidelines for Forensic Psychologists*.

Andrews, D., & Bonta, J. (1995). *LSI-R: The Level of Service Inventory-Revised*. Toronto: Multi-Health Systems, Inc.

Andrews, D. A., Bonta, J., & Wormith, S. J. (2004). *The Level of Service/Case Management Inventory (LS/CMI)*. Toronto: Multi-Health Systems, Inc.

Appelbaum, P. (1993). Foucha v. Louisiana: When must the state release insanity acquitees? *Hospital and Community Psychiatry, 44,* 9–10.

Appelbaum, P., & Grisso, T. (1995). The MacArtur treatment competence study. I: Mental illness and competence to consent to treatment. *Law and Human Behavior, 19,* 105–126.

Appelbaum, P., & Grisso, T. (1998, October). *The MacArthur treatment competence study*. Paper presented at the Competency, Coercion and Risk of Violence conference, Marquette University Law School, Milwaukee, WI.

Arbisi, P. A. (2003). Review of the HCR-20: Assessing Risk for Violence. From B. S. Plake, J. C. Impara, & R. A. Spies (Eds.), *The fifteenth mental measurements yearbook*. Lincoln: University of Nebraska Press.

Arbisi, P.A., & Ben-Porath, Y. S. (1995). An MMPI-2 infrequent response scale for use with psychopathological populations: The F(p) Scale. *Psychological Assessment, 7,* 424–431.

Archer, R., Buffington-Vollum, J., Stredny, R., & Handel, R. (2006). A survey of psychological test use patterns among forensic psychologists. *Journal of Personality Assessment, 87,* 84–94.

Arias, I., Street, A. E., & Brody, G. H. (1996). *Depression and alcohol abuse: Women's responses to psychological victimization*. Presented at the American Psychological Association's National Conference on Psychosocial & Behavioral Factors in Women's Health: Research, Prevention, Treatment, & Service Delivery in Clinical and Community Settings, Washington, DC.

Association of Family and Conciliation Courts. (2007). Model standards of practice for child custody evaluation. *Family Court Review, 45,* 70–91.

Association of State and Provincial Psychology Boards. (1991). *ASPPB13 code of conduct.* Montgomery, AL: Author.

Association of State and Provincial Psychology Boards. (2005). *ASPPB code of conduct* (rev.ed.). Montgomery, AL: Author

Association of State and Provincial Psychology Boards. (1991). *Canadian code of ethics for psychologists.* Ottawa: Author.

Augimeri, L., Webster, C., Koegl, C., & Levene, K. (2001). *Early Assessment Risk List for Boys: EARL-20B. Version 2.* Toronto: Earlscourt Child and Family Centre.

Babcock, J. C., Roseman, A., Green, C. E., & Ross, J. M. (2008). Intimate partner abuse and PTSD symptomtology: Examining mediators and moderators of the abuse-trauma link. *Journal of Family Psychology, 22,* 809–818.

Barnard, G. W., Nicholson, R. A., Hankins, G. C., Raisani, K. K., Patel, N. R., Gies, D., & Robbins, L. (1992). Item metric and scale analysis of a new computer-assisted competency assessment instrument (CADCOMP). *Behavioral Sciences and the Law, 10,* 419–435.

Barnard, G. W., Thompson, J. W., Jr., Freeman, W. C., Robbins, L., Gies, D., & Hankins, G.C. (1991). Competency to stand trial: Description and initial evaluation of a computer-assisted assessment tool (CADCOMP). *Bulletin of the American Academy of Psychiatry and Law, 19,* 367–381.

Baron, I. S. (2004) *Neuropsychological evaluation of the child.* New York: Oxford University Press.

Bartel, P., Borum, R., & Forth, A. (2000). *Structured Assessment for Violence Risk in Youth (SAVRY): Consultation Edition.* Tampa: Louis de la Parte Florida Mental Health Institute, University of South Florida.

Bathurst, K., Gottfried, A., & Gottfried, A. (1997). Normative data on the MMPI-2 in child custody litigation. *Psychological Assessment, 9,* 205–211.

Baxtrom *v.* Herald (1966) 383 U.S. 107.

Beck, J., & Bonnar, J. (1988). Emergency civil commitment: Predicting hospital violence from behavior in the community. *Journal of Psychiatry and Law, 16,* 379–388.

Beech, A. R., Fisher, D. D., & Thornton, D. (2003). Risk assessment of sex offenders. *Professional Psychology: Research and Practice, 34,* 339–352.

Behrends, K. (2005). *Convergent validity of the Personality Assessment Inventory with the Child Abuse Potential Inventory: Implications for the use of the PAI in child access evaluations.* Unpublished doctoral dissertation, Chicago School of Professional Psychology.

Bell-Pringle, V. J., Pate, J. L., & Brown, R. C. (1997). Assessment of Borderline Personality Disorder using the MMPI-2 and Personality Assessment Inventory. *Assessment, 4,* 131–139.

Ben-Porath, Y. S. (1995). *Case studies for interpreting the MMPI-A.* Minneapolis: University of Minnesota Press.

Ben-Porath, Y. S. & Tellegen, A. (2008, December). MMPI-2 FBS (Symptom Validity) Scale Bibliography. Retrieved August 24, 2009, from http://pearsonassess.com/NR/rdonlyres/A25DB8F8-435F-4066-801B-B641978A97DA/0/MMPI2FBS.pdf

Ben-Porath, Y. S., Greve, K. W., Bianchini, K. J., & Kaufmann, P. M. (2009). The MMPI-2 Symptom Validity Scale (FBS) is an empirically validated measure of overreporting in personal injury litigants and claimants: Reply to Butcher et al. (2008). *Psychological Injury and Law, 2,* 62–85.

Bender, S. D. (2008). Malingered traumatic brain injury. In Rogers, R. (Ed.), *Clinical Assessment of Malingering and Deception* (3rd ed., pp. 69–86). New York: Guilford.

Berry, D. T. R., & Schipper, L. J. (2008). Assessment of feigned cognitive impairment using standard neuropsychological tests. In Rogers, R. (Ed.), *Clinical Assessment of Malingering and Deception* (3rd ed., pp. 237–252). New York: Guilford.

Bersoff, D. N. (2008). *Ethical conflicts in psychology* (4th Ed.). Washington, DC: American Psychological Association.

Beyer, P. (1996). *The development and preliminary validation of life satisfaction in children: Post divorce.* Unpublished doctoral dissertation. Wisconsin School of Professional Psychology.

Binder, L. M., & Rohling, M. L. (1996a). Money matters: A meta-analytic review of the effects of financial incentives on recovery after closed-head injury. *American Journal of Psychiatry, 153,* 7–10.

Binder, R. L., Trimble, M. R., & McNeil, D. E. (1991). The course of psychological symptoms after resolution of lawsuits. *American Journal of Psychiatry, 148,* 1073–1075.

Binder, L., & Willis, S. C. (1991). Assessment of motivation after financially compensable minor head trauma. *Psychological Assessment, 3,* 175–181.

Disbing, S. B., & Firestone, M. (1993). The role of the neuropsychologist and neuropsychiatrist in head trauma litigation. *Trial Diplomacy Journal, 16,* 225–242.

Bischoff, L. (1992). Review of the custody quotient. In J. Kramer & J. C. Conoley (Eds.), *Eleventh mental measurements yearbook* (p. 254). Lincoln: University of Nebraska Press.

Blake, D. D., Weathers, F. W., Nagy, L. M., Kaloupek, D. G., Gusman, F. D., Charney, D. S., & Keane, T. M.(1995) The development of a clinician-administered PTSD scale. *Journal of Traumatic Stress, 8,* 75–90.

Blanchard, E. B., Jones-Alexander, J., Buckley, T. C., et al. (1996). Psychometric properties of the PTSD Checklist (PCL). *Behaviour Research and Therapy, 34,* 669–673.

Blanchard, E. B., Hickling, E. J., Taylor, A. E., Buckly, E. C., Los, M. R., & Walsh, J. (1998). Effects of litigation settlements on posttraumatic stress symptoms in motor vehicle accident victims. *Journal of Traumatic Stress, 11,* 337–354.

Boccaccini, M. T., Boothby, J. L., & Overduin, L. Y. (2006). Evaluating the validity of pain complaints in personal injury cases: Assessment approaches of forensic and pain specialists. *Journal of Forensic Psychology Practice, 6,* 51–62.

Boer, D. P., Hart, S. J., Kropp, P. R., & Webster, C. D. (1997). *Manual for the Sexual Violence Risk – 20: Professional Guidelines for Assessing Risk of Sexual Violence.* Vancouver, BC: The Institute Against Family Violence.

Bonnie, B. J. (1990). The competency of defendants with mental retardation to assist in their own defense. In R. W. Conley, R. Luckasson, & G. N. Bouthilet (Eds.), *The criminal justice system and mental retardation* (pp. 97–120). Baltimore: Paul Brooks.

Bonnie, B. J. (1992). The competence of criminal defendants: A theoretical reformulation, *Behavioral Sciences and the Law, 10,* 291–316.

Bonnie, B. J. (1993). The competence of criminal defendants: Beyond Dusky and Drope. *University of Miami Law Review, 47,* 539–601.

Bonnie, B. J., & Grisso, T. (2000). Adjudicative competence and youthful offenders. In T. Grisso & R. Schwartzs (Eds.), *Youth on trial* (pp. 73–103). Chicago: University of Chicago Press.

Bonnie, B. J., & Monahan, J. (2005). From coercion to contract: Reframing the debate on mandated community treatment for people with mental disorders. *Law and Human Behavior, 29,* 485–502.

Borum, R., Swartz, M., & Swanson, J. (1996). Assessing and managing violence risk in clinical practice. *Journal of Practical Psychiatry and Behavioral Health, 4,* 205–215.

Borum, R., Bartel, P., & Forth, A. (2003). *Manual for the Structured Assessment for Violence Risk in Youth (SAVRY): Version 1, Consultation Edition.* Tampa: Louis de la Parte Florida Mental Health Institute, University of South Florida.

Borum, R., Bartel, P., & Forth, A. (2005). Structured Assessment of Violence Risk in Youth. In T. Grisso, G. Vincent, & D. Seagrave (Eds.), *Mental health screening and assessment in juvenile justice* (pp. 311–323). New York: Guilford.

Bradley, K. A., Boyd-Wickizer, J., Powell, S., & Burman, M. (1998). Alcohol screening questionnaires in women. *Journal of the American Medical Association, 280,* 166–171.

Bricklin, B. (1984). *Bricklin perceptual scales.* Furlong, PA: Village Publishing.

Briere, J. (1995). *Trauma Symptom Inventory professional manual.* Odessa, FL: Psychological Assessment Resources.

Briere, J. (1996a). *Therapy for adults molested as children: Beyond survival.* New York: Springer-Verlag.

Briere, J. (1996). *Trauma Symptom Inventory Checklist for Children professional manual.* Odessa, FL: Psychological Assessment Resources.

Briere, J. (1997). *Psychological assessment of adult posttraumatic stress states.* Washington, DC: American Psychological Association.

Briere, J. (2004). *Psychological assessment of adult posttraumatic stress disorder* (2nd ed.). Washington, DC: American Psychological Association.

Briere, J., & Runtz, M. (1993). Childhood sexual abuse, long-term sequelae and implications for psychological assessment. *Journal of Interpersonal Violence, 3,* 312–330.

Brodzinsky, D. (1993). The use and misuse of psychological testing in child custody evaluations. *Professional Psychology: Research and Practice, 24,* 213–218.

Brown, D., & Lamb, M. E. (2009). Forensic interviews with children a two-way street: Supporting interviewers in adhering to best practice recommendations and enhancing children's capabilities in forensic interviews. In K. Kuehnle & M. Connell (Eds.), *The evaluation of child sexual abuse allegations: A Comprehensive guide to assessment and testimony* (pp. 299–325). Hoboken, NJ: Wiley.

Bryant, R. A., & Harvey, A. G. (2003). The influence of litigation on maintenance of Posttraumatic Stress Disorder. *The Journal of Nervous and Mental Disease, 191,* 191–193.

Buck, J. A., & Warren, A. R. (2009). Jurors and professionals in the legal system: What they know and what they should they know about interviewing child witnesses (sic). In K. Kuehnle & M. Connell (Eds.), *The evaluation of child sexual abuse allegations: A comprehensive guide to assessment and testimony* (pp. 501–530). Hoboken, NJ: Wiley.

Buchanan, A. (2006). Competency to stand trial and the seriousness of the charge. *Journal of the American Academy of Psychiatry and the Law, 34,* 458–465.

Buist, A. and Janson, H. (2001). Childhood abuse, parenting and postpartum depression : A three year follow up study. *Child Abuse and Neglect, 25,* 909–921.

Burgess, P., Bindman, J., Leese, M., Henderson, C., & Szmukler, G. (2006). Do community treatment orders for mental illness reduce readmission to hospital? *Social Psychiatry and Psychiatric Epidemiology, 41,* 574–579.

Butcher, J. N., Gass, C. S., Cumella, E., Kally, Z., & Williams, C. L. (2008). Potential for bias in MMPI-2 assessments using the Fake Bad Scale (FBS). *Psychological Injury and Law, 1,* 191–209.

Butcher, J. N., Graham, J. R., Ben-Porath, Y. S., Tellegen, A., Dahlstrom, W. G., & Kaemmer, B. (2001). *MMPI-2 Manual for administration, scoring, and interpretation* (rev. ed.). Minneapolis: University of Minnesota Press.

Call, J. A. (2003). Liability for psychological injury: Yesterday and today. In I. Z. Schultz & D. O. Brady (Eds.), *Psychological injuries at trial* (pp. 40–64). Chicago: American Bar Association.

Carmen, E. H., Reiker, P. P., & Mills, T. (1984). Victims of violence and psychiatric illness. *American Journal of Psychiatry, 141,* 378–379.

Carr, G. D., Moretti, M. M., & Cue, B. (2005). Evaluating parenting capacity: Validity problems with the MMPI-2, PAI, CAPI, and ratings of child adjustment. *Professional Psychology: Research and Practice, 36,* 188–196.

Carter, M. B., Bennett, B. E., Jones, S.E., & Nagy, T. F. (1994). *Ethics for psychologists: A commentary on the APA ethics code.* Washington, DC: American Psychological Association.

Cascardi, M., O'Leary, D., Lawrence, E., & Schlee, K. (1995). Characteristics of women physically abused by their spouses and who seek treatment regarding marital conflict. *A Journal of Consulting and Clinical Psychology, 63,* 616–623.

Cassels, C. (2009). Substance abuse main driver of violence in schizophrenia, psychoses. Medscape Medical News. Retrieved September 10, 2009, from www.medscape.com

Cauffman, E., & Steinberg, L. (2000). Immaturity of judgment in adolescence: Why adolescents may be less culpable than adults. *Behavioral Sciences and the Law, 18,* 1–21.

Cauffman, E., & Steinberg, L. (2000). Reasearching adolescents' judgment and culpability. In T. Grisso & R. Schwartz (Eds.), *Youth on trial: A developmental perspective in juvenile justice* (pp. 325–343). Chicago: University of Chicago Press.

Ceci, S., & Bruck, M. (1993). Social policy report for the Society for Research and Child Development in 1993. *Child Witness: Translating Research Into Policy, 7,* 1–30.

Center for Sex Offender Management. (2001). *Recidivism of sex offenders.* Silver Spring, MD: Center for Effective Public Policy.

Center for Substance Abuse Treatment. (2005). *Substance Abuse Treatment for Individuals with Co-occurring Disorders.* Treatment Improvement Protocol #42, CSAT, Washington.

Chambers, A., & Wilson, M. (2007). Assessing male batterers with the Personality Assessment Inventory. *Journal of Personality Assessment, 88,* 57–65.

Clark, C. R. (2009). Professional roles key to accuracy and effectiveness. In Kuehnle, K., & Connell, M. (Eds.), *The evaluation of child sexual abuse allegations: A comprehensive guide to assessment and testimony* (pp. 69–79). Hoboken, NJ: Wiley.

Committee on Ethical Guidelines for Forensic Psychologists. (1991). Specialty guidelines for forensic psychologists. *Law and Human Behavior, 15,* 655–665.

Connors, G. J., and Volk, R. J. (2003). Self-report screening for alcohol problems among adults. In: National Institute on Alcohol Abuse and Alcoholism. *Assessing Alcohol Problems: A Guide for Clinicians and Researchers* (2nd ed., pp 21–35). NIH Pub. No. 03–3745. Washington, DC: U. S. Dept. of Health and Human Services, Public Health Service.

Conroy, M. A., & Murrie, D. C. (2007). *Forensic assessment of violence risk: A guide for risk assessment and risk management.* Hoboken, NJ: Wiley.

Cooper, C. (2003). Review of the HCR-20: Assessing Risk for Violence. In B. S. Plake, J. C. Impara, & R. A. Spies (Eds.), *The fifteenth mental measurements yearbook.* Lincoln: University of Nebraska Press.

Cunnien, A. J. (1997). Psychiatric and medical syndromes associated with deception. In R. Rogers (Ed.), *Clinical assessment of malingering and deception* (2nd ed., pp. 23–46). New York: Guilford.

Daubert v. Merrell Dow Pharmaceuticals, Inc., 509, U.S. 579, 113 S Ct. 2786, 125 L. Ed. 2d 469 (Supreme Court 1993).

Demare, D. (1996). *The childhood maltreatment questionnaire: Examining long-term correlates of childhood maltreatment.* Paper presented at the 104th Annual Convention of The American Psychological Association, Toronto, Canada.

Dent, H. (1992). The effects of age and intelligence on eye witnessing ability. In H. Dent & R. Flin (Eds.), *Children as witnesses* (pp. 1–14). Chichester, England: Wiley.

Detecting malingering with psychological tests (1989). *Clinicians Research Digest, 7,* 2.

DeYoung, M. (1986). A conceptual model for judging the truthfulness of a young child's allegation of sexual abuse. *American Journal of Orthopsychiatry, 56,* 550–559.

Dezwirek Sas, L. (1992). Empowering child witnesses for sexual abuse prosecution. In H. Dent & R. Flin (Eds.), *Children as witnesses* (pp. 181–200). Chichester, England: Wiley.

Douglas, K. S., Ogloff, J. R. P., Nicholls, T. L. & Grant, I. (1999). Assessing risk for violence among psychiatric patients: The HCR-20 violence risk assessment scheme and the Psychopathy Checklist: Screening Version. *Journal of Consulting and Clinical Psychology, 67,* 917–930.

Douglas, K. S., Hart, S. D., & Kropp, P. R. (2001). Validity of the Personality Assessment Inventory for forensic assessments. *International Journal of Offender Therapy and Comparative Criminology, 45,* 183–197.

Downs, W., Smyth, N., & Miller, B. (1996). The relationship between childhood violence and alcohol problems among men who batter: Empirical review and synthesis. *Aggression and Violent Behavior, 1,* 327–344.

Drob, S. L., Meehan, K. B., & Waxman, S. E. (2009). Clinical and conceptual problems in the attribution of malingering in forensic evaluations. *Journal of the American Academy of Psychiatry and Law, 37,* 98–106.

Durham, M. L., & LaFond, J. Q. (1988). A search for the missing premise of involuntary therapeutic commitment: Effective treatment of the mentally ill. *Rutgers Law Review, 40,* 303–368.

Dusky v. United States, 362 U.S. 402 (1960).

Drope v. Missouri, 420 U.S. 162 (1975).

Edens, J., Skeem, J., Cruise, K., & Cauffman, E. (2001). Assessment of "juvenile psychopathy" and its association with violence: A critical review. *Behavioral Sciences and the Law, 19,* 53–80.

Edwards, R. (1996). Can psychologists predict violent behavior? *American Psychological Association Monitor, 27,* 10.

Egami, Y., Ford, D., Grenfield, S., & Crum, R. (1996). Psychiatric profiles and sociodemographic characteristics of adults who report physically abusing or neglecting children. *American Journal of Psychiatry, 1953,* 921–928.

Elbogen, E. B., & Johnson, S. C. (2009). The intricate link between violence and mental disorder. *Archives of General Psychiatry, 66,* 152–161.

Elhai, J. D., Naifeh, J. A., Zucker, I. S., Gold, S. N., Deitsch, S. E., & Frueh, B. C. (2004). Discriminating malingered from genuine civilian Posttraumatic Stress Disorder: A validation of three MMPI-2 infrequency scales (F, FP, and FPTSD). *Assessment 11,* 139–144.

Epperson, D. L., Kaul, J. D., Huot, S. J., Hesselton, D., Alexander, W., & Goldman, R. (1998). *Minnesota Sex Offender Screening Tool–Revised (MnSOST-R).* St. Paul: Minnesota Department of Corrections.

Everington, C. T. (1990). The competence assessment for standing trial for defendants with mental retardation (CAST-MR): A validation study. *Criminal Justice and Behavior, 17,* 147–168.

Everington, C. T., & Dunn, C. (1995). A second validation study of the competence assessment for standing trial for defendants with mental retardation (CAST-MR), *Criminal Justice and Behavior, 22,* 44–59.

Everington, C. T., & Luckasson, Y. R. (1992). *Competence assessment for standing trial for defendants with mental illness.* Worthington, OH: International Diagnostic Systems.

Everson, M. D., & Boat, B. W. (1997). Anatomical dolls in child sexual abuse assessments: A call for forensically relevant research. *Applied Cognitive Psychology, 11,* 55–74.

Fare v. Michael C., 442 U.S. 707 (1979).

Fazel, S., Gulati, G., Linsell, L., Geddes, J.R., & Grann, M (2009). Schizophrenia and violence: Systematic review and meta-analysis. *PLoS medicine 2009; 6*(8): e1000120

Feiring, C., Simon, V. A., & Cleland, C. M. (2009). Childhood sexual abuse, stigmatization, internalizing symptoms, and the development of sexual difficulties and dating aggression. *Journal of Clinical and Consulting Psychology, 77,* 127–133.

Feldstein S. W., & Miller W. R. (2007). Does subtle screening for substance abuse work? A review of the Substance Abuse. Subtle Screening Inventory (SASSI). *Addiction, 102,* 41–50.

Felthouse, A. R., & Kellert, S. R. (1987). Childhood cruelty to animals and later aggression against people: A review. *American Journal of Psychiatry, 144,* 710–717.

Fishbain, D. A., Cutler, R., Rosomoff, H. L., & Rosomoff, R. S. (2003). Chronic pain disability exaggeration/malingering and submaximal effort research. In I. Z. Schultz & D. O. Brady (Eds.), *Psychological injuries at trial* (pp. 1064–1122). Chicago: American Bar Association.

Fitzgerald, E., & Hume, D. (1987). *Intoxication test evidence: Criminal and civil.* New York: Clark, Boardman, & Callaghan.

Foa, E. (1995). *Post-traumatic Diagnostic Scale manual.* Minneapolis: National Computer Systems.

Foa E. B., Tolin D. F. (2000). Comparison of the PTSD Symptom Scale-Interview version and the Clinician-Administered PTSD Scale. *Journal of Traumatic Stress,* (13), 181–191.

Folstein, M. F., Folstein, S. E., & McHugh, P. R. (1975). "Mini mental state": A practical method for grading the cognitive state of patients for the clinician *Journal of Psychiatric Research, 12,* 189–198.

Forth, A., Kosson, D., & Hare, R. (2003). *The Hare PCL: Youth Version.* Toronto, ON: Multi-Health Systems, Inc.

Foucha v. Louisiana, 504 U.S. 71, 112 S. Ct. 1780 (1992).

Frank, D., Perry, J. C., Kean, D., Sigman, M., & Geagea, K. (2005). Effects of compulsory treatment orders on time to hospital readmission. *Psychiatric Services, 56,* 867–869.

French v. Blackburn, 428 F. Supp. 1351 (M.D.N.C.), *aff'd,* 443 U.S. 901 (1977).

Frye v. United States, 293 F. 1013, 1014 (D.C. Circ. 1923).

Fulwiler, C., Grossman, H., Forbes, C., & Ruthazer, R. (1997). Early-onset substance abuse and community violence by outpatients with chronic mental illness. *Psychiatric Services, 48,* 1181–1185.

Galatzer-Levy, R. M., Kraus, L., & Galatzer-Levy, J. (2009). *The scientific basis of child custody decisions* (2nd ed.). Hoboken, NJ: Wiley.

Garbarino, J., Guttman, E., & Seeley, J. (1987). *The psychologically battered child.* San Francisco: Jossey Bass.

Gardner, W., Lidz, C. W., Mulvey, E. P., & Shaw, E. C. (1996). Clinical versus actuarial predictions of violence in patients with mental illness. *Journal of Consulting and Clinical Psychology, 64,* 602–609.

Gebhart-Eaglemont, J. E. (2001). *Review of the Trauma Symptom Inventory.* In P. S. Blake & J. C. Impara (Eds.), *The fourteenth mental measurements yearbook.* Lincoln: University of Nebraska Press.

Gerard, A. (1994). *Parent-Child Relationship Inventory.* Los Angeles: Western Psychological Services.

Gindes, M. (1995), Competence and training in child custody evaluations. *American Journal of Family Therapy, 23,* 273–80.

Godinez v. Moran, 509 U.S. 389 (1993).

Golden C. J., Hammeke T. A., & Purisch A. D. (1978). Diagnostic validity of a standardized neuropsychological battery derived from Luria's neuropsychological tests. *Journal of Consulting and Clinical Psychology, 46,* 1258–1265.

Golden, C. J., Hammeke, T. A., & Purisch, A. D. (1980). *A manual for the Luria-Nebraska neuropsychological battery.* Los Angeles: Western Psychological Services.

Golding, S. L. (1993). *Training manual: Interdisciplinary fitness interview revised.* Department of Psychology, University of Utah.

Golding, S. L., & Roesch, R. (1988). Competency for adjudication: An international analysis. In D. N. Weisstub (Ed.), *Law and mental health: International perspectives* (Vol. 4, pp. 73–109). New York: Pergamon.

Golding, S. L., Roesch, R., & Schreiber, J. (1984). Assessment and conceptualization of competency to stand trial. Preliminary data on the interdisciplinary fitness interview. *Law and Human Behavior, 8,* 321–334.

Goldstein, A. (2004, April). *Assessing competency for trial.* Paper presented at the American Academy of Forensic Psychology Conference, New Orleans, LA.

Goldstein, G. (1990). Comprehensive neuropsychological assessment batteries. In G. Goldstein & M. Herson (Eds.), *Handbook of psychological assessment* (2nd ed., pp. 197–227).

Goldstein, A., Morse, S., & Shapiro, D. (2002). Evaluations of criminal responsibility. In A. Goldstein (Ed.), *Forensic psychology* (pp. 381–406). New York: Wiley.

Goldstein, A., & Weiner, I.B. (2003). *Handbook of psychology* (Vol. 11). New York: Wiley.

Goldstein, J. A., Freud, A., & Solnit, A. J. (1973). *Beyond the best interests of the child.* New York: Free Press.

Goodman, G. S. (1991, August). *Understanding children's testimony.* Paper presented at the 99th annual convention of the American Psychological Association, San Francisco, CA.

Goodman, G. S., & Aman, C. (1987). *Children's use of anatomically correct dolls to report an event.* A paper presented at the meeting of the Society for Research in Child Development, Baltimore, MD.

Goodman, G. S., & Rosenberg, M. (1991). The child witness of family violence: Clinical and legal considerations. In D. J. Sonkin (Ed.), *Domestic violence on trial* (pp. 97–125). New York: Springer.

Goodman, T. B., Edelstein R. S., Goodman, G. S., Jones, D., & Gordon, D. S. (2003). Why children tell: A model of children's disclosure of sexual abuse. *Child Abuse and Neglect, 27*(5), 525–540.

Gothard, S., Rogers, R., & Sewell, K. W. (1995). Feigning incompetency to stand trial: An investigation of the Georgia Court Competency Test. *Law and Human Behavior, 19,* 363–373.

Gothard, S., Viglione, D. J., Meloy, J. R., & Sherman, M. (1995). Detection of malingering in competency to stand trial evaluations. *Law and Human Behavior, 19,* 493–505.

Gough, H. G. (1950). The F minus K dissimulation index for the MMPI. *Journal of Consulting Psychology, 14,* 408–413.

Gould, J. W. (1998). *Conducting scientifically crafted child custody evaluations.* Thousand Oaks, CA: Sage.

Gould, J. W. (2006). *Conducting scientifically crafted child custody evaluations* (2nd ed.). Thousand Oaks, CA: Sage.

Gould, J. W., Martindale, D. A., & Flens, J. R. (2009). Use of psychological tests in child custody evaluations. In R. M. Galatzer-Levy, A. Kraus, & J. Galatzer-Levy, (Eds.), *The scientific basis of child custody decisions* (pp. 85–124). Hoboken, NJ: Wiley.

Graham, J. (1990). *MMPI-2: Assessing personality and psychopathology.* New York: Oxford University Press.

Graham, J. R. (2006). *MMPI-2: Assessing personality and psychopathology* (4th ed.). New York: Oxford University Press.

Graham-Bermann, S., & Levendosky, A. (1998). The social functioning of preschool-aged children whose mothers are emotionally and physically abused. *Journal of Emotional Abuse, 1,* 59–84.

Green, P. (2003). *Green's word memory test: User's manual.* Edmonton, Canada: Green's Publishing.

Green, P. (2004). *Memory complaints inventory.* Edmonton, Canada: Green's Publishing.

Greenberg, L. R., Martindale, D. A., Gould, J. W., Gould-Saltman, D. J. (2004). Ethical issues in child custody and dependency cases: Enduring principles and emerging challenges. *Journal of Child Custody, 1(1),* 7–30.

Greenberg, S. A., Otto, R. K., & Long, A. C. (2003). The utility of psychological testing in assessing emotional damages in personal injury litigation. *Assessment, 10,* 411–419.

Greene, R. L. (2008). Malingering and defensiveness on the MMPI-2. In R. Rogers, (Ed.), *Clinical Assessment of Malingering and Deception* (pp. 159–181). New York: Guilford.

Greene, R., Weed, N., Butcher, J., Arredondo, R., & Davis, H. (1992). A cross-validation of MMPI-2 substance abuse scales. *Journal of Personality Assessment, 58,* 405–410.

Grisso, T. (1980). Juveniles' capacities to waive Miranda rights: An empirical analysis. *California Law Review, 68,* 1134–1166.

Grisso, T. (1981). *Juveniles' waiver of rights: Legal and psychological competence.* New York: Plenum Press.

Grisso, T. (1986a). *Competency to stand trial. Evaluating competencies* (pp. 62–112). New York: Plenum Press.

Grisso, T. (1986b). *Evaluating competencies: Forensic assessments and instruments.* New York: Plenum Press.

Grisso, T. (1988). *Competency to stand trial evaluations: A manual for practice.* Sarasota, FL: Professional Resource Exchange.

Grisso, T. (1992). Five-year research update (1986–1990): Evaluations for competence to stand trial. *Behavioral Sciences and the Law, 10,* 353–369.

Grisso, T. (1998). *Forensic evaluation of juveniles.* Sarasota, FL: Professional Resource Press.

Grisso, T. (2003). *Evaluating competencies* (2nd Ed.). New York: Kluwer/Plenum.

Grisso, T. (2005). *Evaluating juveniles' adjudicative competence: A guide for clinical practice.* Sarasota, FL: Professional Resource Press.

Grisso, T., & Appelbaum, P. (1992). Is it unethical to offer predictions of future violence? *Law and Human Behavior, 16,* 621–633.

Grisso, T., & Appelbaum, P. (1995). The MacArthur treatment competence study III: Abilities of patients to consent to psychiatric and medical treatments. *Law and Human Behavior, 19,* 149–174.

Grisso, T., & Appelbaum, P. S. (1998). *Assessing competence to consent to treatment.* New York: Oxford University Press.

Grisso, T., & Barnum, R. (2003). *Massachusetts Youth Screening Instrument–Second Version 2: User's manual and technical report.* Sarasota, FL: Professional Resource Press.

Grisso, T. P., Mulvey, E. P., & Fletcher, K. (1995). The MacArthur treatment competence study II: Measures of abilities related to competence to consent to treatment. *Law and Human Behavior, 19,* 127–148.

Grisso, T., & Quinlan, C. (2005). Massachusetts Youth Screening Instrument–Version 2. In T. Grisso, G. Vincent, & D. Seagrave (Eds.), *Mental health screening and assessment in juvenile justice* (pp. 99–111). New York: Guilford.

Grisso, T., Vincent, G., & Seagrave, D. (2005). Mental health screening and assessment in juvenile justice. New York: Guilford.

Grote, C., Kaler, D., & Meyer, R. G. (1986). Personal injury law and psychology. In M. I. Kurke & R. G. Meyer (Eds.), *Psychology in product liability and personal injury litigation* (pp. 83–102). Washington, DC: Hemisphere.

Groth-Marnat, G. (2009). *Handbook of psychological assessment* (5th ed.). Hoboken, NJ: Wiley.

Gurley, J., Kuehnle, K., & Kirkpatrick, H. D. (2009). The continuum of children's sexual behavior: Discriminative categories and the need for public policy change. In K. Kuehnle & M. Connell (Eds.), *The evaluation of child sexual abuse allegations: A comprehensive guide to assessment and testimony* (pp. 129–150). Hoboken, NJ: Wiley.

Halon, R. L. (2001). The Millon Clinical Multiaxial Inventory–III; The normal quartet in child custody cases. *American Journal of Forensic Psychology, 19*(1), 57–75.

Hanson, R. K. (1997). *Development of a Brief Actuarial Risk Scale for Sexual Offense Recidivism.* Department of the Solicitor General of Canada. Public Works and Government Services Canada.

Hanson, R. K., & Morton-Bourgon, K. E. (2005). The characteristics of persistent sexual offenders: A meta-analysis of recidivism studies. *Journal of Consulting and Clinical Psychology, 73,* 1154–1163.

Hanson, R. K., & Thornton, D. (2002). *Static 99: Improving actuarial risk assessments for sex offenders.* Ottawa, Canada: Department of the Solicitor General.

Hare, R. (1991). *The Hare Psychopathy Checklist–Revised manual.* Tonawanda, NY: Multi-Health Systems, Inc.

Hare, R. D. (2003). *Manual for the Hare Psychopathy Checklist–Revised.* Multi-Health Systems, Inc.

Harris, A. R., Thomas, S. H., Fisher, G. A., & Hirsch, D. J. (2002). Murder and medicine: The lethality of criminal assault 1960-1999. *Homicide Studies, 6,* 128–166.

Harris, G. T., & Rice, M. E. (1997). Risk appraisal and management of violent behavior. *Psychiatric Services, 48,* 1168–1176.

Harris, G. T., Rice, M. E., & Cormier, C. A. (1991). Psychopathy and violent recidivism. *Law and Human Behavior, 15,* 625–637.

Harris, G. T., & Rice, M. E. (1997). Risk appraisal and management of violent behavior. *Psychiatric Services, 48,* 1168–1176.

Harris, L. S., Goodman, G. S., Augusti, E. M., Chae, Y. & Alley, D. (2009). Children's resistance to suggestion. In K. Kuehnle & M. Connell (Eds.), *The evaluation of child sexual abuse allegations: A comprehensive guide to assessment and testimony* (pp. 181–202). Hoboken, NJ: Wiley.

Hart, A.N. (1989). Review of the child abuse potential inventory: Form IV. In J. C. Conoley & J. J. Kramer (Eds.), *The tenth mental measurements yearbook.* Lincoln: University of Nebraska Press.

Hart, S., Binggeli, N., & Brassard, M. (1998). Evidence of the effects of psychological maltreatment. *Journal of Emotional Abuse, 1,* 27–58.

Hathaway, S. R., & McKinley, J. C. (1989). *MMPI-2: Manual for administration and scoring.* Minneapolis: University of Minnesota Press.

Hawkins, J. D., Herrenkohl, T. L., Farrington, D. P., Brewer, D., Catalano, R. F., & Harachi, T. W. (1998). A review of predictors of youth violence. In R. Loeber & D. P. Farrington (Eds.), *Serious and violent juvenile offenders: Risk factors and successful interventions* (pp. 106–146). Thousand Oaks, CA: Sage.

Hawkins, J., Herrenkohl, T., Farrington, D., Brewer, D.,Catalano, R., Harachi, T., & Cothern, L. (2000 April). Predictors of youth violence. *Juvenile Justice Bulletin.* Office of Juvenile Justice and Delinquency Prevention.

Heilbronner, R. (1993). Factors associated with postconcussion syndrome: Neurological, psychological, or legal? *Trial Diplomacy Journal, 16,* 161–167.

Heilbrun, K. (2001). *Principles of forensic mental health assessment.* New York: Kluwer/Plenum.

Heilbrun, K. (1992). The role of psychological testing in forensic assessments. *Law and Human Behavior, 16,* 257–272.

Heilbrun, K., Hawk, G., & Tate, D. C. (1996). Juvenile competence to stand trial: Research issues in practice. *Law and Human Behavior, 20*(5), 573–578.

Heilbrun, K., Warren, J., & Picarello, K. (2003). Third party information in forensic assessment. In I. B. Weiner (Series Ed.) & A. M. Goldstein (Vol. Ed.), *Handbook of psychology: Vol. 11, Forensic psychology* (pp. 69–86). Hoboken, NJ: Wiley.

Herman, S. (2005). Improving decision making in forensic child sexual abuse evaluations. *Law and Human Behavior, 29,* 87–120.

Herman, S. (2009). Forensic child sexual abuse evaluations: Accuracy, ethics, and admissibility. In K. Kuehnle & M. Connell (Eds.), *The evaluation of child sexual abuse allegations: A comprehensive guide to assessment and testimony* (pp. 247–266). Hoboken, NJ: Wiley.

Herrenkohl, R., Egolf, B., & Herrenkohl, E. (1997). Preschool antecedents of adolescents' assaultive behavior: A longitudinal study. *American Journal of Orthopsychiatry, 67,* 422–432.

Hershkowitz, I., Horowitz, D., & Lamb, M. E. (2005).Trends in children's disclosure of abuse in Israel: A national study. *Child Abuse & Neglect, 29*(11), 1203–14.

Hershkowitz, I., Horowitz, D., & Lamb, M. E. (2007). Victimization of children with disabilities.*The American Journal of Orthopsychiatry, 77*(4), 629–35.

Hester, R. K., & Miller, W. R. (Eds.). (2003). *Handbook of alcoholism treatment approaches: Effective alternatives* (3rd ed). Boston: Allyn & Bacon.

Hiday, V. A. (1988). Civil commitment: A review of empirical research. *Behavioral Sciences and the Law, 6,* 15–43.

Hiday, V. A. (1992). Coercion in civil commitment: Process, preferences, and outcome. *International Journal of Law and Psychiatry, 15,* 359–377.

Hoge, S. K., Bonnie, R. J., Poythress, N., & Monahan, J. (1992). Attorney-client decision making in criminal cases: Client competence and participation as perceived by their attorneys. *Behavioral Sciences and the Law, 10,* 385–394.

Horowitz, M., Wilner, N. J., & Alvarez, W. (1979). Impact of events scale: A measure of subjective stress. *Psychosomatic Medicine, 41,* 209–218.

Hotaling, G., & Sugarman, D. (1986). An analysis of risk markers in husband to wife violence: The current state of knowledge. *Violence and Victims, 1,* 101–124.

Hubbard, G. (1996). *Validity study of the parent-child relationship inventory for determining child custody.* Unpublished doctoral dissertation. Wisconsin School of Professional Psychology.

Huebner, B., Valentine, D. C., Stokes, S. D., Cobbina, J., & Berg, M. (2006). *Sex offender risk assessment.* Institute of Public Policy: University of Missouri-Columbia.

Hyler, S. E., Williams, J. & Spitzer, R. (1988). Where in DSM-III is "compensation neurosis"? *American Journal of Forensic Psychiatry, 9,* 3–12.

Hynan, D.J. (2004). Unsupported gender differences on some personality disorder scales of the Millon Clinical Multiaxial Inventory–III. *Professional Psychology: Research and Practice, 35,* 105–110.

In re: Athans, 107 Wis. 2d 331, 320 N.W.2d 330 (1982).

In re: Causey, 363 So.2d 472 (La. 1978).

In re: Gault, 387 U.S. 1 (1967).

In the Interest of S.H., 469 S. E. 2d. 810 (Ga. Ct. App. 1996).

Indiana v. Edwards, 128 S.Ct. 2379 (2008).

Inman, T. H., Vickery, C. D., Berry, D. T. R., Lamb, D. G., Edwards, C. L. & Smith, G. T. (1998). Development and initial validation of a new procedure for evaluating the adequacy of effort given during neuropsychological testing: Letter Memory Test. *Psychological Assessment, 10,* 128–139.

Iverson, G. L. & Lange, R. T. (2006). Detecting exaggeration and malingering in psychological injury cases. In W. J. Koch, K. S. Douglas, T. L. Nicholls, & M. L. O'Neill (Eds.), *Psychological Injuries: Forensic Assessment, Treatment, and Law* (pp. 76–112). New York: Oxford.

Jackson v. Indiana, 406 U.S. 715 (1972).

Jackson, R. L., Rogers, R., & Sewell, K. W. (2005). Forensic applications of the Miller Forensic Assessment of Symptoms Test (MFAST): Screening for feigned disorder in competency to stand trial evaluations. *Law and Human Behavior, 29,* 199–210.

Jacobson, G. R. (1989). A comprehensive approach to pretreatment evaluation: Detection, assessment, and diagnosis of alcoholism. In R. K. Hester & W. R. Miller (Eds.), *Handbook of alcoholism treatment approaches: Effective alternatives* (1st Ed.) (pp. 17–53). New York: Pergamon Press.

Jaffe v. Redmond, 116 S. Ct. 1923, 64 USLW 4490 (1996).

Johnstone, L. & Cooke, D. (2004). Psychopathic-like traits in childhood: Conceptual and measurement concerns. *Behavioral Sciences and the Law, 22,* 103–125.

Jones, L., Hughes, M., & Unterstaller, U. (2001). Posttraumatic stress disorder (PTSD) in victims of domestic violence: A review of the research. *Trauma, Violence, and Abuse, 2,* 99–119.

Joseph, S. (2000) Psychometric evaluation of Horowitz's Impact of Event Scale: A Review. *Journal of Traumatic Stress, 13,* 101–114.

Kallert, T. W. (2008). Coercion in psychiatry. *Current Opinion in Psychiatry, 21,* 485–489.

Kane, A. W. (2007a). Basic concepts in psychology and law. In G. Young, A. W. Kane, & K. Nicholson (Eds.), *Causality of psychological injury: Presenting evidence in court* (pp. 261–292). New York: Springer Science+Business Media.

Kane, A. W. (2007b). Conducting a psychological assessment. In G. Young, A. W. Kane, & K. Nicholson (Eds.), *Causality of psychological injury: Presenting evidence in court* (pp. 293–323). New York: Springer Science+Business Media.

Kane, A. W. (2007c). Other psycho-legal issues. In G. Young, A. W. Kane, & K. Nicholson (Eds.), *Causality of psychological injury: Presenting evidence in court* (pp. 325–367). New York: Springer Science+Business Media.

Kaplan, L. V., & Miller, R. D. (1996). *Law and Mental Health Professionals.* Washington, DC: American Psychological Association.

Katz, S. (1989). Hospitalization and the mental health service system. In H. Kaplan & B. Saddock (Eds.), *Comprehensive textbook of psychiatry* (5th Ed.) (pp. 2083–2090). Baltimore: Williams & Wilkins.

Kaufman, A. S., & Lichtenberger, E. O. (1999). *Essentials of WAIS-III assessment.* New York: Wiley.

Keilen, W. G., & Bloom, L. J. (1986). Child custody evaluation practices: A survey of experienced professionals. *Professional Psychology Research and Practice, 17,* 338–346.

Kendall-Tackett, K. A., Williams, L. M., & Finkelhor, D. (1993). Impact of sexual abuse on children: A review and synthesis of recent empirical studies. *Psychology Bulletin, 113*(1), 164–180.

Kent v. United States, 383 U.S. 541 (1966).

Kisely, S. R., Campbell, L. A., & Preston, N. J. (2005). Compulsory community and involuntary outpatient treatment for people with severe mental disorders. *Cochrane Database of Systematic Reviews,* Art. No.: CD004408. DOI: 10.1002/14651858.CD004408 .pub2.

Kisely, S., Campbell, L. A., Scott, A., Preston, N. J., & Xiao, J. (2007). Randomized and non-randomized evidence for the effect of compulsory community and involuntary out-patient treatment on health service use: Systematic review and meta-analysis. *Psychological Medicine, 27,* 3–14.

Klemfuss, J. Z., & Ceci, S. (2009). Normative memory development and the child witness. In K. Kuehnle & M. Connell (Eds.), *The evaluation of child sexual abuse allegations: A comprehensive guide to assessment and testimony* (pp. 153–180). Hoboken, NJ: Wiley.

Koch, W. J., O'Neill, M., & Douglas, K. S. (2005). Empirical limits for the forensic assessment of PTSD litigants. *Law and Human Behavior, 29,* 121–149.

Koch, W. J., Douglas, K. S., Nicholls, T. L., & O'Neill, M. L. (2006). *Psychological injuries: Forensic assessment, treatment, and law.* Oxford: Oxford University Press.

Kolbo, J., Blakely, E., & Engleman, D. (1996). Children who witness domestic violence: A review of empirical literature. *Journal of Interpersonal Violence, 11,* 281–293.

Koocher, G. P. (2009). *Ethical issues in child sexual abuse allegations.* In K. Kuehnle & M. Connell (Eds.), *The evaluation of child sexual abuse allegations: A comprehensive guide to assessment and testimony* (pp. 81–98). Hoboken, NJ: Wiley.

Kozol, H. L., Boucher, R. J., & Garofalo, R. F. (1972). The diagnosis and treatment of dangerousness. *Crime and Delinquency, 18,* 371–392.

Kuehnle, K. (1996). *Assessing allegations of child sexual abuse.* Sarasota, FL: Professional Research Exchange.

Kuehnle, K. (2003). Child sexual abuse evaluations. In A. M. Goldstein (Ed.), *Handbook of psychology: Forensic psychology (vol. 11)* (p. 437–460). Hoboken, NJ: Wiley.

Kuehnle, K. (2006, April). *Evaluating claims of child sexual abuse in child custody cases.* Presented at the Fourth Family Law Conference, Bend, Oregon.

Kuehnle, K., & Connell, M. (2009). *The evaluation of child sexual abuse allegations: A comprehensive guide to assessment and testimony.* Hoboken, NJ: Wiley.

Kuehnle, K., Greenberg, L. R., & Gottlieb, M. C. (2004). Incorporating the principles of scientifically based child interviews into family law cases. *Journal of Child Custody, 1*(1), 97–114.

Kuhmo Tire Company v. Carmichael, 119 S. Ct. 1167 (1999).

Laboratory of Community Psychiatry, Harvard Medical School. (1973). *Competency to stand trial and mental fitness* (DHEW Pub. No. ADM-77–103). Rockville, MD: Department of Health, Education, and Welfare.

LaFond, J. (1994). Law and the delivery of involuntary mental health services. *American Journal of Orthopsychiatry, 64,* 209–222.

LaFond, J., & Durham, M. (1992). *Back to the asylum: The future of mental health law and policy in the United States.* New York: Oxford University Press.

Lally, S. J. (2003). What tests are acceptable for use in forensic evaluations? A survey of experts. *Professional Psychology: Research and Practice, 26,* 54–60.

Lamb, M. E., Orbach, Y., Hershkowitz, I., Horowitz, D., & Abbot, C. B. (In press). Structured forensic interview protocols improve the quality and informativeness of investigative interviews with children: A review of research using the NICHD Investigative Interview Protocol. *Child Abuse and Neglect.*

Langan, P. A., Schmitt, E. L., & Durose, M. R. (2003). *Recidivism of sex offenders released from prison in 1994.* U.S. Department of Justice: Office of Justice Programs, Bureau of Justice Statistics.

La Rooy, D., Lamb, M. E., & Pipe, M. (2009). *Repeated interviewing: A critical evaluation of the risks and potential benefits.* In K. Kuehnle & M. Connell, *The evaluation of child sexual abuse allegations: A comprehensive guide to assessment and testimony* (pp. 327–361). Hoboken, NJ: Wiley.

LeBouorgeois III, H. W. (2007, April 15). Malingering: Key points in assessment. *Psychiatric Times, 24,* retrieved July 10, 2009, from www.psychiatrictimes.com/print/article/10168/54091?printable

Lees-Haley, P. (1997). Attorneys influence expert evidence in forensic psychological and neuropsychological cases. *Assessment, 4,* 321–324.

Lees-Haley, P. R., English, L. T., & Glenn, W. J. (1991). A Fake Bad Scale on the MMPI-2 for personal injury claimants. *Psychological Report, 68,* 203–210.

Leifer, M., Shapiro, P., Martone, M. W., & Kassem, L. (1991). Rorschach assessment of psychological functioning in sexually abused girls. *Journal of Personality Assessment, 56,* 14–28.

Lessard v. Schmidt, 349 F. Supp. 1078 (E.D. Wis. 1974), *vacated & remanded,* 414 U.S. 473 (1974), *order on remand,* 379 F. Supp. 1376 (E.D. Wis. 1974), *vacated and remanded on other grounds,* 421 U.S. 957 (1975), *order reinstated on remand,* 413 F. Supp. 1318 (E.D. Wis. 1976).

Lipsitt, P. D., Lelos, D., & McGarr, L. (1971). Competency for trial: A screening instrument. *American Journal of Psychiatry, 128,* 104–109.

Loeber, R., Pardini, D., Homish, D. L., Wei, E. H., Crawford, A. M., Farrington, D. P., et al. (2005). The prediction of violence and homicide in young men. *Journal of Consulting and Clinical Psychology, 73,* 1074–1088.

Lynam, D. R. (2002). Fledgling psychopathy: A view from personality theory. *Law and Human Behavior, 26,* 255–269.

Maisto, S. A., & Connors, G. J. (1992). Using subject and collateral reports to measure alcohol consumption. In R. Z. Littent & J. Allen (Eds.), *Measuring alcohol consumption: Psychosocial and biological methods* (pp. 732–96). New Jersey: Humana Press.

Malinosky-Rummell, R., & Hansen, D. J. (1993). Long-term consequences of childhood physical abuse. *Psychological Bulletin, 114,* 68–79.

Malloy, L. C., & Quas, J. A. (2009). Children's suggestibility: Areas of consensus and controversy. In K. Kuehnle & M. Connell (Eds.), *The evaluation of child sexual abuse allegations: A comprehensive guide to assessment and testimony* (pp. 267–297). Hoboken, NJ: Wiley.

Marshall, L. L. (1996). Psychological abuse of women: Six distinct clusters. *Journal of Family Violence, 11,* 379–408.

Martelli, M.F., Nicholson, K, Zasler, N.D. & Bender, M.C. (2007). Assessment of response bias in clinical and forensic evaluations of impairment following brain injury. In Zasler, Katz, Zafonte (Eds.), *Brain injury medicine: Principles and practice.* New York: Demos.

Marzuk, P. M. (1996). Violence, crime, and mental illness. *Archives of General Psychiatry, 53,* 481–486.

Mayers, K. (1994). Civil commitment of the severely demented patient. Coercion and ineffective communication. *American Journal of Forensic Psychology, 12,* 55–62.

McAuliff, B. D., Kovera, M. B., & Gilstrap, L. L. (2009). *An updated review of the effects of system and estimator variables on child witness accuracy in custody cases.* In R. M. Galatzer-Levy, A. Kraus, & J. Galatzer-Levy (Eds.), *The scientific basis of child custody decisions* (pp. 125–164). Hoboken, NJ: Wiley.

McCann, J. T., Flens, J. R., Campagna, V., Collman, P., Lazzaro, T., & Connor, E. (2001). The MCMI-III in child custody evaluations: A normative study. *Journal of Forensic Psychology Practice, 1,* 27–44.

McCrae, J. S., Chapman, M. V., & Christ, S. L. (2006). Profile of children investigated for sexual abuse: Association with psychopathology symptoms and services. *American Journal of Orthopsychiatry, 4,* 468–481.

McCusker, P. J. (2007). Issues regarding the clinical use of the Classification of Violence Risk (COVR) assessment instrument. *International Journal of Offender Therapy and Comparative Criminology, 51,* 676–685.

McDevitt-Murphy, M. E., Weathers, F. W., & Adkins, J. W. (2005). The use of the Trauma Symptom Inventory in the assessment of PTSD symptoms. *Journal of Traumatic Stress, 18,* 63–67.

McMillen, C., Zuravin, S., & Rideout, G. (1995). Perceived benefit from childhood sexual abuse. *Journal of Consulting and Clinical Psychology, 63,* 1037–1043.

McNiel, D., & Binder, R. (1987). Predictive validity of judgments of dangerousness in emergency civil commitment. *American Journal of Psychiatry, 144,* 197–200.

Meek, C. (1990). Evaluation and assessment of posttraumatic and other stress related disorders. In C. Meek (Ed.), *Posttraumatic stress disorder: Assessment, differential diagnosis and forensic evaluations* (pp. 9–61). Sarasota, FL: Professional Resource Exchange.

Medoff, D. (1999). MMPI-2 validity scales in child custody evaluations: Clinical versus statistical significance. *Behavioral Sciences & the Law, 17* (4), 409–411.

Meloy, J. R., Hansen, T. L., & Weiner, I. B. (1997). Authority of the Rorschach: Legal citations during the past 50 years. *Journal of Personality Assessment, 69,* 53–62.

Melton, G. B., & Limber, S. (1989). Psychologists' involvement in cases of maltreatment: Limits of role and expertise. *American Psychologist, 44,* 1225–1233.

Melton, G. B., Petrila, J., Poythress, N. G., & Slobogin, C. (1997). Competency to stand trial. In G. B. Melton, J. Petrila, N. G. Poythress, & C. Slobogin (Eds.), *Psychological evaluations for the court: A handbook for mental health professionals and lawyers* (2nd ed., pp. 119–155). New York: Plenum Press.

Melton, G., Petrila, J., Poythress, N. G., & Slobogin, C. (2007). *Psychological evaluations for the courts* (3rd Ed.). New York: Guilford.

Mental Health Division, Public Defender Service for the District of Columbia. (1996). *Representation of persons subject to civil commitment in the District of Columbia and post-commitment representation of persons acquitted by reason of insanity in the District of Columbia* (7th Ed.). Washington, DC: Author.

Mental patients are able to give informed consent. (1985). *ADAMHA News, 11,* 11.

Menzies, R., Webster, C., McMain, S., Staley, S., & Scaglione, R. (1994). The dimensions of dangerousness revisited. *Law and Human Behavior, 18,* 1–28.

Mericle, A. A., & Havassy, B. E. (2008). Characteristics of recent violence among entrants to acute mental health and substance abuse services. *Social Psychiatry and Psychiatric Epidemiology, 43,* 392–402.

Meyer, R. G., Landis, E. R., & Hay, J. R. (1988). *Law for the psychotherapist.* New York: Norton.

Michel, M. K., Gordon, B. N., Ornstein, P., A., & Simpson, M. A. (2000) The abilities of children with mental retardation to remember personal experiences: Implications for testimony. *Journal of Clinical Child Psychology, 29,* 453–63.

Miller, W. R., Westerberg, V. S., & Waldron, H. B. (1995). Evaluating alcohol problems in adults and adolescents. In R.K. Hester & W.R. Miller (Eds.), *Handbook of alcoholism treatment approaches: Effective alternatives* (2nd ed., pp. 61–88). Boston: Allyn & Bacon.

Millon, T. (1997). *Millon Clinical Multiaxial Inventory-III manual* (2nd ed.). Minneapolis, MN: NCS Pearson.

Millon, T., & Davis, R. (1994). *MCMI-III Manual: Millon Clinical Multiaxial Inventory-III.* Minneapolis: National Computer Systems.

Milner, J. S., & Chilamkurti, C. (1991). Physical child abuse perpetrator characteristics: A review of the literature. *Journal of Interpersonal Violence, 6,* 345–366.

Miranda v. Arizona, 384 U.S. 436 (1966).

Moffitt, T. (1993). Adolescence-limited and life-course-persistent antisocial behavior: A developmental taxonomy. *Psychological Review, 100,* 674–701.

Monahan, J. (1992). Mental disorder and violent behavior. Perceptions and evidence. *American Psychologist, 47,* 511–521.

Monahan, J. (2008). Mandated community treatment: Applying leverage to achieve adherence. *Journal of the American Academy of Psychiatry and the Law, 36,* 282–285.

Monahan, J., Redlich, A. D., Swanson, J., Robbins, P. C., Appelbaum, P. S., Petrila, J., et al. (2005). Use of leverage to improve adherence to psychiatric treatment in the community. *Psychiatric Services, 56,* 37–44.

Monahan, J., Steadman, H. J., Silver, E., Appelbaum, P. S., Robbins, P. C., Mulvey, E. P., Roth, L. H., Grisso, T., & Banks, S. (2001). *Rethinking risk assessment: The MacArthur Study of Mental Disorder and Violence.* New York: Oxford University Press.

Monahan, J., Steadman, H. J., Robbins, P. C., Appelbaum, P., Banks, S., Grisso, T. et al. (2005). An actuarial model of violence risk assessment for persons with mental disorders. *Psychiatric Services, 56,* 810–815.

Monahan, J., Steadman, H. J., Appelbaum, P. S., Grisso, T., Mulvey, E. P., Roth, L. H. et al. (2006). The classification of violence risk. *Behavioral Sciences and the Law, 24,* 721–730.

Morey, L. C. (1991). *Personality Assessment Inventory: Professional Manual.* Odessa, FL: Psychological Assessment Resources.

Morey, L. C. (1997). *The Personality Assessment Screener professional manual.* Lutz, FL: Psychological Assessment Resources.

Morey, L. C. (2003). *Essentials of PAI Assessment.* Hoboken, NJ: Wiley.

Morris, G. H., Haroun, A. M., & Naimark, D. (2004). Assessing competency competently: Toward a rational standard for competency to stand trial assessments. *Journal of the American Academy of Psychiatry and the Law, 32,* 231–245.

Mossman, D. (1994). Assessing predictions of violence. Being accurate about accuracy. *Journal of Consulting and Clinical Psychology, 62,* 783–792.

Mossman, D., Noffsinger, S. G., Ash, P., Frierson, R.L., Gerbasi, J., Hackett, M., et al. (2007 Supp). AAPL practice guideline for the forensic psychiatric evaluation of competence to stand trial. *Journal of the American Academy of Psychiatry and the Law, 35,* 53–72.

Murrie, D. C., Boccaccini, M. T., Zapf, P. A., Warren, J. I., & Henderson, C. E. (2008). Clinician variation in findings of competence to stand trial. *Psychology, Public Policy, and Law, 14,* 177–193.

Murrie, D., Martindale, D. A., & Epstein, M. (2009). *Unsupported assessment techniques in child sexual abuse evaluations.* In K. Kuehnle & M. Connell (Eds.), *The evaluation of child sexual abuse allegations: A comprehensive guide to assessment and testimony* (pp. 397–420). Hoboken, NJ: Wiley.

Mulvey, E. P. (1994). Assessing the evidence of a link between mental illness and violence. *Hospital and Community Psychiatry, 45,* 663–668

Mulvey, E. (2005). Risk assessment in juvenile justice practice and policy (p. 209–232). In K. Heilbrun, N. Goldstein, & R. Redding (Eds.). *Juvenile Delinquency: Prevention, Assessment, and Intervention.* New York: Oxford.

Mulvey, E. P., & Monahan, J. (1998, October). *The MacArthur coercion study.* Paper presented at the Competency, Coercion and Risk of Violence conference, Marquette University Law School, Milwaukee, WI.

National Center for State Courts. (1986). Guidelines for involuntary civil commitment. *Mental and Physical Disability Law Reporter, 10,* 409–514.

National Institute on Alcohol Abuse and Alcoholism. (1995). *Assessing alcohol problems: A guide for clinicians and researchers* (DHHS Pub. No. 95–3745). Washington, DC: U.S. Government Printing Office.

Nichols, D. S. (2001). *Essentials of MMPI-2 assessment.* New York: Wiley.

Nichols, D. S. (2006). The trials of separating bath water from baby: A review and critique of the MMPI-2 Restructured Clinical Scales. *Journal of Personality Assessment, 87,* 121–138.

Nichols, D. S., & Greene, R. L. (1997). Dimensions of deception in personality assessment: The example of the MMPI-2. *Journal of Personality Assessment, 68,* 251–266.

Nicholson, R. A., Briggs, S. R., & Robertson, H. C. (1988). Instruments for assessing competency to stand trial: How do they work? *Professional Psychology: Research and Practice, 19,* 383–394.

Nicholson, K. & Martelli, M. F. (2007a). Malingering: Overview and basic concepts. In G. Young, A. W. Kane, & K. Nicholson (Eds.), *Causality of psychological injury: Presenting evidence in court* (pp. 375–409). New York: Springer Science+Business Media.

Nicholson, K. & Martelli, M. F. (2007b). The effect of compensation status. In G. Young, A. W. Kane, & K. Nicholson (Eds.), *Causality of psychological injury: Presenting evidence in court* (pp. 411–426). New York: Springer Science+Business Media.

Nicholson, K. & Martelli, M. F. (2007c). Malingering: Traumatic brain injury. In G. Young, A. W. Kane, & K. Nicholson (Eds.), *Causality of psychological injury: Presenting evidence in court* (pp. 427–367475). New York: Springer Science+Business Media.

Nottingham, E. J., IV, & Mattson, R. E. (1981). The competency screening test: A replication and extension. *Criminal Justice and Behavior, 8,* 471–481.

O'Connor v. Donaldson, 422 U.S. 563, 95 S. Ct. 2486, 45 L. Ed. 2d 396 (1975).

Otto, R. K., Poythress, N. G., Nicholson, R. A., Edens, J. F., Monahan, J., Bonnie, R. J., & Eisenberg, M. (1998). Psychometric properties of the MacArthur Competence Assessment tool-criminal adjudication. *Psychological Assessment, 10,* 435–443.

Otto, R. K. (2002). Use of the MMPI-2 in forensic settings. *Journal of Forensic Psychology Practice, 2,* 71–91.

Otto, R. K. (2008). Challenges and advances in assessment of response style in forensic examination contexts. In Rogers, R. (Ed.), *Clinical Assessment of Malingering and Deception* (3rd ed., pp. 365–375). New York: Guilford.

Otto, R. & Borum R. (2004). Evaluation of youth in the juvenile justice system. In W. O'Donohue & E. Levensky (Eds.), *Handbook of forensic psychology: Resources for mental health and legal professionals.* (pp 871–895). San Diego, CA: Academic Press.

Ozer, E. J., Best, S. R., Lipsey, T. L., & Weiss, D. S., (2003). Predictors of posttraumatic stress disorder and symptoms in adults: A meta-analysis. *Psychological Bulletin, 129*(1), 52–73.

Pagelow, M. (1990). Effects of domestic violence on children and their consequences for custody and visitation agreements. *Mediation Quarterly, 7,* 347–363.

Parry, C., Turkheimer, E., & Hundley, P. (1992). A comparison of commitment and recommitment hearings: Legal and policy implications. *International Journal of Law and Psychiatry, 15,* 35–41.

Parry, J. (1990). The Supreme Court fashions new boundaries for involuntary care and treatment. *Mental and Physical Disability Law Reporter, 14,* 198–202.

Parry, J. (1994). Involuntary civil commitment in the 90s: A constitutional perspective. *Mental and Physical Disability Law Reporter, 18,* 320–333.

Parry, J. (1995). *Mental disability law: A primer* (5th ed). Washington, DC: American Bar Association.

Parry, J. W. (1998). *National benchbook on psychiatric and psychological evidence and testimony.* Washington DC: American Bar Association.

People v. Lara, 432 P.2d 202 (1967).

Perlin, M. (1989). *Mental disability law: Civil and criminal* (Vols. 1–3 and annual suppls). Charlottesville, VA: Michie.

Perlin, M. (1993). 1993 cumulative supplement to *Mental disability law: Civil and criminal* (Vol. 2). Charlottesville, VA: Michie.

Perlin, M. (1995). 1995 cumulative supplement to *Mental disability law: Civil and criminal* (Vol. 1). Charlottesville, VA: Michie.

Perlin, M. L., Champine, P., Dlugacz, H. A., & Connell, M. (2008). *Competence in the Law.* Hoboken, NJ: Wiley.

Petrila, J., Ridgely, M. S., & Borum, R. (2003). Debating outpatient commitment: Controversy, trends, and empirical data. *Crime & Delinquency, 49,* 157–172.

Pfeiffer, S. I. (2003). Review of the Adolescent Psychopathology Scale-Short Form. In B. Plake, J. Impara, & P. Spies (Eds.), *The fifteenth mental measurements yearbook* (pp. 42–44). Lincoln: University of Nebraska Press.

Pipe, M-E., Sternberg, K., Lamb, M. E., Orbach, Y., Stewart, H., & Esplin, P. (2007). Non-disclosures and alleged abuse in forensic interviews. In M-E. Pipe, M.E. Lamb, Y. Orbach, & A-C Cederborg (Eds.). *Child sexual abuse: Disclosure, delay and denial.* Mahwah, NJ: Lawrence Erlbaum.

Pipe, M., & Salmon, K. (2009). *Dolls, drawing, body diagrams, and other props: Role of props in investigative interviews.* In K. Kuehnle & M. Connell (Eds.), *The evaluation of child sexual abuse allegations: A comprehensive guide to assessment and testimony* (pp. 365–395). Hoboken, NJ: Wiley.

Polusny, M. A., & Arbisi, P. A. (2006). Assessment of psychological distress and disability after sexual assault in adults. In G. Young, A. W. Kane, & K. Nicholson (Eds.), *Psychological knowledge in court: PTSD, pain and TBI.* New York: Springer Science+Business Media.

Polusny, M., & Follette, V. (1995). Long-term correlates of childhood sexual abuse: Theory and review of the empirical literature. *Applied and Preventive Psychology, 4,* 143–166.

Poole, D. A., & Wolfe, M. A. (2009). Child development: Normative sexual and missexual behaviors that may be confused with sexual abuse. In K. Kuehnle & M. Connell (Eds.), *The evaluation of child sexual abuse allegations: A comprehensive guide to assessment and testimony* (pp. 101–128). Hoboken, NJ: Wiley.

Pope, K. S., Butcher, J. N., & Seelen, J. (2006). *The MMPI, MMPI-2 & MMPI-A in court* (3rd ed.). Washington, DC: American Psychological Association.

Posthuma, A., Podrouzek, W., & Crisp, D. (2002). The implications of *Daubert* on neuropsychological evidence in the assessment of remote mild traumatic brain injury. *American Journal of Forensic Psychology, 20,* 21–37.

Poythress, N. G., Bonnie, R. J., Monahan, J., Otto, R., & Hoge, S. K. (2002). *Adjudicative competence: The MacArthur studies.* New York: Kluwer Academic/Plenum.

Poythress, N., Lexcen, F. J., Grisso, T., & Steinberg, L. (2006). The competence-related abilities of adolescent defendants in criminal court. *Law and Human Behavior, 30,* 75–92.

Poythress, N. G., Nicholson, R. J., Otto, R., Edens, J., Bonnie, R., Monahan, J., & Hoge, S. (1999). *The MacArthur Competence Assessment Tool–Criminal Adjudication: Professional Manual.* Lutz, FL: Psychological Assessment Resources.

Poythress, N., & Stock, H. V. (1980). Competency to stand trial: A historical review and some new data. *Psychiatry and Law, 8,* 131–146.

Poythress, N., & Zapf, P. A. (2009). Controversies in evaluating competence to stand trial. In J. L. Skeem, K. S. Douglass, & S. O. Lilienfeld (Eds.), *Psychological sciences in the courtroom consensus and controversy* (pp. 309–331). New York: Guilford Press.

Preparation and trial of a civil commitment case. (1981). *Mental Disability Law Reporter, 5,* 201–209, 281–293, 358–373.

Quinsey, V. L., Harris, G. T., Rice, M. E., & Cormier, C. A. (1998). *Violent Offenders: Appraising and Managing Risk.* Washington, DC: American Psychological Association.

Quinsey, V. L., Harris, G. T., Rice, M. E., & Cormier, C. A. (2006). *Appraising and Managing Risk* (2nd ed.). Washington, DC: American Psychological Association.

Rabin, L. A., Barr, W. B., & Burton, L. A. (2005). Assessment practices of clinical neuropsychologists in the United States and Canada: A survey of INS, NAN, and APA Division 40 members. *Archives of Clinical Neuropsychology, 20,* 33–65.

Randolph, J. J., Hicks, T., & Mason, D. (1981). The competency screening test: A replication and extension. *Criminal Justice and Behavior, 8,* 471–481.

Randolph, J. J., Hicks, T., Mason, D., & Cuneo, D. J. (1982). The competency screening test: A validation study in Cook County, Illinois. *Criminal Justice and Behavior, 9,* 495–500.

Renner, L. M., & Slack, K. S. (2006). Intimate partner violence and child maltreatment: Understanding intra- and intergenerational connections. *Child Abuse and Neglect, 30,* 599–617.

Repic, T. (2007). Fear of intimacy among married and divorced persons in association with physical abuse in childhood. *Journal of Divorce and Remarriage, 46,* 49–62.

Resnick, P. J. (1988). Malingering of posttraumatic disorders. In R. Rogers (Ed.), *Clinical assessment of malingering and deception* (pp. 84–103). New York: Guilford.

Resnick, P. J. (1997). Malingering of posttraumatic disorders. In R. Rogers (Ed.), *Clinical assessment of malingering and deception* (pp. 130–152). New York: Guilford.

Resnick, P. J., West, S., & Payne, J. W. (2008). Malingering of posttraumatic disorders. In Rogers, R. (Ed.), *Clinical Assessment of Malingering and Deception* (3rd ed., pp. 109–127). New York: Guilford.

Reynolds, W. M., Wallace, J., Hill, T. F., Weist, M. D., & Nebors, L. A. (2001). The relationship between gender depression and self-esteem in children who have witnessed domestic violence. *Child Abuse and Neglect, 25,* 1201–1206.

Rice, M. E., & Harris, G. T. (1997). Cross-validation and extension of the violence risk appraisal guide for child molesters and rapists. *Law and Human Behavior, 21,* 231–241.

Rich, P. (2003). *Understanding, assessing, and rehabilitating juvenile sexual offenders.* Hoboken, NJ: Wiley.

Richardson, G., Gudjonsson, G., & Kelly, T. (1995). Interrogative suggestibility in an adolescent population. *Journal of Adolescence, 18,* 211–216.

Roesch, R., & Golding, S. L. (1980). Competency research. In R. Roesch & S. L. Golding (Eds.), *Competency to stand trial* (pp. 46–68). Chicago: University of Illinois Press.

Roesch, R., & Golding, S. L. (1987). Defining and assessing competency to stand trial. In I. B. Weiner & A. K. Hess (Eds.), *Handbook of forensic psychology* (pp. 378–394). New York: Wiley.

Roesch, R., Zapf, P. A., Eaves, D., & Webster, C. D. (1998). *The Fitness Interview Test* (Rev. Ed.). (Available from Mental Health Law, and Policy Institute, Simon Fraser University, Burnaby, British Columbia, Canada, V5A 1S6.)

Rogers, R. (2003). Forensic use and abuse of psychological tests: Multiscale Inventories. *Journal of Psychiatric Practice, 9,* 316–320.

Rogers, R. (2008). *Clinical assessment of malingering and deception.* New York: Guilford Publications, Inc.

Rogers, R. (2008a). An introduction to response styles. In R. Rogers, (Ed.), *Clinical assessment of malingering and deception* (3rd ed., pp. 3–13). New York: Guilford.

Rogers, R. (2008b). Detection strategies and malingering and defensiveness. In R. Rogers (Ed.), *Clinical assessment of malingering and deception* (3rd ed., pp. 4–35). New York: Guilford.

Rogers, R. (2008c). Structured interviews and dissimulation. In R. Rogers (Ed.), *Clinical assessment of malingering and deception* (3rd ed., pp. 301–322). New York: Guilford.

Rogers, R. (2008d). Current status of clinical methods. In R. Rogers (Ed.), *Clinical assessment of malingering and deception* (3rd ed., pp. 391–410). New York: Guilford.

Rogers, R., Bagby, R. M. & Dickens, S. E. (1992). *Structured Interview of Reported Symptoms.* Odessa, FL: Psychological Assessment Resources.

Rogers & Bender (2003). Evaluation of malingering and deception. In I. B. Weiner, D. K. Freedheim & A. M. Goldstein, *Handbook of psychology: Forensic psychology* (pp. 109–131). Hoboken NJ: Wlley.

Rogers, R., Jackson, R. L., & Sewell, K. W. (2004). An examination of ECST-R as a screen for feigned incompetency to stand trial. *Psychological Assessment, 16,* 139–145.

Rogers, R., Jackson, R. L., Sewell, K. W., Tillbrook, C. E., & Martin, M. A. (2003). Assessing dimensions of competency to stand trial: Construct validation of the ECST-R. *Assessment, 10,* 344–351.

Rogers, R. Kropp, P. R., Bagby, R. M., & Dickens, S. E. (1992). Faking specific disorders: A study of the structured interview of reported symptoms (SIRS). *Journal of Clinical Psychology, 48,* 643–648.

Rogers, R., Payne, J. W., Berry, D. T. R., & Granacheer, R. P., Jr. (2009). Use of the SIRS in compensation cases: An examination of its validity and generalizability. *Law and Human Behavior, 33,* 213–224.

Rogers, R., Sewell, K. W., Grandjean, N. R., & Vitacco, M. (2002). *Psychological Assessment, 14,* 177–183.

Rogers, R., Sewell, K. W., Martin, M. A., & Vitacco, M. J. (2003). Detection of feigned mental disorders: A meta-analysis of the MMPI-2 and malingering. *Assessment, 10,* 160–177.

Rogers, R., & Shuman, D. (2000). *Conducting insanity evaluations* (2nd ed.). New York: Guilford.

Rogers, R. & Shuman, D. W. (2005). *Fundamentals of forensic practice.* New York: Springer Science+Business Media.

Rogers, R., Sewell, K. W., & Salekin, R. T. (1994). A meta-analysis of malingering on the MMPI-2. *Assessment, 1,* 227–237.

Rogers, R., Tillbrook, C. E., & Sewell, K. W. (2004). *Professional Manual for the ECST-R: Evaluation of Competence to Stand Trial–Revised.* Lutz, FL: Psychological Assessment Resources.

Rogers, R., Hinds, J. D., & Sewell, K. W. (1996). Feigning psychopathology among adolescent offenders: Validation of the SIRS, MMPI-A, and SIMS. *Journal of Personality Assessment, 67,* 244–257.

Rubenzer, S. (2009). Posttraumatic stress disorder: Assessing response style and malingering. *Psychological Injury and Law, 2,* 114–142.

Ryan, L. M., & Warden, D. L. (2003). Post concussion syndrome. *International Review of Psychiatry, 15,* 310–316.

Saltaris, C. (2002). Psychopathy in juvenile offenders: Can temperament and attachment be considered as robust developmental precursors? *Clinical Psychology Review, 22,* 729–752.

Samuel, S. E., DeGirolamo, J., Michals, T. J., & O'Brien, J. (1995). Preliminary findings on MMPI "Cannot Say" responses with personal injury litigants. *American Journal of Forensic Psychiatry, 16,* 59–72.

Sass, L., & Wolfe, D. (1991). *Preparing sexually abused children for the stress of court.* Paper presented at the 99th annual convention of the American Psychological Association, San Francisco, CA.

Sattler, J.M. (1998). *Clinical and forensic interviewing of children and families.* San Diego: Jerome M. Sattler.

Saywitz, K. (1991, August). *Developmental sensitivity in the assessment of child sexual abuse.* Paper presented at the 97th annual meeting of the American Psychological Association, San Francisco, CA.

Saywitz, K. (1995). Memory and testimony in the child witness. In M. Zaragoza, J. Graham, G. Hall, R. Hirschman, & Y. Ben-Porath (Eds.), In *Memory and testimony in the child witness* (pp. 113–140). London: Sage Publications.

Saywitz, K. (1997, August). *Improving the reliability of children's reports.* Paper presented at the 105th annual meeting of the American Psychological Association, Chicago, IL.

Schetky, D. (2003). Juveniles standing trial: Waiver to adult court. *Journal of Psychiatric Practice, 9* (6), 1–4.

Schwartz-Kenney, B. M., Bottoms, B. L., Goodman, G. S., & Wilson, M. E. (1992). *Improving children's accuracy for person identification.* Paper presented at the 100th annual convention of the American Psychological Association, Washington, DC.

Scott, C. (2002). Juvenile waivers to adult court. In D. Schetky & E. Benedek (Eds.), *Principles and practice of child and adolescent forensic psychiatry* (pp. 289–296). Washington, DC: American Psychiatric Publishing.

Scrignar, C. B. (1996). *Posttraumatic Stress Disorder: Diagnosis, treatment, and legal issues* (3rd Ed.). New Orleans: Bruno Press.

Seagrave, D., & Grisso, T. (2002). Adolescent development and the measurement of adolescent psychopathy. *Law and Human Behavior, 26,* 219–239.

Sella, G. E. (1997). Considerations on symptom magnification and malingering. *The Forensic Examiner, 6,* 32–33.

Sellbom, M., & Bagby, R.M. (2008). Response styles on multiscale inventories. In Rogers, R. (Ed.), *Clinical Assessment of Malingering and Deception* (3rd ed., pp. 182–206). New York: Guilford.

Sexton, M. C., Grant, C. D., & Nash, M. R. (1990, August). *Sexual abuse and body image: A comparison of abused and non-abused women.* Paper presented at the 98th annual convention of the American Psychological Association, Boston, MA.

Shackman, J. E., Shackman, A. J., & Pollak, S. D. (2007). Physical abuse amplifies attention to threat and increases anxiety in children. *Emotion, 7,* 838–852.

Shuman, D. W. (1986). *Psychiatric and psychological evidence.* Colorado Springs, CO: Shepard's/McGraw-Hill.

Shuman, D. W. (1994). *Psychiatric and psychological evidence* (2nd Ed.). Deerfield, IL: Clark Boardman Callaghan.

Shuman, D. W. (2005). *Psychiatric and psychological evidence* (3rd Ed.). Eagan, MN: Thomson/West.

Simon, R. I. (1992). *Clinical psychiatry and the law* (2nd Ed.). Washington, DC: American Psychiatric Press.

Simon, R. I., & Shuman, D. W. (2007). *Clinical manual of psychiatry and law.* Washington DC: American Psychiatric Publishing.

Simon, R. I., & Wettstein, R. M. (1997). Toward the development of guidelines for the conduct of forensic psychiatric examinations. *Journal of the American Academy of Psychiatry and Law, 25,* 17–30.

Skeem, J., Golding, S. L., Cohn, N., & Berge, G. (1998). The logic and reliability of expert opinion on competence to stand trial. *Law and Human Behavior, 22,* 519–547.

Skeem, J., Golding, S. L., & Emke-Francis, P. (2004). Assessing adjudicative competency: Using legal and empirical principles to inform practice. In W. T. O'Donohue & E. R. Levensky (Eds.), *Forensic psychology: A handbook for mental health and legal professionals* (pp.175–211). New York: Academic Press.

Skinner, L., & Berry, K. (1993). Anatomically detailed dolls and the evaluation of child sexual abuse allegations: Psychometric considerations. *Law and Human Behavior, 17,* 399–421.

Slobogin, C. (1996). "Appreciation" as a measure of competency: Some thoughts about the MacArthur group's approach. *Psychology, Public Policy, and Law, 2,* 18–30.

Smith, G. P. (2008). Brief screening measures for the detection of feigned psychopathology. In R. Rogers (Ed.), *Clinical assessment of malingering and deception* (3rd ed., pp.323–339). New York: Guilford.

Somer, E., & Szwarcberg, S. (2001). Variables in delayed disclosure of childhood sexual abuse. *American Journal of Orthopsychiatry, 71*(3), 332–341.

Spilsbury, J. C., Belliston, L., Drotar, D., Drinkard, A., Kretschmar, J., Kreeden, R., Flannery, D. J., & Friedman, S. (2007). Clinically significant trauma symptoms and behavioral problems in a community-based sample of children exposed to domestic violence. *Journal of Family Violence, 22,* 487–499.

Stafford, K. (2003). Assessment of competence to stand trial. In A. Goldstein & I. Weiner (Eds.), *Handbook of psychology: Forensic Psychology* (Vol. 11, pp. 359–380). New York: Wiley.

Staines, G.L., Foote, J., Deluca, A., & Kosanke, N. (2001). Polysubstance use among alcoholics. *Journal of Addictive Diseases, 20,* 4 53–68.

Stanhope, V., Marcus, S., & Solomon, P. (2009). The impact of coercion on services from the perspective of mental health care consumers with co-occurring disorders. *Psychiatric Services, 60,* 183–188.

Steadman H. J., Cocozza J. J. (1974). *Careers of the Criminally Insane.* Lexington, MA: Lexington Books.

Steadman, H., Mulvey, E., Monahan, J., Robbins, P., Appelbaum, P., Grisso, T., Roth, L., & Silver, E. (1998). Violence by people discharged from acute psychiatric inpatient facilities and by others in the same neighborhoods. *Archives of General Psychiatry, 55,* 393–401.

Steadman, H., & Robbins, P. (1998, October). *The MacArthur violence risk assessment study.* Paper presented at the Competency, Coercion, and Risk of Violence conference, Marquette University Law School, Milwaukee, WI.

Stefan, S. (2001). *Unequal rights: Discrimination against people with mental disabilities and the Americans with Disabilities Act.* Washington DC: American Psychological Association.

Steffen, L. & Ackerman, M. (1999). Essentials of juvenile assessment. In M. Ackerman (Ed.), *Essentials of forensic psychology assessment* (pp.165–207). New York: Wiley.

Substance Abuse and Mental Health Services Administration. (1997). *A guide to substance abuse services for primary care clinicians* (DHHS Pub. No. SMA 97–3139). Washington, DC: U.S. Government Printing Office.

Swartz, M. S., Burns, B. J., George, L. K., Swanson, J., Hiday, V. A., Borum, R., & Wagner, H. R. (1997). The ethical challenges of a randomized controlled trial of involuntary outpatient commitment. *The Journal of Mental Health Administration, 24,* 35–43.

Swartz, M. S., & Swanson, J. (2004). Reviewing the empirical data on involuntary outpatient commitment, community treatment orders and assisted outpatient treatment. *Canadian Journal of Psychiatry, 49,* 585–591.

Swartz, M. S. (2007). Can mandated outpatient treatment prevent tragedies? *Psychiatric Services, 58,* 737.

Sweet, J. (1997, April). *Evaluation of insufficient effort and malingering.* Paper presented at the spring conference of the Wisconsin Psychological Association and the Society of Clinical and Consulting Psychologists, Oconomowoc, WI.

Sweet, J. J., Condit, D.C. & Nelson, N.W. (2008). Feigned amnesia and memory loss. In R. Rogers (Ed.), *Clinical assessment of malingering and deception* (3rd ed., pp. 218–236). New York: Guilford.

Swisher v. United States, 237 F. Supp. 291 (1965).

Tardiff, K., Marzuk, P. M., Leon, A. C., Portera, L., & Weiner, C. (1997). Violence by patients admitted to a private psychiatric hospital. *American Journal of Psychiatry, 154,* 88–93.

Teisl, M., & Cicchetti, D. (2007). Physical abuse, cognitive and emotional processes, and aggressive/disruptive behavior problems. *Social Development, 17,* 1–2.

Tellegen, A., Ben-Porath, Y. S., McNulty, J. L., Arbisi, P. A., Graham, J. R., & Kaemmer, B. (2003). *MMPI-2 Restructured Clinical (RC) Scales: Development, validation, and interpretation.* Minneapolis: University of Minnesota Press.

Teplin, L., Abram, K., McClelland, G., Dulcan, M., & Mericle, A. (2002). Psychiatric disorders in youth in juvenile detention. *Archives of General Psychiatry, 59*(12), 1133–1143.

Tharinger, D. (1990). Impact of child sexual abuse on developing sexuality. *Professional Psychology: Research and Practice, 21,* 331–337.

Tombaugh, T. N. (1996). *Test of memory malingering.* Tonawonda, NY: Multi-Health Systems, Inc.

Torrey, E. F. (1994). Violent behavior by individuals with serious mental illness. *Hospital and Community Psychiatry, 45,* 653–666.

U.S. Department of Health and Human Services. (1991). *Family violence: An overview.* Washington, DC: Author.

U.S. Department of Health and Human Services. (1992). *Child abuse and neglect: A shared community concern.* Washington, DC: Author.

Ustad, K. L., Rogers, R., Sewell, D. W., & Guarnaccia, C. A. (1996). Restoration of competency to stand trial: Assessment with the Georgia court competency test and the competency screening test. *Law and Human Behavior, 20,* 131–146.

Veltkamp, L., & Miller, T. (1995). *Clinical handbook of child abuse and neglect.* Madison, CT: International Universities Press.

Viljoen, J., & Roesch, R. (2005). Competence to waive interrogation rights and adjudicative competence in adolescent defendants' cognitive development, attorney contact, and psychological symptoms. *Law and Human Behavior, 29,* 723–742.

Viljoen, J. L., Roesch, R., & Zapf, P. A. (2002). Interrater reliability of the Fitness Interview Test across four professional groups. *Canadian Journal of Psychiatry, 47,* 945–952.

Viljoen, J. L., Vincent, G. M., & Roesch, R. (2006). Assessing adolescent defendants' adjudicative competence: Interrater reliability and factor structure of the Fitness Interview Test–Revised. *Criminal Justice and Behavior, 33,* 467–487.

Vitacco, M. J., Rogers, R., Gabel, J., & Munizza, J. (2007). An evaluation of malingering screens with competency to stand trial patients: A known-groups comparison. *Law and Human Behavior, 31,* 249–260.

Walfish, S. (2006). Conducting personal injury evaluations. In I. B. Weiner & A. K. Hess (Eds.), *The handbook of forensic psychology* (3rd ed., pp. 124–139). Hoboken NJ: Wiley.

Walters, S., Holmes, L., Bauer, G. & Vieth, V. (2003). *Finding words: Half a nation by 2010: Interviewing children and preparing for court.* Alexandria, VA: National Center for Prosecution of Child Abuse.

Webster, C., Douglas, K., Eaves, D., & Hart, S. (1997). *HCR-20: Assessing risk for violence, Version 2.* Burnaby, Canada: Mental Health, Law, and Policy Institute, Simon Fraser University.

Weiner, I.B. (1989). On competence and ethicality of psychodiagnostic assessment. *Journal of Personality Assessment, 53,* 827–831.

Weston, D., Ludolph, P., Missile, B., Ruffins, S., & Block, J. (1990). Physical and sexual abuse in adolescent girls with borderline personality disorder. *American Journal of Orthopsychiatry, 60,* 55–66.

Wetzel, L., & Boll, T. J. (1987). *Short Category Test: Booklet format manual.* Los Angeles: Western Psychological Services.

Widows, M., & Smith, G.P. (2005). *Structured Inventory of Malingered Symptomatology (SIMS) and professional manual.* Odessa, FL: Psychological Assessment Resources.

Wildman, W., White, P., & Brandenberg, C. (1990). The Georgia Court Competency Test: The base-rate problem. *Perceptual and Motor Skills, 70,* 1055–1058.

Williams, A. D. (1992). Bias and debiasing techniques in forensic psychology. *American Journal of Forensic Psychology, 10,* 19–26.

Williams, C. L., Butcher, J.N., Gass, C.S., Cumella, E., & Kally, Z. (2009). Inaccuracies about the fake bad scale in the reply by Ben–Porath, Greve, Bianchini, and Kaufman MMPT–2 *Psychological Injury and Law, 2,* 182–197.

Williams, K. R., & Houghton, A. B. (2004). Assessing the risk of domestic violence reoffending: A validation study. *Law and Human Behavior, 28*(4), 437–455.

Williams, S. M., & Nicholaichuk, R. (2001, November). *Assessing static risk factors in adult female sex offenders under federal jurisdiction in Canada.* Paper presented at the 20th Annual Research and Treatment Conference of the Association for the Treatment of Sexual Abusers, San Antonio, TX.

Wilson, J. P., & Moran, T. A. (2004). Forensic/clinical assessment of psychological trauma and PTSD in legal settings. In J. P. Wilson, & T. M. Keane (Eds.), *Assessing psychological trauma and PTSD* (2nd ed., pp. 603–636). New York: Guilford.

Winnick, B. J. (1997). *The right to refuse mental health treatment.* Washington, DC: American Psychological Association.

Wolfe, V. V., Wolfe, D. A., Gentile, C., & LaRose, L. (1997). *Children's Impact of Traumatic Event Scale-Revised.* Unpublished manuscript, University of Western Ontario, London, Ontario.

Woolard, J. L., & Harvell, S. (2005). MacArthur Competence Assessment Tool–Criminal Adjudication. In T. Grisso, G. Vincent, & D. Seagrave (Eds.), *Mental health screening and assessment in juvenile justice* (pp. 370–383). New York: Guilford.

Wrightsman, L. S., Nietzel, M. T., & Fortune, W. H. (1998). *Psychology and the legal system.* Pacific Grove, CA: Brooks/Cole.

Wrightsman, L. & Fulero, S. (2005). *Forensic Psychology,* (2nd ed.). Belmont, CA: Thomson/Wadsworth.

Wyatt, G., Guthrie, D, & Notgrass, C. M. (1992). Differential effects of women's child sexual abuse and subsequent revictimization. *Journal of Consulting and Clinical Psychology, 60,* 167–173.

Young, G., Kane, A. W., & Nicholson, K. (Eds). (2006). *Psychological knowledge in court: PTSD, pain, and TBI.* New York: Springer.

Young, G., Kane, A. W., & Nicholson, K. (2007). *Causality of psychological injury: Presenting evidence in court.* New York: Springer.

Youngjohn, J. R. (1995). Confirming attorney coaching prior to neuropsychological evaluation. *Assessment, 2,* 279–283.

Zander, T. K. (2005). Civil commitment without psychosis: The law's reliance on the weakest links in psychodiagnosis. *Journal of Sexual Offender Civil Commitment: Science and the Law, 1,* 17–82.

Zanni, G. R., & Stavis, P. F. (2007). The effectiveness and ethical justification of psychiatric outpatient commitment. *The American Journal of Bioethics, 7,* 31–41.

Zapf, P. A., & Roesch, R. (1997). Assessing fitness to stand trial: A comparison of institution-based evaluations and a brief screening interview. *Canadian Journal of Community Mental Health, 16,* 53–66.

Zapf, P. A., & Roesch, R. (1998). Fitness to stand trial: Characteristics of remands since the 1992 code criminal code amendments. *Canadian Journal of Psychiatry, 43,* 287–293.

Zapf, P. A., & Roesch, R. (2001). A comparison of the MacCAT-CA and the FIT for making determinations of competency to stand trial. *International Journal of Law and Psychiatry, 24,* 81–92.

Zapf, P. A., & Roesch, R. (2006). Competency to stand trial: A guide for evaluators. In I. B. Weiner & A. K. Hess (Eds.), *The handbook of forensic psychology* (3rd ed,. pp. 305–331). Hoboken, NJ: Wiley.

Zapf, P. A., Roesch, R., & Viljoen, J. L. (2001). Assessing fitness to stand trial: The utility of the Fitness Interview Test (Revised Edition). *Canadian Journal of Psychiatry, 46,* 426–432.

Zapf, P. A., Hubbard, K. L., Cooper, V. G., Wheeles, M. C., & Ronan, K. A. (2004). Have the courts abdicated their responsibility for determinations of competency to stand trial to clinicians? *Journal of Forensic Psychology and Practice, 4,* 27–44.

Zapf, P. A., Roesch, R., & Viljoen, J. L. (2001). Assessing fitness to stand trial: The utility of the Fitness Interview Test (Revised Edition). *Canadian Journal of Psychiatry, 46,* 426–432.

Zimring, F. E. (1991 November). Firearms, violence, and public policy. *Scientific American,* 48–54.

Zinemon v. Burch, 494 U.S. 113, 110 S. Ct. 975, 108 L. Ed. 2d 100 (1990).

Zlotnick C., Mattia J., & Zimmerman M. (2001). Clinical features of survivors of sexual abuse with major depression. *Child Abuse and Neglect 25*(3), 357–367.

Zuckerman, E. L. (1995). *Clinician's thesaurus* (4th Ed.). New York: Guilford.

Zuckerman, E. L. (2005). *Clinician's thesaurus* (6th ed.). New York: Guilford.

Zuravin, S., McMillan, C., DePanifils, D., & Risley-Curtiss, C. (1996). The intergenerational cycle of maltreatment: Continuity versus discontinuity. *Journal of Interpersonal Violence, 11,* 315–334.

Annotated Bibliography

Ackerman, M. J. (2006). *Clinician's guide to child custody evaluations* (3rd ed.). Hoboken, NJ: Wiley.

This text is a comprehensive guide for clinicians to utilize as a road map for performing appropriate child custody evaluations. It includes significant controversial issues regarding placement, alienation, maltreatment (domestic violence, sexual, physical, and psychological abuse), and overnight placements for children under 2 years of age.

Ackerman, M. J. (2008). *"Does Wednesday mean mom's house or dad's?"* (2nd ed.). New York: Wiley.

This book is written for the parents who are divorcing or are already divorced to aid them in making the major decisions associated with child custody cases. Highlights include helping children through divorce, parental "dos" and "don'ts" in divorce situations, and how to deal with changes in circumstances associated with divorce cases.

Ackerman, M. J., & Kane, A. W. (2005) *Psychological experts in divorce actions* (4th ed.). New York: Aspen Law & Business.

The authors of this book were primarily concerned with providing attorneys with information to help them adequately examine and cross-examine psychological experts. Each chapter ends with cross examination questions that cover the contents of the subject matter covered in that chapter. The book is written from the perspective of informing attorneys about all areas of child custody evaluations and the underlying theory.

Bersoff, D. N. (2008). *Ethical conflicts in psychology* (4th ed). Washington, DC: American Psychological Association.

Not much more could be said about this book other than it is written by the foremost psychological ethicist in the country. The author has both a law degree and a PhD in psychology, and previously served in the General Counsel of the American Psychological Association.

Grisso, T. (1998). *Forensic evaluation of juveniles.* Sarasota, FL: Professional Resource Press.

This source provides an excellent resource on the assessment of adolescents for the courts. It combines both theory and research and is written in a straightforward manner.

Grisso, T. (2003). Evaluating competencies: Forensic assessments and instruments (2nd ed.) New York: Kluwer/Plenum.

This book offers both a conceptual model for understanding competencies and a practical guide to performing assessments. It also reviews a number of specialized forensic assessment instruments.

Grisso, T. (2005). *Evaluating juveniles' adjudicative competence: A guide for clinical practice.* Sarasota, FL: Professional Resource Press.

This guide incorporates a legal and developmental perspective for conducting evaluations. It also has a CD-ROM included with reproducible practice forms.

Hester, R. K., & Miller, W. R. (Eds.) (2003). *Handbook of alcoholism treatment approaches* (3rd ed.). Boston: Allyn & Bacon.

This handbook is a complete reference to various approaches to the treatment of alcoholism. It reviews the literature to conclude what are evidence-based practices. The treatments described run the gamut from 12-step programs to individual and family therapy.

Ksir, C., Hart, C., & Ray, O. (2006). *Drugs, society, and human behavior* (11th ed). New York: McGraw-Hill Higher Education.

This is an excellent collegiate text and general review of a variety of subjects related to drug pharmacology and their context in our society. It is comprehensive, balanced, and very well illustrated in color and includes many sidebars, self assessments, and web sites for more information. Thoroughly footnoted.

Kuehnle, K., & Connell, M. (Eds.) (2009). *The evaluation of child sexual abuse allegations: A comprehensive guide to assessment and testimony.* Hoboken, NJ: Wiley.

Kathryn Kuehnle previously wrote the single best book about sexual abuse allegations. She has now teamed with Mary Connell for this edited edition, which is thorough and provides seemingly endless current info about the subject.

Melton, G., Petrila, J., Poythress, N. G., & Slobogin, C. (2007). *Psychological evaluations for the courts* (3rd Ed.). New York: Guilford.

This comprehensive text is in its third edition and is the first text that forensic practitioners should have in their library. All areas that are discussed are supported by relevant, current research or literature. The authors have clearly made an effort to cover both sides of controversial issues.

Monahan, J., Steadman, H. J., Silver, E., Appelbaum, P. S., Robbins, P. C., Mulvey, E. P., Roth, L. H., Grisso, T., & Banks, S. (2001). *Rethinking risk assessment: The MacArthur Study of Mental Disorder and Violence.* New York: Oxford University Press.

Rogers, R. (Ed.) (2008). *Clinical assessment of malingering and deception* (3rd Ed.). New York: Guilford.

The best single source of information regarding malingering and deception. Rogers is arguably the most expert researcher on the topic, and additional chapters are authored by other top experts.

Young, G., Kane, A. W., & Nicholson, K. (2007). *Causality of psychological injury: Presenting evidence in court.* New York: Springer Science+Business Media.

This book contains a wealth of theoretical and practical information regarding psychological assessments in personal injury contexts, including the most thorough review of malingering research of which I am aware.

Index

A

Ackerman-Schoendorf Scales for
    Parent Evaluation of Custody
    (ASPECT), 51–56, 64, 65
    Interpretation, 51–52
    Reliability, 52–58
    Research on, 54
    Validity, 52–58

Acute Stress Disorder, 74

Addiction Severity Index (ASI), 243

Adolescent Psychopathology Scale,
    221

Alcohol or Other Drug Abuse, 29

Alcohol Use Inventory (AUI), 243

American Psychological Association
    Ethical Principals of Psychologists
    and Code of Code of Conduct,
    4–17, 22, 25, 271
    Assessment (9.0), 11
    Avoiding Harm (3.04), 7
    Bases for Assessment (9.01), 11–12
    Boundaries of Competence (2.01),
    6–7
    Conflict of Interest (3.06), 8
    Conflicts between Ethics and Law,
    Regulations, or Other Governing
    Legal Authorities (1.02), 6
    Explaining Assessment Results
    (9.10), 15–16
    Fees and Financial Arrangements
    (6.04), 11

    Informed Consent (3.10(a)), 9
    Informed Consent in Assessments
    (9.03), 13
    Interpreting Assessment Results
    (9.06), 14
    Maintaining Confidentiality (4.01),
    10
    Maintaining Test Security (9.11),
    16
    Maintenance of Records (6.01), 10
    Multiple Relationships (3.05), 7–8
    Obsolete Tests and Outdated Test
    Results (9.08), 14–15
    Release of Test Data (9.04),
    13–14
    Test Scoring and Interpretation
    Services (9.09), 15
    Third-Party Requests for Services
    (3.07), 8–9
    Use of Assessments (9.02), 12–13
    Withholding Records for
    Nonpayment (6.03), 10–11

General Guidelines for Providers of
    Psychological Services, 5

Guidelines for Child Custody
    Evaluations in Family Law
    Proceedings, 5, 17, 19, 22

Guidelines for Psychological
    Evaluations in Child Protections
    Matters, 5

Patients' Bill of Rights, 5

Record Keeping Guidelines, 5, 17

C

About the Author

Marc J. Ackerman, Ph.D., is a licensed psychologist in the state of Wisconsin who has been involved in over 2500 family law and personal injury cases in Wisconsin and throughout the United States. He has testified in hundreds of family law, personal injury, and sexual abuse cases in over 30 states. His practice today is largely a forensic psychology consulting and assessment practice. Dr. Ackerman co-developed the Ackerman-Schoendorf Scales for Parent Evaluation of Custody (ASPECT) and the Ackerman-Schoendorf Scales for Parent Evaluation of Custody-Short Form (ASPECT-SF), published in 1992 by Western Psychological Services, and authored *Clinician's Guide to Child Custody Evaluations* (Wiley, 2006), *Does Wednesday Mean Mom's House or Dad's?* (Wiley, 2008). In addition, he has co-authored *Psychological Experts in Divorce Actions, Fourth Edition* (Aspen Law & Business, 2005) and *Psychological Experts in Personal Injury Actions, Third Edition* (Aspen Law & Business, 1998). Furthermore, he has over 50 publications and has presented over 150 seminars and workshops throughout the world.

Dr. Ackerman has served as a founding faculty member and Dean of the Wisconsin School of Professional Psychology from 1981 to 1987, and is the former Director of Clinical Training at the Wisconsin School of Professional Psychology. He is currently a full clinical professor and Chair of the Forensic Psychology Program. He has served as both the president of the Wisconsin Psychological Association and the Milwaukee Area Psychological Association and was a member of the Board of Governors of the Wisconsin Society of Clinical and Consulting Psychologists. In addition, he has served on the Wisconsin Psychological Association's Ethics Committee for seven years, chairing the committee for one year. Current president of the Wisconsin Psychology Foundation, Dr. Ackerman is co-chair of the Interdisciplinary Committee, sponsored by the Wisconsin Psychological Association and the Wisconsin Bar Association.

Until recently, Dr. Ackerman was co-director of North Shore Psychotherapy Associates and is a member of the National Register of Health Service Providers in Psychology, the American Psychological Association, the Southeastern

Psychological Association, the Wisconsin Psychological Association, and the Milwaukee Area Psychological Association. He has received awards from the Wisconsin Psychological Association for outstanding contributions to the advancement of psychology as an applied profession and for outstanding leadership. Lastly, he serves as a member of the University of Georgia Graduate Education Advancement Board.